Beloved Spirit

By

Celeste Anand

1663 Liberty Drive, Suite 200
Bloomington, Indiana 47403
(800) 839-8640
www.AuthorHouse.com

This book is a work of non-fiction. Unless otherwise noted, the author and the publisher make no explicit guarantees as to the accuracy of the information contained in this book and in some cases, names of people and places have been altered to protect their privacy.

First published by AuthorHouse 07/12/05

ISBN: 1-4208-3820-2 (sc)

Printed in the United States of America
Bloomington, Indiana

This book is printed on acid-free paper.

Beloved Spirit

Other Books
By
Celeste Anand

*

Beloved: Pt. I–The Garden Message
&
Pt. II–In The Still Of The Evening

I could not have completed these books without the love, prayers and assistance of my Beloved Father. He has blessed me with a wonderful husband, and family. In addition to the loving support of my husband Robert, my mother, children, grandchildren and friends I must give thanks to all of them and you who have sustained me with their heartfelt prayers.

I also received the honored blessing of my friend John Eagle White. We knew we were to lay our hands in prayer upon this inspired book in order that all who read it may be blessed by the Beloved Great Spirit of our Father who knows and sees all of His people everywhere.

I lovingly dedicate this book to all my beloved friends and family members. My beloved husband has staunchly stood there beside me.

It is my belief His Beloved Spirit has guided and directed me throughout my entire life. We are taught our Father is a Spirit. Therefore, we must "worship Him in Spirit and in Truth". His Beloved Spirit is my All In All. I must strive to love and serve Him with my whole heart, mind, body and soul. It is my belief He will be attuned to the voices of His children forever. We are His Beloved Children.

A BLESSED MESSAGE FOR ALL

There are no words to describe the ecstacy of the union of our souls with the Soul of the Universe. There is a new movement of the Divine Spirit to draw the Children of God again into remembrance of their roles in the Kingdom of Heaven as the Priests and Priestesses of divine lineage. They are the siblings of the Divine Son of God who was called Jesus the Christ, now known to many as the wonderful Cosmic Christ of all the families of the Earth and the Cosmos. He is coming soon and we will be with Him again.

There exists several types of relationships with the All-Encompassing Spirit. We can become Monks, Mystics, and Lovers of God even in our diversified roles as ordinary men and women. Small children, the aged, and all the souls of humankind are capable of entering into relationships with God wherein we come into Communion as One Spirit with That One. We can feel complete At-onement with All That Is.

There are Dark Nights of the Soul, as are mentioned by St. John of the Cross. There are also times when we are allowed to share Co-Creatorship experiences with the Omnipotent, Omniscient, and Omnipresent Creator Deity/Deities. We can walk as closely with Him/Her/All That Is, however we find ourselves able to define the Holy One, as we allow ourselves to venture into the Shekinah Glory of the Presence.

In the beginning of our love relationship, we learn of the Fruits of His Divine Spirit, and of the mighty and marvelous Gifts of His Holy Spirit, the Counselor He sent to comfort us in our Earthly lives. All powers of miracles are His. His greatest Gift is that of His Divine, All-Encompassing Love as He offered Himself as our Beloved and Treasured Savior. He is also as close as our own soul. He dwells within our Hearts if we will but allow entry. He is our Beloved. We are His.

When we leave this present Earthly reality, we will return to the Light of That One. We will once again enter into the Presence of the Beloved, our Lord and Savior, wherein dwell the souls of all those who glimpsed and loved Him as their own. We will once again drink of the fruit of the vine together, as we place our hands in His. O, what sweet delight long missed. Thank You, Dear One, for being our Beloved.

Seek Him. He said He would be ours forever. It is possible for us to experience all manner of holy ecstasies and miracles as His disciple, brother, sister, priestess, priest, monk, nun, or as one who seeks only Him, and not any role of notice or power. To have Him as our Beloved is enough.

Christ is the Lover of our souls. Each of us can share a divine spiritual romance with the Lord and be able to truly say:
"I am my Beloved's, and He is mine."

(Wise King Solomon/Songs of Solomon)

* * * * * * * * *

His Message: December 14, 2004

"The Gift of Faith is an elusive Gift.
Hold strongly to it or it will be gone."

WHO WILL BE THE GREATEST LUKE 9:46-50

An argument started among the disciples as to which of them would be the greatest. Jesus, knowing their thoughts, took a little child and had him stand beside him. Then He said to them, "Whoever welcomes this little child in My name welcomes Me; and whoever welcomes Me welcomes the One who sent Me. For He who is least among you all–he is the greatest."

BELOVED SPIRIT

Part I

In The Spirit Of The Beloved

Table of Contents

****
PART II TEARS OF OUR BELOVED FATHER
****

A SPECIAL MESSAGE:

THE MESSAGE–OUR FATHER'S TEARS

There are several reasons for writing this book. It was finally the message I received July 16, 2004 which has disturbed me to the point of making me know I must share it with others.

I was allowed to experience the overpowering, all-encompassing grief of our Heavenly Father. It was much more than can be understood spiritually or physically by humankind.

Many of us have been shown this vision of our Father's Sorrow. We must care enough to attempt to understand why He is sorrowing, and is seemingly not being comforted. The Message has become an overpowering obsession with me. I must know what we can do to relieve the sorrow of my Beloved Father.

This book is a personal research project to explore this question. It is also my never ending personal project to understand myself and others better. In my many years as a personal journalist, I have learned much about myself and others, as well as the world in which we live at this time. I have noticed grave changes in our culture. Not all of them are positive and advantageous. Many of them are recessive traits to the lower human behavioral and social norms. It is my concern that we are also accepting lower, even atavistic, ethics and norms in all of our societal and cultural domains–whether business, health, religious or secular. Many consider, trends towards theocratic domination to be similar to times of terror in former centuries. Many of us observe all of these things and are very concerned. I'm going to attempt to see if we can discover some of the major reasons for causations of the extreme sorrow of our Heavenly Father. The fact that He has been sharing His feelings with many of us makes me sure this is a very important time for Him and His Family. If my earthly father weeps, I try to help him. If our Heavenly Father weeps, we all must take notice of His concerns for they are ultimately our concerns. Perhaps it is because of our lack of love and our return to ancient evils. Let us remember the sins against those we now call saints. Example: St. Joan of Arc

****

Dear Spirit of the Beloved Father,

We will await the coming forth of Your anointed words at this time in order to assist in the healing and blessing of all of us.

You will lead and direct us as we attempt to bring forth Thy holy words.

You are the author and the finisher of all things wise and wonderful.

You know the plans You have for this work.

Thank You for Your Beloved Holy Spirit to teach, counsel and protect us.

Amen

****

My Beloved asks me to remind everyone of His Return.

"My daughter, remember to tell them I am coming soon.

All is now ready and soon to be finished.

I have waited too long for your company.

I will return to bring the Father's Kingdom of Peace to this world.

I will wipe away every tear from your eyes and all who are awaiting My coming will say,

"Amen, even so come Lord Jesus, with healing in Your wings."

SECTION I
THE AGE OF INNOCENCE

INTRODUCTION

Wonderful Visions of Heaven

While many were in exhausted sleep during these darkened hours, He has come to many with special insights which we wish to share with those who seek to know Him better.

We have been exploring the awful sorrows of this world. It is now time to explore the wonders of Heaven and Earth. All is not sorrow. It will pass after the Son has arisen with healing in His wings. A new day will dawn suddenly and all that is sad will soon be gone. He wants to offer us hope and joy, bliss, love and peace for the ashes of mourning and sorrows.

It is the mission of this fellow world traveler to share at this time some of the wonderful knowledge I have gained from my spiritual experiences in the powers of His Holy Spirit. These anecdotes will offer an antidote to pain and sadness.

It is now time to take a journey into some of the wonderful mysteries of our Heavenly Father's Home. It is possible everyone will not agree on upon some of the topics herein. Is it possible to ponder these things together? If we attune ourselves to the Holy Spirit we can be led into great knowledge and joy. It is also possible some few souls prefer the bliss of non-knowing. The exploration of Heaven and our Heavenly Family is wonderful. As always, Love is the key to the Father, for He is Love.

Remember, "I am coming soon." This is His own message at this time to all who love Him and await His return as their Beloved Lord and King.

Some of topics we will explore in these pages are ones received by the Scribe who simply records His Messages received in dreams, visions, and heavenly dictations. This is a small list of some possible topics in the following chapters:

His Words & Messages
&
Who is Jesus?
Who is God?
What are angels like and what do they do?
The Great Crowd of Witnesses.
The Halls of Learning.

SECTON I-THE AGE OF INNOCENCE

I write in the Holy Spirit as always. It has been a long time since I last shared some of my spiritual experiences with others. Perhaps there are some who would again like to walk in the Garden in the still of the evening. (Beloved: Parts I The Garden Message & Part II In The Still Of The Evening") I love being with Him. He is my Beloved and I know He wants to commune with each and every one of His children. It's a beautiful and contemplative walk. The breezes are gently blowing. I can see the ocean surf in the distance and the boughs of the big trees are rustling. Beyond the surf line we can imagine the whales swimming south blowing spume as they negotiate their paths through the mountainous waves of the Pacific Ocean. If you prefer you can paint another word picture. This is mine this early morning. We are able to walk and to talk whenever and wherever we wish to imagine ourselves to be. The ultimate walk will be when we are Home at long last. It is my desire that we all fill our sojourner roles in beautiful ways until it is time for our return to our Heavenly Home.

As I mentioned in "Beloved: Parts I & II", it has been a long time ago since He first gave me the large Message in 1967. Since then many things have happened in my life. When I came into this world I was injured at birth and required heart surgery in 1953 to repair the damage to my heart.

My pioneer ancestors must have genetically infused me with the spirit of adventure. Mine has not been a dull life ever since I was born again as a healthy young woman at age 15. Many of us met our local sweethearts and married young in 1957. I was the wife of a U.S. Naval Aviator by the time I was 21 giving birth to a beautiful son in Pensacola, Florida. Twenty months later I was again mother of a beautiful daughter born in Memphis, Tennessee.

When I was age 29, I was born again as a Child of God. I learned to love and to seek Him with all my heart, mind, body and soul. Sophia, the goddess of Wisdom became my delight. I listened to His scriptures and sought her with all my strength for, in her, I knew were His Ways. I began to desire to know Him with all my will and desire. I wanted His will above all else in my life. However, as I have mentioned before, my will was the last thing I gave to Him. One does not give one's self to a stranger. He had truly proven Himself to be my Beloved Lord and Savior. I give all praises and glory to Him. He is the author and finisher of my Faith. However, I am determined to seek Him and His path only. He has told us the way to please Him is to follow His teachings. His teachings are pure and without blemish. When I started my walk with Him, the Father told me to make sure I follow whatever His Son said and did. I was not to be led astray by teachers or religious pathways other than His. I have found those to have been very wise injunctions for my life. He is my Lord and Master. I am His disciple. One cannot hate and slander if one follows my Lord. He came not to destroy the Law nor the prophets, but to fulfill all. I am thrilled and joyous to be His beloved sister. We are told He is the "firstborn of many brethren (and sisters)". When I share as I do in these pages, this is simply a foretaste of those things which are personally available to anyone if they will seek to know Him. He has told us to tarry until the Counselor will come to us. I sought to be baptized in His Holy Spirit. I have never been disappointed. I have had the close companionship and counseling of the Holy Spirit of the Beloved since I made those decisions so long ago in the Mojave Desert of California. I have never regretted these decisions. I was reborn as Celeste, Child of God and He gave me a very special message for my long and adventurous life:.

"AS I WAS WITH MOSES SO SHALL I BE WITH YOU."

In January 2000 when I was awakened with the strange words, "You are like Cassandra", I have made many changes in my life. At that time, I did not write for publication. I still cannot imagine I write to share my life with others. I am a private journalist and feel no desire or need to share. He seems to have deemed His messages to belong to all of us, not only to me. If this is the case, I must share. They are too wonderful to hug to myself as a treasury of great worth.

I explained about the ancient story of the Trojan prophetess Cassandra, the priestess of Apollo, the Sun God. She asked for the gift of prophecy. (So did I when I asked for the prophetic message again in 1967.) She and I were both granted our gifts of prophecy. We both neglected to walk on together with our Givers of the Gifts. One can read her story and its seemingly sad ending. The alternative legends of Cassandra speak of her as not being killed with Agamemnon by his wife Clytemnestra. Instead, she survived and had a long life until she was finally known as Alexandra, helper of mankind. This is my desire. I must turn my life around and help others to know Him, even as I know Him. He is my Beloved. He is also That One who came to seek, save and love all of us who desire Him to come into their lives. We are living in a new era. He wishes to come very closely into our lives to share our walk even as we live in troublous times on our planet. He also gives us His angels to lead, guide and protect us from all (d)evils. St. Michael's shield says "Who Is Like Unto God". We are His Lambs and He is the Lamb who was slain and is our Good Shepherd.

I walked on with Him until I became a completely involved scholar and student of His path. I completed religious studies at several schools and universities, at the same time I was attempting to perfect my knowledge of human beings in all facets of their beings. I desired to be a helper in all ways for the good of humankind. I still do. If we do not love and help one another, this is a Hell world. We can bring Heaven to Earth only by living a life of altruism and compassion–or selfless love. He came in this fashion to offer His life as the Servant King for our salvations and release from the endless cycles of rebirth in worlds of suffering. It is only by following His pure ways and teachings that we will be able to enter His Father's House with thanksgiving in our hearts, even as Little Children, "for of such is the Kingdom of Heaven". What is harder, seeking to be loving, or to seek to become as trusting and as sweetly open and delighted as a Little Child. He says we are responsible to be as we would wish to be to Him to the "least of these". This includes the lowest downtrodden person of the Earth to the guileless and pure Little Child.

It is my desire to share as you desire me to share. From my perspective, I see that others might like to know what some of us are seeing as possibilities of things which could be happening on Earth. There are also wonderfully fantastic worlds within worlds to explore. My walk with Him has in no way been a dull walk. It has been more than exciting. I am thrilled and blessed each day I walk in His Spirit. It is important to take His hand and to be led carefully through some of these adventures. We are so closely connected to Him that we often find we are walking behind the Veil, on the Other Side, and in realms we have not yet dared to enter. I have never used mind altering drugs. It is the teachings of the holiness people that we try to keep the vows of the Nazarites of partial or even complete abstinence from mind altering substances. If we are to be filled with the Great Spirit, we must not try to also fill our human vessels with other spirits which can damage our abilities to hear His still, small voice. We want to be led only by His Holy Spirit–none other. The things I have been taught did not come to me because I asked to learn of Death, the Other Side, and other Mysteries. They are given to me because I asked to draw closer and to know Him. This is my only desire. I simply want to be completely His. When I look back over my life I am amazed all He has shared with me. I can also see patterns of instructions. He has been teaching me for years of these times and of the things we must know of others in order to better help each other to survive and grow in His grace. I will start with things like prophecies in messages and dreams. I know the messages I was given. You may have different workings of the Holy Spirit in your life. God is manifold. He speaks to each of us as He is able to do so. I do not put Him "in a box", so to speak. Who am I? Who is He?

We continue our walk with the Lord of Hosts. This is not intended to be a staid and scholarly sharing of technical information. Most of my spiritual experiences have been shared with no real intent to obtain or to experience them. However, I realize I have been dreaming with clarity, lucidity and awareness. Prior to 1987-1988, I was not a person who could consciously remember dreaming at all. However, every few months or even years, there I found I remembered several of my precognitive and prophetic dreams for myself or society. There are many professional writers who have done a wonderful job of writing technically detailed books which at least attempt to describe, catagorize and give detailed statistical data regarding dreams, psychological and spiritual episodes and experiences. These writers are listed in the Suggested Spiritual Reference. Many of these reference books were read by this author later (AFTER) I had personally received and used unsought spiritual experiences; e.g. they wrote books on step parenting AFTER I had learned and used many of the same techniques in my own life. This is the way to live an exciting–never dull and boring–life...whether in, or out, of the Spirit. I prefer, as always, to live my life "in the Spirit of the Beloved".

It is my joyous realization as I am impressed to share my personal spiritual path with others of the enjoyable times we have in the Spirit in wondrous childlike play times, friendly interchanges of divine mysteries, and the loving communion of souls. Occasionally there are real prophetic messages of real portent for personal, family and friends. There are also warnings of events coming upon the Earth. It is my belief we are allowed to share close relationships with those in Heaven, if we are willing and happy to do so. The simple and childlike soul is able to experience such fun times. If one is too grown up and adult, too staid or wise in the technological and learned ways of the world, one may not be able to have the qualifications needed for such happy times with the Beloved.

I am one of those people who is thrilled by the simplest of things, in childlike joy and praise to my Father. I love interchanges with my Friend. We have known each other for so long. How can we act as if we do not know each other? It is impossible to not enjoy Him as simply and as happily as we would any other. However, He is loyal and fair in His unbelievably wonderful love. When I was an invalid child, I dreamed of the ecstasy of flying. What a logical form of escape from my sedentary state of existence. As mentioned earlier in the text, I had my heart surgery at age 15, I married and gave birth to a son and a daughter. It was at the request of my holiness/pentecostal mother I became an active member of my local Assembly of God Church in about 1965. It has been my great joy to be baptized in water, His love and His Spirit. Some would say I am a born-again, spirit-filled charismatic Christian. I simply say I believe and know He is my Lord. I love Him as no other. We can enter Heaven if we become as a Little Child. He is childlike. We are told by Jesus "of such is the kingdom of Heaven". I have heard of those who have had visions of Christ as a young boy with whom they were at play together. What an ecstatic playtime that would be! It is my desire to let everyone know there is "joy unspeakable and full of glory" for each and every one of us who desire to be in the company of the Beloved. It is my belief some of you will remember times spent in Heaven with Him. Others must be reminded. This is why I dare to share such times with you now. Otherwise, I seek to simply be in the Spirit of the Beloved. I do not like to share my private playtime with anyone else. I am eager to introduce you to our Beloved Friend only because He is so wonderful and I believe He likes those who are selfless, loving and sociable, not given to jealousy and low self-esteem. He tells us we are His Friends. We can no longer feel sad and alone. We are His Friends. If He loves and shares with us, we know ourselves to be His.

When I began to type the manuscript of Beloved: Parts I & II, I found a prophecy He had given for my whole lifetime of working with agencies involving the mentally ill, and other disadvantaged minorities such as the Afro, Native and Asian American communities, the homeless, poor, women and many others. Our society is much like the Grecian world when only those who were deemed to be perfect were adjudged to be acceptable citizens worthy of praise and notice. They wished to avoid interaction with all matters involving the aged, children, death and disability, anything and anyone deemed to less than perfect, beautiful, healthy and fit, and wholly wonderful. Does this remind us of our own national values?

My work was blessed by this message as I discovered it lost and forgotten in the stacks of handwritten notes taken by this scribe in 1967. It is located in Part I of Beloved, Section 52, page 77.

52. A SPECIAL PROPHECY

"Yea, I am thy God, Master of all Creation. Surely I love thee and givest thee blessings without number. Hear My Voice now and pay heed to My cry. There is so little time left. Open wide thy heart to bold forgiveness, as I said to you once before. Give thy love and thy heart to thy friends and the Lord shall pour out His blessings without number upon thee and thy friends.

Thy friends shall be the beasts of the Earth, the dregs of this society, the filth of all mankind. Surely thy presence shall be felt in their numbers and My name glorified. I will use you greatly, but your power must be Mine. Without Me thou wilt never be able to stand. Shew forth My love in this darkened place, this place of milk and honey. Judge not what I say at this hour. Wait until the scene unfolds.

Lo, I am thy God, Maker of all Creation, Keeper of a few who see My face in a better place, a place that My hand has made."......

Later, in probably 1968-1970, I remembered prayerfully asking to be made capable of helping others. This is the meaning of the name Alexandra. The Greek prophetess Cassandra became known as Alexandra in those few stories which said she did not die at the hands of Agamemnon's family.

In many parts of this book I will use other forms to describe my own experiences, whether written as non-fiction or as fiction. I become the fictionalized Celia, as well as names I have been given to describe my roles in life by the Lord such as Cassandra and Wowetsin. I also use Indian totemic names because certain creatures have come to me to help me understand the messages at each time they have appeared for my life. In fact, as we walk and play with our Beloved in His Spirit, we enter into play times when we pretend we are someone else in order to better understand our life roles. He teaches us His mysteries in delightful ways. School in Heaven must really be fun!

I am soon to be a Great Grandmother. That is biologically old, but I feel very young at times. I imagine I will always be learning until the day and moment I leave to return to my Heavenly Home. I am here to tell you this is not a bedtime story. It is an adventurous story of my life lived "in the Spirit of the Beloved". To a child, life is serendipity. The Child is also wise and shall lead them, for Jesus tells us "of such is the Kingdom of Heaven.". I invite you to enter my wise, joyous and funny world. I simply share. I am not seeking critiques, edits, approval or judgment. I share to be a good Child of our Beloved Father. If you enjoy my world you may share this with me. Otherwise...leave me to my happy times...and go along on your own pathway.

Your Sister Celeste

PREFACE:

I. *Beloved (Parts I & II).* It was my intention to share the joys of communion and at-onement of our souls with That One, the Holy One by whom we were created and have our existence. It was a book full of the wonderful joy of relationship with the Divine Lord Jesus and His Father.

II. *Beloved Spirit.* This book is written to share the teachings and counseling of the Divine Holy Spirit.

I will not attempt to define the Holy Spirit or to discuss the definitions of the Trinity of Father, Son and Holy Spirit. These are learned discussions of religious scholars of all faiths. This is a compilation of personal teachings and messages from the Holy Spirit–however She/He is defined.

Again, I feel impressed to attempt to share with others who have desire to know about the miraculous operations and ministry of the Holy Spirit. *Jesus Christ said to tarry to be endowed with this ever present Spirit of Comfort, Knowledge, Wisdom who will come and fill each of us with His/ Her divine presence. He told us This One was sent as a Comforter and a Counselor to let us know He had not left us alone like so many sojourning lost sheep without their Great Shepherd.*

The Holy Spirit will be with us and we will know we are not alone. There are levels of growth with the Father that are taught to us by the Teacher who has been sent to tutor us in the divine mysteries of our Heavenly Father. *We are told to seek to know Him. If we seek, we shall find. If we knock the door will be opened to us.*

Many of us took His instructions to seek to be filled with the Holy Spirit of truth and wisdom very seriously. We are to study to show ourselves approved, His works who need no correction. We have been studying very hard to know Him.

This is a collection of the personal heavenly educational experiences outlined as the stages of the author's long and full lifetime. This book contains many very special messages received in my lifetime of attempting to walk in His Path as His daughter. As stated in my first book *"Beloved: Parts I & II"*, I consider myself to be a very ordinary, often fallible, woman. These are the notes of the busy lifetime of a busy "Super Mom" American wife, mother and great grandmother who has walked a very long and arduous pathway attempting to follow *"In His Steps"*, as in the original book of that title. I am not the perfect "Pilgrim" of *"A Pilgrim's Progress"*. I am so very prone to error and sin, I wonder why I dare to share such a common life with others. However, it is my belief that many of us would rather share over a cup of coffee with a friend like ourselves than with a stranger unlike ourselves. I don't know about you all, but when I sin, I truly make a horrible mistake. I've learned so much by my mistakes this is why I am able to think a book full of these disclosures may be appealing to those who like truth, honesty and a non-contrived story of one of his daughters who loves Him.

My life has been stranger than fiction, as are also many of yours. I love Him and His ways so much. However, for all my prayerful efforts, I do not think I am the "perfect woman". In addition to my own imperfections, I sin because I do not trust someone who seems obsessed with their own hypocritical virtues. In fact, I am truly sure some of these dear souls are "so humble, they are not without pride in their own humility. I find it hard to believe some few souls actually feel they can actually call themselves truly virtuous and without sin. I believe most of us are simply attempting to do His will as best we can. In fact, one morning several years ago I had a dream which said something about the " feeling of one's self as perfect is truly imperfection." Therefore, those who can think "I'm humble and I'm proud of it" must surely lack that which they believe themselves to be therewith endowed. Why, if this is the case, have they not been taken from this veil of toil and pain?

If I were ready and perfect, I surely would love to escape and return to my Heavenly Home. As with the scriptures which describe the "Vision of the Sheet" the Lord showed to Apostle Peter, I believe we have come to a place in our own Christian walk when many of us need to have Him once again show us that "Sheet" and let us realize there are many who we may deem to be unclean. However, if we will closely examine our own hearts and lives we may, perchance, see some small "mote within our own eyes", thereby making us aware of our utter fallibility before Him. It is time to remind ourselves that we can become just as legalistic and orthodox in our thinking as "Born-Again Christians" as did that dear very Orthodox Jew we now call St. Peter. There are very few perfect people, religions or denominations. It seems we could have terrible things happening with so much fear, ignorance and pride in our own infallibility as humans who are simply attempting to learn how to follow Him. After all, we know the Father hates our pride. "Pride goeth before a fall"–God forbid! Many of our human houses of worship are simple gathering places in which we are penitently attempting to find the simplicity of His ways in order that we might find our own feet walking in the footprints of the Steps of our Master. Lord, lead and guide us always, please. None of us are perfect. We simply desire to know and to be near You. This is not "*The Gospel According to Garp*" (or ME). Who am I? We need You to lead and direct us, Beloved Lord. Amen.

Our Lord Jesus said there will come a time when His Spirit will be poured out "upon all flesh". Let us not be so busy in our own conceits we are unable to see Him in this great outpouring upon all nations, kindreds and tongues. Babel separated us. He will re-unite His children in the fullness of times. Are we ready to accept everyone as having a piece of His wonderful blessings within their lives? Let us be as accepting and loving children. Children are not racist or judgmental unless they learn these things from frightened parents who do not understand how wonderfully loving and big is our Father. We must become trusting and childlike as the "Little Child" who is the like the Kingdom of Heaven. He will do new things if we are able to see and accept them into our hearts and lives.

Also, there are more books which could be written of the fullness of His glories. It is possible each reader has a story which could be shared with others. This family's close relationship with the Spirit of God began with the miraculous healing of my crippled grandfather, a hard working farmer with an injured back suffered when he fell from a hay mow. He attended a local holiness meeting in Northern California many decades ago. He went in on crutches. He came out shouting the praises of God for his divine healing, running and walking without any injury or crutches. This is a manifestation of the divine healing ministry of the Holy Spirit of the Father. (Mark 16:15-18.) He said to them (1)"Go into all the world and preach the good news to all creation. Whoever believes and is baptized will be saved, but whoever does not believe will be condemned. (2)And these signs will accompany those who believe: In My name they will drive out demons; they will speak with new tongues; they will pick up snakes with their hands; and when they drink deadly poison, it will not hurt them at all; they will place their hands on sick people, and they will get well.

I Corinthians 12:1-11. Now about spiritual gifts, brethren, I do not want you to be ignorant. You know that when you were pagans, somehow or other you were influenced and led astray to mute idols. Therefore, I tell you that no one who is speaking by the Spirit of God says, "Jesus be cursed," and no one can say, "Jesus is Lord," except by the Holy Spirit.

There are different kinds of gifts, but the same Spirit. There are different kinds of service, but the same Lord. There are different kinds of working, but the same God works all of them in all men.

Now to each one the manifestation of the Spirit is given for the common good. To one there is given through the Spirit the message of wisdom, through another the message of knowledge by means of the same Spirit, to another faith by the same Spirit, to another gifts of healing by one Spirit, to another miraculous powers, to another prophecy, to another distinguishing between spirits, to another speaking in different kinds of tongues, and to still another the interpretation of tongues.

All of these are the work of one and the same Spirit, and he gives them to each one, just as he determines.

Other scriptural readings: I Corinthians 12:12-31; and I Corinthians 13 & 14. Chapter 14 defines the gifts of prophecy and of tongues. Chapter 13 Love covers all. Without love, all of these gifts are as nothing. I Corinthians 13:13–And now these things remain: faith, hope and love (a.k.a. charity).

" BUT THE GREATEST OF THESE IS LOVE"

We can have all types of powerful prophetic and healing gifts, yet He will not know us if we have not love. There is nothing as important to Him as Love, one of the Fruits of His Divine Spirit. We must show forth His Fruits to the world. They need to see His Spirit living in us and be comforted.

We are told there are not enough books to contain all that has been said and done by our Beloved. *Beloved Spirit* is simply one small attempt to share His wonderful teachings and counseling with others. I can truly see patterns and a divine plan for my life and the lives of others.

The many lists of our prayers have all been answered in one way or another. The lists of Prayers are long enough to fill other books. We are blessed. It is by counting our blessings "one by one" that we are allowed to see "what God has done."

The Holy One is so beautiful and His Spirit opens the Doorway into the wonderful mysteries of Other Worlds. Many authors have attempted to share these mysteries in fictionalized stories because people have not been ready to hear them as a reality of their "modern world". My directives are to share with others as if they are now ready to learn a few of the wonders of All That Is. His ways encompass many nations and religions. He is indeed Omniscient, Omnipotent, Omni-Present, All Good, The Just, Merciful and Compassionate, Protector and Provider, Healer and Comforter, Advocate, Friend and Beloved. To know Him is to know Truth which will set us all free to love one another with His Love and Peace which passes all understanding. His Kingdom will become a reality and we will "Live like there's Heaven on Earth". The Lord's Prayer will be answered. We will be able to come to Him as His Own.

Truth sets us free to know the complexity of the Divine Ones. We can be divided and be conquered by our fears and violence. These are often caused by our lack of knowledge. The natural person fears anything until the light of truth is shown upon the darkness of ignorance. We can also choose to pray without ceasing and to know communion and at-onement with All That Is. The Creator is in all His Creation. We worship with all the zeal and adoration of a charismatic Christian or Sufi. In spite of our great desire to know and to do His will and way in our lives, we know ourselves to be so fallible as human beings. He is pure. We are but sojourning pilgrims walking a dusty pathway.

Evil exists without end for those who will not see the Beauty of Wholeness. His holiness is "Joy unspeakable and full of glory." We are invited to exchange our mourning garments for garments of praise and joy. We are invited to a gala family reunion the likes of which we cannot imagine. One side of my family boasts over 2,000 members at their annual reunion in Pennsylvania. Imagine. What will our heavenly reunion be compared to here on Earth? We sing, dance, eat and share as do those who are part of the Earth–the ones who know the Great Spirit is in all of us and His divinely blessed creation. This will be the biggest 'pow-wow' of and for all.

Those who have love one for another will be able to hug, kiss and bless each other with Divine Love. It will not matter how we express our love to Him. Each relationship with Him is a divine romance of one soul again joined in union with His Spirit. Some cannot imagine romance without the filth of the world. We experience the ecstasy of being in the Presence of Our Father who loves all His children. Some children are playing church in one part of the world. Some are in another area. Each has made a place of worship in their own lands. Above all, we all share the knowledge of our private relationships with Our Father within the Secret Gardens of our hearts. We know we are His. We recognize others who love Him with their whole hearts, minds, bodies and souls. We know Him and His voice. We no longer wonder if we are His.

We have this blessed awareness as our reality. Therefore, we can say we have knowledge (gnosis). If we seek and are able to realize the immensity of All That Is and always has been, we sometimes feel as if we are living in a world which does not always share our desire or value Wisdom and Knowledge. Our Lord Jesus was considered by many to have been closely associated with Gnostic, Essene and Nazarene religious communities. Hypocrisy, ignorance and lies are the pathways of those who inhabit this world and the nether worlds of half truths. The Truth and Light of the Beloved will set all free to Know His Love. Let us decide to seek to be brave enough to seek Truth and Wisdom. To know them is to know the Beloved Father. We may not like the things we learn, but we will also know we must attempt to discern the Spirits of Evil and of Truth. We are each to "work out our (personal) salvations with fear and trembling". We will each be personally accountable for the efforts and salvation of our own soul. We are part of Him seeking to find our Path back to Him with our own accounts of our 'adventures' while on our seemingly "impossible mission" (as from the television series "Mission Impossible"). *However, all His teachings are about simplicity and about becoming as a "Little Child". We may study and ponder many deep studies. However, we can also know without any doubt, in utter child like simplicity, that the more one knows the more there is to learn. We are humbled by our very humanity as His "Little Child" which must live in each of our hearts in order to truly be His Child.*

My journey began a few short decades ago when I opened the doorway to a closer walk with Jesus in 1967. I have gone through several stages of insightful experiential research as a human woman. When I was an invalid child I read everything I could find from Elsie Dinsmore, to the romantic historical novels and biographies of the people of the world for many centuries of life on this planet.

My personal life has become a study of what has been happening on this planet in the 20th Century. I am a student of the diverse studies of human beings. From my studies of the social sciences I am able to see myself objectively from several social and personal psychological stances. I can see how myself and others are viewed as human statistics on bureaucratic reports as to our marital, financial, religious and political roles in life. The most simply led life has been recorded in the statistical reports of this planet. It seems q uite logical to me in this age to realize we each have files which contain detailed recorded data about our body, mind, emotions and soul. What have each of us been doing with our lives? Are we learning and growing or going backwards into oblivion and death of our eternal souls? These are questions each of us could be asking ourselves.

When I began a personal journal in 1967, I was doing it to keep my sanity and to sort out my life. Later, as I progressed on my daily life, I realized I was indeed being led and guided by the Spirit of the Holy Father I had sought with tearful prayer for all of my life. It is my ongoing desire to know and to love Him with my whole heart, mind, body and soul. Sometimes we must study to know how to know our fellow travelers in life. Loving is not logical. Forgiveness and acceptance of one another as fallible and sometimes very imperfect adventuring souls is important. None of us came with easily accessible User Manuals. Many of us were forced to leap off the precipice into the great unknowns of life. Most of us had no memories of anything except the here and now. What do we do–sink or swim? Many of us tried to swim without any lessons. We almost drowned ourselves and others with us. We were not malevolent; we were like little children lost in a scary world full of many unusual unknown human entities of heaven and earth, along with unusual appearing and behaving wildlife, flora and fauna, each of which could each be dangerous until proven otherwise. Our parents were also learning. It's obvious that each soul must strive as to spend their whole lifetimes attempting to learn what this world is all about without being maimed, murdered or robbed, while attempting to provide for the survival needs of itself and its family. All of this is expected with seemingly very few, if any, real guidelines. If we are not able to learn from the historical records or from each other of the rules of daily life, we are in dire troubles. Life is not a picnic.

Truth is stranger than fiction. Those of us who have lived life more abundantly–or less abundantly–know this is a true statement. Personally, I can say my own life has been at least as unusual as several of the socalled fictionalized episodes I have read. Those of us who are avid readers know these things are true. Those who have been actively living life know that those who participate will learn more–as well as be blessed more or less, and suffer more or less–than those to whom others are not drawn. Therefore, attractive men and women get into more interesting life relationships and experiences–for better or for worse. If our lives are long, we have that many more levels and numbers of experiences. Therefore, if one wishes to learn, choose to study with someone let it be with and from an interesting person "who'se been there and done that". However, much to my chagrin, after prayerfully seeking to be an example so others wouldn't have to suffer themselves, I found God's Kids are all "Do it your self-ers", even if they should not be. I found my journals were full of 'Signs' of the Times and guiding watchwords along a blessed and protected, sometimes thorny, rough and landmine laden, path of life.

Above all, as directed to share with others, this busy and adventurous life is one full of divine instructions and messages for how to make it through all of these memorable events in life. Evidently, some of us are here to learn a lot.

If we can help others by letting them know they are not alone in their traumas that is something I feel may be helpful to some few who like to read of the adventures of people like themselves. Sometimes I have problems with that. I never read all those "How to" books written by the careful souls who wanted to read a lot of boring data before I'd lived it. Generally, living life at a fast pace requires one to spend a lot of time 'punting', as one runs through all types of unusually interesting times and ages in one's own personal life.

In addition to those things for which we must take responsibility, there are also those 'other' events over which we have no control, such as the psychological, cultural and spiritual upheavals in our local religious and cultural communities, our nations and world. These are those major events such as wars of all types, economic recessions, medical epidemics, plagues and the like.

When one is not battling one's own personal 'wars', we find we are also forced to face those terrible fears engendered by all types of human machinations of others " to keep us all on our toes". We find ourselves seeking to keep ourselves and others safe from the realities of others– even if not our own. We feel threatened and terrorized by the real, or imagined, fears of ourselves and others. The human psyche tends to go into dangerous modes of thinking if it leads a life which is 'too exciting'. Psychological, emotional, physical and spiritual traumas do each take their tolls upon our personal selves. Some of us tend to run on adrenolin and it keeps us alert and hyper in order to be safe-- if not sane. Sometimes they make us lose our memories if they prove to be too intense for us to retain and still function in our busy lives. Sometimes we find ourselves becoming catatonic with fear. Life can be made to feel like a Chamber of Horrors rather than a preparation for Heaven. It does make one wish to be shown the exit from this House of Mirrors, Labyrinth or Chamber of Horrors. In addition, we also suffer from simple physical 'accidents' in life. If we fall on the back of our heads as some of us do on occasion, this can add headaches and back aches to our list of 'battle scars'. Some of us begin to suffer the pangs of old age and death. All of these are but other adventurous stages in life. Some of us have adventures we discuss only with our Heavenly Father. Confidentiality is good for our souls and the souls of others whenever we realize we are able to do well with keeping our secrets if they will help no one else–not even ourselves.

If we take time to be conscious and mindful, we may find we are overjoyed to find that each of the messages and experiences in life have been given to us for our guidance and edification. We have not been alone as we faced each of these dangers in life. We have been blessed over and over again by the leadings and guidance of the Comforter. We have been counseled such as when the still small voice of the Spirit said, "You can forgive and bring blessings to your children...or you can become an embittered old woman who no one wishes to be around, or you can see great blessings...." Another time as a young mother, there was a concern over how to be able to later rear teenaged children. The immediate message was "If you are just (fair) and loving all will be fine." Later, as a court appointment loomed, wonderful strong scripture message of Jeremiah 1 was given. He and His forces will be there to support us. We are never alone. If we draw near to Him, He will draw near to us.

It is obvious when observes the dates of the messages received that each was a relevant piece of an ongoing research project. Now we can see what the Divine Weaver was attempting to show on our Tapestry. We saw the knots on the back of the tapestry. Now we see there has always been a Divine Plan and Purpose for our lives. We are led and directed to show us the pitfalls and dangers. We are also shown the opportunities and blessings. It is obvious to me in reviewing the patterns of events of the world that much of my life has been lived to let me learn that we are not alone. We are led and guided even until the End of Time. This is the Message of the Beloved Spirit. We are children being led by a Loving Parent. He tells us "You have not because you ask not." Let us ask to know Him and to be led and guided by His Spirit. We need comfort, guidance and protection. Logic tells us we cannot live in this world, yet not of this world, like sojourners on a strange planet. We need to see order and reason in His universe. We need to know it was His intention for this world to be a blessed place in which to live. Instead, we have added conflicted spiritual forces to this perfect creation. He has never stopped His attempts to infill us with His blessed Holy Spirit and to teach us of His Spiritual Fruits. He is Good. He is Love. He is able to forgive all of us for our errors and to set us free from the bondages of this world. He wishes to prepare us for our Return to Paradise. This is an ordered and well governed world. He is the Living God. He knows and is known by those who seek Him. He knocks at the inner door of our hearts. We must ask Him to come in and sup with us. He is very gracious and polite. He will counsel and comfort our hearts.

May we all be blessed and made whole in His Beloved Spirit. Our Lord said He would leave but that The Comforter would come to lead and guide us in all manner of ways. The Beloved Spirit is with us each as we travel through our Earthly lives.

This is but one of the messages contained herein. In the case of the author, I have broken my life into segments showing the type of path upon which I was traveling at each time in my life. It is obvious there each event was a carefully planned teaching experience. We all know "experience is the best teacher." To enter the reality of a human being is a great adventure for this soul. Every other part of that life is one which has taught other levels of awareness to this inquisitive soul. "Curiosity killed the cat." Yes, and souls often going adventuring into the realms evil into which "Angels fear to tread." This can be done with intent, or by purity, innocence and ignorance. This is why it is good to ask for guidance and protection at all times.

After awhile as we go, some of us find ourselves using symbolic and mythological terms to define roles and events in our lives. This helps us to be able to stand back outside ourselves to see a macrocosmic plan for our lives,and then to enter in closely to see a microcosmic view of our own lives. This helps us to learn from our own mistakes as well as to see beauty and holiness in our own lives. If we stand afield, we can see the Divine Weaver working upon our own life Tapestry. (See the sections on divine spiders, etc.) This is why the author dares to share. Perhaps we need to comfort and help one another from time to time. Perhaps we can see Him more clearly as we share together. Oftentimes, we can learn from one another from His Treasures.

Many years later, I am able to see the beautiful messages of the Holy Spirit has been fulfilled in His own words, "A place made with My own hand". I am thrilled and blessed. He teaches, warns and protects us from ourselves and others–even on a cosmic scale. He is the Alpha and the Omega, the Beginning and the Ending, the Author and the Finisher, or your life and mine. He is our All in All. It matters not how we name or define This One, the multi-faceted, Manifold Go(o)d, the Beloved Spirit. He simply is and always has been. We will be led and guided to find ourselves "Lost in the (Beloved) Spirit". Many of us asked to be His, to be lost in His Holy Spirit, and to be "Taken Out" before all manner of dreadful prophetic events occur upon our planet. Perhaps "Glory is coming down". Perhaps we are becoming more and more enraptured by Him as we see Him. He will be "Coming soon". We will study with our hearts full of His Love, seeking His Truth and Wisdom. We will be filled to overflowing with His Spirit even as He has promised.

Joy, Peace and Love are the Gifts of Our Beloved Heavenly Father. Please accept His invitation to take His hand and walk into the beauty of His Eternal Bliss. This is but a foretaste of Heaven Divine. It is time for all of us to share one with another. Let us build each other up in our Faith. Let us comfort one another, even as we are comforted by Him. The Truth shall set us free from all doubts and fears. He rested and said "It is good." Let us assist in the reconstruction of a wonderful new time as prophesied by the angels at His birth of Peace on Earth and good will to all." Sacred time, space and safety can be ours. We are His Children. He is our Beloved Father. Darkness will be no more. His Light will overcome all that is not of the Holy Spirit of the Beloved.

Sometimes as His, we are allowed to suffer with the world in which we find ourselves. We are a watchword to others. If we see a larger macrocosmic view of life, we may begin to experience the woes of our society as a prophetic person. He tells us to "Fear not , for I am with you, to bless, keep and to save." We must hold on a little longer. He is coming soon. He iswith us forever.

SECTION II
THE WORLD VS. WISDOM

SECTION II –THE WORLD VS. WISDOM–1970-1982

THE PATH OPENS–MESSAGES FROM HEAVEN

THE CALLED-OUT ONES

THE CALL

I had grown older and had left my days of youth behind me. I was a married women with beloved children of my own and also my husband's former life. My life as a young divorcee had ended and I had been remarried nine years. We all know about those wonderful years of attempting to be a super woman with teen aged children. We attempt to burn the candle at both ends being the best wife and mother ever. Some of us even tackle higher educational pursuits while working in our family accounting firm. We each have our reasons for every part of those unbelievably stressful times of seeming overwork. Our goals and accomplishments are many especially if we begin to realize how short the lengths of life. We were living lives unknown to many of our mothers who had not been forced to become sole parent and provider for our children.

That night so long ago, in probably 1981, it was a night like any other homemaker's tired sleep. I was sleeping soundly until I heard the first words:

"REMEMBER, I AM COMING SOON."

I seem to remember going back to sleep before the next words awakened me from my sleep that selfsame night:

"COME OUT FROM AMONG THEM, AND BE YE SEPARATE."

I forgot about these enigmatic messages until I again became a woman alone.

At that time, I began to attempt to understand the meanings of these two, very interesting, even auspicious, messages. What did they mean to me, then and now? What do they mean to others who also receive such "A Call"? I Peter 2; II Peter 1.

I see a great new trend in our nation in the past few decades of polarizations between religious, spiritual, and political views in our nation. America has always placed great value on being "One Nation, Under God"; however, hopefully not to the exclusion of healthy and needful dialogue between those of even opposite perspectives. There has been so much emphasis placed upon the values of only one faction of our society and upon one religion that it has fragmented our people much as if we have had an invisible Civil War. We have been divided by those who do not realize everyone of us have our own divine set of values within our souls. If we have love one for another we will share our views and have a peaceful society where each of us are deemed to be able to share our beautiful insights and values with each other. We do not have attitudes that we are higher or more holy than one another. We are all divine children of God. Ethics and values are individually shared by all. Each of us see a different view of society. Some of us share all the values of others. One group has a list of important issues to solve. Another group may see theirs and more moralistic values even than a socalled 'moral majority'. The Father's List is long. It can be corrected by the loving and prayerful efforts of all of His beloved globalized children. We live on a round planet. We must ask for His divine guidance in order to heal such deeply festering wounds.

In the midst of these societal oppositions, there are those souls who have received their own, personal, calls to stand apart and thereby attuned to the Master's Voice. They might be called the so called Mystics, or the American secular monks and nuns who are living as invisible Sannyasin, on the order of the spiritual withdrawal made by the philosophically and spiritually inclined people past the ages of the householder roles in India. After all, we are in mystical union with Christ, in spite of the misguided and ignorant belief among some Christians that "one cannot be a mystic and be a Christian". We must take time to learn the meanings of words and their usages. There is a whole vocabulary of spirituality which is being misunderstood by many wonderful, truly seeking, souls. If one errs, or makes an honest mistake, it is nice to err, if we must judge another, upon the side of liberality, kindness, and love. One would not wish to slander, libel, or in any way injure another simply because there is a lack of insightful dialogue.

Words, symbols, dreams and all types of values do have very deep meaning in my life now. I will attempt to reiterate some of the meanings I have received over the next 22 years for myself, and others. At this time, I now see them clearly as my call to discipleship to Lord Jesus, my Master and Counselor, Teacher, Healer, and Savior as I progress on my spiritual quest as a Seeker of Truth & Wisdom, found in Him and His mysteries. He has remained closely beside me, dwelling within my heart's center. He is always my Savior, who gives me Advocacy as a blessed, sometimes poverty stricken, very ordinary woman, who is also His Child.

He is still my Master. I am His disciple, child, and sometimes foolish one who walks as a wealthy or as a poor woman, even as my Master ordains for my life pathway. He is my best treasure who dwells in my heart. His Fruits and His Gifts are my gemstones. His Home is my Home.

I will attempt to outline some personal and scriptural messages which I have used throughout my life in order to keep myself on the Path of Love, Light & Wisdom.

After my initial introduction into receiving prophetic messages in 1967, I also began to become a copious writer of journals. I realized we do not seem as concerned with our own feelings and spiritual growth as we do about cooking, cleaning, our various collections of jewelry, books, or movies. Therefore, I believe this is why He has led some of us into much more detailed record keeping of the well beings of our own souls. We have no more important treasures than those of our eternal souls. Of course, one must believe in souls, and some degree of an organized plan and purpose for the universe and our everlasting souls in order to believe there is also a Divine Creator who cares to communicate with our souls even as His/Her created children.

I continued walking by faith. It seemed the only way for me to go. In the midst of my spiritual path, I also began walks with others in relationships which were not always the best for me. They evidently had special roles outlined for them in my personal life plan destiny. Remember we are speaking of a woman with a strictly fundamentalist Christian heritage. Since then I have become a multi-cultural inter-faith mystical contemplative charismatic Christian who also sees great beauty and power in the teachings of the Buddhist and Native American people. He is in all people everywhere. He has given each dear tribal group a special piece of His beautiful plan for peaceful life on Earth. Love is our Key to Peace on Earth, goodwill to all human beings. The creation was blessed by the Creator. So are we.

I did not seek masters, guides and teachers. When I was ready, as is said, they simply began to come into my dreams and waking messages, along with my higher university studies in comparative religion and the social sciences. I always desired to be someone who worked with others to get through their hard lives. Much of my many years of working has been in the settings of Human Services, Mental Health and with educational facilities such as colleges and universities. It might be said that humans and the human condition are my passion and great love of my life. How can one learn of only one or two facets of these involved creations without also realizing religious institutions and spiritual experiences are very important in the progression of humankind from atavism to enlightenment.

Religious studies is an all-encompassing passion for those of us who have become enamored with Sophia, the goddess of Wisdom. She is interested in us all becoming “Knowers”, not simply “blind followers” and “true believers”. We are told in the scriptures to “study to show yourselves approved, workmanships which need no corrections.” I utterly believe we are to Seek, Find,and bear witness to the Truth. It is Truth which will set us free. (Jesus Christ)

As I relive my spiritual experiences in living, dreaming and visionary states, I am aware of the fact that the Spirit has been teaching and guiding me for years to be conversant with the various paths of enlightenment available to us at this time. I have only begun to scratch the surface of the great wealth of information we have with which to work. There seems to be appearing a pattern of instruction since the middle of the 1980’s. This is of the coming great trials and tribulations prophesied to come upon this planet. It seems obvious to me that most are simply accepting all the aforementioned chaos, without any prayerful pleas for changing of the programmed formats into which humans have organized themselves. If we will not alter our human proclivities for violence, greed, envy and jealousy and war there will be no way of altering this destructive course for annihilation of ourselves and others. Perhaps the dwellers of the cosmos do not agree. Some of them are coming to some of us to let us know we must wake up and speak forth the warning messages we have been given.

MESSAGES FROM HEAVEN

1. HEAVEN'S SWINGING DOOR

Dream - Early 1980's

The dreamer was sleeping soundly until she was terribly stunned to realize she had just run through the "Swinging Door" into Heaven. She made herself speak quickly to the Father and said "Stop, stop, dear Father, don't let me forget this. I must tell them about how easy it is to enter this swinging door into Heaven!"

The next scene was of the anteroom directly inside the door. It was filled with others as blissfully ecstatic as herself to have actually "Made it into Heaven". It was indeed "Joy unspeakable, and full of glory" which no words can describe herein. One person stood out from all others because she was weeping heartbrokenly because she was desirous of a relationship and a small amount of money–not desiring to be deceased and in Heaven, in the very Presence of the Lord. The dreamer began to weep with her, for her sadness, and found herself becoming Christ. His tears became overpowering and she awakened, still weeping unrestrained tears for the one who was so unhappy.

There were many messages received from this dream. 1) The younger weeping woman would have her own free will to choose to be wherever she desired to be. She would not be forced to stay in Heaven's glory. There was spiritual realization that her desires were both for mediocre things. The man of her affections was not worthy of her love and the amount of money was a small amount like $700.00. We each have free will to choose where and whom we will share our life realities.

2) Christ is concerned about each and every one of us. He weeps for us.

3) Many people talk of the unknown realms and beings. Few can give coherent and real data from Heaven, about Heaven. Few also know about the deity and majesty of the rulers of these realms. Many people try to act like hardcore salespeople with hardened sales spiels about Jesus, the Father, Heaven and Hell, and all manner of divine events and sights. They try to sell others information about entities and property about which they know nothing. They are very concerned for others to the point of attempting to make things as they wish them to be, rather than as they are in all truth.

4) At the end of the dream, the dreamer was given a cut-away side view of the slightly inclined Tunnel through which many have seen themselves walking into Heaven. She was shown a prophetic view of herself leading a long line of others into their Heavenly Home. This was a thrilling ending to some very insightful messages within the first Message. Evidently, this was simply a foretaste of the joys that will be ours when we enter our Heavenly Home once again.
****

SECTION III
SEEKERS OF WISDOM

SECTION III–SEEKERS OF WISDOM

PART I

METAPHYSICAL & ESOTERIC TRAINING INTRODUCTION.

In the early 1980's I asked to know about the prior two decades I seemed not to understand at all. The reply was "Alright, you will be shown many things of which you will be very frightened at times." This is a great understatement. It was as though I had personally opened Pandora's Box. Out of it flew all manner of evils except Hope. I cling closely to Hope, even as my own mother, also named Hope. We must keep our hopes high if we are to walk "atop the waves" through these coming Earth changes without sinking into an abyss of pure panic due to the horrific things we see coming upon the planet. This is sometimes a veritable Labyrinth laced with land mines. The times are treacherous. Our Lord has not changed. Therefore, I cling ever tighter to His beloved hand, attempting to walk completely in the Spirit of the Living God. No. He is not dead. Only humans dare to say The Living God is dead while they are walking zombies following dead beliefs of devils in human forms. Let us soon make our escapes from such prisons. It is time.

I find my adventures to be interesting and even frightening. You will make your own decisions. I am not going to go into great learned dissertations about every incident and message. The reason for writing is to make each reader think of their own personal reasons for belief and their own personal paths. Some of my experiences are completely inter-faith and global–given from behind theVeil of the Cosmos. You will think the same when you meet the visitors who have come to me in my own or the messages of others for me and perhaps all of us. They generally are speaking of their own research. They are sharing it with us again in this century. I thank our Divine Father so very much for His loving kindness in letting them come on brief instructional visits to help us through these times.

Early in the 1980's, I began to resceive instruction from many wise teachers including the Zen Patriarch Bodhidharma and other Zen masters, Native American totems and messengers, as well as words and messages in ancient and foreign languages such as Sanskrit, Aztec, Meso-American and Runic languages. It might be noted at this time of my own personal studies of Greek, Hebrew, Russian and other "dabblings" in unusual languages, symbols, mythology and codes. I tend to have a very short memory for all these involved items of data. However, I had never studied any of the lives and languages I received in my metaphysically intuited messages. I had never heard of any of the words which came to me in the Spirit. I was required to re-read about Niccolo Machiavelli when I awakened to the word "Machiavellian" which I believe came to me early in 2002. A friend was given the word "atavism". Both are descriptive words for this time in which we are living. We have both been shocked to realize the messages we have received to assist us in our understandings of these times. My brain is on over load. Recently, I read the autobiography of St. Therese. I was overjoyed to hear even such a special soul as herself also had a short memory. I think I have forgotten more than I remember. This is what can happen which one becomes deeply involved and in love with Wisdom and Truth.

MESSAGES FROM HEAVEN

2. THE GREAT CROWD OF WITNESSES

Dream - mid 1980's.

In the midst of a heavy load of university classes, this student began to get overtired with class work and her own overburdened life. She started to count all the things she had learned and suffered in her attempts to try to help others. She began to feel overcome with all of her unusual testings and trials she had been experiencing.

Shortly thereafter, in the midst of all this traumatic soul searching and gut rending analyzation of her unusually stressful personal destiny, the student dreamed she had arrived at a classroom in session in one of Heaven's centers of learning. This was like no other classroom she had ever seen (or felt).

She knew the students as her friends and the instructor was a very dear woman friend of hers in Heaven. They were acting as those who help to orchestrate our life destiny plans. She could feel their terrible sorrow, as if their hearts were breaking, and their internal parts were twisted in agony, over her life. They were truly traumatized, as was she. There was a great and wonderful feeling of ancient bonds of kinship and love. She was comforted in the midst of her extreme surprise and awe at her glimpse of this crowd of witnesses who were working with her in her traumatic lifestyle. It was amazing to experience their trauma over her own traumatic life. Is it possible our Father sits in on those sessions with our Witnesses?

She spoke to her friend who was leading the group and asked, "I'm so tired. Can't I please stop all these hard learning experiences?"

Her friend replied, "Alright, then let's just go have coffee."

They left the classroom together and walked into a coffee shop area with natural stone wall from which beautiful ferns grew. She later remembered this as "The Fern Grotto Coffee Shop". (The dreamer is a coffee house/shop person in Heaven...even as on Earth.)

She and her old friend walked directly in front of a table at which one of her close relatives was seated without stopping. She was shown this is how it would be when we return to Heaven. We each gravitate to those with whom we have spiritual affinity–not necessarily our friends, or even relatives, which fill our lives on the Earth plane at this time.

The dream ended with her realizing that we do not walk through the joys and hardships alone. We truly do have a "Great Crowd of Witnesses" assisting us as is mentioned in the scriptures.

At the time of this dream the writer/dreamer had never studied about life plan destinies, empathetic healing and feelings, or being able to meet friends and relatives from this and other lifetimes on this Earth plane. The Great Crowd of Witnesses was also a topic she had not explored. It is indeed a wonderful experience to know we are surrounded by so many who love and care about us. We are truly not alone. Every hair of our heads is numbered. We are special children. He weeps for our sorrows. He also blesses us with His joys. I know this was one of those special treasured messages sent from Heaven to comfort me.

Later, when I began to study more of His divine mysteries, I began to dream and to receive waking messages in the Spirit. I have never consciously sought to receive messages from the Beloved Father or His Son Jesus. Neither have I ever attempted to request information from the deceased or from other angelic beings. The only time I asked for the Message I felt I should have given in church was the one I requested as a young Christian. This is the special message of my other book entitled *Beloved.* When I began to prepare the manuscript for publication, I was reminded of the many times I had received messages from Heaven regarding deceased family members. These dreams had also revealed things about the Other Side, at least on some of the dimensional planes therein. I will include several of them in this book. Perhaps some of my readers have also seen these same scenes. It was only when I began to read books about these topics I remembered the dreams scenes I had already seen over the prior decades of my life. I was very surprised to realize I had been shown about many of my loved ones prior to, or soon after, their deaths. I had never thought of myself as one who seeks to know such mysteries. I sought to know Him and He began to teach me the mysteries of the Earth and of the Heavens. In fact, since I asked to know Him and to have Him dwell within my heart so many years ago, I have lived such an exciting dream life I could describe my life as being "just a dream", as in the old song "Life Is But A Dream".

I will begin with a wonderful dream of a deceased auntie.

3. UNIVERSITIES IN HEAVEN?

Dream: Mid-1970's

The Dreamer had briefly glimpsed and exchanged greetings with a deceased aunt amidst a crowd of people entering a large stone columned building she sensed to be a place of higher learning. Her aunt was youthful and was wearing a bright red cardigan sweater. It was a time of wonderful confirmation of her good health and happiness in Heaven.

It might be noted the Dreamer had never heard of institutions of higher learning on the Other Side, much less seeing deceased loved ones entering therein.

****

4. HEAVEN'S MEADOWS

Dream: Mid 1980's

Three of our family's women were walking together through flowery meadows in Heaven. They had each earned their victory garlands and were happy to be together again.

The huge vividly colored orange and red daisies remain in the Dreamer's memory. What a wonderful shared message of divine peace and love this was to the Dreamer. One of these has crossed over. Soon the other two will follow no doubt.

****

5. NEAR DEATH EXPERIENCE (NDE)–11 YR. OLD BOY

1964

This is an account of the personal near-death experience of my husband in his own words. He was 11 years old. It is written in his own words in order to not leave out any details of the things he experienced while on The Other Side.

Once, at age 11, as a lad I was playing high jump on a swing set where you set the bar on chains by dull hooks. It was dinnertime. I had been called to come to dinner, but decided on a last attempt.

I made it, but hit my head and caught my right forearm on a hook. I felt a sharping stinging and a tug. My arm was wet. I later realized it was from blood, and that my shirt was torn.

I didn't know what to do. I was in shock when two Vishnu appearing beings descended from the sky, or heavens, and began talking to me telepathically, telling me to go inside and tell my parents.

I did this as best I could. They wrapped a towel around my arm and drove me to the doctor. On the way I swooned, and, like switching on a lamp I was outside my body in a golden light field while my thoughts bubbled up like in a cartoon. I was not alone either, as other beings inhabit this netherworld–or in between world.

My mother must have slapped me to awaken me, for I awoke with a start, only to perceive the bago of "odour and vomit" we call our bodies. A garbage heap I resigned myself reluctantly into as a life dwelling. Why I wanted to stay, I don't know–duty perhaps, or a "bloom where planted" philosophy akin to piety.

I took short forays to discover more of the realm I had surprisinglly entered. When we reached the doctor, my mind was vivid and greatly expanded. I argued with the doctor only later realizing that absolute terms were inapplicable to the world and only frustrate one if seeking to apply them to human society, culture and intelligence.

Next, I remember being given a shot and being on a gurney dreamily awaiting an operation. A nurse sought to reassure me though I waited long.

I went into the operating room and everything shone brighter. I guess I was seeing auras and more. I had psychometric vision. (He later expanded this description to state "Along with auras, you begin penetrating into the nature of objects like clouds expressing their true natures (the souls of things), e.g. everything shone brightly and I became aware of the essential nature of objects.").

I took the ether and had a horrible nightmarish fall and chase. I believe I was in the recovery room when I had the series of experiences.

I had done a perceptual field shift resembling a tunnel, but, actually, it was a translation to heaven. I was met by a real being of wonderful beauty. A light of gold surrounded me, embraced an enveloped me, even seeming to penetrate me, but with perfect love and acceptance–a kind of love that humans dream about, but that rarely exists in the practical dog-eat-dog world of compromise on Earth. Love is the law, but who wills it to be and acts on it? They would be surprised by its success, but I'm sure it would be successful and is much needed here.

In a vision I was shone a beautiful Muslim city in the distance, and I was told I would enjoy it someday. I didn't understand. I thought it might be the Ancient One's temple monastery home. (Dr. Strange Comics)

I saw an ankle high cloud bank and some beings saying they were relatives sent to meet me, and that I couldn't stay, but that I could look around.

I saw, but didn't comprehend the huge columned building, a tower, plazas and throngs of people in simple white robes, living uncrowded in a sparsely occupied area. I was told I would have a hard life, but to persevere as best I could. They would help me recover with special therapies. Also, I saw what a happy life and place it is.

My Life Review

At the time of crossing, I had my life relived in exact detail and experience. I was made aware of the results of my deeds. The attendant "Judge" was a high spirit of fairness and spiritual wisdom, dutiful in office.

Being a child, I had no sin to be blamed for as I was only a child; but was told my future would displease my parents and cause their repute to suffer, and we would be estranged. The seeds of this already existed.

I remember a white cloaked, faceless, figure of high standing and great power. He commanded the prophetic gifts and revealed things in the future I might see or play a role in. It was singularly complex, bu orderly, as in a Plan, with every contingent outcome weighed and dealt with. I then came back and awoke to see my parents in the room. I asked them, "Did I die?" They laughed and replied "No."

I also had continued to try to leave my body at will and saw a glimpse of my white, shining, spirit form as it went though the wall while I swooned.

When I got home and back to my life, I was changed. I had telepathic and clairvoyant gifts. I would even concentrate and generate ectoplasmic substance or force, and create synchronistic effects. I felt tuned in to the divine music, or mind, that controls events. I could sometimes know things before they happened. I could tell when friends who had enlisted for the Viet Nam war would not come back. I sometimes tried to tell them, but now the VFW Hall is named for them.

My family was not able to nurture these nascent abilities and I floundered without guidance. Church became a place of excitement initially, but a disappointment ultimately, as my understanding and approach, even my visions, were not understood. I would clap with joy at a verse reading and be shushed, or I would see spirits or even a glorious light surround the pastor as he read and preached. I believe he was a truly holy man who had joy in his faith.

MESSAGES FROM MASTERS

As spiritually artistic souls we do not know as much as we would like to know about how we are able to receive wonderfully insightful inspired messages. We do not know how or why the actual soul of the entity comes to us. Some of the insightful messages I have received could have been given to me by the tutorial or guiding angels who do those things for human beings. I do know the information which we receive is pertinent, wise and wonderful as is the soul of the wonderful personages who deliver them to us.

I have come to realize there are those special beings who become our teachers in their own fields of research. My interests are in ancient worlds and in prophetic worlds to come. I write. Therefore, my messages are from those writers of those very topics in metaphysics, political and social sciences. I even had the name of Pindar come to me when I simply wondered what type of writing is in my first book. The next morning, I awakened with his unfamiliar name. He wrote copiously in all types of writing forms. Strangely, I feel very comfortable automatically calling him "Old Pindar". Later, I was told this is a common title given him by his students. The works of Oswald Spengler and Niccolo Machiavelli have been given to let us to recognize and to know the similar eras in which we are living at this time. I am eternally grateful fo these dear souls for coming to me in dreams and waking awarenesses to direct me on my spiritual path. If you, too, desire to learn their mysteries you must read their giant tomes of learning. You, too, will know we have no excuses for not writing books. Many of them wrote their huge books of wisdom in their own handwriting. Typewriters and computers had not yet been invented for some of the finest, most well loved and revered writers. Some of the best and most prolific were Manly P. Hall and Helena Petrovna Blavatsky.

I also feel a very close kinship and love for Helena Blavatsky. I do not know why. Love is not logical. It simply exists. The Father knows my relationship to this dear lady and her work. Helena Blavatsky wrote all of her own books in her old age and in poor health at times. She had no computer...perhaps not even a typewriter. She is one of my beloved archetypes of wisdom.

It is at this juncture when the author must share the fact that she has become quite sure our Holy Bible and many other holy books are quite plain in their teachings of reincarnation. We are taught as Christians that this is a false teaching. It is not until we learn it was written out of Christian doctrines at the one of the several Councils of the Catholic Church many years after Christ. If we re-read His scriptural messages again with a knowledge that many of His age did believe in reincarnation, we will find more understanding of many of His statements. It was a commonly held belief at the time of Christ that John the Baptist had returned in the "spirit of Elijah". The doctrine of reincarnation seems to explain His messages.

He said He will return because we are all eternal souls whom He did know before and know would be His when He came to find His followers. (Read Romans 8:29-30.)

When He healed to blind man He spoke to the crowd who thought the man must have done something karmicly evil to be born blind and told them this was not so. He told them this man had been blind in order for him to be the wonderful miracle man of His own ministry. Their comments let us know they believed in reincarnation in order to work out our karmic destinies as well as our Life Plan Destinies in the Divine Will for His glory and honor.

It is my belief many of the lost teachings will again be known and His teachings will be as they should have been understood in order for us to know the full glories of His redemptive powers. He came to pay the price for our sins. He took our karmic debts upon Himself and gave us forgiveness. This is why His Gift of Salvation is so wonderful.

Of course, His salvation is not the only reason I love and serve Him as my Lord. I sought Him and fell in love with His teachings, as well as the reasons He lived and died for us. If He had indeed continued to live, married or single, as some legends tell us, I would still serve Him. He is my dearest Friend. I love Him dearly as my Beloved Lord. He is too wonderful to ever find in Him any fault.

The doctrine of reincarnation is not of utmost importance, but it does add much to His Gospel. His words are much more understandable with it as part of our belief system. Human leaders were concerned the belief in reincarnation would let the souls of many free to not be dominated by evil tyrants. One who believes in divine learning destinies and several lifetimes has even more courage to be able to die for worthy human rights causes. They also know they have a merciful God who cleanses them from sins and offers them instructions on how to overcome any errors showing at their life reviews of their prior lives when they enter into Heaven once again. They know they are the immortal souls our Holy Book tells us we were eternally created to be in Him. He said His creation was blessed and good. Others have left a huge pall of darkness upon all the works of the Father. Much of this is not from Him. These are false doctrines of devils. He is very sad we have been separated from His company. He misses us and desires to be with us all once again.

6. HELENA PETROVNA BLAVATSKY (H. P. B.),

"Beloved Lady, No One Like Her"–How does one describe a legend?

About 1988

My dear friend is a charismatic minister and is a college professor. At the time she dreamed of Helena Blavatsky (HPB), she and I were both university students. It was a remarkable message. It is with the wisest of all metaphysical women I will begin our walk into the wonderful halls of wisdom.

My friend and I had met in our university classes in 1987. She and I found ourselves both being taught divine mysteries in dreams, visions and educational classes. At this time, I had not yet begun to be a dreamer, much less a researcher of dreams. Therefore, HPB came to her in a dream.

"The Old Lady, like an aunt to me", came to my friend in a dream and said she had her "Library" and a house full of jewelry and trinkets she wished to share with me. She quoted a special "Stanza" of her book "The Secret Doctrine". The amazing thing about all of this is that neither of us had ever known of HPB, her "Library", or the topics of her research which is about root races and beginnings of life on the planet, as well as deeply esoteric studies of Tibetan wisdom from Tibetan masters, lamas and avatars. She knew her great tomes of wisdom concerning my own research was needed for my usage. The "Stanzas" she gave were not known to us. In fact, the usage of a term like "Stanza" is not common to those who study Biblical "Scriptures and Verses". We were being taught by the Mistress of high metaphysical lore. She and other well known metaphysicians had founded the Theosophical Society. They had traveled extensively to uncover these ancient truths, even into Tibet. HPB left this plane of existence in the last decades of the 19th Century. This was not a time when travel was by airplane and automobile. She is considered to have been (and still is) one of the strongest of souls to have accomplished so much in her lifetime. As we can see, she has not ceased teaching. I fell in love with this woman and her great wisdom. I have not had time to this day to really study her work as I would like to be able to do. She remains a beloved and inscrutably wise woman. A person to whom she referred me has become my closest and dearest Teacher. The mystery schools teach "When the student is ready, the teacher will come.". I am honored to have been called ever more deeply into the deeper mysteries of esoteric studies by the beloved Grande Dame herself. Her picture remains in my own library as a sphinx like face of one of my beloved mentors.

As a Christian I have been taught to be careful of esoteric deeper mysteries. However, by this time I had been also been deeply drawn into the deeper workings of the Gifts of the Holy Spirit. I believe He had allowed HPB to come to share her wealth of wisdom with us. Perhaps she and I know each other as friends on the Other Side. Perhaps I study with her there. There are many things we do not know.

I am sure she came to give me her Library because in her writings are the keys to the creation, the ages of life upon this planet, and the reasons and causes of the things to come. She came to share these truths with us because she knows we need them at this time in the history of the Earth. She was the first of several who have come to share their wise research with us at this crucial time.

Those who chose to misconstrue her messages about the Aryan races and the usage of the backward Hindu swastika cross never knew her or the teachings of her Theosophical Society which were so helpful in the furtherance of studies of Buddhism and Hinduism in the West.

7. "A WILLING VESSEL"

Dream–September 25, 2004, 5 a.m.

We are attempting to learn what we need to know in order to be able to teach others.

The problems is with the need to use a finite human being. In fact, in my case, I am a very busy hardworking and older vessel. I am willing. However, I know it's hard on my spiritual teachers because my body and brain are exhausted with physical and emotional stressors. I am also only able to grasp teachings based upon my own abilities to describe concepts with which I am at least partially able to comprehend. Sleep is very useful as a therapy for body, mind and soul. It is possible to alter time in order to obtain maximum amounts of sleep.

Most of the time I am learning as I teach others. They must make me conversant with data new to my mind. Then I must teach myself a concept in order to explain it to others.

The goal in all of this is to show the painstaking care given to instruct the willing and obedient soul in a "course of miracles" or any other course upon which we are to be instructed.

We must hear, learn and reason it all out to the best of our prayerful abilities. Then we must try to teach others. This is very hard to do as many topics are not sought nor completely understood by the recipient of the divine mystery.

The teaching is taught during deep, often exhausted, sleep and dream states.

Even if the student is willing and ready as a soul, their human fleshly vessel may be very tired, poorly nourished and rested.

It is no easy thing to be a divinely taught soul who is then to teach others. The key is loving and obedient willingness upon the part of the Seeker of Wisdom and Truth. There must be a complete loving and submissive desire to know the Good, the Whole and the All-Encompassing Beautiful One(s). The dedication to become a Soul who is attuned to the Highest, who earns access to the Presence and Unction of the Most Holy Spirit is to be highly commended.

To be able to teach others who are often unwilling and ignorant souls is an unbelievably hard, sometimes impossible, task.

To be able to retain incoming data and be led to expound upon it is a disciplined treatise written in Divine Love for the good of all.

Thus will each new student learn from the Great Teachers.

None have learned without dedicated discipline to Truth and Wisdom.

The Vessels, even as this one, are finite and sometimes very humble. Their merits are their loving dedication to the well being of their own soul coupled with their dedicated desires to learn so they are able to teach and counsel others.

He uses willing souls who love Him and are dedicated to learning His teachings in order to love Him. He has directed His followers to obey His commandments. This is their willing desire. They are also told they must share His teachings with others.

His education is such that the student may learn the Most or the Least. It is based upon the desires and abilities of the able and willing soul.

The question is ours to decide. Do we choose to learn the mean and menial or the mysteries of the Highest?

His Ending Message was a surprise to me:

"Say goodbye, Sleepy Soul, for tomorrow is another day in which to learn, in which to share and to teach mysteries with the others who desire to know Me.

I love you all." (Jesus, the Christ)

The author's thoughts about this message:

Evidently He wanted me to have these insights. They also made me think of the way HPB agreed to be used by the Mahatmas in order to bring their messages to us via her willing vessel. They even inferred her vessel was hard to use because she was weak and older. I realize the same things at times. However, one time I heard Ben Kincheloe of the 700 Club say, "All He needs is a willing vessel." There are those who feel led to offer themselves as living sacrifices for the Cause of Wisdom, Truth and Love of the Holy One(s). There are many who do not realize we may be asked to consciously offer ourselves to the Father to be used according to His purposes.

8. HPB IN RUSSIA

My Dream–about 1992

I was in Russia surrounded by a large group of people who seemed to be hanging on every word I spoke. I noted and was thrilled to see the adoration of a young handsome man with glowing dark eyes. He seemed completely engrossed in the topic of my conversation. I was still enjoying my popularity when someone asked me to please play the piano for them. I was so engrossed in my role I actually thought I could play for them even though I do not play any musical instrument. I looked down at my beautiful vest and reticule in black satin brocade decorated with precious onyx or jet stones and realized I was not able to play the piano. If not, who was the person in the dream?

I awakened realizing HPB had allowed her student to become as if I were herself. It was and awesome experience like nothing I had ever experienced before or since. No one ever hung raptly upon my words at that time...or perhaps ever shall. I found I liked being known as a wise woman. What an amazing woman she was and is to this day. I am still able to experience the warm glow and the thrill of being allowed to experience this one day in the life of HPB, my beloved Teacher.

9. WILLIAM QUAN JUDGE

Dream–a few days later in 1992

I dreamed this virtually unknown name:

"WILLIAM QUAN JUDGE"

Then I heard him say, "Beloved Lady, no one like her." In my research I discovered this is the way HPB's dear friend, William Quan Judge, often was known to describe her. She was considered to be the most unbelievably unusually wonderful (and strange) woman of her era.

William Quan Judge was one of her closest friends. He accompanied her because this was his role throughout the many years of their friendship.

10. BODHIDHARMA

Dream: 1992

One morning while I was studying Hinduism as my Core Senior Project as a student of Religious Studies at my university I awakened with this word:

"BODHIDHARMA"

I was exhausted so thought of this word as simply another type of meaning of the Hindu word "dharma". Much to my amazed consternation, I was shown this word is the "Name" of the original Zen Patriarch Bodhidharma. Why would "He" wish to come to me in a dream. I was later told one is led to Zen by the intuit of Zen Masters.

At that time, I realized I had dreamed the day before of two bizarre dark robed and black haired men standing in unusual stances...which I thought of as "mudras of the their bodies". It was immediately obvious these mysterious beings were being shown to me because Bodhidharma was the original founder of the martial art of Kung Fu.

These auspicious beings, Bodhidharma, HPB and William Q. Judge were the ones who truly opened the doorway to Buddhist studies for me. This had also been part of their mission in life. They helped to bring the study of Buddhism and other eastern religious studies to the western world.

I was impressed by the teachings of Bodhidharma in "The Gospel of Bodhidharma". One of my favorite sayings is, "If the meanings are understood, there is no more need for words (to describe the meaning)"–thus allowing for us to be spared the divisiveness of languages.

11. THE ZEN SWORD OF TRUTH

It was from this dream of the martial artists I was shown deeper esoteric peaceful weapons of the Spirit over a period of a year. One must never wield this invisible sword without being in complete wholeness with no anger or emotional biases. This is a sword which brings light and balance out of chaos. Therefore, we must never wield it in wrath or hatred. Rarely does one ever use it. Then it must be used only after deeply soul searching contemplative meditation and prayer. It is mighty to bring order and truth out of chaos. The secret is to be mindful and peaceful. Otherwise, it can be dangerous to the one who wields it. Weaponry is dangerous, even if it is a peaceful sword of truth.

There is much to be learned about swordsmanship and the other weapons of Zen.

12. ZEN ARCHERY

Dream: 1992

"You are a Zen archer." (I'm still pondering the meanings implied by this message.)

The interesting thing is that I found archery was one of the few sports in which I could participate in due to the fact it didn't require coordinated running skills. When this message came I was very surprised. However, I had been accurate with placement of my arrows in the target. This was many years ago. I knew the Zen Art of Archery requires one to be so skilled as to have spontaneous accuracy–as one must also be with the Zen Sword or Tea Ceremonies. I found this a very interesting message because I have no idea of my own prowess with any such weaponry.

As a Seeker of Wisdom and to be walking on the Path of my Destirny, I have always practiced the art of "flowing in the Spirit". We are taught to live so closely connected to the Master as to be able to speak in the Holy Spirit, accurately in the Spirit and with His unction. Zen and charismatic Christians practice prayer and meditation if they desire to grow and to flow in the Spirit of the Living God–my Beloved, as the Cosmic Christ's Beloved Spirit speaks through us as the Father gives utterance to instructions regarding His Will and Way.

13. THE HIEROPHANT

Dream: May 15, 1992

I awakened with the message:

"STOP, DON'T RUN OUT INTO THE STREET INTO DANGER. YOU ARE THE HIEROPHANT!"

I am still pondering all the ramifications of this very special mysterious message received on the morning of my own Taurean birthday, May 15, 1992.

First of all, I realized the word was one from the main arcana of the Tarot deck even though I am not a Tarot reader. The term "The Hierophant" speaks to us of the role of the High Priest who submits to bearing the ills and sins of many for the good of the world. This is very much the role Jesus Christ and Buddhist Bodhisattvas take upon themselves. It is also the birth sign, #5, 'The Hierophant", the astrological sign of Taurus the Bull. I had not known this is my own natural Tarot sign.

It was at this time I began a summer filled with divinely given spiritual training in divine empathetic healing. I feel it can be one the highest and hardest, and the most frightening, of all the healing arts used for effecting the healing of another. As a mother, one often offers one's self for the good of another. It is a natural role for an Earth Mother Taurean female.

This training was very dangerous and very insightful. I knew I would only live this way briefly under strict supervision. If one even slightly empathizes with another in their illness–of any sort–from cancer to death--one can draw it into one's own temple, thereby weakening one's own divine temple. However, if the temple be indwelt by the Spirit of the Most High, who can endanger us? We must also learn the protective practices of those who work closely with the bodies and souls of others. We must ground ourselves and also be able to transmute the manifested symptoms of another out of our own vessel through our crown chakra at the top of our head. No novice healer should ever attempt to work with these arts without guidance of a master healer. Since I consider myself to be a novice, I only allow myself to dare to work with someone if I feel I have the complete unction and protection of the Holy Spirit of the Father. I do not believe we are given gifts with which to dabble and attempt to prove ourselves as magicians or in order to obtain followers–unless there is a real need for us to play such roles. In fact, I am interested in sharing so that others may know the mysteries of the Holy One which are available to them. I do not seek to be anyone's guru or master teacher. "Seek and you shall find. Knock and it shall be opened to you."

This was a year when I was unable to find paid employment. I worked hard as an social worker's assistant with a local family homeless shelter. When I wasn't there, I was at my mother's home practicing my healing skills privately on the physical and emotional ailments of my own family members.

Each day was a new training session. When I had reached the time of menopause in my early forties I had been impressed to pray for my feminine problems as if they were unnecessary illnesses. Indeed, one night in northern Europe with our local church group to the Middle East in 1979, two of my dear friends told me they had felt impressed that I needed prayer. They were right, but I never told them it was from pre-menopausal hot flashes. I thought I was going to expire with them. The next day I was fine and have continued to hold myself up for healing from any of these "dis-eases" of our middle years. Therefore, since I felt I had been healed, I dared to ask if I could help others with their "heating up" problems. One particular day I "pulled" the hot flashes of two women who were in my own family and had been complaining of these problems onto myself. I knew I could take these ills upon myself through my solar plexus and transmute them out the top of my head by using the ritual words I had been given in a dream earlier in the summer after my "Hierophant Dream" on May 15. I asked to have divine healing come through my request. The women gladly said I could pray for them. However, as is common with healing–especially by a family member, the next morning when I showed them the proofs of my victory–namely my own hair drenched with perspiration, they simply acted as if they didn't know what I was saying. I can see why Earth never progresses beyond a certain level of intelligence and belief in themselves and others. Also, Jesus cautioned His own disciples that they should not attempt to prophesy or heal others if those others know them too closely. It is very hard to be the first college graduate, writer or artist, politician, healer or prophet in one's own country. They called Jesus the "son of Joseph" and refused to be blessed by anything He said or did. In fact, they even attempted to kill Him in His own home town of Nazareth.

Also, after that unusual summer of healing arts training as "The Hierophant, I realized how very important it is for those of us who practice earth-centered shaman healing arts to stay closely linked with our closest spiritual friends who are also healers and light workers. This is indeed one of the most stressful of the healing arts and should only be practiced by those who are careful to guard their private time and space from intrusions from darkly negative and dangerous energy forces. This dream was also connected with the wonderful Zen Sword of Truth and

Healing. This training had been given in two sessions. The year prior I had been shown Bodhidharma and his martial artists. The following year I was given the Sword and it's ritualistic "Dance". I was also given a word used by early Christian healers for healing powers of this variety. Even so did Jesus give forth His divine energies for the good of all. He also knew the effects of such work–the stresses and the dangers of such practices without the full covering of His Father's Holy Spirit. Thus, on my selfsame birthday, the urgent warning of my dream, "STOP, DO NOT GO OUT THERE ALONE!!!"

I was amazed by the messages of this dream. I am not a student of the tarot. I know virtually nothing about it until I receive these unsolicited special teaching messages. After spending many years in institutions of learning, I have almost 200 semester units of formal education, as well as business training courses in my almost 40 years of paid employment. Our community volunteer and elected roles teach us many things. We also are capable of being taught great and wonderful lessons for life while we sleep. Edgar Cayce learned from placing a book under his pillow, as well as in the special messages he received in his sleep. I was not a dreamer until the mid 1980's. At that time, I evidently entered another time of education from Heaven in dream state. There are some very interesting books one can study. I do not have much time to read until I must ask for guidance and be led to the proper book which may further inform me of the meanings of such messages. I am still seeking to know the complete meaning of this and other special messages. I do know it is a scripturally based message from the Father, given to me in my sleep. It opened the doorway to an unbelievable walk with the Master. We are not alone. If we must walk apart for awhile, He leads and guides us. We are spoon or bottle fed by the hand of the Father. We are surrounded and kept by His angels. We are the lambs of the pastures of our Great Shepherd. We are His little Children.

When I was a young mother I seemed to envision a time in the future in which we would need to know healing arts because we may need them in order to survive in a time when there is a need for doctors. At that time, with medical and dental care for most of us, I could not understand my strong feelings of concern. Now I understand. Many of us have lost our medical and dental care. Some of us have some benefits. Our world has lost a variety of wonderful benefits. I would rather have been wrong. We now thank the Father for our dreams of medical insights. He told us He would never leave nor forsake us. We thank Him for all His many blessings. There is no part of our beings about which He does not care. We are His treasured and Beloved Children.

DESCRIPTIONS OF SPIRITUAL GIFTS OF THE FATHER'S HOLY SPIRIT

It is at this juncture I feel impressed to insert others of His healing messages to share with you at this time.

Part 13-
A. Healing Arts

We will each be allowed to know many of the mysteries of God when we seek to know God. God is all Wise, Loving, Kind, Knowing, Discerning, Merciful, Fair and Just. There is no other Healer, Counselor, Advocate or Attorney, Judge or Jury, such as are the Holy One(s). If we seek, we will be given even more than we ask for. We will be infilled to overflowing with all of the good Gifts in the Divine Treasure Chest of Gifts.

Each religion and culture offers the highest of spiritually esoteric gifts to humankind. The secret in all of them is to follow in the footsteps of the Master(s) in order to know There are a variety of healing techniques available to human beings. I have read of over twenty methods used by a certain Native American woman healer in Northern California. When I compared her list to mine, I realized that I, too, had been taught far more ways of administering healing than I had thought of prior to that time of comparison. In fact, we are given access to the spiritual gifts and mysteries of other times, and of other Earth cultures, religions, and times, as well as from unseen worlds.

I had always been taught to pray, even prior to my training time in Christian churches which had doctrines which encompassed the training in, and usage of, the so called Gifts of the Holy Spirit, such as healing, exorcism, discernment and knowledge, prophecy, speaking forth and praying in inspired, unknown, heavenly and earthly tongues, and the interpretations thereof.

Each of the Gifts of the Holy Spirit require detailed training by the Holy Spirit, and human beings who have been trained in these so called Gifts for our healing and edification from our Heavenly Father. Charismatic, Spirit-filled, born again Christians are taught we are now eligible to participate in the divine gifts of God's Spirit. We are to offer ourselves as instruments of healing, edification and warning to others who also need to be blessed, informed, and healed. These Gifts are part of our inheritances as Children of God. As we are blessed, so, too, are we to go out to bless and to heal others so we may all share the treasured Gifts of

Heaven with others as that all of our lives may be full, joyous and healthy ones. There are Gifts to heal each person completely in their minds, souls, and bodies. If we are ill, perhaps we should begin to ask for guidance to be able to once again be healed, as in former times, when people knew they could be healed in every way by the hand of our beneficent Creator(s). In times when we are too busy to read even our holy books, we are too busy. We must take the time to re-learn our own healing arts. The arts are still ours to learn by divine intuition and instruction and by taking time to request help from our elders. Only in devout prayer and humility can we be taught. The Gifts of the Spirit fell spontaneously upon those original souls who humbly asked to know God. They had no pre-planned desires to obtain as yet unknown powers and gifts. They simply had intense desires to know their God. In divine love, they were not given a stone. They were given healing and eternal life. Their lives were full of power and joy, full of the Divine Spirit and Presence of the Holy One(s). Heaven came down. So, too, can Heaven come into our lives whenever we prayerfully seek to know God. The Holy One desires to infill and to overflow out of our lives to others.

The first night I attended the Assembly of God Church in 1965, I received a healing touch. When the call for those who needed to be healed came forth, I went forward for healing for a bladder infection. That night I received a group prayer for healing. In faith, I believed that prayer could initiate a healing in my body. I learned of , and claimed, gradual healing that night. My condition had been such that my doctor had told me I would need medications in order to be healed. I had been planning to go in for treatment at the Clinic the next day. Instead, I was inspired and intuited to hold fast, pray and believe for complete healing. Indeed, within a couple of days, all symptoms and illness had disappeared from my body--from that time to this, over 36 years later. That was the first, of many, healing lessons I received. However, very soon I was inspired to believe I, too, could lay hands upon the sick for their healings. The inspired prayer of faith can heal us. We are shown exactly how to facilitate healings for ourselves and others by the direction of the Spirit of God in us. By the directives of the Spirit, we are shown who needs healing and exactly the methodology needed to cure the particular illness or injury, of mind, body, or emotions of each person to whom we are directed. The laying on of hands is a real healing art which still used by those who have received awareness to use it.

Sometime after those first years of training, I found I also had another healing gift. This one sneaked up on me. I had never heard of it, nor had I, to my conscious knowledge, ever received training of any sort in usage of such a specialized healing gift. Indeed, I found it is a frightening experience to received awareness of one's ability to empathetically receive and experience the illness of another.

It is now almost 30 years since I first became aware of the fact I had unintentionally empathetically received a male relative's symptoms from his cancerous, pre-death, illness. I suffered as he must have felt while he was in a coma. I even had a momentary loss of speech as if I had brain damage from the cancer. Other bodily functions seemed to be impaired. I was taken to several fine doctors and clinics. There were no illnesses found in my body. Finally, AFTER I learned of his symptoms and devastating illness, I realized I had been intuiting, feeling, and empathizing with him in my own body, mind, and emotions. It was years later, after other experiences of this type, that I began to recognize my seemingly new healing art. To me, my socalled Empathetic Healing Gift seemed to be a frightening gift, since I found I was unconsiously able to continue to receive the symptoms of illness and injuries from others. These symptoms of illnesses and injuries of all types could be as simple as a hot flash or a cold, and as deadly as cancer or even death. Indeed, I truly KNEW my gift was a specialized gift to me as soon as I was given the dream of The Hierophant on my own birthday, May 15, 1992.

Part 13-
B Prophecy, Wisdom & Knowledge Gifts

When one seeks, prays, and waits, one can often have a great infusion of special spiritual gifts. The key is seeking to know the Giver of all Gifts. The Giver, who also is the Divine Creator(s), seems to be very pleased to be sought out. The Giver loves to give good gifts to the Children of God. "Seek and you shall find, knock and it shall be opened to you." We were always told to seek to know God. Seeking is finding. We must gratefully thank God for all of our blessings of the material and spiritual realms. We are indeed blessed to know the Divine. Divine are the Gifts of the Holy One(s). Life will never be dull or unfulfilled. It will be hard to have enough moments in one's lifetime to be able to complete all that one wishes to do for That One, and those who love and seek the Holy One(s). When we are given Gifts, much is expected of us. We are to use them to bless, heal, inspire and delight others as well as ourselves. Giving is the secret of receiving - at least in the world of miraculous gifts. The rule of receiving is to give forth to God and to others. "Ask and you shall receive." King Solomon pleased God because he sought Wisdom above all the wealth of the material world. God was so pleased at his request He also blessed him with wealth, fame, and the honor, at that time, of being one of the wisest of men on Earth. We are to seek Wisdom with our beings, even as we seek how to access the Gifts which are our heritages as Children of God. Seeking the Creator is the ultimate request. The improper seeking of power gifts for self-empowerment and aggrandizement alone are not acceptable reasons for receipt of the powerful Gifts of the Spirit of the Divine. Bounteous Gifts can be received by those who seek to know the Creator and if one is given the unction of God's Spirit to use these Gifts for the edification and healing of others. These Gifts are Helping Gifts to be used for the healing of the healer, others of pure and right spirits, and of our Earth.

My experience was to suddenly know things I had never before known to be possible. I was intuited in the usage of prophetic, knowledge and wisdom gifts. I became obsessed with my desire to know God, and to be filled to overflowing with His Spiritual Gifts. One becomes accustomed to walking with the breath of the Spirit upon us. We long to be close to God. We want to love and to serve the Divine Will in the Presence forever. We want to show forth His prophetic messages and teachings for all to share and be blessed thereby.

As a young woman, I was very busy with my life as a wife and a mother. When I began to reach my thirties and forties, I began to long to know God more and more. I desired to know who I was and my role in the greater Divine Plan and Destiny for which I was born. Dream and prophetic messages began to come to the non-dreaming woman. I continued to seek wisdom, to know as much as God wants me to know, and more. Sometimes we are infilled with divinely beautiful mysteries. At times, God lets us even open the doors to chambers of horrors--which may only be the figments of sin-sick minds of humankind. However, unless we dare to learn, we will not be able to heal ourselves or others. Sometimes we are shown things in the Spirit which we do not wish to know ourselves, much less to share with others. However, if we walk in the Spirit, we can be warned of highway dangers, and much more. We can be forewarned and thereby armed even for real battles and wars upon the planet. We need to be very cognizant and aware of the directives of the Holy Spirit of God, our angels and guides. We learn the hard way, by trial and error, and sometimes great suffering, if we do not listen to that still, small, warning voice, that we truly should have listened to instructions. We are not left without warnings if we walk in the Spirit. The Lord told us He would never leave us uninformed even until the End of the World. Listen with an open, unfettered, heart and mind, to the Voice of the Silence.

Prophecies, wisdom, and knowledge are given to us in various ways. We can dream insightful dreams. We can hear music, or read books, which give us divine leadings. The very Earth speaks to us. We are all part of All That Is, the Holy One(s). I have had warnings in dream clouds, creatures, sea, sand, rocks, winds, seismic actions, fires, and more which give us warnings and messages on the Earth and in the Heavens. After all, we are told, "The Earth is the Lord's, and the fullness (of powers) thereof. " We are not alone. We are led and guided by these blessed gifts even as we have always been guided. We are NOT alone. If you have need of prophecy, knowledge, or wisdom, they will be yours.

As you read through some of my dream prophecies, and the wise messages in the Spirit, you will know these are not from my own mind or soul. I was simply seeking to be filled with the Spirit of God. I had no preconceived ideas of what was coming upon the Earth. Neither did I want to be a negative person or prophetess. As with anyone born of the love of God, we do not want to know the horrors of the evil ones. We would rather be able to tell forth the bounteous blessings of Heaven and Earth, but not have words which will frighten or disturb others. However, to withhold insights can often be very detrimental to the salvation of our lives and souls. The life of a wise knower of prophetic things is a hard one. Prayer is our mainstay. Without the Divine One, we could not bear to stand. Constant prayer for divine wisdom, knowledge, love, justice, the will and protection of the Divine is our only key to standing strongly braced before the winds of change coming upon this planet at this time. We seek, we find, and are given to by the One we adore. We must then pray for abilities to rightly discern and use these Gifts of the Spirit.

Gifts have not been taken from the Earth. Neither are they gifts from the evil one. They are the Gifts of God's Holy Spirit, which always have been the inherited rights of those who seek to know God. Those who do not have these Gifts, cannot discern the workings of the spiritual gifts. If one has no pre-cognitive gifts, and no inspired, or learned, wisdom and knowledge, they cannot rightly discern these gifts in others. Only those who are infilled with God's Spirit and show forth these Gifts in their lives, can judge what is holy, right, and of God. Each must be prayerfully filled with the Love of the Divine and of each other, as themselves. Love is the divine Key. He is Love, Wisdom, Knowledge, and is known as the All-Knowing, the All-Encompassing, One. Judge not, lest you also be judged by your lack of insight and wisdom. Judge not, lest you also be judged for your unholy, prideful, unawareness of the gifts of others. Those who seek, DO find all things are possible as gifts in their lives. Great and wondrous is the Holy One(s), who knows all - the Beginning and the Ending, and who shares these things with His servants and handmaidens. His wisdom and knowledge are not of this world, thereby making Earthly gifts as nothing. Hold tightly to His divine hand. The End is not yet, even though the days seem to be increasingly far spent. "Look up, for your Redemption draws near." However, some of us have witnessed His Sign in the Heavens, at least in our dreams, so we do wonder if He is coming sooner than we think. Let us ask to be wise, and knowledgeable of His divine ways. Of such is the Kingdom of God. However, above all else, our God, who is Love, will be there. I desire loving interchanges with Him and our loved ones above all else. Friends can share. If we are unaware and untaught, we will have much to learn. Let us strive to ALL be One in the Spirit of Wisdom and Love, as prophesied.

By opening the doors to Wisdom, we open the doorways and gates to other worlds within worlds. We meet divine creatures and entities. We begin to enter Heaven's Gate before we cross over. We begin to access the Heavenly Realms. After that happens, parallel worlds and matrixes become ours to explore, if only cautiously.

Our Wisdom, Knowledge and Discernment Gifts becomes expanded until we can truly be able to work, in oneness with God in the Creative and Healing Arts, to assist in these heretofore unseen worlds of the infinite realities of minds, souls and bodies far beyond our current finite abilities and realities. In other words, as we seek to be infilled with Knowledge, Wisdom and Discernment, we are able to be Seers of the worlds of the Infinite. We prophesy things unseen and unknown to others because these awarenesses are ours to see, know, and to discern events and entities which are not yet visible to the finite mind and soul. The Book tells us we have not seen, nor can we understand, the worlds beyond this finite world, unless God so reveals them to us. The Wisdom Gifts can be used to heal others even as can be the Gifts of Healing.

As Healers, if it is so desired, we can acquire temporary symptoms of mental illness in order to know how to be helpful in the worlds of the insane. If our hearts are broken, we can help to mend broken hearts. If we have been disabled, we can perhaps share the heartbroken plights of those who are unable to function in a healthy body in this word. It has been stated, "Only the wounded (and healed) physician can heal (others)." Empathetic healing again. We also can sense the need to heal ignorance.

Prophecy, Wisdom, Discernment and Knowledge can heal us of our false securities in this material world. The ultimate gifts are those which require Love. If we have love, we must seek to help to set captives free by our Truths. Truth sets us free.

There are also those who are ignorant of their own latent spiritual gifts. Some of these dear souls may tend to ignore, denigrate or even openly assail others with these gifts as being either insane, evil or taken over by devils. Ignorance is bliss for all but those who are forced to suffer from well meaning or even malevolent spirits in some who would rather judge others unjustly than to learn of their own possibilities as Children of God. His Gifts are still ours, even if we are not always applauded and understood when we use them.

There are also some few people who do not seek medical help when it is needed. There are also some who handle snakes and drink poison to prove their faith. As we know, there are many souls and many ways of thinking and acting. So, too, in the world of spiritual gifts are those who would rather shock others and who seek followers of themselves. Many are the varieties of spiritual experiences.

If one is not a seeker of the Holy Father and His Fruits, perhaps it is better to proceed slowly–or not at all–into the realms of deeper spiritual powers and truths. When I began my spiritual quest for His Gifts, I was obliged to wait until He showed me I must first seek Him–the Giver of all Gifts. This is the first and most important message when one begins to attempt to learn of the multitude of spiritual gifts with which we able to help others receive all types of healings and the gifts of knowledge, discernment and prophecy. Thank You, Father, for giving good gifts to your Children. As the wise Father, You require us to follow certain guidelines before You anoint us with the Oil of Thy Holy Spirit. We seek Your unction before we ever aspire to use any of Your Gifts.

Part 13-
C He Is Our Breath Of Life

May 22, 2003 - Day 229 of My Prayer Vigil

I went to bed heartsick with concern for the health and welfare of my beloved family members and for the well being of our whole planet, and the Family of God, whoever, and wherever, they abide in the Holy One.

A restless nite was mine, including awaking from a seemingly breathless sleeptime, with a pain in my left chest, as if my heart was literally aching with lack of air to keep it beating safely and in health. This is not the first time I have felt this way. Many of us are gravely unhealthy and bordering on congestive heart failure. Perhaps we cannot blame our dis-eases upon our high altitude lifestyle here in the Rocky Mountain state. Indeed, I awakened completely with a Message of Life and Health from the Lord:

"HE IS OUR BREATH OF LIFE"

I felt He had more to say about this wonderful statement. He seems to be telling us of how we can be whole and healthy in Him. I will repeat His Message as follows:

HIS BREATH OF LIFE MESSAGE

(I wish to state at this time, I have never been, and am not, a member of an Eastern religion who uses yogic or meditative arts.)

I.

Inhale Life.

Exhale Death & Disability.

In Him alone is Life.

II. Affirm Life & Life's Blessings by speaking and using Him as our Breath of Life to accept our healings. In order to be healed, we must first seek to be filled with the Spirit of the Great Healer. He was the One who first breathed His Spirit & Life into our ancestor Adam. His Breath is our breath.

1. a. Speak: "I love You, Jesus."
   b. Inhale & Receive: His divine Love
   c. Exhale & Release: Hatred, Fear & Heartache

2. a. Speak: "Dear Lord, I accept You and Your Wholeness (Holiness)."
   b. Inhale & Receive: Wholeness (Holiness)
   c. Exhale & Release: Illness & Death

3. a. Speak: "I accept health, prosperity & all that is whole from You."
   b. Inhale & Receive: His health, blessings and joyful wholeness.
   c. Exhale & Release: All disease, sadness & losses.

4. a. Speak: " I see Your walls of protection surrounding me and my loved ones."
   b. Inhale & Receive: His protective covering and safety from all evil.
   c. Exhale & Release: All the evils of the age, which surround and entrap all of us within the very real bonds of fear, terror, horror, which consequently cause our lack of balance and wholeness in the Lord. These fears literally cause our hearts and minds to fail us--as He prophesied would occur before His Return. Since we are not well, we are indeed ill. We are suffering from our broken hearts and our insanity. Because we are not holy (whole and balanced in Him), we unintentionally are influenced by our illnesses. Ignorance, prejudices, fears, cause us to

react, rather than think logically. Our out-of-balance emotional responses may not bring about sane and sound choices and decisions within our personal lives, nor in the governmental decisions of the international communities. We all suffer with each other. The blind cannot lead the blind. The ill cannot heal themselves. WE NEED OUR GREAT HEALER!

5. a. Speak: "I claim release from all that hinders and separates us from You and Your Spirit, Lord Jesus."
   b. Inhale & Receive: Only Him, His Wholeness, Love & Safety, Health & Life for ALL my family & friends, and also those who are also His in every part of our Earth.
   c. Exhale & Release: All evil from our hearts & our world.

III. PRAYER FOR REJECTION OF ALL EVIL:

A. "Please record this decision, Lord.
I believe for complete from the bonds of ignorance, disability, death, poverty and unwholeness (not of Thy Divine Will) for our lives.
I want You, only, in my life.
I reject fear, hatred, unforgiveness, injustice, and more, for our family and for the peoples of Thy world, Lord." Amen.

B. I will remember and repeat this precious thought:
"HE IS OUR BREATH OF LIFE.
IF WE DO NOT BREATHE HIM INTO OUR LIVES,
WE WILL SURELY DIE.
HE IS OUR LIFE."

C. PRAYER OF THANKS:

"I thank the Lord for giving Himself, and His Last Breath of Life, to save and keep us from all evil forever. He said He would never leave nor foresake us. He now gives us instructions on how to survive the Great & Terrible Day of His Return. We believe His Words and walk in health, peace and safety, even in the midst of chaos. Thank you, Lord Amen."

III. ROUTINES FOR DAILY LIVING:

1. Take time to breathe, pray, and meditatively await His response.
2. Arise, perform daily hygiene ablutions.
3. Eat carefully, mindfully, and nutritiously.
4. After eating, take moderately high doses of vitamin and mineral supplements--emphasizing anti-oxidants such as Vitamins C & E.

5. Drink several glasses of water each day.

6. Rest as needed.

7. Sleep therapy requires at least 8 hours of nightly sleep in order to alter health patterns enough to reduce high blood pressure, increase oxygen, and favorably alter other vital signs in our bodies.

8. Make sure to walk, love each other, dance, sing, visit with loved ones, commune with your animals and the creation. Take time to rest serenely secure in His healing and loving arms.

9. Above all, seek to be in His Divine Will, led by His Divine Spirit, infused with His Wisdom to be enabled to know and appreciate His Divine Mysteries and Secrets as received in our hearts, minds and souls by His still, small, voice and in our dreams. He told us He would never leave nor forsake us, even until the End of Time. He has not left us. We have left Him and His teachings.

Remember, we are sick because we have been robbed of our lives by our fears and our ignorance. They take away our breaths with their horrors. We therefore stop inhaling because we are subconsciously in traumatic shock. The years go by and we forget we stopped breathing.

He is Sanity, Love,Joy, Peace, Justice, Wholeness, Temperance. He has never failed us.

It is now time to exhale all those fears and traumas from the past years.

We have retained death, illness, horror, fears, terror, broken heartedness and heartache. We are retaining these dis-eases close to our hearts, in our minds and souls, where they can injure and kill us.

"WE MUST BE FREED.
KEEP BREATHING AND LIVING IN HIM.
HE IS OUR WAY, OUR TRUTH, & OUR LIFE.
HE IS THE BREATH WHO BREATHED LIFE INTO THE FIRST MAN.
HE IS STILL OUR BREATH OF LIFE...
HE IS OUR LIFE..
AND OUR TOTAL HEALER.

REST IN HIS ARMS. BREATHE QUIETLY & REST IN HIM, DEAR ONES." Amen.

Part 13-
D Aphorisms & Affirmations For Aging & Disability

(Special Note: If you are very aged and disabled, you may find it harder to alter your thought patterns and to reverse the effects of biological aging. However, if you are a 'young soul'–no matter your biological age–- you may be able to see 'miraculous' changes in your appearance, brain activities and bodily health. Time is not part of Heaven.)

It is my personal notion that for some 'Aging is an attitude'.

If we do not spend our time thinking of time we may not be aging as rapidly as those who spend their time continually letting their minds dwell upon illness, aging and death. Now this is not to say that all of these are not part of the human condition. We do know our minds play a large role in how we live, feel and believe ourselves to be. We will be much more healthy if we believe we are healthy.

It is also my belief as an optimistic realist that one cannot change some things. Neither do I believe it is righteous, fair or loving to accuse someone who is very ill of being the singular causation of their own illness. There can be many factors beyond our control which are capable of sabotaging the best laid plans for health and happiness in life. We can find ourselves caught in changes such as epidemics, famine, war, poverty and the greed of neighbors and global rulers which are generally far beyond our human control.

One might remember that Job was the most righteous man of the ancient times in which he lived. Even righteous Job was tested and tried. He was victorious but not before he had lost his health, several beloved family members and property. There were those who told him he should curse God and die. He refused and continued to bless and thank God for everything, no matter how horrible. His life became an example for all ages. He was one of the most righteous and beloved of God's human beings, yet he was not exempt from suffering from the testings of his faith or the grave death defying assaults upon his heart, mind, body and soul. He strongly stated to the Father, "I will still serve You even if You kill me!"

However, in some cases, we are capable of initiating some degree of healing of our minds and souls in order to activate very powerful energies to combat illness and premature death.

We "expect miracles". We accept them gladly as our rightful due as children of God.

We must think in terms of Heavenly Destiny and our roles in our own Life Plan Destinies. We are so busy doing His Will and living as He wishes us to live, we have no time to think of things like "Aging". Some sadly distraught souls spend their whole lives thinking of their bodies being too fat or thin. Others think of every piece of wrinkled skin or greying lock of hair. Instead of taking each day as a gift from God, it is a slow dying of our body. Some people are 'OLD' at 15 years old. There are who feel youthful at very old ages.

Life is too short to spend time wasting it upon these energy draining thoughts. If we forget about 'Time' and 'Self', we seemingly are able to acquire an ongoing 'Ageless Attitude'. We 'Forget' our daily concerns about our biological age and live in our true earthly role as an 'Eternal Soul'.

Occasionally, we take a few moments to be stunned by seeing our children and grandchildren dancing with other adults and think, "This is shocking!". One does have to do an attitudinal adjustment of one's biological clock when one of these younger people say "You're a Great Grandma!" My own mother went into instant 'amnesia' when she was told "You are a Great-Great Grandma!" This is all wonderfully exciting and uplifting. However, it is like being hit with a stun gun at close range. "My God, I am rather older, aren't I!"

Babies and older people are all blessed and thrilled by the wonderful stages of our lives. We must also remember we will not live until the ages prophesied by our Lord by spending every day of our lives thinking of our advancing ages. We think of 'Life' and of it more abundantly and joyously. We truly live because we are not continually thinking of 'Age'. We are truly 'Ageless Beings'. We are not the 'Body'. We are an 'Eternal Soul' inhabiting a body made of 'clay'. We are not simply our 'Body'. We are His Souls created for His Indwelling Spirit. We are incarnated in human bodies in order to live in the dimension of this world. We will be known as we are known in Heaven. We will all recognize each other because we have all known each other for a very long time. Some of us may have been with Him in the Beginning. We are told He knew which of us were His-- then and now. (Romans 8:29 and 30)

If we think of each of us being an 'Eternal Soul', we might be thinking of entities who are incredibly ancient. Many of us are unbelievably "Old Souls".

One day I was thinking of seeing Christ and realized He is many thousands of years older than the 2,000 biological years of age of which we are told. If we live in the Spirit, we walk in the Spirit of the Eternally Living God. We think with His thoughts and live each day unto Him, as "one day at a time, Sweet Jesus". This is wonderful. He is wonderful.

Let us keep our hearts and souls intent upon doing the good will of the Father. Nothing else matters except to be His and to do His Divine Will. It is for this purpose we are born into this world of sin and sickness. We are Children who are attempting to bring His Light, Love and Peace to those lacking in all of these attributes of His Kingdom. We believe it is time for His Kingdom to come and His Will to be done–not as some would legislate by the theocracies of humankind. Heaven is wonderful. Let us live as citizens of Heaven as if it were already here. Perhaps we will find we can simply enter that world based upon our own will in times to soon come upon this world.

Perhaps there will be many who will simply be "Changed in a moment, in a twinkling of an eye." There may be those who will truly be able to say, "Beam me up, Scotty", and it will be so. Some will enter an airplane and find they are being taken off Earth in a huge airship of the Divine. Who can tell what on Earth may happen to each and every one of us. Let us live as if we are eternal children in a magic world of His making. We are.

"Age is an attitude" which fits a finite world of human beings. We simply become older as gracefully as we can. Sometimes this is not possible. However, we must not forget our first estate is that of being the 'Eternal Children of the Living God'. He asks us to forget all else but His ways and live as His Family. We are to assist others to know our Beloved Lord.

"Age is an attitude." It is an earthly attitude. We are citizens of Heaven's Glory. We can be beautiful souls in spite of the aging signs of our earthly bodies. He lives within our hearts and souls. We are part of the Divine Spirit of the Beloved Father/Mother/All That Is.

We die to the earth plane to be resurrected as an 'Eternal Soul' returning to a Family Reunion with all of our loved ones. It is a blessed time. There is no sting in death. We are victors over our sins and sicknesses. Disability and death are conquered.

His Kingdom is one which encompasses all with His Divine Love, which is the Key to Eternal Life. Nothing else matters as much as knowing Him as the Lover of our Soul.

We are His eternally ageless Children.

Therefore, He can help us to be and to do many things others would tell us are not ours to do. Imagine and dream "Impossible Dreams". You can do anything if He desires you to do so. He can also help us to live through all types of events in life.

If we live as disabled aging adults for a long time, we will pray to be able to do so bravely and well. Many of us would simply like to have a "good death". To be able to simply leave in our dream world seems a humane fashion in which to end it all gracefully. I truly like the idea of truly feeling "this is a good day to die". A parade or a party befits death. It is a celebration and reunion after a well lived human life plan destiny. In other words, I'd invite loved ones to toast my life, dance upon my grave and have a wonderfully happy party and parade someplace nice. Death can be a beautiful and well-earned reward at the end of a long well-lived life. Let us pray this may be so. We can also pray to be kept from the evils to come upon the Earth. If nothing else, let us be hidden in Thee, Dear One. Amen

14. THE GYUTO MONKS OF HIS HOLINESS THE DALAI LAMA

A Special Performance At My University–early 1990's

It was my great desire to attend the performance of these wonderful monks who are able to chant in a variety of tonal levels. They are marvelous. However, their performance was sold out before I could pay to see them perform. The lines were still long.

There were those Christian groups who felt they had to demonstate their lack of respect for the Buddhist way who were there to make sure everyone was aware of their displeasure. In spite of all this, those of us who wanted to hear and see the monks were not to be deterred in our efforts to see them. When I was told I could not see them I contributed my hard saved money I had for the tickets to their performance to the Tibetan cause and attempted to mention this to others in the lines, thereby blessing the monks even if we could not attend the performance.

The Dalai Lama and his people were forced to leave Tibet in the early 1950's when he was a very young man. He travels the world teaching the divine teachings of Buddha. They have locations in America and in Nepal, India.

I was preparing to return home without seeing the performance. Instead, there were several of us who decided we would see if we could find a place to be where we could at least listen to the chanting monks. We located a stairwell beside the stage. There were about 10 of us seated on the stairs listening to the performance when a theater person came by and offered us all a special treat.

He led us upstairs above the stage to the platforms where the stage lighting was located. We were allowed to quietly sit down upon the floor and where we were able to look over the edge directly upon the monks in their colorful robes and head dresses chanting with their dorjes and bells in their hands. The monks' chorus of deep throated chanting is like none other the world over. We were thrilled to be so honored to be in the company of such men.

It was one of those magical and enchanted experiences in life. I was seated beside a young Eurasian man holding a phur-bu (known as a miraculous dagger for stabbing demons--*The Buddhism of Tibet*, Author: L.A. Waddell, W. Heffer & Sons, Ltd., 1971). We had both not given up our goals to participate in the performance. We both felt wonderfully blessed to be able to observe them in this ingenious fashion.

I felt a little like Helena Blavatsky must have felt when she was allowed to be in the company of the famous people she met in the exotic parts of the world in which they lived. She was a woman far beyond many people of her time. She traveled around the world in the days when there were no airplanes, automobiles and taxis. She went in carriages, carts and on horseback, when she was not walking. She is still seen to be one of the most uniquely advanced souls who ever lived on Earth. I am able to say I know her spirit is still alive and continues to communicate her wisdom to us.

As I said, it was an enchanted experience that evening which is not to be forgotten.

15. THE EIGHT CHINESE IMMORTALS & THREE HEAVENLY BASKETS OF FLOWERS OF TRIPITAKA

Dream: 1991-1992

I saw three huge baskets full of divine flowers. These were the baskets of Tripitaka. Each basket of flowers had their own divine music to match the flowers in the baskets. There was one black flower in one of the baskets. I was shown this was a token of one of the Eight Chinese Immortals. These baskets and their floral musical bouquets were like nothing I had ever experienced before or since. I think of these baskets as having their own divine "Music of their Spheres". This was the term used by the Greek Mathematician Pythagoras who defined the music befitting each person's soul as "The Music of the Spheres (Souls)".

I read and studied much of the Buddhist and Hindu teachings at that time in my religious training. I believe sincerely our Heavenly Father has given us divine pieces of wisdom in each of the teachings of the Divine Masters. All are not our Savior as is Christ Jesus. Others also came to teach and to lead souls to Him as they were able to do so. I believe many of us could be well benefited in our pathway with Christ by incorporating Buddhist methods of prayer and contemplation into our own Christian devotions. In fact, I consider myself to be a contemplative, meditative and prayer person who is a disciple of my Master Jesus Christ. I believe He also knows we can be helped to follow His teachings by listening to the wise ways of Buddha. He teaches us how to live as Christ instructs and wants us to live on His own pathway. The Buddhist teachings of mindfulness, awareness, clarity, and of seeking to be freed of the lower human emotions and urges are very helpful in learning how to follow our Master Jesus Christ.

16. MESSAGE OF THE ZEN MASTERS

Dream: August 29, 2004, 6:34 a.m.

I was walking through an Asian garden expecting to see an Asian teacher with raven hair. He suddenly appeared, along with two others, also with raven hair garbed in jet black robes of advanced masters.

He showed me I was to use a long wooden rod with which to connect myself to the ground. I have drawn off illnesses and even death from others to myself in my desire to help others. I was shown in the Spirit I was to transfer them from myself to Jesus Christ through the top of my head. It is obvious I also need to learn how to ground myself, thereby making it possible to transmute these dangerous pollutants from myself into the Earth. I must learn to shield myself with the powers of Jesus Christ by asking for His coverings. I must also learn the usage of healing light to protect myself from all injuries.

A word was given to me:

"MISANTHROPE"

The meaning of this word is "Hatred of mankind".

The dream ended and I began to realize we are all full of hatred of mankind. Our hatred varies according to our own view of life. If we do not hate individuals, their nations or religions, we abhor and detest their obsessive love of ignorance and lacks of loving wisdom and merciful justice. This planet is a horror to many of us who hate the evils of Earth life. It is a miracle if any of us are able to love one another and the Father when we hate the gross evils of this life so much? Note: Avitchi* is another name for Earth. This means the "Hell Dimension" in Sanskrit. Buddhists consider it the lowest Hell. (*Other spellings are avichi and avici.)

It was made very obvious to me that we must take time to cleanse our vessels each day. It is even more important for those of us who empathetically care for and absorb the problems and illnesses of others. We must be cleansed each and every day in order to avoid the dangers of illness and disability which literally "plague" this sin-sick planet. Hatred is one of these awful plagues which also causes other illnesses and death. Hate will destroy us.

It is evident there is only one way to be healed by His divine love. Only His Love will set us free from our bondage to the evils of this world.

"WE MUST LOVE ONE ANOTHER. LOVE IS THE KEY TO HIS HOUSE."

As for myself, I must admit I am also suffering from this dis-ease of my soul. I came to this world as a little child who loved everyone and saw them through 'rosy spectacles'. Now I am sad and upset over the cares of life and of the inordinate fixation some people have on idolatry of themselves, their lusts, greed, fears of everything and everyone they do not know, while insisting consciously in believing their lack of insights and ignorance is the path of choice in order to be holy. Some souls also wish to destroy all wisdom not of their own, especially if they are unable to comprehend it. Soon we will return to a primitive fear state of our own natures–not of the higher mind. Is it any wonder our Heavenly Father weeps?

Those souls who treasure wholeness, wisdom and selflessness are not happy in this current world climate of terror and obsessive compulsive behaviors of the lowest forms. I find myself actually detesting such behavior. I am hating. I came as a child filled with divine love for everyone, accepting and forgiving. Now I am dis-eased with hatred and am trying hard to forgive others who persist in their worldly illnesses of their souls. I am also ill by my associations with such illnesses.

I remember seeing the staff held by the Zen Master. I bought a long walking staff and am now preparing to use it whenever I need to 'ground' myself to release these poisons from my system in prayer to the Father. I will raise my other arm to Him to transmute the remainder of these horrible and unhealthy vibrations and poisons to my Great Healer. I can see we must all practice prayerful cleansing of our vessels. This is the planet where they would kill any saint who dares to think it is a safe world in which to live. This is not true. This is known as a world of jealousy, violence and hatred–a sin-sick world of chaos–if we do not seek to be cleansed in the healing powers of our Father.

(It is always so amazing to realize how closely He is working with us to keep us safe. He has told us not a hair will fall from our heads without His knowledge. I didn't call upon Zen Masters. They came to me. We are not alone. We are guided and protected by His love.)

****

It is obvious to me the teachings of Christ and Buddha were very similar at times. We are taught in many paths that we must cleanse our vessels of all the vices of the natural human being. This is for our own health and safety. Karma does not end with one lifetime. It sometimes goes on from one generation to the next for several generations.

After working with Afro and Native American people for decades I cannot imagine we are free of karmic injustices perpetrated against these people. Some of us are directly descended from Southern military leaders who were also slave owners who may have brutally abused or killed their slaves. Some of us have those who were actively attempting to make sure all the Indians and their holy buffalos were destroyed. There were those of our ancestors who perpetrated atrocities against the Chinese and Asian immigrants pioneers of America. I am only referring to the sins of the American white supremacists of the past centuries.

These studies became my obsessions after I asked to know about the events of the two decades prior to the 1980's. Pandora had many evils in her box.

After my message from the Zen Masters I was given the following message to help us to know how we are endangered by these ancient karmic hatreds.

WE MUST BE FREE

Thoughts: August 30, 2004

I want to be freed from all of these earthly bondage to a Hell world of suffering:

Lust and greed.
Illness and disability.
Poverty.
Anger and jealousy.
Violence and wars.
Darkness and ignorance.

I must walk the Good Red Road speaking and living Beauty all around.
I must arise, thank and bless the Earth and her Creator.
We must be freed and forgiven from all our Sins.
The Sins which torment our Heavenly Father are many:

THE CURSES OF KARMIC DEEDS

The Abuses of all people who are enslaved and ruled by us and/or the Curses placed upon perpetrators of such Abuses and Atrocities by the suffering captives and all other victims of an endless list of slavery, inquisitions, invasions, wars and genocidal purges of those hated simply because they exist designated as the "Minorities", who are truly the "Majorities":

Africans
Native Americans
Aborigines
Asians

Jews and Arabic
Poor
Women
Children
Aged
Disabled
Animals and other wildlife.

Earth–Her damage and destruction at the hands of human beings.

The curses of the victims, their families and tribes are upon those who will not bend their knees to the laws of family, community and tribe or be governed by the guidelines of religious faith and/or institutions.

The curses upon the perpetrators can rest also upon the heads of the innocent descendants of these those who harmed others. We want to see healing upon them and their planet.

The Voices of the Innocents cry out to the Father from under His Throne asking Him, "How long before our sufferings and deaths are vindicated?"

17. THE BLACK "DOT"

Dream: September 8, 2004, 1:34 a.m.

I was lying in bed asleep or half awake. I'm not sure.

I suddenly saw a "Black Dot" with two other pale green "Dots" behind it. I "entered" the Black Dot and was encompassed by it until I realized I may have entered the state of death.

At first I was startled and then thought I'll just be calm and "let it happen". It seemed to me to be fine even though I knew I was possibly leaving my earth plane life.

As suddenly as the dots appeared and I entered the Black Dot, I was out of it and was simply abed–not dead or dying. My heart seemed to me to be beating at a slightly elevated rate of speed.

I arose and then became concerned lest my mother be facing death at that time. I am very empathetically connected to her because she is so closely related to me genetically. Also, as her daughter and care giver, I often received spiritual messages of her illnesses and possibly death defying episodes. I wanted to call her but didn't want to awaken her from erratic sleep to attempt to reach her phone. She is also very deaf. I would wait until morning to check on her.

I wanted to share this with my husband and hear his wise comments. I decided that would be too traumatic a topic for him to face in the middle of the night.

When I arose in the morning, I checked with my mother. We did discuss this dream state experience the next morning. As my dear and wise teacher that he is my dear husband referred me to a very wonderful book on dream yoga. The visions of dots of different colors have special meanings in dream yoga practices.

Note: I had never heard of such teachings before I experienced the teachings of this dream. Anyone who says they know everything, is simply too ignorant to know the unbelievable variety of religious experiences one can share and the seemingly endless mysteries of our Father.

18. OSWALD SPENGLER

Dream: Early in 2002

I awakened with this message:

"IF YOU WILL OPEN TO SPENGLER STATE HOUSE YOU WILL KNOW WHAT THIS IS ABOUT."

This seemingly inscrutable mystery message was evidently given to me to understand the dream I had been having prior to the waking message shown above. None of the words of the message made any sense to me. However, I do believe in the power of God to teach us new things. After all these years of dreams and their research I have learned to obey His messages and I will be shown great and wonderful things. It is obvious I now knew I was being trained by wise masters of ages past. This morning's message was no different. The answers were always given to me–no matter how hard or long I looked. This time was no exception to this rule.

The word "OPEN" seemed to be the key to the location of the words in the message. We had just installed a new gift computer the week before. Following my whim, my husband typed in Spengler State House into the "Search" area of our newfangled machine. We were both shocked to find anything to do with any of the seemingly isolated words–much less ALL of the words on the page that came up on this new electronic device. By this time in the Earth's technological history this was a commonly known fact. We were stunned. What sort of strange world had we entered?

The message seemingly referred us to Oswald Spengler and his well known book entitled *Decline Of The West*. God talking? Yes. It is time to learn from history. If we do not take time to read, we will be destroyed by our own lazy stupidity. If we do not seek the Father, He will not be able to show us warning signs of dangers we face in the history of our planet.

There are many more notes regarding the involved implications of this message. I have saved proofs of the exact computer entries and dates, etc. In fact, when one reads his book, one finds he mentions the dangers of racial wars. He also gave my husband and me personal warnings and insights of the harassment we may face due to the beautiful spiritual name we chose when we married as our nom de plume.

Our resolve only becomes stronger to seek Him only and His divine will for our lives. We evidently came here to help during these very dark times. For those of us who seek Him, He is also everywhere to be seen. He has not left us all alone. He will warn and protect us as He is able to do so. We must think like a creative child and be willing to listen to unusual ways our Heavenly Father speaks to us–by whatever means He is able to give us His messages. Imagination, creativity and scholarship are all His inspirations.

It is my impression this warning message was given by those who wish to let us know of the very real changes in this nation and upon the planet. I fear we may be watching the demise of the "Great American Empire", much as we know of the great and terrible collapses of the Greek, Roman and Babylonian Empires thousands of years ago. We must learn from history. "If we do not learn from history, we are doomed to repeat it." (Herodotus, Greek Historian)

19. RENAISSANCE PEOPLE

Dream Message: May 5, 2002 & May 6, 2002

I received two messages regarding advanced men of the era of the European Renaissance which occurred over two hundred years ago. These messages came in the same time frame as did the message regarding the research of Mr. Oswald Spengler.

First, I received messages regarding Sir Thomas More. I read his book entitled *Utopia*. I read of his life and death. I studied the types of people and ideologies which were held at that time.

The next day I was shown the image of a very handsome man, with curly silver hair, wearing a baby blue velvet coat such as from the Renaissance. He definitely seemed to be a nobleman of that era. I was impressed to realize the ancestors of that era are wanting us to take notice of that age. We, too, are living in an era called a Renaissance. We are living among people who are sometimes frightened when they see the changes coming into their lives. I was made aware that it was a wonderful and dangerous age. So, too, is our current age.

The next day, I stumbled upon the lives of my own ancestors. They were noted men who participated in the formation of the United States of America's Declaration of Independence. They had signed the document. They also authored books during that time.

I can see great and grave similarities between that Renaissance Era and this one in this new century. We think we are modern. We are also to be wise. We are still dealing with supreme ignorance in many fearful souls even in this 21st Century.

Seemingly, as at that time, we cannot share our wisdom with all. We must be very circumspect. Fear is again robbing some people of all reason, logic and literacy, as well as the courage to love one another with the love of the Father. For the fearful, this is not a golden age of progressive changes and renaissance. It is a dire and frightening age of doom and destruction of long held world view and social norms. Some souls would rather "fight than switch", so to speak. They would rather kill others than to fear the loss of their own identities and world views, no matter how outdated, inequitable or obsolete and useless to serve the greater good of humankind.

This age is no different than the prior Renaissance. Begin your studies of these eras immediately. We must again study the history of our ancestors in Europe and America. We must begin to look again to the messages of our ancestors for the keys to this modern world in which we live. History does repeat itself. If we have the penitence and humility to seek the Divine Teacher perhaps we can avoid reliving the horrors of that age. It takes bravery to enter the "Promised Land" and to create a "Brave New World"–like unto the Utopian dreams of Sir Thomas More. We will be forced to wander in "The Wilderness" of ignorance and fear. We will instead be defeated, before we set forth, by the "Giants" we think we will face in the New World. Fear is not of God. Yet, too, a normal degree of paranoia is needed to survive in this dark and dense world of death and war. It is dangerous to be on the cutting edge of the cultural and political changes in society. We must pray much for peace , wisdom, love and justice. The Father has said "Vengeance is Mine". We are not to spend our efforts on creating chaos and genocides by our pre-judgement of people and ideas. Prejudice is a dangerous tool in the hands of babes. This is perhaps why God retains those decisions for Himself in His all-knowing wisdom. It is my memory that our Savior Jesus Christ gave us a long list called The Beatitudes to tell us who He believes are His brothers and sisters. They do not judge. They believe in peace, love, mercy and justice for all. They also believe in the rights of all who serve the Wise One, the Beloved Spirit.

We must seek to be led and directed in wisdom by the Holy Spirit of the Father.

If Sir Thomas More was not safe then, no one is safe in this world at this time. I believe we are being directed to walk carefully in the paths of Light. When some of us are having our hearts and minds fail us with fears of these things coming upon the Earth, let us be kind one to another. Let us love one another. Let us be slow to quiet speech. Let us pray without ceasing for all. Let us comfort, nurture and love others with His love. Let us be the wise men and women of this noble name–Renaissance. Love will overcome fears. Our goal is hard to accomplish but we do not walk the pathways of life alone. We are guided and guarded by our Creator.

19- A PROPHETIC WARNING OF WORLD RECESSION

Dream: April 8, 2002

I was given the strong impression there was a grave financial and economic recession over a large area of Earth.

We were to spend our time purifying ourselves in all ways. We would be fine if we did so and stayed in close communication prayerfully with God.

20. NICCOLO MACHIAVELLI

Dream: Early in 2002

I awakened with the word

"M AC H I A V E L L I A N"

First of all, it had been so long since I had studied political science and Niccolo Machiavelli's views I had to search out my reference books in order to even recognize his name. I had read his controversial book "The Prince" of the Italian Renaissance in my class studies years before. This time, when I read the book I found we seemed to be facing political figures in our nation who made the word "Machiavellian" have real meaning. I re-read Mr. Machiavelli's book with renewed interest and recognized the reasons I had been given this word. Indeed, his book was considered to be so awful as to cause the author to be excommunicated from the Catholic Church at that time. His name became a stereotypical word used to describe the most sinister and covert of "hateful" political words and deeds. It has come to define one of the most selfish words ever written on paper. Mr. Machiavelli simply wrote a book to show the evils of his own society at that time. Unfortunately, the author's name became a living byword for the worst ways to live.

About this same time, a friend was given an equally insightful word:

"A T A V I S M"

This word is equally disturbing, especially when these are the dual attributes of one of our nation's political parties. Those of His sheep who hear His voice find these to be words of warnings to those who will hear and learn from their meanings the atmosphere into which our lives have been thrust. "Natural brute beasts" are known to inhabit primal worlds.

As a combination these are very dangerous words. Covert and malicious evil and a primitive mentality are frightening defining words.

They are the antithesis of this beautiful word:

"A L T R U I S M"

This holy word is the word for selflessness which describes the way we are to live, loving our neighbors even as we love ourselves. We are to pray for our enemies. It's a heavenly way to treat each other. It will help us to "Live like there's Heaven on Earth".

21. "OLD PINDAR"

Dream: Early in 2004

I had been wondering about the types of writing used in my book "Beloved". I didn't pray or even strongly think of it as a question needing an answer. In the night I was given a word:

"PINDAR"

As usual, I was forced to search out the meaning of the word. It is the name of an ancient Greek writer who wrote about the different forms of writing in which he expressed himself. I am still researching his writings at this time.

"Old Pindar" came in responses to my prayer request. Finally, on October 6, 2004, I was able to find a copy of his Pindaric Odes. There are only four books of his odes left to us. He hated war and was a peaceful soul. I feel very honored when one of the ancient masters comes to my rescue. I know I could spend the rest of my life sitting under the teachings of this dear renowned master linguist of the literary world. I can only thank whoever guided me to him.

I truly believe my adventures in the Spirit are available to anyone who seeks to know Him. In all honesty, I have never sought spiritual gifts or the help of metaphysical and historical writers. "Seek ye first the Kingdom of God and His righteousness and all will be added unto you." When I was a new charismatic Christian attempting to receive spiritual gifts, I was allowed to tarry and travail in tears for many months–possibly a year or more. By the time, I finally got His message. He wishes us to seek Him, the Giver of His Gifts, BEFORE we selfishly and thoughtlessly seek gifts for their own self-aggrandizement alone. To know Him is the key to His spiritual gifts and mysteries.

It is obvious one has no idle thought without being given an answer. He has told us He hears us before and while we are yet speaking. This has truly been the case in my life.

SECTION IV
SIGNS & MESSAGES FROM THE EARTH AND THE HEAVENS

SECTION IV–SIGNS & MESSAGES FROM THE EARTH AND THE HEAVENS

INTRODUCTION

I was once again a woman alone, older, wiser and knowing I needed as much wisdom as I could obtain in order to survive on this very volatile and sometimes backward planet "Where they kill saints." I had taken a civilian employee position on a local military base.

In the Fall of 1985 when I asked my Heavenly Father to be shown the things I hadn't understood in the prior decades. Somehow, I felt as if my busy years had robbed me of all types of cultural insights. Evidently, it was time for me to learn these things. I immediately began to be taught about all manner of large topics which had become part of our American lives:

Covert Intelligence Operations
UFO's and Extra Terrestrials
Inner Earth Theories
Human Rights Agendas & Leaders
Multi-cultural Studies of the Afro & Native Americans, Asians & Other Minorities
World Religions
Human Disability and Mortality

THE INVISIBLE BEINGS OF INNER EARTH

It is now perfectly obvious to me there is a great deal of unrest in this nation because most people do not have the desire or opportunity to learn about these ultra important people and their issues. It is obvious we have a problem with those from other worlds when we do not know about our neighbors on Planet Earth. If this is the case, how can we desire to interact with those who attempt to visit us from other planets in the cosmos? One of my most shocking thoughts was of the theories these visitors are also from inner Earth locations, thereby causing them to be called 'intra-terrestrial' beings. In the end of the 1960's, I was horrified when I read a book entitled *Invisible Residents*. It's awful to not realize we may be sharing the Earth with a whole race of unseen and unknown inhabitants who live inside the Earth. The access to these worlds are through the many vortexes around the globe. Is it possible those lost at sea in the ominous Bermuda Triangle are alive within our own planet? My blood ran cold when I read that book.

Fears have also kept us from exploring the many theories regarding advanced cultures living within our own planet. Fear keeps us from wanting to know, even when they come to visit us. Our own Holy Bible tells of inner Earth planes of existence such as Sheol, Hell, Tartarus and other areas unknown to most of us. Admiral Byrd and other explorers have sought to explore the Antarctic and Arctic wildernesses, believing that these lands are keys to why and where these worlds exist. The vortexes such as the Bermuda Triangle, and the one in the Bay at Kuwait which is called the entrance to Sheol, are believed to be some of the entrances to these inner planetary worlds. These worlds may be incomprehensible to some of us. As we know, there are a variety of diverse theories which are not believable by everyone. This does not mean they do not have truth intermixed with fantastic legends. There have been writers who have fictionalized (or "Sugar Coated") unspeakable realities.

Native people of the planet all have entrances to these worlds in their legends. Studies of these primitive cultures is of the utmost importance. I cannot tell you how broadened and freed I have become since I have entered the worlds of the descendants of American Negro slaves, the Native Americans and the aboriginis of the lands down under. They are still connected to the Earth and her mysterious hidden lore.

THE WATCHERS FROM THE HEAVENS

They also open the doorways to advanced dream state studies. They have always known of the Watchers and of their flying crafts. Is the Garuda of Indian legends a huge bird or a huge airship? What of the Moth Man and other frightening creatures not described in our text books? The Indian people of North America know of the Watchers and of the Star Maps of the Heavens. Those who live close to the Earth spend every night of their lives gazing at the beauty and the blackness of the cosmos. They knew of ancient space explorers and visitors to this planet. These beings came to supervise the beings of this world, even as they watched over the other planetary Gardens. ("Keepers of the Garden", Dolores Cannon)

PLANETARY RULERS & HIERARCHIES

Our ancient holy books all tell of powerful hierarchies of governing groups of each planet, universe and cosmos. Why are we so surprised? These organizations remain in existence at this time.

What do we know of the obscene machinations of supreme ruling hierarchies of the heavens and of the earth? If one doesn't want to explore secret and covert operations, please do not begin to explore these areas. They are not just "grey". They are comprised of earthly and other worldly groups which are of the purest and most holy to the nether worlds of the deepest of dark organizations and entities. One does not slap a monarch. If one treads upon a snake it may turn and strike you with its venom. The scriptures tell us there are those things and entities which are not approached to even by a strong and wary angel. There are evils dealt with by only the Most High One(s). There are situations and times when one is to become like a submarine and "Run silent. Run deep." One should remember to be "Wise as a serpent (of wisdom) and as harmless as dove (of peace)."

The lists of references for these topics would fill pages in separate bibliographies. If and when one dares to face one's deepest fears, one is rewarded with insights beyond one's deepest understandings. The mysterious wisdom of the Most High is beyond human comprehension. Perhaps you are one who feels many of these topics are not yours to explore. This was my own personal decision UNTIL my curiosity overcame my hesitation and fear. Now I know I have been taught of some very awful and horrifying topics. The secrets of the dark side are better left uncovered. I do not believe in giving place to evil so that it can come into my life and destroy me. However, it is necessary to explore and face some of these dangers if we are some of those who pray and seek wisdom as Peaceful Warriors. We need to dare to face one of our biggest enemies–fear. We are told "fear is not of God" and "Fear is torment." Fear rules this planet because human beings remember and sense more than they realize of the unseen and unknowable evils. Many choose to stick their heads in the sand like an ostrich and pretend they are alone and safe even though they have exposed the greater part of their bodies for all to see. Others choose to loudly state their fearlessness thinking this will make it go away. If we dare to bring this enemy to us, we will squarely face and conquer it eventually. ("The Art Of War", Sun Tzu)

I do attest at this time in this book that my prayer was heard. The answer was "We will show these things to you, but they may frighten you." Let me say right here this was the most awesome truth I have ever heard. I have been horrified to the highest degree of horror. My fears changed to panic. The awful, unspeakable things are not seen by all because one must be prepared before one can ever open the doors to these worlds. One may think one is ready. One simply does not know anything about these things we are told to not explore unless we must. They are the dark secrets upon which the doors generally are closed to all. To know is to scream. To scream is to wish one had never known. I believe these comments refer especially to the latter studies of the evil machinations of the powers who control us all. Logic and control of our emotions must be conquered or we will be defeated. Someone said "We have nothing to fear but fear itself." Also, the wise soldier knows fear. Fear can be a protection against carelessness. It is the basis of bravery.

FEARS OF THEM AND THE OTHER–GLOBAL AWARENESS.

It is my belief we all should learn and know of all manner of cultural and theological truths. It is only by banishment of our fears that we are able to know and to love our neighbors as ourselves.

In 1985, when I met the 7 ft tall black soldier at Monterey, California, who told me (as if he were Uncle Sam) "I want you", it was because it was time for me to begin the work with human rights issues as I had arranged to do when my life destiny was planned for life in this world.

I feel like I was inducted into the national human rights movement. I began my studies in Afro-American studies shortly thereafter. I have never regretted it. In fact, the Father let me learn so deeply and empathetically the lives of Black people that my own Black professor told others this white woman thought and felt as if she were a white woman in a black skin–an "Oreo Cooky". I took over 25 units of Afro studies, as well as over 25 unit in Native American studies. Americans need to study about gender and ethnic studies. If we do not, we are missing knowing many of our wonderful Hispanic, Afro, Asian and Native Americans neighbors.

From that stance, I found my heart completely ready to study the religions and spiritual experiences of the whole world. I feared I would lose my faith in Jesus Christ. Not so. I only found my awareness of Him and the Father to have broadened into seeing Him as the "Manifold God" and the "Cosmic Christ". They became even more wonderfully my treasures. I am so proud to be His child. So, too, should everyone attempt to know Him as He is–HUGE. Do not even begin to put our God into a small box. He will not fit into a tiny compartment where He is to sealed hermetically as a dead deity. He is the Living–All Seeing and Knowing–God.

These studies began in the Fall of 1985 with those of covert intelligence and UFO's. The next steps were to get me out of myself and into the worlds within our worlds. To explore the depths of awareness of our own world is enough to keep us busy forever. Beyond this, there are other worlds and dimensions.

It is here I will introduce the creatures of the Earth to you. Our Holy Bible speaks of the trees and creatures of Earth dancing, singing and clapping hands . When He is teaching us His mysteries, He also teaches us the symbolic mysteries through which He can communicate with us. Please remember I was like a table rasa. I was a blank sheet upon which to write the messages contained herein.

It was at this time in my life I began to dream of horses, wolves, hawks, dragonfly, cloud omens and other messages of the Earth's simpler, yet so beautiful, ways of communication. The very creation speaks to us of Him.

You will have your own impressions and beliefs. These are a few of mine. Please let this be a pleasant time of contemplation of another's spiritual experiences. He may yet speak to you through them.

There are many profoundly unique and diverse topics as yet to study. Some of these studies are presently incomprehensible to most finite minds. One must practice expansion of one's understanding in order to be able to live in the world of the 21st Century. The 20th Century was perceived to be one of miraculous inventions and changes. So, too, will this current time seem like a primary level of human advancement.

The disadvantages to our developmental growth patterns are our deeply ingrained primal fear of the unknown and of forcing ourselves to admit we have many things yet to learn. These are traits which will keep us in the Dark Ages forever.

One must be courageous in one's pursuit of wisdom and faith. Both are the pathways to transcendence of the bonds of this world. If we could exchange our fears for courage, our weaknesses for strength and our mindlessness for an actively seeking and working brain we would see ourselves in much the roles of those heroes of The Wizard Of Oz. There have been many attempts to fictionalize and fantasize ancient truths. Some of the major teaching tools have been books and movies such as "Lord Of The Rings", "Harry Potter", "The Stepford Wives", "The Manchurian Candidate" and many others. It was so easy to relate to the Tin Woodsman, the Lion, the Scarecrow and to Dorothy. The entire story of the Land of Oz and the realization by Dorothy that "There's no place like home." We all want to go somewhere "over the rainbow". We all want to find that special one who could help them as they walked "The Yellow Brick Road" to see "The Great Wizard of Oz". Alice had many thought provoking adventures in Wonderland. Also, one's ability to "Step through the Looking Glass" opens real or imaginary gateways to other dimensional and parallel worlds of life.

CONSPIRACY THEORIES AND COVERT ORGANIZATIONS

Each of the world's governments have their covert spy organizations and the many conspiracy theories which occur when one deals with so many different secrets. We are warned to not be part of secret organizations. There is a reason for this. However, one also must know something of these political and religious organizations of all types. There is a constant war of ideologies and rulers.

If one does not belong to the ruling power structure, one is often labeled as renegade or terrorist. One may simply be foolish enough to think their lives are their own. We may be living in a time when all are monitored for their beliefs. If one does not belong to the accepted group, one may be harassed, ostracized and even destroyed. These historical times of extreme inquisitions and genocidal holocaust may not have ended. One must continually guard one's self from fear and bigotry. Those who dare to attempt to educate their neighbors may be suspected of treasonous acts of subversion.

This nation is one that has named itself, "One nation under God, with liberty and justice for all". Prior to this time it was definitely not our desire to be other than a nation conceived and birthed for safety and freedoms for all. It is time to examine ourselves lest we become no greater than the lowest of the low. Pride and ignorance are a lethal combination. The spoiled and lethargic may not act quickly enough to prevent their own destruction. Those who will not learn from history may repeat it, to their own destruction.

I am one like Rip Van Winkle. I awakened. Did I awaken in time to save myself and others?

Mind games may have conquered the unwary. Fools dare to go where angels fear to tread. The Mad Scientists are still playing with lethal toys.

DEATH, DISABILITY & OUR OWN MORTALITY–THE FINAL TEST OF FEAR.

Death comes to all, unless one is translated in a Rapture or is whisked to safety off this planet in a space ship. This is a basic reality one should learn before anything else. However, it is the last thing we wish to face. Why? All must face their biggest fear. Death is our biggest fear in spite of all efforts to pretend it does not exist for anyone, much less ourselves.

Many of these concepts are definitely mind benders. If we do not face them, and ourselves, how can we then say we are ready to face death. No one escapes Death. Death does not have to be the "Grim Reaper" or Yama, the death god. We must face our fears in order to be able to accept and live with our fears. If we face fear, we can face death. Do we fear death or our own fears of the unknown realm(s) to which our souls will find their own paths, as they have before?

Personally, I do not fear the Other Realm because I believe I go back and forth in my dream states. If we are at peace with our own deaths, we can actually long for the peaceful beauty of the world which we originally called Home. Death has no fearful sting for me. It is simply the concerns over what will happen to our physical bodies before death.

Indeed, in analyzation of my fears of disasters such as earthquakes, I finally went through so many quakes I realized it was the terrible surprise–the "shock" of the earthquake–which terrified me the most. My secondary fear was that of being caught upstairs in a building and having troubles getting to ground levels due to my personal acrophobic fears of heights. During this time, I found I was exploring ideas of how to safely escape using rope ladders and the like. I realized my fear was of injury from trying to escape high structures. Also, one must face the fact when driving that the roadway may be gone. Bridges may have spans missing over very deep and cold waters.

If we face our fears, they often tend to become lessened or may even disappear. My concern is not an easy death in my sleep. It is of being forced to experience years of disability and pain, uselessness and imposition upon my loved ones. If I face death at the hands of evil people or world destinies, I do not wish to suffer hugely before I die. Death and crossing over has not been upon my mind whenever I have faced death. Yes, I have faced death. In fact, I have faced death in plane crashes of small airplanes, as well as a gunman in Izmir, Turkey. It is the fear of what it will feel like when a plane is blown asunder. What will some human devil do to us before we die? These are hideous things to think about. If we face death in an open and fearlessly detached fashion we may find it holds no fears. In fact, as I said, one can even welcome it with open arms. I have been warned of impending deaths of loved ones. I have seen them in the Other World. I believe in eternal paradisial worlds, as well as others realities of existence far beyond the knowledge and comprehension of most souls here at this time. It is the horrors of pre-death and a premature burial which cause many of us to fear death. Death can even be a welcome solace after a hard and sad life. We can even reach a level of acceptance so we are able to agree with the beloved Indian Chief "It's a good day to die." I have known those who have had near death experiences early in their lives. They have gone there, and done that, and tell me "I will never again fear death." Then, when it was time for them to go Home again, they simply prepared themselves and said, "I'm ready. Let's go!" I would love to go through the "swinging door" and find it was time to stay in the Presence of the Beloved. I long for and miss Him and our Home.

HUMAN DEPRAVITY, IGNORANCE, FEARS & JEALOUSY

Some of these truths have always been known to those who were able to assimilate and use them. However, there were a vast majority of souls for whom all new topics of awareness have been too much for them to understand and use in their daily lives and societal norms. It is common for human beings to prefer to denounce the bearers of good news and to "Kill the Messengers". It is very frightening for some souls to admit errors and to be able to say, "I didn't know that. Please teach me." This is why our world is so steeped in superstition and fear. The Truth will set you free–free indeed." (Jesus Christ)

It is not possible to forget or disbelieve our own truths, education and spiritual awareness. They simply become part of our realities. I cannot say I do not know these things. I asked and I received many answers to the larger, more frightening, questions of this age in which we all live. I have been shown many things of heaven and earth. I have been horrified, terrified and, also, uplifted to Heaven's Door, to the very Presence of the Living Spirit. I do not regret projecting my awareness out beyond the Rainbow. I would rather become a Butterfly than to stay in the chrysalis as a simple worm. I wanted to grow into a Butterfly. I was willing to change like the Dragonfly. I flew to the Great Spirit as the Hawk. I see Him in everything. I know why the trees "clap their hands". (Old Testament) I know we can levitate, walk upon water and move mountains. The question is that of "Do we have faith?"

We do not do these things because of our fear. We have lost abilities known by the ancient cultures. Our world shows signs of advanced life far beyond the understanding and acceptance of many. These cultures know of many ages of genesis and destruction of life upon this ancient biosphere. We only receive our freedom when we overcome our darkness by the light of Truth. Truth will set us all free. It's worth facing the dangers contained within Pandora's Box. It is my desire to spread these words of joyful truth to all who will hear. We are in bondage to our fears. They have disappeared if we recapture them and return them to Pandora's Box.

Some other thoughts about our Fears are

What is real?
Which fears are real?... AND
Which of our fears are based upon others' fears?

What is real. This is the biggest question?
Who and why are we here. Do we really want to know?

Who are our creators and ancestors?
What are their plans for us?

Where are we really?
Do we want to know?
Since we do not know, are we listening to the delusions of our minds?

Do we want to know more about our real or invented enemies?
Do we want to face them within ourselves or others?

There are those who wish to keep us fearful and ignorant.
Thereby keeping us quarreling among ourselves.
We will kill ourselves and others thereby never realizing who were our real enemies.
Insane "Bullies" (like the Minotaur perhaps) are happy we are afraid of them.
If we are brave enough to stand up against them, they may flee.

DO WE HAVE THE GIFT OF FAITH TO BELIEVE WE CAN BE SET FREE
FROM THIS WORLD OF IGNORANCE AND FEAR?
OR

IS ALL ILLUSION?
WE ARE SIMPLY ATTEMPTING TO SEE THROUGH DARKNESS OF OUR FEARS AND IGNORANCE?

SECTION IV. SIGNS & MESSAGE ON THE EARTH & THE HEAVENS

PART I NATIVE MESSAGES

INTRODUCTION

We begin our personal spiritual walks when we are born. Some of us blithely walk along without any thought of what we are saying or doing as a person or soul. We have no concerns about our roles in our world. Some never concern themselves with anything except "making it". Many people survive in whatever manner they can do so in order to make sure they obtain as much of the good things of life which are possible for them to have. Many people never realize the real essence of their beings is their own inner soul which may live far beyond the biological ages of their human bodies.

Some of us have become introspective students of life and their own places in their personal worlds of existence. Faith is a Gift which is elusive, yet it does come to many. It is a divine blessing. It also requires one to ponder the meanings of one's faith. If we experience and study many aspects of a spiritual walk we wonder about and seek out deeper mysteries and wisdom along our spiritual paths. We have not material wealth to share with our children and others. Instead, we share as we are able the treasures of the Holy Spirit.

Many souls accidentally, or on purpose, restrain themselves from seeking because of their reluctance to learn things which are frightening or they do not understand completely. Another group of souls may be drawn to learn of anything to which they are led with little, or no, restrictions. The author is cautious. However, after my long years of explorations of the many of the cultural, political, religious and spiritual groups of the world it now seems to be time to do a personal analysis of all my studies. Perhaps they will interest some readers.

This analysis has simply shown there are a variety of helpful and non-helpful aspects to each of these several topics which have been researched.

This research simply seems to show us the many stages of advancement upon the Earth, as well as the many ways we have dealt with the wisdom gained. Oftentimes, out of our shocked concerns, we have destroyed the good along with the bad. We have murdered the messengers and saints of each group if they frightened us. Such is the behavior of the natural beast in each of us. It is the concern of the writer to help us to understand these facets of our own personalities and to help us to be obedient loving children of God.

There are other ways of looking at religious and political systems of each cultural and racial group. The Father wisely allowed each group of His children to learn and to grow to know each other, the world and Himself as they were able to do so. One learns about these aspects of human socialization in physical and cultural anthropology courses. At the center of each political group there was a core of idealistic ardor held by a large group of leaders regarding their reasons for believing in their political path–whether democratic, republican, socialistic, monarchal or by elections of, by and for the people. The same holds true for each religious path. Each religion teaches certain core beliefs which creates a viable path upon which followers may walk. Perhaps He created each political and religious group and each has a viable reason for being. It is important to allow freedom of adherents to these paths their own free will choices in life as long as they are not a danger to themselves or others. If their doctrines and tenets, their laws and rules, are not of Him they must be discarded. The whole belief system may not be deemed worthy of destruction. We must sort out the good.

It is a well known fact in the business world that each new boss or manager will feel they must make drastic changes in operations and employees. This is very unwise if done too soon or in a fashion too aggressive for acceptance by those they intend to lead.

These have also been the reasons for destruction of the holy writings, icons and buildings of conquered nations of the world. At the Church of the Nativity in Bethlehem the doorway is so low as to prevent horsemen to ride into the edifice in order to raze it at times of war. The builders of the Church were hoping to save the holy site by making the height of the door too low for entry by the mounted soldiers. One can only wish someone had been able to saving the burning of the Library at Alexandria, Egypt. The manuscripts of the antiquities were lost forever to the world. It seems to be human nature to completely clear away the remnants of another faith, their thought and their edifices. Why? Are we not able to attempt to learn from others and synthesize all into an even more wonderful understanding of Him? Perhaps the jigsaw puzzle paradigm is a good one for usage by some of us. It takes many carefully seeking hands working peacefully together to complete a large puzzle with many pieces.

When will human beings be ready to work peacefully together upon the questions of the various faiths and political parties? We are wasting valuable insights which are useful to furtherance of a better, more peacefully loving and wholesome world.

One does not "throw out one's beloved Baby with its bath water". We are wasting our valuable resources of knowledge and wisdom, as well as killing others simply because they find valuable truths in their own political and religious paths. Perhaps we could all share the wonderful things and analytically reject those unuseful aspects of each religious and political groups. It would be cost efficient in the savings of holy writs, divine laws and in the lives of our brothers and sisters of His Family.

God is not one certain political party. Neither has He reached evildoers in all but our own religion and denomination. It is perfectly obvious there are many ways to find Him. His teachings are contained within all the holy books of the world. If we have His agape love we will explore these books and beliefs to find which ones we can add to our own. If one is a careful stenographer, one knows it is easy to miss a definitive word or phrase. If we will admit we are fallible people and seek Him humbly as souls, we will find Him dwelling in more hearts than some of us are able to admit possible. This is wonderful. Fear not, for He is with us all.

If one becomes His student, they may be able to see the comparisons and relate the beauty of His Manifold Path. The author is of the opinion that these 'Hard Puzzles of Life' are as easily put together as are hard jigsaw puzzles by groups of loving people all working to make sure the pieces fit together into one huge beautiful picture. The attitudes of those who are asleep to wisdom are illogical and do not deserve to be validated by anyone who values truth and wisdom. If the pieces do not fit, they may eventually be discarded. However, one never completely throws away a piece of a jigsaw puzzle. One never knows where it may eventually fit in the Whole Picture.

When I evaluate my PERSONAL spiritual walk, it is obvious my walk has only grown more complete by incorporation of the beliefs of several faiths together–because they are all part of the One. Examples: How does one pray if one does not meditate? How can one heal if one is not personally healed? One is drawn to prayer by music, chanting and incense. Stringed instruments lend themselves to romance. They also lead one into meditation and prayer. Candles are a beautiful reminder of His Light and Truth. Candles light His Way. Christmas trees may be from the remnants of earlier religious beliefs. The evergreen tree is a symbol of everlasting life as is the ankh symbol of the Egyptians. The reason for the Season is because He was born–even if not in December or

January. We do not wish to forget His birth. The reason for deification of either Mary is because they were beloved to Him. He is known as the "Beloved of Women". Some believe His disciple Thomas went to preach His Gospel in India. There are those who believe Krishna and Christ have some things in common–as with their female followers. *NOTE: THIS IS MY PERSONAL WALK AND VIEW. HE ASKS THAT EACH OF US PERSONALLY SEEK HIM.*

Those Christians of the Western Hemisphere of Earth may wish to study the ways of the people who were native to these continents before the arrival of the white man. They came boldly into this land without asking to know the ways of these people. They had very beautifully and viably sound government and religious values. They believe in the One Great Spirit who is in all His creation. They do not believe anyone can own the Earth, thus their unselfish attempts to 'share' the land with our pioneer ancestors. They performed ritualistic dances based upon the heartbeat of the Earth, thus the cadence of their dances. Their ancient oral histories contained records of the times when the Earth's axis had shifted. They felt they must perform dances in their attempts to keep 'their Mother' balanced upon her axis. The usage of the peace pipe was brought to them by White Buffalo Calf Woman. Her messengers to the Indian nations were Deganaweda and Hiawatha. Example of White Mens' logic: "The only good Indian is a dead Indian." Fear and ignorance had been the causation of such belief systems. The historical records of Earth are full of genocidal actions against anyone one does not look like, or agree, with us. Let us "divide and conquer" others. One example of this with the Native Americans was the removal of small children to the white man's schools several states away from their own homes, thereby separation of each child from their own family, language, religion and culture. They often married a person of another tribe, thereby dividing all structures of their societies. *NOTE: OUR PEOPLE FELT THESE PEOPLE WERE REQUIRED TO RELINQUISH THEIR PERSONAL RIGHTS TO LIFE, LIBERTY AND THE PURSUIT OF THEIR OWN RELIGIOUS AND POLITICAL HAPPINESS.*

The same things were done when slave owners sold Black families apart. They also bred lighter skinned slaves by the use of a Black slave with lighter skinned sexual partner. Breeders made more money on the lighter skinned slaves. Many books have been written about the ethnic cleansing done to many of the various ethnic groups of people here in America. Every group has its personal set of oral, if not written, human atrocities done to them by their Anglo American neighbors. *NOTE; THIS IS THE SAME VIEW OUR PEOPLE HELD FOR THE LIVES OF ALL*

PEOPLE OVER WHOM THEY GAINED CONTROL. OTHERS SEE THIS AS THE DOMINATION OF WHITE SUPREMACISTS.

These are a few simple examples of racism perpetrated upon the cultural religious and political systems of the Natives of North America. Many of the younger Anglo Americans have come to learn and to realize the beauties of Him in these wonderful people. There are evil ones in each racial group. However, their wise and peaceful ways were long taught and were sound. There are tribal fire pits over 4,000 years old all across this nation. Their burial grounds and holy sites have been desecrated by their Anglo neighbors. The souls of those who sleep in the Earth cry out to Him along with all the rest of the martyrs of the world. One cannot worship Him without offering the blessings offered by these beautiful believers in Him. The noble faces of these people speak to us of Him. Jesus told us how we can recognize those who are His.

If we are His, why would we wish to destroy completely the lifetime pathways of our neighbors? If we are filled with His Holy Spirit and are filled with His Love, it is possible to have wonderful peacefully balanced exchanges of information between ourselves and our neighbors. By so doing, we may find we wish to incorporate their wise teachings into our own valued religious, political and cultural systems.

Some of us feel this would make our Father laugh happily. We would stop our quarrels over possessions and simply get along together as one, happy and loving family group. Is this bad? We all love Him and seek His ways. What could be more wonderful?

"If one shares the meanings, one no longer needs the words." (Bodhidharma, Zen Patriarch) Words can be descriptive. They can also be divisive. Labels can define something or someone. They can also stereotype and denigrate others as to race, religion, cultural or political group.

If we have love, we will wish to talk to one another. If we have dialogues and communication, we will become friends. Friends care about friends. They do not make war on friends. As long as we see another as 'The Other', there will be 'The Enemy'.

The Native people hope for a return of the ancestors and a time "when men and animals could talk together" as they did in the Beginning. They also believe the white men may kill themselves, thereby returning the land to those who love it. Perhaps they are right.

Do we wish to have peace on Earth, or war in the Heavens forever? His Love is the Key.

Do we wish to learn truth and wisdom from others, or do we wish to learn from our own mistakes? Do we wish to complete the Divine Puzzle, or do we wish to have many pieces of this beautiful Puzzle strewn asunder forever in order to think we are wise in our own conceits? His Love is ours to use to complete this wonderful Puzzle.

Stephen King tells us the best writing is to "keep it simple". Perhaps the Divine Plan is as simple as we are told. We do not need to become prejudiced against another's religious or political groups. If we have our minds and hearts in His, we will love one another and attempt to find His truths in our own and in our friends' ways. If we become one in His Spirit we will surely become ready for the return of the Prince of Peace. His Love is the Key to the Heaven world of Our Beloved Prince.

Love covers all, including this book. It is not written to cause disagreements. The author is interested in everyone treating one another with the unconditional acceptance in His Love. We may find we are pleasurably surprised at the similarities of purest, most holy, doctrines of the each of the world's religions of loving and peaceful co-existence.* If we share one with another, we may complete a larger, even more beautiful, Tapestry of our lives, which may yet become an spiritually artistic masterpiece diagram for our peaceful Earthly lives. The author stresses becoming as a Little Child, who, He tells us, is to lead us. He tells us, "Of such is the Kingdom of Heaven." Children are trusting and teachable. They love their parents and family. Parents love and pamper their beloved children. We are all divine children of the Holy One.

The choice is ours. Do we divide and conquer one another forever? If not, we may yet give place to the Angels of Light and Truth, rather than the Dark Angels of ignorance and error. It is the author's desire to help others realize their full potential in the Divine Kingdom of Light and Truth. The essence of the Beloved Spirit is Manifold. He does not fit inside the bonds of self serving power groups. He is our Universally Beloved Spirit–the Great Spirit of All.

The author is attempting to learn about Him and to know what He wants for herself and His whole family. It is her desire to seek to know Him in order to learn what is His divine will and way for her own life. In so doing, it is hoped other will glean something from this tome filled with the conversations shared with the Father as she has tried to keep step with Him as His "Little Child".

Perhaps she has learned much, but there may be much more to learn. However, we do not want to make an idol of our education. He is to be the goal. We do not wish our means to come between Him and ourselves or others.

Some of His Laws and Rules for our lives are listed in the References. They help us to quickly refresh our memories if we've forgotten where some of them are located in our Bibles. These are Universal Laws which are included in each of this world's holy books from the Code of Hammarabi to the last of the Paths to Him.

We desire to be led only by His Holy Spirit. We do not wish to be led by delusions of our own finite minds even if we do not use psychedelic drugs, liquor or even prescription drugs, as in the case of the author. It is the intention of the author to keep these writings freed from self and the effects of mind altering additives to her own body.

These messages have been received and offered to all with never ending prayers, tears and joy of His Spirit as much as is possible. Obedience to His Call is the author's only desire. However, she would rather receive no messages than to lead others astray by them. It is her understanding that it is time to attempt to become brave enough to share them with others. It is obvious there will be many views upon the views of the author expressed in these writings. They are received with tearful prayers. It is the desire of the author that each reader will take a few moments to meditate and pray before opening the pages of this book and the others written by the author. We want to be led by His Spirit as we write and read these messages.

We can study. He must open His words to us. He must speak to our hearts each day. We must relax and accept His love. This and His Gift of Faith are our first gifts as His children. We do not need to worry about the words in this book. This is a personal walk with Him. It is shared in attempts to help others desire to seek their own personal walks with Him. This is the ONLY reason for sharing. Otherwise, the writer is most happy to keep all her personal messages between the Lord and herself. His will is my first desire. I hope and pray you will also desire Him and His will above all else. There is nothing else but Him for me. We are His orphans for whom He weeps. He can also bring us to a place safely within His Presence wherein we weep and fear no more. The Accuser of our souls is forever silenced. We rest in His Peace which passes all Earthly comprehension. C.A.

(*We know some of these selfsame Holy Books also contain more radically violent material. These are not the universal laws of peaceful co-existence practiced by those who wish to share this planet in peace with their neighbors.)

WOWETSIN

This was a Native American personal prophecy I received upon awaking on the morning of April 24, 2000 at 5:47 a.m.

This message–as well as all of my messages from Him–was written with great emphasis on clarity and accuracy. It is written to me or someone like me who will read and know this.

I am to assist to plant, grow and water Indian land.
I am to help Indian women become prosperous.
I am to help them to be known.
I am to make sure there are good ponds of water and grass in the rolling hills.
I am to grow as fat and well-watered as the hills of my women.
I am to know the paths of peace, beauty and blessing.
I am to be known as "Wowetsin, Maker of Dreams To Come True, and known only to those who seek truth, justice and healing of the land".
I am a daughter of the plains. My heart is buried at Wounded Knee.

I build grasses for the buffalo.
I walk with the buffalo.
I am Buffalo Woman's helper. I am Buffalo Woman to my people.
I know the ways of peace. I am peace.
I am health. I walk in health.
I hate evil. I abhor evil and shun it as a plague.

(<u>Message from/about the Great Spirit</u>)
Know you not the ways of old? Learn them and be free.
All ways are not good. Shun ungood ways.
Make my paths wide and fertile. Make my paths grow and flourish.
Make my people serve me. Make me grow.
I am good. I am truth. I am the Way of healing.

I will be lifted up and brought down from the tree.
Even as Sundancers are torn, so, too, was my flesh torn. I gave my life for all life.
I am Indian. I am Jew. I am Gentile. I am Me, the Living God.
I am whole even as we/ye are holy. Be ye holy and well-watered fields and hills.
Walk ye in the Paths of Righteousness (Right Ways).

And you will see beauty and peace in my lands.
We will no longer dance as ghosts, but as living souls–alive and well-watered at last.

Amen.

My Notes: The Good Red Road is Cherokee. Is this the peace of the Cherokees or the Sioux–or both? The name "Wowetsin" was given to me in the dream as my own? In my studies of the assistants to a Hunka, as outlined in my book of Lakota Rituals, is this word related to wawasi and walowan, which mean assistants to a Hunka healing person. I have asked a Native American shaman if he knows what this name means to him, and to me. I am still attempting to research this special name. I do know my desire in life has always been to be able to help others in whatever ways I am able to do so. I see myself as an "assistant" in many different roles.

In the mid-1980's I awakened with Meso-American, Aztec or Incan names given for me to use to decipher and gain an understanding of the ways of the people of this continent where we have been placed to live. I also was given Sanskrit and Runic words during the era of my initiatory training in the socalled "mysteries" of the Father.

Beginning in probably 1981, I began to have dreams of the major arcana of Tarot, as well as seeing and hearing the creatures of the Earth and the Heavens give me messages of the times in which we are living. He literally began to teach me how His whole creation is alive with His Voice. He speaks to us in the still, inner, small voice. He also lets us know the messages of the trees, clouds, streams and wildlife (the four-leggeds), insects, and birds (two-leggeds, like humans). Native legends talk of the days when men and animals could talk. They expect this to occur once again. So, too, do I. This is the world where darkness impedes the light of truth. Jealousy rules over loving blessings for the joys and victories of each other. I have become attuned to the natural ways of the Tao, Zen, and of the creation. I believe the Father blessed His handiwork. The creation still speaks to those who have ears, eyes and all the senses He gave us to commune with nature. This has been shown to me over and over again in my dream and visionary messages. He is attempting to help us to re-connect to His creation and to Himself. If we become as joyously carefree and eager to learn as the Little Child, we will be eager to learn of these treasured truths. It is in these sections I will share my messages from the creatures, the heavens and the earth. We are all part of His cosmos.

As women, we are part of the creation. We bring forth life from our own bodies with–or without–the assistance of our natural counterpart the male of the human species. We are all part of Mother Eve, our human mother archetypal role model.

PART II TOTEM CREATURES

22. SHE DREAMS OF WOLVES

(This is an Indian name by which I define my connection to the Wolf.

23. WOLF--THE HERMIT & THE WOLF/DOG

Dream: Early 1980's

I was appalled to see a dark robed figure I thought of as The Angel of Death enter my home through a huge hole in the side of my home. I saw myself as the mother become the size of small children. It might be noted that my own children were teenagers at this time.

I began to rise toward Heaven as if in an ascension of Rapture. I looked above me and saw a large silver UFO. In the midst of my ascension, I stopped as if to reject entry into such a vehicle.

This dream was to tell me of the human state of development called the "Philosophical 40's stage of contemplation and university studies. In fact, as if to usher in this stage in grand fashion, my life as a full-time working student began with the ending of my marriage shortly after this dream.

The prophetic message of the regression or return of the mother to the size (or era) of her children was exactly what happened to me. I had always refused to date a man even one hour younger. Now I found much younger men wanted to date them. I was mistaken for a young man's wife, rather than being old enough to be his mother.

This was truly a prophetic dream used to define a stage in my life plan destiny. This was also my first "Wolf" dream. The wolf-dog is the psychopomp which accompanies The Hermit on the tarot card. At the end of my marriage, I actually cared for such a creature briefly. He looked at me as if he were a deeply wise, all-knowing, human soul who knew we had met for a divine purpose. He was also a messenger sent to prepare me for my new life of monastic time of metaphysical study, contemplation and prayer. I considered myself to be like a nun for Christ.

The Wolf Totem means one is a counselor, teacher or family and tribal person. The Wolf Clan is a Peaceful Warrior clan. This was indeed my era of working with multi-cultural social services of all types. Native American Studies and Afro-American Studies became great support systems in my life.

Even the UFO in this dream speaks to me of my desire to leave this planet after spending so many years here trying to not feel like a misfit. I know we do not have to be so angry, hurt, mean and ignorant. Many of us are sure there are planets where these ways of existence are not allowed even if they were part of the thought patterns of those who occupy those worlds.

My first feeling when I saw the large silver spacecraft was to think, "I don't want to believe we will be taken to Him in a spacecraft." As the years passed, I continued to dream of leaving the planet in a space ship. In these dreams I was with husband, mother, deceased grandmother, and others such as the military couples I knew in my life as a Naval Aviator's wife. This dream came in the early 1980's. Now I am at peace about the spaceship. Perhaps many of us would not mind returning to our Father in a space conveyance–especially if we're still in human forms. Now it is 2005 and I would be overjoyed to exit this world any time soon, before things get worse. However, I believe we are to peacefully occupy our roles in life and to live fearlessly in His Beloved Spirit. We are so grateful for His loving Presence. We long for our Heavenly Home.

24. WOLF--THE WOLF AT THE DOOR

Dream: about 1990 perhaps

I was shown a dream image of a wolfen face looking like "The Wolf At The Door". I found a picture postcard which was the same face. I prepared for the harder times prophesied in this dream message. This wolfen creature did indeed give us the message of hard times ahead.

25. WOLF--THE CHEROKEE COMFORTER WOLF

Dream Visitor: 2001

I began to do much research into the Other Side. I had been reading late in Sylvia Brown's wonderfully descriptive book *"Life On The Other Side"*.

I went to bed after weeping copious tears over my great longing to be there again some day. I awakened in the night to the most unbelievably tactile and real dream I had ever experienced.

In my dream, there was a ring of a telephone and the distant sound of an unintelligible male voice. I reached out my left hand and touched the heavy coat of a large husky type wolf/dog standing by my bed. The feel of his hair still remains in my memory. It was very real and heavy hair such as the strong "ruff" hairs around his head. I reached my left foot out and touched his huge hindquarters at the end of the bed. It was at this point I began to verbalize my shocked response to this large canine apparition from another world. I awakened thinking perhaps this was an ancient pet from my own home in Heaven. He was allowed to visit me because I was so homesick for Home the night before. This is still one of my personal belief options about how to describe and make any sense out of this wonderful–and frightening–dream.

A few days later, while at work, I mentioned this manifestation to a Native American couple. They were of the opinion it may have been a wonderful Divine Messenger known by the Cherokee people as The Comforter Wolf. They believe there is a wolfen dream messenger who comes to comfort those who are unhappy and mournful. I can also believe this is true. I only know that this was a shockingly "real" entity. Whether it was my pet "Omar" or the Comforter Wolf I do not know.

It also made me think of having experienced dream messages which were olfactory, as with the Three Flower Baskets and auditory as with the "Music of the Spheres" which matched the flowers. It also made me aware of the places I have also seen in Heaven, even as have been seen and described exactly by others. In this dream, I was allowed to have an example of tactile touching of a living creature from the Other Side. After all of these mysterious manifestations of the divine creation I am now ready to believe we are soon coming to a time when the Veil will be opened into Heaven. We will go back and forth even as the angels upon Jacob's Dream Ladder to Heaven.

Wolf has made a large impression of his totemic role in my life. Wolf is the symbol of counselors and teachers, as well as being the totem of the Sioux Wolf Clan of the Peaceful Warrior–strong but trained as are the martial artists in control without rage. Wolf mates for life. It is also a symbol of the family and the clan loyalty we need to care for one another in our tribal lives. I do realize we are all part of tribes even if we have no proven Native American lineage.

26. DEER--GENTLE DEER'S VISIT

Dream: Spring, 1993

I dreamed of a beautiful doe deer who had come to grace my life with her Holy Presence. Indeed, she stood by my dining room table and ate from a plate upon the table as my honored guest.

When she was finished, she gracefully rose into the air and ascended through a round exit near the ceiling of my dining room to return to the Great Spirit. (It was later when I realized this hole was the birthing entrance or exit of a Native American sweat lodge. I realized I had been graciously blessed by a Heavenly Visitor. Thus did Deer enter my life as guide and totem creature.)

Shortly after I went to work at a Forest Service Laboratory in a redwood grove she came to actually manifest herself to me as an actual doe. She came directly up to the glass walled office and stood in quiet communion as my friend and guide. We shared several minutes of social interaction. I knew she was a confirmation of my dream message. I also knew I would see this deer one more time before I left my job with the Lab. In the three and one half years at the Lab I never saw any other deer until she walked across in front of my car as I left work on one of the very last days of my employment.

I have no doubt Gentle Deer was sent to me as a Messenger by my Heavenly Parents to guide me, their daughter, into my perfect employment position. I never stop praising God for divine leadings and directives. I live my life as a simple, faith-filled woman, who believes in the Great Spirit/Our Holy Father, and that He leads us by forces of nature, and the messages of the creatures of the Earth and the Heavens.

Another divine message regarding this special job position was that of The Feathered Wind, which is included next.

27. THE ANGELIC FEATHERED WIND

Dream: Spring, 1993

This is the other of the two dreams I had before my unexpected job offer from the local Forest Service Laboratory.

This dream began with a hard and nasty Dust Storm. (This means family problems, etc.)

Next, I saw a huge Whirlwind. (This signifies for me the Deity.)

The last wind was a fantastic wind I called The Feathered Wind because it has to do with being carried by that wind, as if by angels with feathered wings, to the entrance of the very same large glass building in which I worked for three and one half years until the governmental cutbacks of 1996. At the time of this special dream, I had not ever seen the two-story laboratory with its huge glass windows. I guess one might call this remote sensing via dream state.

This auspicious dream was one which was a truly wonderful epiphany. I knew I was being cared for in a miraculous fashion.

REMOTE VIEWING?

Dream: 1995-1996

I had little knowledge of the work done by those who worked with remote sensing using our viewing satellites for tracking of wildlife and the preparation of topographical maps for usage in the work done by scientists all over the planet.

When I had this dream I had no idea it was an actual remote viewing of a governmental agency in the Denver area. I had never been to Denver until I moved to Colorado in June of 1996. It was probably the following year when several of us filled out applications to be considered for work in the selfsame fields in which my co-workers had been involved at the Research Laboratory...as cartographers and scientific data analysts that I recognized this all from my dream of a couple of years prior. I felt badly–as I did in the dream–with the realization I had no chance of having this type of position.

In my dream, I was stunned and absolutely amazed to be in classes regarding these types of training even though I am not a mathematician or a science person. I was shown the buildings in which we met for our introductory seminar. I was also given the name of the large road shown as "25". Imagine my extreme surprise when I discovered Interstate 25 is located within a short distance of the buildings of the Auraria College

Campus where the applications were being taken for the training positions which were being offered. I realized the tall tower I thought of as a "light house" in the dream was the tall tower at Elitch's which is also visible from the same location I viewed in my dream. I saw all the buildings and the freeway as well as experiencing all the same feelings I had in the dream. Why was I here?

The human mind is a great computer, worthy of great and awful usages. I can see how our ancestors used their God-given gifts to span time and space in order to reach loved ones. It is my belief there are many more unknown and seemingly miraculous things to be learned than we can imagine at this time. We must stay open to new information and technology. We may become completely obsolete human beings if we do not open our minds and hearts to new ideas. Perhaps it is time to stop hating one another and to concentrate our efforts upon releasing our fears and ignorance and re-programming our minds and souls to freely soar adventurously into this new millennium to be part of the advanced gifts of the Creator.

28. HAWK--RED EAGLE, THE RED-TAILED HAWK OF WORLD LEADERS

Dream: Probably 1996

It was sometime in the mid-1990's when the world's leaders seemed to me to be even more confused than usual. I went to my bed very concerned for the good of all the people of the world. Before I retired that night I found myself gravely concerned enough to began praying in a serious and heartfelt fashion for wisdom and well being of our world's leaders and rulers. I drifted off to sleep.

I had a very insightful dream about the role of hawk in relationship to world rulers. Until I had this shocking time of insight brought about by this dream, I never knew the symbolic meanings of Hawk.

I lead such a busy life I hurriedly must research each dream as it comes. I do not sit around reading reference books because I have too much time on my hands or because I feel I must know everything there is to know in life.

I drove into an ordinary farm yard. Suddenly, I heard this loud shriek of a red-tailed hawk. He was in flight to the upper eaves of the farm house. He definitely had gotten my undivided attention with that loud noisy shriek, which I had not even realized was his normal sound. It was still echoing in my ears while I awakened completely and began to study about Hawk.

Much to my great surprise, I found Hawk is known as the Guardian of Kings and of all the Earth's rulers. Indeed, we know many of the Egyptian Pharaohs and the Native American Chiefs wore Hawk head dresses over their heads as a sign of the authority of the Hawk. (Read about Horus and other Hawk symbols.)

God knows the creature's role. Therefore, the Hawk was allowed to visit me and to make his role and powers known to me because I, too, was attempting to be a seer and a guardian to assist Earth's rulers, which is his own mission. The creature is a symbol of divine sight. With his piercing eyes he sees all, far and wide. A red-tailed hawk is called Red Eagle by Native Americans. He flies to divine heights to where the Deity is said to dwell. Again, I was profoundly surprised and amazed to learn accurate wise information in daily instructions from our Divine Teachers in Heaven.

Hawk gives us abilities to have foreknowledge as seers of the future, to be forewarned to lead our people safely through life. To me, this Divine Creature, one of the signs of the Seer, speaks to us of the All-Seeing Eye of God. May we all be so blessed, so we may bless and protect our loved ones. May our world leaders be blessed with divine insights and all manner of heavenly wisdom. Great are their roles and responsibilities. I was made aware of our responsibilities as citizens of the world. We must pray for rulers and nations. We must all attempt to be actively participatory in the care of our planet, our leaders and of our respective kingdoms.

29. DRAGONFLY--DANCING DRAGONFLY'S MESSAGE

A Real Dragonfly Performance–probably early 1996.

"Dragonfly, please keep on with your splendid performance."

This was my entranced, silent message to the Divine Dragonfly sent to capture my attention that day in the crowded parking lot of the Golden Harvest Restaurant.

He was much more than an ordinary dragonfly, wonderful as they can be. His head was like brilliant sparkling pink and green gemstones. He was intent on his active dance up and down between the 20-foot row of cars in the lot. He always returned to his position directly in front of me, as if intent on making sure I could see and acknowledge his presence–and his message. I made sure I let him know I was intent upon watching his wonderful dance. He reminded me of the bejeweled and magical owl of the Goddess Athena in the movie "Clash Of The Titans". By this time, I was able to recognize this Dragonfly was also a Divine Messenger.

Later, I realized he had been sent to confirm several major life-altering changes occurring in my life and the lives of my whole family. We were considering a family "Exodus" from California to Colorado. This was an extremely hard decision for descendants of the original Anglo-American pioneers in Northern California of the 1860's.

It is now my belief the Holy Great Spirit leads us by all types of creatures and in all manner of ways. Dragonfly was a Divine Messenger of Change for me that day. (Read more about the creatures.)

Those of us who have experienced the dance of the Divine Dragonfly are prone to feel an ongoing connection to these wonderful tiny creatures. We're the ones who buy dragonfly lamps, and who watch and buy movies such as "Dragonfly" with Kevin Costner. I met one woman who had dreamed of Dancing Dragons, which are said to be ancient mythical and magical creatures akin to the Dragonfly. Both creatures are marvelous creations. All these marvelous creatures are manifestations of our Creator. I never cease to be amazed at the manifestations of the Divine.

HORSES & UNICORNS

30. HORSE--THE GIANT DARK ROAN (OR RED-BLACK) HORSE

Dream: Probably in the early 1990's

I was seated atop a huge horse the size of a magical titan sized dark reddish black horse with a matching mane and tail. I looked far down on the ground and saw a mediocre man.

The message of this wonderfully empowering dream was that I was no longer endangered from those men who continually threatened me in lustful fashion. This gigantic creature upon whom I was seated was the symbol of my feminine empowerment and the protection of the divine.

I have heard of other women who have also ridden this horse and were also blessed as I have been blessed. This Horse was one of the first of several I have been given as dream messengers.

The Horse is one of the power symbols.

31. HORSE--VISION QUEST

Dream: Early 1990's

I had been visiting in the Rocky Mountains. It was at that time I dreamed I had come to the mountains to make a vision quest of enlightenment. I was no longer to take insults from those who made it their mission to degrade me. I was to be still and calm. I was to let "The mountain come to Mohammed" and was not to any longer humbly lower myself for abusive behavior. My testing had ended. I had given all I was allowed to give of myself to such abuses.

Whenever I think of this message I am shown myself as an Indian riding his horse to the top of a high mountain on a Vision Quest.

32. UNICORNS--GODDESSES RIDE UNICORNS

Dream: About 1991

I was shown a dream vision of myself and two other beloved women no longer riding beribboned bicycles. Instead we were each shown astride white unicorns with ribbons in their manes. We were all dressed in long white gowns with floral garlands on their heads.

33. HORSE--THE MUSE OF THE WRITER, THE WHITE & BLACK HORSE

Dream: Early in 2002

I was in a state of writer's block. This was an unusual state of being for me at that time. In this dream I saw a wonderful white Horse with black mane and tail. He was so darling. He walked directly over to me and dropped his huge head in my arms. I hugged him and felt my inspiration had returned. This beautiful creature remains in my most pleasant memories of wonderful creatures. It was one of those truly ecstatic moments. I felt as if he was truly a Messenger from the Divine. It is hard to say if it was an epiphany or a theophany. I never cease to be joyfully surprised by the whimsical ways our Father helps us along the hard paths in life.

SECTION IV. SIGNS & MESSAGES FROM THE EARTH & HEAVENS

PART III
FANTASTIC CREATURES

WE MUST DARE TO BELIEVE IN OUR POWERFUL DREAMS

At this time, I am going to attempt to connect all of my dreams messages into one coherent, connected, ongoing, insightful and informative, picture of my life as a spiritual woman. Since I am an Ordinary Woman, mine will probably look more like a Patchwork Quilt, tied together with broken threads, than a fine Renaissance-era Tapestry.

I call this section Love Covers All, because love does cover all of us as one special creation of very special creatures.

34. DREAM #1 - THE STRIPED HUMANOID (1996)

When this dream came to me, I was understandably shocked. In the dream, this unusual two-striped, seemingly unisex being (which was seemingly wearing no visible clothing other than a seamless, form fitting, covering, like a wet suit for scuba diving) came to me desirous of me holding it close to my heart in a loving embrace. In other words, it simply needed a hug.

When this dream apparition came to me I thought of it as a socalled "Alien", yet also as a human being, seemingly, expected to be embraced. It came as if knowing I would spontaneously, and automatically, be able to hold it close to me in the loving embrace it so desired. I did so. How can one refuse someone who is desirous of the touch of holy, non-sexually motivated, love?

I must attempt to describe this special entity. This humanoid being had an amazing appearance. It had human shape. However, it was striped with darker blue on it's back, while it was a lighter blue-white color on it's front. The stripe ran the length of it's body, as if it was divided lengthwise, with the color division coming at the exact 1/2 of the torso, all limbs, and the head.

Perhaps, though we have not made acquaintance with this being, except in dreams, it is really one of our kinfolk. Indeed, it may be an unseen neighbor with whom we share our planet. Are we ready to do the neighborly thing and say, "Hello, so nice to meet you."

35. DREAM#2 - THE HAIRY RHINO (1996-1997)

I was in an area with a wilderness preservation reserved for the conservation of certain species of animals. I found myself seated atop a small truck as I was being driven through this area. Suddenly, a huge, hairy rhino came up beside me where I was seated with my legs dangling off the truck. He let me know he expected me to pet and hug him, even though he was a huge beast on the ground below me. I felt deeply honored by his desire for my touch and affection.

When I researched the symbolic and totemic meanings of this creature, I learned the meaning of the Rhinosceros is that of Ancient Wisdom. I was again made to feel very honored to have such a special one desire my human contact. Later, I met a woman who loves rhinos. She told me of her beloved and endangered Malaysian Hairy Rhino, who, she verified to me, does exist in a Nature Reserve in Malaysia. some of them have been brought to other countries, including our local zoo, to which she belongs as a long-time member. Indeed, she makes monetary contributions for this special rhino.

After sharing my dreams with these wonderful creatures, I began to wonder about our telepathic connections to others, including even the non-human creatures and beings, as with the Striped Humanoid, the Hairy Rhino, the Divine and Bejeweled Spiders, the Snow Leopard, and others. Was there an almost extinct, hairy, and lonely rhinoceros, far off in Malaysia, who was dreaming of wanting love from this human being? Initially, at the time of my dream, I was under the impression that he was a prehistoric, ancient rhinosceros. Therefore, I will continue to believe his meaning for me will always be that of "Ancient Wisdom".

In addition to my thoughts of telepathic connections to the creatures with whom we have communication, if we but see them as kindred souls, I also had several other thoughts about the meanings of these dream visitors:

1. All the creatures are divinely created, no matter how diverse their appearances.
2. All were needy, and desirous, of the warmth of loving touch.
3. All the creation, two-leggeds, four-leggeds, or multi-leggeds, all need the warmth of touch. Therefore, we all seem to need to be hugged and embraced.
4. If this is the case, why is it sometimes so hard for us to love those who look like us? They are genetically our own species. Yet, in spite

of this fact, we do not easily share our hearts, minds, or our bodies with others. If these creatures desire our love, how much more must our loved ones be needy of our touch.

5. It is obvious to me this day, that God is the God of love in ALL facets of the meaning of love. Love is an action, as well as a symbolic shared ideation of our minds. He gave us human bodies which require touch to sooth our fears and loneliness, as we co-habit with all the species here on Earth, in the blackness of the universe as His Creations--ALL. We ALL require Bodily Touch, even as we require the Love which comes from our Hearts, Souls, and Minds. All are needed to completely encompass us in all the love available to us as living creations, residing on the face of a living world--The Creation of the Creator who is Love.

****

36. THE HOLY SNOW LEOPARD & OUR IMMORTAL PET

Dream: 1996

I was given a dream in which there was a Tibetan Snow Leopard and our beloved long-deceased pet Debbie Dog. She died in about 1969 or 1970. In the dream, her eyes were bright green. Seemingly, I was providing sustenance enough to be able to even feed "special creatures" such as these.

At the time of the dream, I took this to mean we would be able to provide abundantly for their material world food needs. I also felt it meant we would be well cared for as a human family as well as an over abundance enough to be able to share with others of the wilderness creatures as well as of the Other Worlds.

I was reminded of the manifold meaning to the words sharing and caring. We are to share and to provide sustenance for even those creatures of the spiritual realms if need be. This is a concept not currently known or understood by human beings at this time. Perhaps we do bless God and His manifold creation with our love, our prayers and communications, our touch, our thoughts, our souls. We share more than food, warmth and survival needs. These creatures are deemed by us to be beyond such needs. They do need our acceptance, honor and mindful awareness. They need us to know we all are co-existent forever.

I believe the Great Commandment of the Great Commission includes, first of all, loving God with our whole heart, mind, body and soul; (2) our neighbor as ourselves; and (3) –even loving these creatures as neighbors and as friends, even as we love ourselves and our human neighbors? Adam and Eve walked and talked with God, each other, and those other creatures with whom they shared the Garden of Eden. Are we ready for the Gardens of Heaven? Do we want the Return to the Paradisial Garden? The Native Americans speak of the times in the beginning "when men and animals could talk". They believe in the immortality of the soul.

AGAIN, I SEE HOW TRULY LOVE AND SHARING COVERS ALL!

Perhaps we may return to a time when we carry on telepathic communication with our pets and the wild beasts become our friends also. It is quite a well known fact the creatures appreciate our recognition of their heavenly natures. They often dare to interact with us in socially relaxed ways if we relax our dominant stances.

In fact, I am quite sure "Friends eat and talk with Friends." They do not make their "Friend" wait until they are done eating. After all, every young child is taught "It's not polite to eat in front of another person if they do not have something to eat." Perhaps, since we are told He sees every feather of a tiny bird and every hair of our own head, He also observes how we treat "the least of these". He has told us we are judged by how we treat the "least of these"–to the point where our Lord tells us we are doing unto Him, even as we do to one of these. Therefore, it is my belief we should add a new rule to our book of new things to learn–"Friends eat *with* friends."

It is also possible to begin a bonded relationship you have never before known with our pets if we treat them as if they were another beloved 'soul'. They will adore you.

PART IV
SIGNS IN THE HEAVENS AND UPON THE EARTH

This is a collection of various Signs we have been seeing in the Heavens and experiencing upon the Earth. Last night's lunar eclipse would very likely been recorded in ancient times as a Sign of a dire prognostication of an event to come. Sometimes we notice these eclipses even in our modern times. If we don't, perhaps we should ask the Native Americans or the Aboriginal Tribes of Australia of these planetary signs. They are very aware of the Watchers and of their own Star Maps. Some tribes see maps in the heavens showing the designs of their own villages. Many people have felt close affinities with certain planets and stars. We have the studies of astrology as well as those who believe their ancestors came from Sirius or the Pleiades.

It has been my ability to see certain of these heavenly manifestations in my dreams, as well as having personally witnessed sightings of unusual flying objects in the skies.

Dreams and visions of earthquakes, winds, floods and other earth signs have come to me as well as having lived through several very frightening earthquake experiences.

I will start off with my memories and studies of the creation of the planet. There were signs at that time. Our Lord Jesus Christ told us to beware of the things which are soon to be coming upon the Earth. He mentioned the changes in weather, the raging of the seas and also of the dangers to those who think they are safely dwelling in coastal areas. It is now obvious to most people on the planet His warnings were correct. It is now 2,000 years later and we are beginning the Third Millenium of the Gregorian Calendar after the birth of Jesus Christ. At this time, there are many everyday citizens, as well as scholars, scientists, world governmental, military and theological leaders who are pondering grave concerns over the safety of Planet Earth, our dear Gaia, at this time. There are validly grave concerns over "Global Warming" and the validity of the theories the Earth is 'wobbling' and is preparing to experience a cyclic "Axis Shift". These have been noted concerns for several decades in the Western World. To this very age there remain ancient records showing this readjustment of the Earth upon her axis has occurred several times. The Meso-American records show this is the beginning of the Fifth Sun, or the Fifth Axis Shift. Each time there have been "Signs in the Heavens and upon the Earth" to give warnings to the human populations who have forgotten these things. The highly technological world of the powerful nations of the modern world are some of those who are skeptical of these theories even though Earth's rocky structure shows sedimentary signs of these events.

Is it any wonder those who do not desire to learn anything about even their own world of today, do not care about such ancient historical Signs of the Times? There are those souls who do not care to know anything about the personal bodies, minds and souls of themselves or their loved ones. Therefore, His words or warning also included the prophetic warnings there would be those living a the times when the earthquakes came who would be completely involved in the cares and stresses of daily life. They will be "marrying and giving in marriage" until the day comes when they are all swept away–as at the time of the Deluge described in the world records of a man the Bible calls Noah and his family who escaped in an Ark. There are stories of this event in the ancient scriptures of many of the religions of human beings.

I will insert some of my thoughts about these topics herewith. It is my belief this book is primarily for my use in evaluation of my personal life research studies. It's simply an collection of my interests as a Seeker of Truth and Wisdom as a Child of God. My roles have been those of a human woman with a large family. It isn't like any of the prior wonderful Christian books such as *A Pilgrim's Progress* or *In His Steps*. Mine is a pionoeer woman's story such as *Sarah, Plain & Tall*. This is simply who I am and the several topics about which I am interested. I truly believe in attempting to "Study to show thyself approved, a workmanship which needeth no correction." Since I am such a simple and ordinary woman no one should feel competitive or frightened in any way. After all, what changes could a weak soul such as myself initiate? Personally, I am quite taken with a plain and simple angelic soul named Michael. He wears an ugly workman's cap and looks tremendously 'scruffy'. However, he speaks for the simple soul who seeks to assist in our concerns over losts rights of everyday people. Such people need advocacy of those who are "Mad as Hell" who are not "Going to take (it) anymore!"

Some of the things I have learned in my long years of dabbling into many topics of interest is that there is so much to dabble in that many souls become overcome with the immensity of information through which they are to sort that they simply give up with the pure shock of it all. Many have said they hate school, learning, reading and the like. Many are simply overcome with a great mountain of garbled data. It is my intentions to "keep it simple". It's a very hard thing to do when one has been bombarded with such huge amounts of knowledge so fast. They have named this the Information Age. This is true. However, all is not truly interesting or worthwhile information. It is simply "out there" being bounced around upon the air waves as if it is truly "Lost in space". Read on if you are still able and willing to do so. Otherwise, as I said, this is a collection of my own research which may refresh my aging memory when I grow too old to want to work so hard anymore–whenever that is I cannot imagine! I intend to concentrate my life energies upon all manner of positive and uplifting energies and data, relationships and such. Above all, I intend to walk as closely with my Heavenly Father as I am allowed to do so. I truly love and miss Them and a world I only see and remember upon special occasions. I hope some of the things mentioned herein will help someone in some age even if all of this only ends up discarded by some busy housewife in a toilet bowl. Perhaps it will be found 2,000 years later as at an archaeological dig as a treasured tome of wisdom–by a relic hunter. This is the world according to Celeste, a simple woman–plain and plumpy–a great grandmother and "crone". She loved the Deity with all her heart, mind, body and soul. She also tried to love her neighbors with His love...if they would allow love (and wisdom) into their lives. We live in troublous times. May it not always be so. We pray and believe for miracles. They are truly needed.

"May the scales fall off all eyes and senses re-awaken to see and to know the Living God indwelt among you."

"Memories Of The Alpha & The Omega"

MEMORIES OF THE ALPHA AND THE OMEGA

I. Genesis Memories

My life has at times been stranger than fiction. So, too, is the story of our planet stranger than fiction. This is also the story of our Beloved Planet Earth. This book is my attempt to make sense out of the things I have been led to learn about to jog my memories of things I already know about, but have simply, and gratefully, forgotten. However, I do realize I am a daughter of Earth, a human woman who has lived long enough to know there have been a great many unbelievably interesting things happening upon Planet Earth from the very hours of her formation as the beautifully Edenic world of our ancestors to the present world facing all types of doomsday prophecies. These prophecies are not retained only in the Holy Writs of those religious followers of Yahweh, Jesus, Allah & Mohammed. They are extensively described in the Torah and the Kabbalistic records, as well as in the Old & New Testament books of the Holy Bible of the Christians, and the days of Kalki and the Kali Yuga of the Upanishads of the Hindus. Indeed, all of Earth's peoples, including the African, Native American, and Australian Aboriginal tribes, have their "Story" of the birth of Earth and humankind, as well as the stories of the horrific dangers of her demise. The holy writs and traditional oral tales of universal memories also tell of the possibilities of life ending as human beings know it now, but that life does continue on. After all, Gaia, our Earth, has been a living entity for at least 50 million years. There have been many eras of her life. (i.e. the Land of Nod where Cain found his wife.) The Aztecs believe this is the time of the Fifth Sun. Prior eras of Earth's long lifetime have ended life--as known by humanbeings--in various ways. The Aztecs tell of the ends of these eras in several different ways including wind, animals and/or jaguars, deluge and fire:

Fourth Sun	Deluge (as in other world apocalypse records)
Fifth Sun	Fire (as in other world apocalyptic prophecies)

Indeed, the Aztec Calendar ends in 2012 A.D. There has been a great deal of speculations about this abrupt calendar ending. The major concern is that this date is in our near future.

There is a commonly known belief that some of us who are now on Earth were predestined to remember our forgotten memories in order to be able to warn others of the truth of the ancient stories of the ends of these prior ages and to warn those living now of the impending dangers of the current Apocalyptic Age of the Fifth Sun.

These memories were triggered in my recognition in the summer of 1985 while I was working as a civilian employee secretary at a U.S. Army base on the west coast of the United States. I had always been an actively reading and researching student of the teachings of the Bible and other Judao-Christian literature. Evidently, I was ready to know the things I had so long desired to understand. There was a short set of verses in the first part of the first book of Genesis in the Old Testament of my Christian Bible which had always remained as an enigma in my memories. These were the verses quietly placed in there about the mating with the daughters of men by the Nephilim of the Elohim. There were also other stories of the Sons of Anak, the Giants who were in the Land until the Deluge at the time of Noah. Even the Giant slain by the Shepherd King David was seemingly a descendant of the Sons of Anak, an Annakian.

These verses sat there in my memory until the fateful day in the summer of 1985 which I now believe was the day ordained by the Holy One as my day of remembrance of all the memories I had forgotten and need to remember in order to tell others.

Indeed, a Black Apache Viet Nam veteran, an officer of the U.S. Army told me, "I WANT YOU (TO REMEMBER TO LEARN, AND TO TELL ALL YOU HAVE FORGOTTEN AND MUST TELL OTHERS BEFORE IT IS TOO LATER)!!!" In the words of the symbol of the United States armed forces recruitment offices, I now realize this memorable instant in time was my "Message" to remember who I really am and to realize I had been recruited to remember what really happened here on Planet Earth in The Beginning, at the time of Genesis. I am not the only soul sent here to warn of the things which must be remembered in order to save as many humanbeings as possible from destruction when this planet prepares to change it's rotation on it's axis, as some believe it has done every 10,000 years or so from the beginning of it's creation so long ago. There are many of us who have been intuited to remember the things we have forgotten while in these bodies on Earth. One has only to read a few of the books listed herein to realize something big is soon to happen on Earth. My personal 'Research Project' began that day. It has not ended. It only becomes more real as a necessary subject for study. Much to my surprise, this strange and forbidden topic has now become one of the must important, and openly discussed, topics of this age.

Also, my 'Recruiter', the 7 ft. tall ('giant') American veteran soldier, also knew he was here for a reason, living, and perhaps dying, at this Time. He believed and knew he would be here at the End. He said he knew he would be fighting as a human soldier, or as a resurrected warring angel--a descendant of the Nephilim perhaps, against those who had destroyed the Earth.

He and I intuitively knew he was speaking truth. Human scientific and governmental agencies will destroy this planet even before her time is near to bring forth new life. There are many ways in which human life has destroyed her health and upset her balance. We have destroyed our own species, probably with our mindless misuse of Mother Earth and her resources, as well as by their experiments of mass destruction used in the name of science and progress to save the Earth. Instead, our unrestricted and careless usage of underground nuclear bomb detonations, and experiments with Earth's electromagnetic fields have only caused Gaia to know she must destroy us before we destroy her. This is her eternal way. We have speeded up our own destruction. Our destructive ways have only added to Gaia's renewed efforts to be freed from the dangerous virus known as humankind who cling so tightly to her breast. In order to live at all, she will shake us all off like so many fleas off a dog's back. If this doesn't work, she has been known to use her other powerful natural resources such as strong winds, floods, wild animals and jaguars, and more ways than we perhaps shall ever know. She is our nurturing Mother. She can also be like Kali or Shiva, who will destroy us if need be.

Indeed, back in the 1980's I awakened one morning with the words, "The Voice of the Planet". I found this was the name of a popular radio and television program involving the dangers to life on Earth if we continue to abuse our planet. William Shatner, of Star Trek fame, was the human talking with Gaia, our Planet. The gist of the broadcasts was to educate the populace into the dangers of not caring properly for Earth. When I received this waking intuit, I took it as a serious warning. After all, if my Lord had awakened me with the voice of an angel to let me know of this very special documentary, I realized I must take heed to that voice speaking to me as from the Earth herself.

I continued to learn and to grow as a student of comparative religious studies, as well as a student to whom 'The teacher had come', as a student of esoteric and metaphysical lore--the mysteries and secrets of God. We are taught we are to ask to know God, His mysteries, and His wisdom. I took these messages seriously from a young age. Actually, I realize now I was never allowed the life of a careless child. I have always studied, prayed, and meditated. My spiritual path has been one with no beginning and, hopefully, no ending. To be in the Presence is my one, greatest, desire forever.

However, now I see we have all been sent here with very hard missions for these possibly End Time Life Destinies. If I had known all of this was expected of me, I'm sure I would have been terribly concerned and frightened about coming. Also, if we do not come here at this time, to remember, and to explain each of our sets of memories to others who cannot remember, how can we help them? This, evidently, is my reason for being here. None can be lost. My heart breaks with concerns for all of us. This was also the reason the Masters and Avatars have always come to Earth. How can we bear to not assist others. Jesus also felt this great calling to try to seek and to save others from destruction.

Gone is the time to argue over who is the most omnipotent, the most powerful, the most renowned, the holiest, the Truest Believer, the follower of the Only Guru, or God. We must use all of our gifts of the Holy Spirit of the All-Encompassing Holy One. Let us, in the words of the Zen Patriarch Bodhidharma, forget the words and stand as One Spirit all knowing of the meanings of the divisive words of humankind. Let us no longer be lost to each other by the divisive words of Babel. Let us quit babbling and prating of self interests and goals. Let us acquaint ourselves with the Divine Spirit of Love, Forgiveness, Wholeness, Goodness, Mercy, Non-Judgment, Non-Prejudice, Faith, and Peace. Let the Peace of God be upon us as a world, working together for salvation of all the peoples of our world.

We are all the Children of God. We are eternal, everlasting, souls. We were known and predestined to come to Earth, to learn, grow, and to assist one another to pass this world of trials and testings, to obtain our degrees in how to be advanced students of His Way. We are to love enough to care for each other as our neighbor, as Jesus told us in His Great Commission to His disciples. We are to love our neighbor, and even our enemy, as ourselves. We are to forgive without ceasing. Thus are we forgiven and loved by our Heavenly Parents. We must forgive in order for ourselves to be forgiven.

We all have access to the Gifts and the powers of mind and soul of the Creator. However, as we will see from our Memories of our Studies of Earth Life, we were sidetracked at the time of Enoch by the warrings of factions of the angels of God. These who fell to Earth at the times of Earth's creation, mated with the daughters of men, thereby breeding those who were giants at that time on the Earth. We are a hybrid race. We have the eternal bloodlines of angels, as well as the mortal bloodlines of Earth's animals, in our hereditary human bloodlines. We are attempting to outgrow our ancient heritage of tainted genetics. We may be ready to transcend. There is much to be learned. Many of us will never stop learning. However, above all else, I believe we must be Seekers of Truth and Right Ways (righteousness). It is more important to be desirous of the Will and the Ways of the Divine than of any self-empowering, questionably holy, gifts from any god other than the One All-Encompassing and Manifold God.

Many of us have great, as yet untapped, powers of minds, emotions, and souls. If we could take time from our daily burdens of survival from the elements and human warring, perhaps we could see the emergence of the eternal kingdom on Earth.

One must not denigrate another's spirituality, wholeness, cultural, racial, and divine heritage. We are all One in the Spirit. Love is the Key to Life and Light.

Jesus is a Teacher of Light, Wholeness, and Cosmic Salvation. Others brought other messages. He was called the only begotten Son of God. Others have come as Sons of God, even as we are the Sons and Daughters of God. We are told we are the siblings of the firstborn son of God, Jesus. Our inheritance is His. We are His brothers and sisters. We are a royal generation, and a holy priesthood. Our roles in His Family are amazing.

We simply must remember this fact in order to be ready to take up our mantles and to lovingly care enough to teach His Ways of Peace and Love to a dying planet. We must teach each of our Paths to All, so that the pieces of this wonderful puzzle will be joined into one, complete, picture of Life As It Is--with many Paths to the Center. We must have love in order to complete this picture of the Whole Plan for All People. We will find great unity out of our diversities.

Many of us have attempted to bring forth the Message of Love and Peace to all humankind. Some have heard and obeyed. Others have continued to believe doctrines of divisive souls, thereby inhibiting the spiritual growths of the Divine Children of God. The hourglass is overturned. The Sands of Time are running out. Let us use our time wisely and well.

I believe I will record my Memories so that they'll be here to read, if, and when, all memories are forgotten at the time of the Polar Shift. May there be some of my descendants, and even myself, who will need to read the written thoughts and intuitions of this simple Twenty First Century woman. I have spent my life in seeking God, His Divine Will and Ways. It has been my mission to share these insights with others, even if they are unable to listen and to believe.

God forbid we should again lose all our memories of our lives and of this world at the seeming upcoming times of the Axis Shift. However, we are told this has happened every time the Earth as re-adjusted her rotation. Thus, those survivors are found in a land called 'Nod' (forgetfulness or sleep), where our ancestor Cain is said to have gone to get his wife. As we can see, our genetic heritage perhaps includes that of those humankind from the previous Earth Age, as well as from the creative efforts of God and Fallen Angels. What creations we mortals be! Who are our ancestors? Who are our relatives and friends in the Heavenlies? These thoughts open the door to many more insights which many of us have not realized or dared to think as part of our heritages as human beings, also known as the Children of God, some descendants of the socalled Sons of God who mated with the Daughters of Men in the times when the Creation and the Creator communed in the Garden and earlier.

II. Revelation & Apocalypse Now

This can be a time of great and wonderful insights and beauty or it can be a time of abject horror and terror with" human hearts (and minds) failing them for fear of the things that are coming upon the Earth. "

It can be a time to go into our prayer closets, our caves, ashrams, or whatever. We can take this treasured time to seek the Heart and Breath of the Divine with our whole hearts, minds, bodies and souls. We must seek to be completely infilled with His Indwelling Holy Spirit. We can be taught of the Merkaba of the Flower of Life. We can seek to know and be filled with the Glory of God, rather than the Darkness of Destruction. Let us choose Life and Light, and It more abundantly.

On July 10, 1967, when I asked to have the prophecy I neglected to speak forth to my church congregation, I was given a very special Message I called *The Garden Message*, in a book entitled *Beloved*. At that time, I learned many things. The one, all- pervading Message was that we are loved intensely by our Heavenly Parents. Indeed, we will never be left without His leading, and guiding, Spirit of Comfort. He will always be with us, even until the End of Time (as we know it).

We are the fruits of His planting, seemingly gone awry at times of the Nephilim. God is the All-Pervading, All-Encompassing, Manifold, Omnipotent and Omnipresent One. We are His, even if we feel alienated, forsaken, and alone in a dark world of densely ignorant and out-of-balance energies. We are Children of the Higher God. We are His Divine Plantings on Planet Earth. We come here as His beloved children who are on a 'Mission Impossible', as Sojourners, and Space Travelers on a Divinely Planned Earth Tour or Star Trek. We have had many write and show us small bits of our Earth Tours. When we start to be thoughtful, mindful, prayerful and contemplative we will realize we have been in training for many years to remember and realize the Roots of our Racial Heritage. We have much to learn. We will scratch the surface of our memories at this time. It is only after we ascend and transcend this present time of Earth's laborious delivery of the New World and the New Personages, that we will continue to know and to grow in the wisdom and grace of the Divine.

We "must study to show ourselves approved, "workmanships which need no correction". Thus were we ever taught to seek God, "working out our salvations with fear and trembling", prayerfully seeking Truth and Righteousness in order to come completely through our "Dark Night of the Soul" (St. John of the Cross), into oneness and communion with the Divine Spirit into the Presence in the Heavenlies.

Jesus warned us to "beware of dwelling in the coastlines(--feeling ourselves dwelling there--) safely". Now His words have come alive for us in this time when global warming and destruction of the ozone layer are known realities of science.

When we were told of the deaths of life in the oceans we knew nothing of oil spills.

Currently, our world rulers are those of a small number of powerfully rich families. It is said, they, too, realize they cannot overcome these gigantic dangers of world changes. Therefore, they may even seek to be part of the ranks of the lowly ones they dominate in order to escape the grave dangers of annihilation of all life at the time of the Earth Axis Shift which may be eminent.

At any rate, there are real reasons for feeling as if one could go insane and lose all calm with the stories of the cataclysmic devastations prophesied to be occuring within the next few, short, years. It is also very important to face these fears, study to show ourselves approved, accept death as a normal part of life, and then go back to the place of one's ancestors--wherever that Edenic world exists for you--if need be. By facing our demons of fear, we can look them in the eye and stare these bullies down.

After we have faced our worst fears, we again arise, wipe away our tears, brush ourselves off, and go on living--until we die to this Earth plane. We are eternal souls. Our souls have always lived. We knew Them before we came to live this life. Many of us have lived many lives. These, too, many of us are beginning to remember. In order for us to be able to come here to this Life Destiny, I believe we all were sprinkled with amnesia dust by our loving Parents. They knew this world was too scary for us to bear. We have heard of the Bardo planes in the *Tibetan Book of the Dead.* Perhaps this world is like one of those Bardo planes. If we remember it to be one of our worst fears, it will become a world of Light and Life.

I believe we must seek to have good, wonderful, wholesome and sane visions of life here. We must see ourselves to be the Children of God. We must take our lives and roles seriously. We must see a wonderful New Heaven and a New Earth. We must see ourselves as Dwellers Of At Least Two Worlds, if not many multi-dimensional and parallel worlds. We are much more than we know ourselves to be. We must learn to think and to believe BIG things for ourselves and others, our entire world, galaxy, and universe. We are Star Children. (B. Steiger) Some of us are Indigo Children. Some of us finally know we have things to do and places to be in the divine order of things. We all need to try to remember what we have forgotten. Only then will we be able to function as one Family of God.

Get ready for a trip Home. Many are the dreams and messages from Home. We have simply been separated from Home too long to remember the details of the Other World(s). We need to prepare to our Rapturous Return. He may be coming for us soon.

In addition, some of us may have other lives and soul adventures to live for the glory of the Holy One.

1. My message for this Age is to never stop believing in the goodness, glory, power, beauty and holiness of God.

2. Seek, Study, Show forth the Wonders of even this Age of Apocalypse.

3. There is a Divine Reason and Plan for Everything, including our lives NOW.

4. Facing of our worst fears, will bring a relief from horror and shocks during this Age of Rebirth. - It has been said, that the prepared, right breathing and thinking birthing mother has a less laborious birth than one that is fearful. Thus are we to be using our trainings to help with our own Earthly birth pangs at this time.

5. Our fears and pains will be gone when we see Him & our New Worlds even as a new mother's woes are forever forgotten and ended when she sees her newborn babe.

6. All these things have been before. The Earth, and humankind, have survived other Earth Ages of Birth and Rebirth.

7. We are not alone. We have a great Crowd of Witnesses in the Heavenlies and upon the Earth, who are working with us through these dire times of danger.

8. We are Children of God. We will overcome all evil and dangers by accepting their reality, their reasons for being, and our need to know about these Fruits of Knowledge of Good and of Evil.

9. We believe in Life Everlasting in the Presence of the Divine.

10. We believe all nations will be healed by Fruit of the Tree of Life in the Gardens of Heaven. We will be able to bear our Knowledge of the Tree Of Good and Of Evil.

11. We will be able to be trusted with Eternal Life because we have completed our Advanced Studies in Heavenly Life and Mysteries and are allowed to don our bridal garments to be part of the guests at the Marriage Supper of the Lamb of God, who washed away all our Sins (Errors) forever with His Blood, as the Sacrificial Lamb of God. Much like advanced university students, we are able to wear our robes, ribbons, and tassels with honor. After all, we are called by many wonderful names by our Heavenly Family.

12. He said He would always be with us, even until the End of Time, and/or our last Earthly Walk through the Valley of the Shadow of Death. His Spirit, our angels and guides will always be with us. WE ARE NOT ALONE! OUR SOULS AND OUR FUTURES ARE IN THE HANDS OF THE BELOVED.

13. Think and live like an Immortal, yet learn the arts of dying a good death, whether by End of the World as we know it, or by natural causes, in our sleeping dreamstate--simply leaving this dimension for the Other Side.

14. There are many who simply live without fear, unaware of frightening prophecies. They live, breathe, and commune with All That Is as naturally as if they had no fears of living or of dying. These are full of Prana--the Breath of God. May we all be so blessed and favored by the Gift of Faith, simply and humbly accepted.

III. Signs of the Times

I must have agreed to be born in the middle of the Big Worldwide Depression of the 1930's for some reason. There can be no other reason for coming in at the beginning of Hitler's World War II Holocaust, to then face the threat of World War III for all of my adult life, culminating in what is prophesied by all known prophets to be the worst wars of the fundamentalist True Believers of Islam, Christianity, and Judaism, the Christian and Islamic radicalists and fundamentalists, and the Jewish Zionists, or a mixture of all, stirred into one anti-Semitic, racist, hodgepodge of extremism. We see dangers from resurgence of Nazism and pro-Aryan thinking.

We see ourselves balancing upon the brink of worldwide nuclear destruction again. This time, as prophesied in the scriptures, one small part of the Middle Eastern nations - Palestine and Israel - are the center and crux of most of the world's unrest. Those who know history and politics, know and are concerned about the dangers of fascist tyrannies which often result from our current governmental systems. We have some very powerful governmental systems which are classified as theocratic, plutocratic, and oligarchic. Into this all, mix a large dose of Machiavellian machinations by the selfish and elitist world leaders. This era is known in scriptures as the time of the Natural, Brute Beast/Age of Self people.

Out-of-balance and selfish people with the anti-social behaviors of the most depraved and violent, unholy, impure, greedy and gluttonous sociopaths are bad enough without also being made worse by having their already sick behaviors exaggerated and intermixed with the unbalanced electromagnetic fields of Planet Earth. Since we know we have a dire problem with the wobbling gyrations of our planet we should have no problem wondering why we find ourselves polarized, seeking peace and wholeness, in a world which makes us sometimes think we are dwelling amidst a true bedlam of worldwide insanity.

Where does one find light, truth, wisdom, peace, and sanity? We sincerely wonder and ask, Where has God gone? God is not dead. We know He still lives. We are having our own, often hard, personal battles of spirit and soul. Our world sits on the brink of World War III. If we, even as a reigning religious monarch, such as our Pope, United Nations, or other major world leaders are not heard, how then can the scholarly and the peacemaker citizen expect to be heard to even quietly and wisely interject words against the Powers That Be. We are called all types of derogatory names attributing all manner of evils to us if we dare to disagree with the status quo at this particular theocratic time.

We only tell the truths at least one half of our people believe they know to be true. We are stifled and stymied when we say wars are expensive, our leaders are duping and lying to us, and our economies are failing. Our people seek sustenance and employment. Our disabled, aged, children and single people suffer great deprivations and lack of concern by a sick, frightened, and unfeeling, and wrongfully judgmental government and society. There are few who are allowed to speak credibly and well to defend the free speech rights of the many who are being unheard, as well as being reviled, for their defense of the human rights of all. There are reasons for these imbalances.

It is also true we are also living on a lurching, sick, and wobbling Earth. We try desperately to keep our minds, souls, and bodies balanced with His Breath of Life. Our peace and safety is within the Garden of our own souls, alone with the Beloved. We can be one of those who love Christ. In Him we find inner peace. He is my only solace from the cacophony of our sometimes insane world.

We read ancient prophecies, as well as comparing the many types of messages being received by spiritually aware souls who are seeing the soon occurrence of many of the cataclysmic dangers coming upon this world. It has been several decades since these warnings have become pandemic in their frequency and intensity. Thoughtful seekers of truth are rightly concerned by the things we see coming upon the Earth.

The warnings are in the heavens and upon the Earth, even as prophesied by all of the world's great Holy Ones. All the great religions have their creation and apocalyptic stories. They are in agreement upon many aspects of these shared stories.

Jesus warned of the destruction of Jerusalem in 70 A.D., as well as the events to occur at the time of His Return. He mentioned many strong earthquakes in diverse places on Earth as being some of the signs of the birth pangs of the New World to come at His Second Coming, His Return to Earth for His Bride.

He mentioned the roaring of the ocean tides, and the dangers of living near the rising ocean levels. Many are the seacoast city ports of the world. There will be great changes upon the Earth. In the movie, *Water World,* by Kevin Costner, he is trying to warn of the gravity of the dangers of inundation from rising ocean waters.

In addition to the dangers of earthquakes, global warming and destruction of the ozone layer, there are also many volcanic warnings of additional unexpected eruptions of the world's major volcanoes, as well as formations of new volcanic cones and mountains. Many of these, even in our own hemisphere and continents, are not mentioned in our local and national broadcasts unless they occur in the United States. Those citizens in the plains states know very little of the true dangers facing the inhabitants of California, or, even yet, the dire prognostications of G. Scallion, Edgar Cayce, Nostradamus, and Native American prophets such as are in the Hopi and Sioux tribes. People are generally too frightened of the dangers they face in their daily lives to want to know of the doomsday prophecies some of us have studied for many years.

PROPHETIC MESSAGES & LIFESTYLE:

I have always been a Seeker of Wisdom, and most especially since the 1970's, when I seriously returned to university studies as an adult female. It is my belief those who are those who live in His Beloved Spirit should try to abstain from usage of mind altering substances. I believe I can take a glass of wine or some such drink on a rare occasion. There are many people have had a need to use peyote and such substances to enhance their abilities to have spiritual experiences. In my case, I believe in the Vow of the Nazarite, such as the strong man Samson followed. Those of us who are His need to stay as pure and as whole as we can be in the healths of our minds, bodies and souls.. However, because we enjoy and experience the beauty of nature and the fellowship of the creatures, both two and four legged, there were those who truly believed we have need of foreign substances to be able to achieve spiritual insights and the bliss and foolishness of the happy-hearted devotee. It is sadly the case that many people do not know that the Gifts and the Fruits of the Spirit cannot be bought with money.

Salvation is a gift. It, too, is not purchased . It is a free gift offered by the Redeemer of our Souls, Jesus Christ. For those who do not believe in the need for redemption, they, too, must explore this question to their own satisfaction. As a Christian, I know Christ is my Saviour, Lord, and King. He is my Master, Teacher, Counselor, Rabbi, and Advocate before the throne of His Father. I believe in a Cosmic Christ who is the Brother of all Humankind who call upon the Father.

The Jesus known to many of us is so wonderful we can hardly comprehend how some people in the world today say they follow His teachings and yet do the hideous things they do to one another. I believe they follow ancient doctrines and laws which are no longer valid for the person saved by His Grace. He came not to destroy the Law or the Prophets, but the fulfill their meanings and prophecies. If we take warnings from the words of the seers, perhaps we can change our ways and prevent the horrible apocalyptic events from destroying our planet. Are we listening to the words of the Prophet and the Teacher I know?

What Book are some True Believers reading? It is not the Words of the manifested Word of God I am hearing. He was in the Beginning. I know His Voice and His Words. Instead, I sometimes think I am hearing the doctrines of men and of nations, not of the Ruler of Heaven.

Our spiritual ancestors would be disturbed if they could see and hear what we are being taught as the theological tenets of our faiths. Perhaps others of the world's great religious paths find greatly blasphemous changes in the purity of the messages of the Masters, even as I, as a student of my path, also have discovered to be evident. Who has been minding His flocks? He was eclectic, symbiotic, open hearted and minded. He, to me, is my Zen Master--inscrutably mindful and peaceful, wise, able to turn away harsh words with the deftness of a Zen swordsman, full of divine love and wholeness. However, He did warn of a time when His teachings would bring warfare into even the homes of the elect. We must re-discover Him. Who is our Master?

We are peaceful warriors who want to follow all the teachings of Buddha and Christ. We see the Father in the universal truths taught by

Hinduism, Taoism, and Native Americans. The Holy Ones dwell among us in the forms of Krishnamurti and others. It is my belief that all holy paths lead to the center of our beings--our heart relationship with the Deity. We must learn each other's beliefs and teachings, our rituals and rites, our feelings and heart responses to the Holy One(s). If we share our experiences, in love, we will reap a harvest of heartfelt responses as a community of believers of all races, kindred, cultures and tongues. We will find Heaven has come to Earth.

Many of us may be considered to be unitarian in our beliefs. We are One in the Spirit, in the mystical relationship with the Divine. We are told we cannot be mystics and be Christians. Is this a false doctrine? Always has our relationship been a mysterious, wonderful, mystical experience between those who love and give liberally and our loving, liberal, mystical Lord, who, by His mystical offering of His Body and Blood, gave Himself as a substitute sacrificial Unblemished Lamb slain for the salvation of our souls from death and the grave forever.

We are told He will come as the Prince of Peace to end all wars. They will burn their weapons and beat them into plowshares. The blood of the Last Great War will be up to the horses' bridles. The soldiers will melt--probably from nuclear or laser attacks. Indeed, the world "will melt with fervent heat". The plagues will be released upon various parts of the world. Are we ready to listen yet? What must happen to get our attention? These prophecies are ready to occur. Can we learn from history so we do not have to repeat it?

Read the newest of the Prophet Daniel's hidden texts saved for the invention of the computer. Check out two new books entitled *The Bible Code I* and *The Bible Code II*, by Michael Drosnin. If we have gone through the Photon Belt and are still able to read our own language, we must seek copies of these priceless books. The opening of these sealed scriptures are fulfillment of ancient prophecies given by the angel to Daniel "to be sealed until the End of Time".

Already, the weather patterns have been unbalanced upon the planet for several decades. The heat of the Sun seems to be increasing, thus killing many by it's very intensity. There are global warnings to use sunblocks and coverings for our skin. Yet, in the Scriptures, it says "even then they will curse God", rather than taking responsibility for causing these woes by their own actions, while they suffer from skin cancers and other related damage to their skins. These are quotes from End Time scriptures.

The hurricanes and tornadoes are increasing in strength, thereby causing unheard of flooding and destruction of property. Insurance and

Federal funds for natural disaster damages are running low. The Red Cross is overloaded with work, and lacks funding. These Winds, like the Quakes, are just the birth signs - not the final possible cataclysmic sinking of parts of continents into the oceans of the world due to these disasters.

Wildlife is no longer frightened by humans, probably because of the encroachment of human habitats into the natural habitats of the wild creatures. There are many stories of the big cats chasing and killing joggers. The hungry post-hibernating bears are having troubles locating food. They wander far into large cities seeking food. The wildlife was prophesied to become unnaturally aggressive in attacks upon people.

Our rivers and lakes are polluted by human wastes, as well as by the ash from volcanic eruptions and gigantic wildfires. Many of us suffer from respiratory ailments caused by the dense smoke of uncontrolled wildfires. These events are part of the End Time prophecies.

Many people care more for the preservation of Earth's whales and seals than for sufferings, health and welfare of their own families and neighbors. People are lacking in natural affection for even their own children and aged parents. These are the times which were prophesied to be afflicted with a dire lack of natural loving and caring abilities in humans.

We are now living in polarized, isolated and insular, groups. Many are so afraid of learning anything they would rather be ignorant, prejudiced, and discriminatory, even slanderous and libelous, than to check a dictionary for the meanings of words and ideas they do not understand. Where have all the teachings gone about using our talents to seek wisdom? I would like to know why these old values have been ignored, and become obsolete, in the vocabularies of many who feel they are God's 'Chosen Ones'. We are living in the End Times spoken of for it's selfish and foolish, non-spiritual, people. 'Atavism' was a word given to someone I know who walks in holiness and purity to define the changes coming upon this world. We searched out the meaning of this word and found it means among other things, 'reversion to a primitive type', or 'resemblance to ancient ancestors'. This is frightening to know we are regressing, rather than progressivly forging forward in our human developmental stages. This is truly another warning word which defines the Signs of the Times of the awful changes which come to the humanbeings as the Earth changes positions on its axis.

After being to the Holocaust Museum in Jerusalem, I wondered, briefly, why it was necessary to have such a sad memorial. Shortly after I returned home, there were those saying these things had never occurred. As a child of the WWII era, I remembered the pictures of the horribly emaciated prisoners in the death camps, as well as massive open graves piled high with naked skeletal bodies. How can one ever say these things did not exist? However, we must remember those who do not read history will repeat the same historical errors over and over again.

Unfortunately, these times are part of the prophecies for this age. Will humanbeings ever learn? Seemingly human nature never changes, unless there is a great desire for regeneration, enlightenment and transcendence of the evils of this plane and world. God help us all. We seem Hell-bent on creating Apocalypse Now--again and again.

I would rather not be a naysayer or a seer of doom and gloom. However, if these things are real warnings, it is my heartfelt desire that everyone take a few moments to look around with wide-opened eyes, and attempt to alter the awful course of destruction. Let us awaken before it is too late to do anything. We can pray, if we can do nothing else, before it is TOO LATE to alter our pathway to Doomsday.

DESCRIPTIONS OF SOME OF THE "SIGNS IN THE HEAVENS & UPON THE EARTH"

This section may be entirely for refreshment of my own horrific memories of the warnings and the events of this age showing forth "The Signs of the Times". As I have said, I came as a very naive and innocent soul wearing "rosy spectacles". Every step of my Life Plan Destiny has been a new experience which has often been very horrific. Many of the events of my life have left me as a battle scarred and traumatized soul. It is my belief I know nothing of worlds such as Planet Earth. It is simply too exciting and full of awful energies for my liking. I have always felt like "A stranger in a strange world". I know now I am one who knows why the brave Afro-American heroine of the Civil War era called herself "Sojourner". The brave Negro heroine Sojourner Truth had a mission to assist her friends and relatives become free people. I feel I must fulfil my call to be one of those to assist others to be set free with the Truth, even as my Lord Jesus Christ came "to die to make them holy" . (Battle Hymn of the Republic) He tells us "The Truth will set you free–free indeed."

We are lost in a world of half truths and lies. The Father hates lies above all else. Blasphemy against the Holy Spirit is tantamount is the one thing that may cost us our immortal souls. This is why it is so very important to know " the still small Voice" of our Father of our Great Shepherd Jesus Christ. Many holy sainted souls have died to attempt to accomplish this seemingly impossible task. Great are the powers of those theocratic hierarchies who fear the losses of their great powers over the minds, bodies and souls of the races, cultures and religions of the world. We are told those who love Him will obey His Commandments. We will "Worship Him (the Father who is a Spirit) in Spirit and in Truth". We are not told to worship world leaders, their governments or churches. We are not told there is only one temple made with hands in which to assemble ourselves. We are the "Living Temples of the Living God." He is not dead. He is an Eternal Spirit. We are immortal souls, part and parcel of His Spirit. We worship Him in our highest level directly in the realm of our hearts. He becomes the Center of our Hearts. We are like Golden Temple Urns. He resides within the hearts of each one who invites Him to enter into their Heart's Center. This is a mystery, much as is the understanding of the Trinity. Great and wonderful is He–the Spirit of Truth and of Wisdom. We do not boast of our temples. We glorify Him by our Raptures of Joy at the final understanding of Who and What indwells our human vessel. We are truly His own Family. We are no longer servants. We are the "Many Brethren (and Sisters)" of the "Firstborn of Many Brethren" (Jesus Christ).

He told us He would never leave nor forsake us. He warned us of the things that would happen upon the Earth before His Return. He told us His Kingdom would come shortly after He left, which is now over 2,000 years ago. His Kingdom is a Secret Kingdom. The planet is still ruled by the "Ring Lords". His own Prayer requests the Kingdom of His Father to come and His will to be done, on Earth as it is in Heaven." Those of us who love Him and await His Return in peaceful power and glory, fervently pray His Prayer with great desire. We love and miss the Father and the Son. Then there is a forgotten, often unknown, entity called by Him, the Comforter, the Spirit of Truth and of Error, the Holy Spirit. Some speak of this entity as a feminine spirit. Some see the Holy Spirit as masculine. Rabbinical studies have often described a feminine Spirit known as The Shekinah. There are many mysteries about which we desire to have knowledge. It is not an evil word or entity. This is so very sad. So sad. My heart breaks for the great losses of those who are too frightened to open the doors of their frightened minds and souls to see the Beauty of Wholeness (Holiness). The most beautiful of words have been labeled as evil. The language of the Holy Ones is in symbolic truths and the meanings of the Words of God. Christianity has often been prone to bury His Truths under piles of sometimes inane platitudes and trivial human laws known as doctrines and tenets of each denomination or branch of the Faith. There are several major branches of Christianity–Roman Catholic, Greek Orthodox, Anglican, and, additionally, a whole other group of small denominations which call themselves Protestants in an over-simplified fashion. Each denomination or group of believers–no matter how diverse or cultic-- has made their own set of Doctrines and Tenets of their faiths. One can see how there may have occurred grave changes to His teachings. They have not kept it simple. Each group has set up its own leadership and governmental laws. It is hoped that the original Good News of the Gospel of Jesus Christ has not been adulterated in His name. There are many people who have no idea of the great libraries that have been burned to conceal ancient truths, the Truths that would have set us free.

Neither do they know how many of the early church fathers had grave biases against women and others with whom they had no contact. When the translations were made, there were many questions of the veracity of each statement. In my studies of original Greek texts for translation of the New Testament, one begins immediately of the many questions of the translators. If one desires to study other ancient texts, there are many to be read and researched. It is fascinating. Why were many of these marvelous records not included in our Holy Bibles–Catholic or Protestant?

His truths will set us free. Many of the most strong statements of faith were written to control those who asked real questions the leadership did not desire others to know or did not know how to answer. The teachings of reincarnation were deemed unfit for usage by the Church. After all, this gives hope and empowerment to the souls of His people. His teachings are also more understandable if these insights had not been deemed as untrue. He asked us to follow His Teachings. Some of them are missing.

We could be rapturously alive in the Spirit of the Living God. Open the doors of one's heart of Him and be surprised for a wonderfully alive and well Savior. He is altogether desirable and is truly the Beloved. He is our All in All. We love Him with the full entirety of our minds, bodies and souls. This is His First Commandment and the Last Commandment as well. Any other worship of church, state, human leader or ruler of the heavens is the purest of idolatry for those who know Him. We desire Him, His Will and Way above all else. We know Him as Love. He is our Beloved. He is our just and merciful Heavenly Father who "is not worshiped in temples made with hands, but in mens hearts". These are His teachings. Try to remember. Ask Him. He will not give you a stone.

I will continue on with my Memories of the Signs of the Times as I experienced them.---Perhaps there is coming a great amnesia upon the world. Perhaps it is already here. Is it caused by the ancient electromagnetic energies of the 'wobbly Earth', or, instead, by the questionable experiments of the "Mad Scientists", even as they seemingly dabbled in dangerous experiments at other times in the Earth's long history.

At this time, Hebrew scholars may have once again unearthed a great key to this age. There are at least two marvelous books entitled *"The Bible Code I & II"*, by Michael Drosnin. It is believed there scholars have discerned prophetic truths buried in the 'exactly recorded and maintained–change not one jot or tittle' lines of the Torah, the first five books of the ancient Judaic records. When one uses certain formations of letters in the Torah, the unadulterated words of the Holy Texts contain the names of well known people and leaders, as well as their actions and the events, such as wars and assassinations, of this present age. What a marvelously insightful gift. Can it be possible our Father has saved the the Sealed Prophecies of Daniel 12:9 for our usage at this very dangerous time in world history?

This new prophetic key also tells of plagues, earthquakes, nuclear and biological wars upon various nations of the world at this time. It also speaks of locations of ancient relics buried in the Middle Eastern deserts which will give us keys to the mysteries of Genesis.

After a lifetime of prophetic study, I find this a marvelous Spiritual Gift to His frightened children who feel as if they are dwelling in the times of The Apocalypse. He has come forth with His unerring Divine Synchronicity to provide the very powerful computer technology which makes it possible to translate the Sealed Prophecy exactly at "The End of Time" when we need to attempt to prevent these events from occurring. Perhaps we can pray and act as a force for the good of all. (Gregg Braden, *The Isaiah Effect*)

There is a whole library of pertinent prophetic literature for this momentous age in which we are all living. We must use all of our training as His people to offset the evils with our good. We are told the prayers of holy people "avails much". It is my belief there is potent power in the prayers of even one or two believers agreeing together for the perfect will of the Divine. We do wish to make our Weeping Father happy. I cannot bear to see Him in tears.

In the following personal records of the observations of those of us who have been part of these "Signs" it is not my desire to frighten. It is the writer's desire to show how wonderfully we are guided and protected in spite of all these frightening things which are coming upon the Earth for the past few decades. I will relate these events in the order in which they occurred in California and Colorado.

****

SIGNS OF THE TIMES

These are my shortened notes of each event as it happened. Detailed notes are retained in my files.

37. EARTHQUAKE - DECEMBER 21, 1954 - 6.0- 6.5 RICHTER SCALE

The first time I felt an earthquake was December 21, 1954. The initial quake had a 6.0 to a 6.5 Richter reading. I was in my teens. The family had been reading in a cursory fashion of there being prophecies that this was the day the Earth was to shift on its axis. We all made it safely out of the old wooden frame family home. Miraculously, we all managed to avoid being hit by household items or with bricks from the chimneys falling all around us. We all stood in the yard with the car radio on. Immediately, we all remembered the newspaper stories. Our terror was my first initiation into the literal fear that "This day was to be the End of the World". Many people fled to other states after this mighty California earthquake. Perhaps we are those known as " The Earthquake Generation".

38. PROPHETIC DREAM –THE EARTH AFLAME–1970'S

In this dream, I saw the Earth as if I were viewing it as a globe from the stratosphere. I saw us all safely standing atop a high mountainous area of the Earth. I could see the glow of flames beginning to encompass the darkened Earth. We could feel the warmth of the distant flames from our safe refuge.

As I watched from my vantage point atop the mountain peaks, I saw the Earth seemingly engulfed in fire. The scene was very frightening. However, in the midst of this fiery chaos, I knew we were being safely kept high above, and away, from all danger.

This was a memorably terrifying dream, yet also it was very blessed to me. It showed me the strength and powers of God to keep all of us safely, in our faith with Him, apart from all dangers, no matter how grave. (This is a comforting dream to this very dangerous time.)

39. PROPHETIC DREAM "WHEN THE EARTHQUAKES COME" - SPRING, 1980

A beloved young man, one who had always wanted to love and to serve Jesus so much, was having troubles with his choices of friends. His mother was quietly spending a great deal of time in deep motherly prayers for his well being. He was dancing on the edge of an abyss. He was maturing in ways unbefitting the spiritual roles he wished to fill in life.

Two memorable dreams were received by his mother. They alarmed, warned and directed her on how to deal with the dire dangers he was facing.

In Dream #1, he and his closest friend were shown dying together in prison. They were shown screaming in horror as they died together 'WHEN THE EARTHQUAKES COME". This dream definitely upset his mother.

She began to weep and pray for their souls. She was then given a written message of what was to be done to alter the dangerous course of his lifestyle in order to help him to return to the original Plan he had made for his destiny.

His mother then returned to her bed and was given a blessed dream of victory over all of these dangerous times. Indeed, the dream showed he carried only a small band aid under the hairline of his forehead. This second dream reassured her that he and she were to share an even closer bond as mother and son than ever before.

She assisted him to make the needed changes in his life. He and his friend separated and later met again as happy married men with children.

We must praise our Beloved Father who warns us and gives us parental instructions of how to deal with adolescent young people, and then bandages our wounds like a nurturing parent, and forgives us forever–as our Divine Creator.

We do have guides, guardians and protectors. It is my belief we each have Him in whatever role is needed. He is a Divine Parent or Spouse. He told us we are not alone "even until the End of the World". (Jesus Christ)

40. LOMA PRIETA EARTHQUAKE OCTOBER 19, 1989–RICHTER SCALE READING:

This was a large quake with aftershocks centered in the mountains near Santa Cruz, California. The earthquake was so hard it destroyed whole sections of Santa Cruz and San Francisco, California. The Oakland Bay Bridge lost a span and the Cypress Freeway in Oakland, California collapsed with great losses of lives. The author was very sad to hear the charming historic downtown of the City of Santa Cruz had been demolished by the earthquake and the accompanying fires. She had spent many happy hours there with her aunt and uncle.

Communications were damaged in the Bay Area, thereby causing those of us in the Eureka area to need to pass messages between parties in the stricken areas. There were communications out of the area but not between cities for a short space of time. There were grave concerns for the safety of those who might have been driving upon those demolished bridge and freeway sections.

Cooking and food is a comfort so I cooked a lot. Many people came and we ate and worried together. We were very relieved to finally learn of the safety of all of the members of our large family.

The San Francisco Bay Area has been home to many of us. It was our metropolitan center away from home when we lived further north in California. There have been many disasters in California in the past few years. This one was one of the most traumatic events we had ever experienced before or since.

41. OAKLAND HILLS FIRE– EARLY 1990'S

This fire was a terrible thing to watch. This wildfire destroyed many of the most beautiful areas of the Oakland Hills, including coming very close to the Claremont Hotel as it quickly burned completely over into the lovely Piedmont homes.

Prior to this fire, the author had a dream of dogs and cats watching a huge fire from within the safety of automobile tunnels. This may have happened. Many pets ran to safety away from their homes. The roads may have been closed and perhaps I did see the view of the huge fires even as the creatures had viewed them at the time of the massive fire.

My family and I are all descendants of pioneers who settled in northern California in the 1860's at the time of the Gold Rush. Our hearts and lives are very much intertwined in the legendary lore of the native born Californians.

Mother Nature and careless humans can forever destroy all of our illusions of forever experiencing beautiful serentiy and safety.

42. PETROLIA EARTHQUAKE - APRIL, 1991--RICHTER SCALE RATING:

The author had been having dire warnings of an impending earthquke in the weeks prior to the quake. My messages from the Lord were that the clouds at that time would be darkly ragged ominious clouds would be in the sky. I felt it was soon to occur.

The morning of the massive earthquake I was reading Ignatius Donnelly's book "Atlantis–The Antedeluvian World". Needless to say, the quake seemed a little too coincidental. My mind was literally boggled' with the pure surprise of it all. We found ourselves unable to stand without holding each other erect. The kitchen cabinet drawers had all slid out six inches, coffee cups and books were all toppled, along with all manner of piles of miscellaneous indescribable items.

Many of the family members converged upon my mother's home which seemed as if it were built on rock and didn't exprience the earthquake motions as did our own homes. It was early the next morning after escaping again before another massive aftershock that we knew Petrolia or othe adjacent areas would be experiencing further damage and destruction. The Post Office burned and the additional damage occurred.

There was massive destruction of older Victorian homes and the like in the town of Ferndale, California, as well as the great losses in the town of Petrolia. One of the charming "Victorian Ladies" leaned like the Tower of Pisa, while others had fallen over.

43. SAN ANDREAS EARTHQUAKE–DECEMBER 16, 1996–RICHTER SCALE RATING: 5.

By this time, we were being told by the local University's scientists and earthquake specialists we were to evacuate our homes and immediately flee to higher ground when an earthquake hits the area due to the grave dangers of earthquake induced tidal waves (tsunamis). This earthquake hit in the wee hours of the morning. Therefore, we were atop the closest hills as fast as we could do so. As we sat shivering with the shock and fear of it all in the dark car at about 5 a.m., callers to the local radio station were talking of a large meteoric streak of light which fell into the Pacific Ocean near Ferndale and Petrolia at the place where the San Andreas Earthquake Fault lines runs out into the ocean. Callers from all over California had seen the fireball fly over them. Local callers had seen it fall into the ocean before the earthquake.

A friend atop Kneeland Prairie high above the Ocean was thrown from her bed and saw a huge fireball out at sea. She spoke of thinking it was a nuclear explosion. Another man sleeping in Eureka said the nails sounded as if they were being pulled out of the walls. It felt as if a truck had hit his building.

Large brass candlesticks were thrown from cabinets in my living room about five feet across the room. This felt more like an impact than the rolling motions of an earthquake. The ground floors suffered grave structural damage and loss of window glass in all adjacent cities and towns. Upper floors had not been moved back and forth as usual with an earthquake.

Several of my family members had already moved 1,500 miles inland from the ocean. The rest of us moved to the Rocky Mountains in June, 1996. This was the last of the earthquakes I had experienced, until I went to California in 1999. I was only there less than a week and we experienced a moderately hard earthquake. Many of us are still recovering from our deeply ingrained earthquake traumas. Indeed, do human beings who have suffered deeply shocking traumas all completely recover in one lifetime? I do not think so. Studies have shown that past life memories of traumatic events may remain with us until a healing is received.

44. GLOBAL DISASTERS

Dream: Mid 1990's

A large earthquake had occurred. The dreamer had managed to rescue her red Honda Prelude from the garage of her burning apartment building. As she stood outside on the curb with other evacuees, she realized the fires would be stopped and then everyone would go back into their damaged buildings as if nothing had happened.

She was shown the same type of scenario involving an Asian family. They seemed to be living on another continent. The disasters had become so commonplace in every part of the world until the human psyche was adapting itself to traumas of large magnitude. The Asian people were also returning to their damaged houses and apartments.

The message of this dream was that human beings were becoming inured and were adapting themselves to earthquakes and other natural disasters. This is really not what is happening. People are simply so stunned and traumatized they cannot realize how unsafe are their attitudes regarding natural disasters. They do not wish to admit the lives of themselves and their families are threatened. Their denial of clear and present dangers is causing many to accept dangerous living conditions as part of their everyday living standards. We are told of the great adaptability of humans. At this time, there are many who are migrating inland to higher elevations of the Earth. At the same time these people are relocating themselves and their families we are being shown the others–like many of us have been–who see the Signs of the Times as being too horrifying for their comprehension.

It was obvious to the Dreamer there were indeed events occurring upon our planet which were causing the hearts (and minds) of people to fail them. These ongoing natural disasters are capable of causing great global trauma.

45. A DARKENED WORLD

Dream: 1992

The Dreamer and her close friend were inside a darkened house with other minority people. We were looking carefully and fearfully around the edge of the blinds to see the unusually frightening events happening in the outside world.

The animals were seated atop the unmoving vehicles. The sky was dark, lit only by Stars which were falling like a fireworks display from the Right. It was a bleakly terrifying and depressing world.

It was a prophesy of economic and political events at that time yet to come. In fact, there were massive cutbacks in Federal employment which did occur in 1996. The 'Stars' turned out to be those who called themselves Ken Starr's people who tried to impeach then President William Jefferson Clinton in the times which followed.

46. "A NEW HEAVEN AND A NEW EARTH"

Dream: Early in the 21st Century

The dreamer was shown a frightening scene of a great crevice filled with volcanic fire slicing its way across the land. It ran past a lovely ranch style home in a green pasture. One wondered what on Earth was happening. Evidently, the Earth was showing forth her feelings about the continued rapine and murder of herself, the creatures and her resources? This truly appeared to be an apocalyptic devastation.

The dreamer was then shown a scene of a beautifully pristine forest in which stood a lovely young deer. This message was one of renewal and rebirth of the planet. This part of the message was one of hope and joy. The dreamer knew the world as we know it may end, but all like was not ended. This beautiful young deer was the proof of ongoing life.

Indeed, when we study more completely, we realize the Earth is still intact even after dire prognostications of doomsday have been fulfilled. After all, we are told, "The meek (the native people, etc.?) shall inherit the Earth."

47. THE AUTHOR'S EXPERIENCES WITH DISASTERS

We know for sure the Holy Spirit leads and directs us. We can be kept safely from whatever dangers which are coming upon the Earth. We do not fear death. We simply fear the things which can happen before one has a peaceful flight to Home.

The Signs seem to bode no good for those who dwell along some of Earth's coastlines feeling ourselves to be safe from the inundation of the ocean's tidal waves. Whether these be waves of actual ocean currents or of mountains of spiritually filthy exoteric waves of hate, ignorance and horrors unspeakable, they are still often shown as "Waves", or "Waters". The "Monsters of the Deep" can be an actual reptilian draconian monster; or, instead, they can also be the inventions of our own fears. The natural human "Brute Beast" is lead by all manner of human weaknesses. We may be our own worst monsters and devils. We each have our own darkest angel with which to do battle. That angel can drown us in the filth of the world until we are drowning in filthy waters of dense darkness.

It had been an intention of the author to share many more interesting Signs of the Times in which we live at this time. There are many more interesting tales to tell of the Signs in the Heavens and upon the Earth. We will discuss more of these things later, if it is His Will.

Many of us have seen, experienced and are very much aware of there being many unidentified entities and objects upon and surrounding our planet. We should take heed to the warnings before we destroy ourselves and Earth. The Earth is showing her unrest. We must observe and beware of her messages. She is beginning to shudder and shake with the heating of the molten lava of volcanic action. Beware the "Ring of Fire". The Natives of North America feared the tidal waves more than the quaking of Mother Earth. Whale bones are atop mountains. Redwood groves are buried deeply in silt. There are Watchers in the skies. The children of Mother Earth who live much outdoors have always known we are not alone. It takes only the stupidity of modern humans to think they are the first to see Them. Some of these "Horrible Signs" are meant for good. Others are simply better left undiscussed until it is the right time to share with all. Remember, we are told there are some things which are too much for even the angels to encounter.

It is the desire of the author to simply share this much of our walk together in the Beloved Spirit at this time. There are more things to discuss in another walk which continues on with our attempts to discern between

the Spirits of Truth and of Error. It is our desire to pursue the paths of Truth and Wisdom, Love, Beauty and Blessings. It is our desire to walk upon the Good Red Road of the Beauty of the Great Spirit.
****

TIDAL WAVE DREAMS & MESSAGES

1.

As a young girl growing up in the northern California Redwood Region along the Pacific Ocean, I was familiar with the story of the bones of a whale being found upon the hills surrounding the ocean. This speaks to me of a very high tidal wave. There were also records of a full sized redwood grove buried in the "jelly soil" of the farmlands adjacent to my hometown. However, I didn't know anything about this until years later, in the end of the 1990's, while employed at the Forest Service Research Laboratory studying earthquakes and soil of my home area.

2.

In the next few years it also came to my attention from the Yurok tribal records of the day several people had gone to pick berries high above the shore line of Crescent City. These people returned to their village only to find it had been washed out to sea.

3.

In the 1960's, a local charismatic Christian prayer group met regularly in the northern California town which is located at sea level. They had visionary messages of the city being inundated by a large tidal wave. These ladies were simply seeking to be close to the Lord and these startling messages came to them. They were under the impression they would need to be in Nevada to escape the dangers of the ocean.

4.

At the time of the huge Alaskan Earthquakes in 1965, the small city of Crescent City suffered loss of property and lives when an earthquake induced tidal wave rolled into parts of the sea level town. There were also some losses of the lives of those washed out to sea.

5.

There was another dream in the early 1980's in which the author was attempting to rescue her whole family from a tidal wave which was ominously approaching from the West. Her family automobile was parked at the curb by their lovely beach front home as was shown to her in the dream. She noticed the ocean surf had receded unnaturally far out from the usual line where it usually broke on the beach near their home. She knew this meant there was a tidal wave soon to arrive on their shores. She was very concerned and distraught about escaping in time and tried to keep hurrying her teenaged daughter to get ready and to leave with the family. When it became obvious they weren't going to make it to safety unless she left her daughter behind, her daughter appeared. Miraculously, or so it seemed to the author in this dream, she managed at the very last moments before the wave arrived to rescue all of her children in the large sedan and take them to higher ground.

6.

In the 1980's, while I was also an adult university student, I dreamed I had recently moved to an area with high mountains. My 'husband' and I were living in a home which was sodden with dampness and snow. He was wearing snowshoes.

(At the time of this dream, it was my intention to never marry anyone. The thought of a husband was not a topic of interest to me in any way. I also had no idea one used snow shoes at times when snow is very deep because I know nothing as a California seacoast woman of knowing about snow OR snow shoes. We never had snow. I had never lived in it until we arrived in Colorado in 1996. I learned about the usage of snowshoes when we had the Blizzard of 2003, the hardest since the early 1900's.)

The shocking message content of this dream was that the mountain face was sheered off from the high top of it to where it entered ocean waters. I noted there were no coastal beaches or roads at the base of the high mountain. This seemed to be a message of a greatly disastrous event which had occurred. We were safely atop the mountain, but we were apart from a section of the world which had been brought about by displacement of a large part of land.

7.

This messages was received by a well known local minister, now a local college professor. She dreamed she was rescuing her neighbors in their small northern California coastal town which was situated atop a high rocky outcropping along the Pacific Ocean. A huge tidal wave had washed over the town. This seemed amazing because the town is nearly 200 feet above the ocean shoreline.

8.

This dream was received in the early 1990's by an adult psychology student at the local university in northern California. She was seated in one of our popular cozy coastal cafes located in a small coastal harbor. She realized a very beautiful gigantic wave was about to submerge the whole café. As she watched she was entranced by the beautiful blue color as she watched others in the restaurant attempting to flee to escape the advancing tidal wave. She also realized she was safely able to see the wave from an artistic perspective due to the fact she was not at that time in a waking state in the real world. Immediately upon her recognition of her own safety vs. the dreadful dangers to others, she was overcome with sadness for them and the others who would suffer great losses from such a wave.

9.

This dream was one received in 1995 by a local adult university student in northern California. He was made aware that a tidal wave had come ashore from as far north as the lagoons north of the small city by the Bay. He was involved in digging people and their vehicles out of waist high mud along a main thorofare from a tidal wave which had come into the city.

10.

This dream showed a vision of the San Francisco Bay Area near the entrance to the Delta. The Dreamer knew she was observing the after effects of a large earthquake. The waters were very high in the Bay and she watched a large ship being inundated and submerged by the huge waves. This Dreamer is a noted spiritual leader.

11.

My husband had a terrifying dream of a monster wave approaching a coastal region near Malibu or San Diego, California. He felt it was at least 200 ft. high. He felt the spray before he saw the wave. This in itself, seemed bizarre he should have unconsciously known the spray would be carried far ahead of the water. This dream came to him in 1997.

12.

In probably 2002, I finally had my own "Wave Dream".

THE DREAM

Dates: August 30, 2002

I was shown the wet beaches of the Pacific Coast–someplace along the central or northern coast perhaps. There were a couple of war vehicles like a camouflage painted tank or truck parked on wet sand at the mouth of a river flowing into the Pacific.

I was on the east side of a very high rock mountain face. I saw a huge tidal wave splash above the top of that very high mountain. I was horrified to see it. However, I realized I was safely kept inside a cave–like The Cleft of the Rock, my Beloved Lord Jesus. This showed a mountain of water in opposition to an actual mountain. I knew I would be safely kept in His Spirit.

The dream message went on into a lengthy discussion asking us "Who We Serve?" You can read the rest of the message later in this book.

I only include this message because it needs to be shown as another warning of tidal wave danger of some type, at some time–hopefully not far inland as prophesied by some Native prophets and Mr. Edgar Cayce.

It is not my desire to needlessly frighten anyone. However, I do feel responsible as one of His children to warn others of His children.

After hearing of these dreams by friends and acquaintances, who are all spiritually powerful people, I was already convinced these "water dreams" either meant an overflowing of exoteric spiritual forces of vast proportions over our nation (which may be in itself now be true), or that we should take heed and realize we are being warned of disasters to come along our coastal areas.

In the early 1990's, our family begin to feel unnaturally endangered by our beloved ocean. It should be noted that we are long time descendants of pioneer families who settled in northern California in the 1860's at the time of the Civil War. We loved the beautiful cool climate, holy redwood cathedral groves, the pounding of the huge winter surfs and watching the migrating whales head to southern climes in the wintertime.

Now, as with the Dust Bowl Oklahomans (also one line of my genetic heritage), we are residing in a world far different from our own California in Colorado. As the rear guard, so to speak, of this pioneer clan who were now to "Go East, young woman, go East", rather than at the Gold Rush Days of "Go West, young man, go West", I sometimes wondered if we had not been led by our fears to make a completely bizarre move to such a new world. At one count, at least 11 souls had been led to move away from the "Land of our ancestors". Several of us still were attracted to the beautiful foggy coastal lands where our great grandparents had bravely settled so long ago. I even find myself missing being with our loved ones in the coziness of the small cemeteries–which I had formerly felt were oppressively imposing themselves into my awareness when I lived there. Now I missed them, our deceased loved ones and the lands we all had loved so very much. There are a couple of younger women who love to walk through old cemeteries. Now I found myself also longing to stroll through these beloved sites with them. I missed the times my dear mother and I went to decorate the grave sites of all the loved ones on Memorial Day. Nostalgia and sadness had overcome me at times.

I thought of the terrible fears, suffering and loneliness of my pioneer ancestors of both sides of my family. I wept with and for them. I was learning of the past by living my own modern day pioneer life. I realized my own great grandparents had spent their older ages in Delta, Colorado. I wanted to take a walking tour of that cemetery with my daughter and grand children. They were the parents of the Dust Bowl people–their children–who moved to the fields described by John Steinbeck in his book The Grapes of Wrath". Undoubtedly, as is done now, these older Oklahomans opted to move to the snowy peaks of Colorado rather than dare to move to the fertile farming communities of the San Joaquin Valley in California where their children settled, worked hard and flourished as a large family. This other branch of my family, like the Pennsylvania "Cousins", held very large reunions of all us "Cousins By The Dozens". I discovered a castle in Ireland owned by some of their ancestors. There is justice! After all the years of scorn, these hard pressed people who bravely moved whole families to California (and Delta, CO, etc.) were vindicated from the shameful labeling given them as "Okies" by some other Californians. I wept and laughed over this piece of genealogical trivia. "The last shall be first."

In the early 1990's before our family moved to Colorado, I had a dream message. The simple words were "The (one branch of my family) would understand." Shortly thereafter, I noticed the local television channel was airing John Steinbeck's movie of his book "The Grapes Of Wrath". I watched it with great interest because I had not really ever known the horrible trials suffered by these simple family people. They had been forced to leave the beloved farmlands which no longer had soil to support the growth of their crops. Their decisions were made to make a long, hard and dangerous 'Exodus' to the sunny lands of California. They were forced, in their great poverty, to load their whole families with their few earthly possessions in their trucks and automobiles. They were not well received when they arrived. Mr. Steinbeck's book shows all of us an accurate picture of the plights of many of the displaced people of the Oklahoma Dust Bowl migration.

Perhaps we had to come to Colorado to know what they suffered. It was not pleasant to find ourselves presented with bumper stickers labeling us as "Californicators". We are family people. The hate stares made most of us quickly opt to change our license plates before we could incur actual verbal or physical abuses. This is hard to take when we came from a land where we are accustomed to accepting many different cultures and ideas. We came because we feel we must in order to attempt to save our descendants–if indeed this is not a time for destruction of all humankind. We have attempted to accept these things quietly, as the spiritually attuned souls who try to understand the reasons why people would say and do such things.

Perhaps those who were ready to judge others should be allowed to walk the pathways of their western relatives. We are all of one family. Oftentimes, we have been separated and alienated by Civil War, weather and other earth changes. This does not mean one should consider another to be 'The Other' and thereby be labeled and stereotyped with all manner of strange appellations. Have you felt the earth shake so hard one could not stand up? The "Earthquakes" are increasing in number, strength and length of time. Whole buildings collapse, are damaged and re-damaged–no matter how well built, how old or new. Soon the whole world may taste of the Earth changes which will effect all, not only Californians and those who dwell in other coastal or inland water domains. Our concerns were due to volcanic, seismic and tidal dangers.

I tried to tell myself we prayed long and hard to be led only by the Beloved Spirit before we ever attempted such a large migration. Many lives would be changed–hopefully for the good of all and in the divine will of the Father. Of course if we didn't listen and were all destroyed as a family we would perhaps not fulfill our destinies in these lifetimes. It is my supreme prayerful desire to never harm anyone or to alter their karmic lives in any ways not of His leading. This is why I was amazed to have the dream about the young boy and girl in my mother's home setting. They were telling me we needed to move to Colorado because of the destiny they were to live. Later, I finally realized these were a dear couple in my own family speaking to me as if when they were children–in the Spring of 2001–of their present adult ages. This wonderfully insightful dream was wonderful for me to hear. It gave me a great deal of solace as a concerned mother to know the major move had been pre-planned–probably before any of us were born. I needed to hear this because my sister and I had been the leaders of this exodus from our Atlantean world to the land where eagles are gathered. After the Attack on America of 9/11, I realized the Black Bull and its Black Bull Calf of War were shown to me to validate the veracity of both messages. It was another of the ways we see the workings of our Beloved Spirit in action. Thank God for His Holy Spirit to guide, protect and comfort us the whole way through our lives.

It is not the desire of the author to lead all so far afield into the personal feelings of this large family. However, I think some few readers may find the episodes of this humble tribal group much akin to their own. Perhaps it will solace some. This is my only reason for daring to share our personal journeys with others.

These were only a few of the personal messages received by the author. There are a large collection of prophetic messages available to others if they are interested in learning more about the dangers facing various populations of people upon the Earth at this time.

Those of us who have lived safely in the coastal regions are leaving only because our lands seem to be endangered from several sources at this time. Global warming is a threat to all of the millions of coastal areas wherein human beings love to dwell.

These are only a few of the reasons there are vast migrations of people at this time. We are told in the Holy Bible we may be experiencing times such as at the times of Noah. It is important to see the comparisons. There are many which are very similar. First and foremost, we are told by ancient writers the world of that time was destroyed due to the 'violence of human beings'. Our violence and hatred are vile energies sufficient to undermine our own safe lodgings upon the breast of Mother Earth.

Many years ago, I was given a vision of her shaking humans off the planet as if she were a dog shaking fleas off its back.

What on Earth is happening? Study and we will see we are causing many things to happen by our own evil attitudes and deeds.

My studies of prophecy began when I was a young wife. Many decades have passed. Unfortunately, these dire prognostications only become more obviously present with us at this time. It is my belief we are living in the time of the Earthquake, Tidal Wave, Tornado and Hurricane, as well as poisoned waters and air, weather and tidal changes, wars and rumors of wars, natural brute beast behaviors, unspeakable evils and crimes, and much more.

When I began to receive dream and other messages, along with many others upon whom "The Spirit has also fallen", we are told by the Lord His Spirit would be poured out "upon all flesh" before He returns. These are simply the "birth pangs" of a wonderful new world He is creating.

****

Yes, and even as we do believe for great and wonderful things to come upon this world as well as evil, we have now experienced one of the Earth's most horrible events.

It is with great sadness I must include the latest of the awful natural disasters at this time within these pages. It was early in the morning of December 26, 2004, after a year of horrendous world events. It was also a beautiful day in the paradisial islands and nations surrounding the Indian Ocean. In the Sea, near Sumatra, there occurred a huge earthquake of the Richter Scale magnitude of 9.0. Immediately, there was forming a huge tidal wave which traveled out at speeds of 500 mph to strike every adjacent coastal area from India and Thailand to even the African and North American continents. The wave was huge near the earthquake but was only about a foot high at San Diego, California. Since that time, we have daily seen the death tolls mount until there is expected to be losses of over 226,000 known dead. There are thousands who are lost or dead. The injured and homeless are unknown. There are at least a million people who have lost homes. Many people were washed out to sea when the waves receded. The losses of lives and property is incredible. Many small islands lost whole villages. The videotapes are awesome memorials to the powers of Mother Nature when she is disturbed. There have been additional 5.7 to 9.2 aftershocks as well as tidal wave threats. Indeed, as much as a month later on January 26, 2005, there were two after shocks recorded at 6.3 on the Richter Scale.

This author has seen far too many natural disasters in California and in the rest of the world to be able to think these are anything but "birth pangs". It is my desire to soon be delivered from this burden of sin so we can once again "walk with Him in the still of the evening." He is weeping out of sadness and anger. Many of us are weeping even if we have not lost loved ones as have these dear people. We are weeping with the Father and our brothers and sistere who live in those areas. May the Father see our need and our desires for His loving protection.

Many of us who believe we recognize these as "Signs" of which our Beloved told us would be our sign to "Look up, for your redemption draweth nigh." Many of us believe He is coming soon. These "Signs in the Heavens and on the Earth" are simply warnings to His people everywhere to let them know they are not alone–even until the "End of the World"(as we know it perhaps). We may be living in gravely troublous times but we will look up directly into His face. He will lead and guide us even "though I walk through the Valley of the Shadow of Death", for "He will be with me". We are comforted by Him. We are His children. He is the Great Shepherd.

Included below is a list of some of His last words to His disciples and His people:

The Holy Bible:
Matthew 23–Church Leaders, etc.
Matthew Chapters 24 & 25 (Signs of the End Times.)
Mark–Chapter 13 (Signs of the End of the Age.)
Luke 21:5-37-(Signs of the End of the Age.)
John–Chapters 15 & 16 (The Holy Spirit and His Return to Heaven.)
Revelation--Chapters 1, 2 & 3 (Regarding the churches.)
Revelation–Chapter 21 (The New Jerusalem)
Revelation–Chapter 22 (Jesus is coming.)

SECTION V
THE DIVINE FEMININE

SECTION V-THE DIVINE FEMININE/WOMEN & GODDESSES/ GODDESSES RIDE BICYCLES

PART I

ISHA WOMAN-CHILD-- BORN OF THE DAWN STAR

Isha is the most descriptive of words to describe "Woman", and women as a gender. To me, it is the singularly most definitive word there is to describe the altogether primordial

"Real Woman", and "all" women, the daughters of the Earth and the Heavens.

ISHA - SHE IS THE DIVINE FEMININE IN EACH WOMAN.

THE WOMAN FORCE WITHIN EACH DAUGHTER OF HUMANKIND,

THE "LIVING" AND "LIFE".

She is born of Earth in the Cosmos who is again capable of rebirth as the Spiritual Daughter of the Dawn Star, the Divine Twin of the Dioscuri, known herein as The White Unicorn.

For those who are Christian, we see Jesus Christ as the Star of the Dawn, the Bright and Morning Star. Many know of the Dawn Star. Indeed, while traveling in Israel in 1979, I visited a kibbutz named Morning Star, where we shared a kosher meal.

Women can also be Knowers and Seekers, Teachers, Counselors, Scholars, Doers, Healers, Wives, Mothers, Grandmothers, or simply co-Creatrixes who bring forth human life, and also in their unlikely capabilities of women who cause deaths, in the their roles of Dark and Light Star Women, known by many archetypcal names to define their various roles.

The first time we are called "Isha" most of us find it to be a personally exciting word. We arise to accept it gladly since it is generally used as it defines us in our new status as a mature and as an adult female--"A Woman" or as "A Real Woman".

Since that time, many of us realize we have become much more a Woman than we ever desired or dared to believe possible. The role is a large one.

May this become our prayer as Women, all "Ishas", of the Third New Millenium of this Age of the Fifth Sun, as the Star-Crossed Daughters of the Dawn Star.

"May all of us be guided clear through the gigantic and circuitous pathway through "The Labyrinthe" of the World with our human cords, as humanbeings and as women tied tightly to the Guiding Light of our Beloved Star of the Dawn."

However, we did not exist without our Father and our Mother the Earth. Before any of us existed who walk upon this Good Red Earth, there was said to be Chaos. From that Chaos came a union of our Father, Creator Force, and our Earth, our First Mother.

From their unity came forth The Word, The Dawn Star, also known by many other wonderful names, for He & His Father bear many names. As life came into being upon this primeval world, there were born men and women, "Ishas".

Women are uniquely multi-faceted, multi-directed and thinking creations. They are very curious. Who else would have been energetic or curious enough to get themselves into trouble over The Apple?

Later, after he took a bite of it at her insistence, he even placed the blame for his own decision upon "her", Eve, the first "Woman"of the living. His ways are still the same.

Thus have the two been separated, as well as joined as a team, for seemingly endless eons of loving unity and polarized differences. She thinks, feels, and talks in a private and openly unique fashion. She has a mind that sees all things in a wide, intricate, diverse, microcosmic and macrocosmic fashion. There are many ideas and many ways to say and to work with those ideas. Therefore, she talks of several topics in one breath, as well as generally being able to think in a wider, more diverse, spatial fashion than man. The thinking patterns of men generally seem to be in a more linear way of thinking, and thereby living, in a way of seeing everything in a well-ordered line, such as of thought, mathematics equations, historical data, and the ideologies of even the widely diverse topics of politics and religion.

Example: The natural woman as mother is concerned with provision of food as well as the preparation, eating, and cleaning up of it. Her roles are many. Due to their greater physical strength, many men have not taken on the multi-faceted, chores and lives of women. They use their "Helpmates" to do all of their chores if possible. This wonderful creation is able to do everything he can except to produce the semen to inseminate her own ovaries. She even attempts to take care of her whole family if need arises-usually due to his death or desertion. Many a divinely protected and guided innocent woman, generally poorly prepared to care for herself, has been so forced to attempt to survive with her children. If this happens, she must fight to survive against all types of odds, with many traumas, in societies dominated by men. If she finds herself placed out there in "His World" attempting to protect herself and her family from the oppressive systems created by men for men, she asks for help from her heavenly Parents, if no earthly parent offers sustenance. She is not too proud to ask for directions or for assistance in life--in spite of all types of degradations and harassment. She is the Divine Mother incarnate in human flesh. However, due to the many hard trials and tribulations, and her many life experiences, she may grow into a very strong, almost Amazonian, woman--a female who could be called a "Woman Who Runs With Wolves" (C.Estes, *Women Who Run With The Wolves*.) The Helpmate has become the Head of the Household, whether she wanted the role or not. This mutable human female creation is quite capable of rearing her family alone, caring for others in her extended family and more. However, all of the systems in her world had originally been created by and for the male. This places extreme hardships upon all other types of people in society. They have lower incomes, less education and work experience, yet have far more responsibilities than any old-fashioned husband who was expected to go out of the home to go to work and return to a comfortable world run by his wife, who was to cook, clean, launder, purchase his food and possessions, rear his children (and others if need be), act as teacher, counselor and spiritual instructor, chauffeur, and exciting sexual partner as his wife. If she has any time left, she might find she had time and could perform simple feats, such as churning all the butter, milking the cows, tilling the fields like a beast of burden, sewing and mending clothing, performing hygiene and medical duties for others, knitting clothing, dyeing cloth, making and weaving cloth and masterpiece tapestries now displayed in museums as unsigned works of art.

God (man) forbid she should not fulfill all of her roles and duties in life. After all, she is told from infancy she was bred for service to herself and others. After all, her title for life is "Helpmate", so named by the Creator God Himself. Perhaps this is why she is so well-suited to willingly accept roles as "Assistant", "Care Giver", "Helper", "Sex Object", "Plaything" and more. If something happens to cause her husband to discard her, she is adjudged by many in the religious and secular cultures of the world to be the reason the relationship has failed. Subliminally, if not directly, all her life she is made to believe she must go through all manner of atrocious treatment by her husband because he is like her human God Almighty. In many cultures, he is taught he is never to be crossed by anyone, much less women, who are considered to be soulless as well as simply slaves created to fulfil his every whim without protest or question. If she is strong and smart enough to confront him for his behaviors, she is often punished or killed. The roles of women have become much better worldwide. However, there are many parts of the world where women are still treated as chattel, owned by men, who are disposed of summarily if they dare to cross men--no matter how brutal, insane, or homicidal. If she becomes too fat, too thin, sick, old, unattractive, or just familiarly boring, she may be discarded like a piece of trash or an old labor-saving device by her husband or family. Some males of the human species will change wives like changing his clothes. He will throw away his whole family if it does not benefit himself to have them with him. To him, survival of himself, the fittest and strongest, using his own systems with which to protect himself, is of the utmost importance. After all, without himself, how would all of life be protected. How indeed? It is very hard for some men to turn to the Divine Father for guidance, sustenance, and nurturing, thereby walking very lonely, frustrated, frightened and fearful as a darkly hostile soul and force in the world. Due to brainwashing of women, monsters have been created in the name and incorrect interpretation of ancient scriptures of God, however named and defined.

Due to the misunderstandings about the Divine Nature, many men truly believe they are the representative of the Divine Father God upon the Earth, whether they are genetically, spiritually or educationally prepared for such a role. Many of them determine at a young age to willingly and forcefully take the role for themselves, whether they are well suited to such a role or not. It is known that power, improperly gained and used, corrupts the soul of those unready to wield the sceptor of ruler.

Indeed, the role of men is a hard and frightening one for young men. Many men have been taught to rule and to dominate all others, including the Earth, other men, all women, children, all humanbeings and creatures, including the two and four-legged, the feathered and scaled creatures of air and sea.

Man is created as a conquering, controlling, species known for his aggressively adventurous, dominating, warlike, hostile and territorially protective nature. He may be known in his community as a protective father and husband, yet he can also become a homicidal maniac who has been known to be capable of killing his own wife, children, family members and neighbors. He is also willing to protect and die for them and, in times of war, he will be willing to fight and to die for whole nations of strangers. Some men will fight just for the fun of fighting. He has been known to attempt to dominate, overcome, and even destroy. his Parents, Father God and Mother Earth. Many men would even dominate and destroy the universal Cosmos if he were able to do so.

The Divine Man, infused with the Spirit of the Divine Creator Father, will make the Natural Man an old-fashioned, out-of-date, role model for his sons. This New Man will be found to be known to have naturally-ingrained qualities of leadership because he is worthy of their love, trust and respect. Such leaders do not have to die at the hands of their own soldiers. They are filling the roles of leadership for which they were born as true Sons of God. The Daughters of God will be able to respect them, as well as be theirs because of the "Bonds of Love' by which they are joined to men.

Indeed, ancient records show the first women were immediately upon creation exploited for her many services by others of the creator gods. Isha was a very useful, appealing and attractive, Model Woman. Many men have continued to find the socalled "Stepford Wife" for his very own robot doll wife, or child-wife, to be enslaved, used, and dominated. Many a man wants his own way, rather than a helpmate, partner and woman-wife--a co-creatrix of life, liberty, and the pursuit of happiness--together.

A wise man once told me that "Women were the first to be enslaved by men, and they will be the last to obtain their freedom." It is my belief this is indeed the case. Women's lives, and the lives of their children, are too closely tied to the man as their father, who will often become incestuously sexual with them, then as their lover, friend, protector and husband. Women must be very selective and careful about chosing the special "significant other" man in their lives. Indeed, men and women in homosexual relationships must also be very careful about the same-sex partner they are chosing for those people often live by the culturally-defined norms of gender roles even in these alternative lifestyles.

Studies of men and women are most interesting and it is recommended that students should take courses in gender roles, ethnic and cultural studies in order to be better prepared to face a rapidly expanding world view. If we are to be living with many different groups of people, we must learn their cultural, racial, spiritual, and political views. It is possible we can become happier and healthier by learning more, rather than by becoming fearful, prejudiced and hostile towards one another--thereby initiating hostilities because of our ignorance and fear. It is possible to be zealous in our desires for peace and human undertanding, even as others have chosen to become zealots for orthodoxy, fear, hatred, prejudice and killing in the names of Holy Ones who came to teach us how to live in love and peace.

Who Am I? This is the question of many women and men. We must learn who we each are as human souls before we can attempt to know others. However, it seems to be that we come to this planet without even basic tools for survival, unless we have extremely wise parents and teachers.

Therefore, it seems to be reasonable to assume we do need to become Seekers of Wisdom and Knowledge. If we do not know how to take care of ourselves, how can we care for others? Many of us have learned completely by insightfully traumatizing life experiences. This is the socalled "School of Hard Knocks", in which many have been enrolled.

There comes a time in the lives of many of us when we, consciously and planned, or not, desire to understand what we have been doing all of our lives, and why. We start our lives as halfway asleep automatons without any clear comprehension of what life is all about. Many of us spend time occasionally wondering "Who We Are". (Example: "Who Am I?") We later find out we are all Explorers, Seekers and even Fools. We are fallible, erring, weak, foolish, ignorant, unholy, even evil, at times. At other times we may have and assume almost divine qualities in our lives. If one seeks to know, one shall be given a teacher who will instruct us. It is the belief of many that there is truly a hidden path unfound by many of us. If one seeks to know what life is about hard enough, one will begin to learn much more than one believes is possible about all aspects of one's own soul, this world and other worlds; including human and other hierarchies, worlds and beings. This is the world of the esoteric metaphysics of the mysteries of the Divine.

MANDALAS

Several years ago, while an older student at a University, I felt impressed to make an artistic attempt to make a circular design of the Stages of My Life. I began with my Birth and ended with my role at that time of a Seeker of Spiritual and Social Truths--a Crone/Shaman-type Single Woman.

JOURNALING

As a woman who feels like she has lived "Six lifetimes in this one lifetime", it seems to again be the time for me to clear out one's lifetime of memories and learning, the so-called "archived memory bank" in our computer-like human brain. At the time when I was left alone to rear my two children, I was literally divinely-led to journaling. However, I didn't recognize this fact until I began to assemble these many memories into the writings I have now began to call "books", or "sections of books", or, "eras, times, or sections of my own life"--not for publication, but for my own therapeutic review and analysis in order to more clearly understand what I now see as the results of this divinely planned and orchestrated Life Plan Destiny for this lifetime.

After a personally-chosen lifetime such as mine, which has been so multi-faceted, it seems to be a necessary part of soul cleansing before one begins one's new life on the Other Side. Perhaps it is a little like the term "garbage in, garbage out", "counting one's blessings, failures and victories", a long overdue "debriefing" as if a returning astronaut, or some such definitive term.

After all, my Life Plan was prepared and executed in a very important historical time on Earth. Some of the most auspicious and worst events and beings have been here co-existing with me and my people in the past 65 years of Earth Life. As a soul who has instinctually, intuitively, and/or consciously sought wisdom and knowledge all of her life, it is important to do research projects in order to mull over, digest, and to, hopefully, learn from my many experiential lessons taken in my Classroom(s) of Earth Life. If I do not understand what all of this has been about, I may have to re-live these karmic lessons until I do comprehend what I have been here to learn. Now, silly as it sounds, after all these years of living, and almost 200 journals later, I may have some comprehension of life and it's many lessons.

It is the belief of many of the souls incarnated here at this time that we are here on a lifetime of cramming as much as we can into one lifetime in order to be able to complete our training before Earth as we now know it comes to an end. (TEOTWAWKI & Y2K=the abbreviated forms of the warnings for the year of 2000 A.D. when many shared very real concerns and expectations of the collapse of all computerization, and "The End Of The World As We Know It".)

It is my fantasy perhaps, but it may be a reality as well, that there were many of us on the Other Side who decided to attempt to fulfil as much of our "Life Learning Experiences" as possible in "ONE" lifetime, rather than many. We planned our Life Plan Destinies to include more stressors than were good for us to do so. However, due to the shortness of Earth Time, we were vying to see who could do the most work possible in these singular lifetimes. It was a fun-filled, convivial atmosphere there. However, many of us may have taken "too much on our plates," thereby glutting ourselves in our overindulgence and zealous efforts to complete our necessary course requirements as soon as we could do so.

Perhaps others can learn from our efforts. However, if no one wishes to share in my socalled "Research Project", I still must do this work in order to understand Life's Lessons, as if I were doing a Ph.D. dissertation in an Earthly university program of higher education. After all, I do believe we are here to learn and to grow in wisdom, in order to be acceptably able to be in the Presence of the Holy One(s). Of course, for some, this sounds like so much religious "superstitious twaddle". However, for those of us who retain and hold memories of "The Other" & the "Other Side", we cannot unlearn, or not know those things that are our own mysterious realities.

Society can be very hard in their judgments of the "uppity" woman who desires more than the role of wifely helpmate to her husband. If she also desires to fulfill her own inspirational, religious, educational or artistic pursuits in her desire for self-actualization she is suspected of being a "Wild Woman", uncontrolled by her men, her society, and intemperate. She is in danger of being suspected of all manner of horrible thoughts, deeds, and opinions. Since many people in those societies see woman as natural brute beast, unworthy of notice except as an enslaved piece of chattel, God forbid a woman should be her own freed woman and soul!

There are still backward societies which believe women are too poorly endowed with souls and minds, as to not be fit for education, the afterlife, or even to be recorded in the birth and death records. If they do not meet all requirements of a theocratic, male-dominated, society, they can be killed by their own family members. In fact, infanticide of female babies, and clitorectomies of girls are still practiced in many of the poorer nations of the socalled modern world.

In fact, I am one of those disgusting Western women who actually believe herself and her sisters to be worthy of notice and recognition as divine souls, minds, and bodies, even as are our masculine husbands. How can a man who sees women as inferior, respect, love and care for his own wife, mother, daughters and female relatives? I suspect the horrors suffered by downtrodden women in such places is unspeakably evil, yet these horrible monsters must see their actions bespeak their beliefs in a god as horrible as themselves. They would rather commit atrocities in the name of the Holy One than to question the unrighteous tenets and doctrines created by ignorant and unwhole men with sick souls.

If we see ourselves as all part of the Divine Family, we can love and assist each other to put on our garments of purity. I dare to believe we all go through specialized stages in our lives. We can better understand some of these times by using symbolic and mythological archetypes as we have learned from the work done by Joseph Campbell, noted author and researcher of these topics. There are also good examples of the usage of seeing ourselves in roles such as goddesses as in Dr. Shinoda-Bolen's books, *Goddesses In Every Woman & Gods In Every Man.*

In my research I have written up my research into several books, or sections, and roles of my own lifetime. I have even fictionalized a short section of these writings in order to attempt to teach others and myself the topics I know others must also desire to learn in life. As a young mother of five-year-old daughter and a seven-year-old son, I actually asked to be allowed to experience anything I could in order to better able to assist my children as a mother. Little did I realize how many things I would suffer and experience in answer to my prayers. Many years later, I realized I needed to modify this original prayer somewhat, for I had asked, and received, exactly those things for which I had prayed--far beyond my imaginations. At one time, when alone with children when their father was on those long cruises on an aircraft carrier with the U.S. Navy, I prayed for patience. When one prays for patience, one must suffer things which cause one to be impatient, in order to be able to learn patience. Faith is a gift, but it is gained from the need for faith given by a wonderful Savior God. There was a time when I prayed for a loved one's soul, even if I needed to give my own life to insure his soul's safety in the Shepherd's Fold.

There are also many of the women of the second half of the 20th Century who have become frightening in their roles of "Amazonian" wives, mothers, and grandmothers. Perhaps this is how any group of women would appear to others who have not lived with the Spirit of God as their husband, and as father to their children. Since they had no other sources of support when they were left to rear their families without fathers, they were made able to strongly carry their dual life roles with grace and power by the guidance and protection of That One, the Ineffable Other, the Divine. Anyone who is touched by the power of the Holy One will never be as others who have no conceptual way of defining such roles. These strong Ishas became strangers to their own children due to their dual gender roles of Householder. They became accustomed to walking alone with the Divine. They truly do not need, nor yet desire, the intrusion of others less concerned and experienced than themselves in such matters. The sad thing about these roles of strength many were forced to carry is that there has always been fear and ostracization of those less understood. This is very sad for loving mothers to bear, especially when they cannot remember ever having had a choice in these matters.

There are "Called Out" women (and men) all over this land. They were called to bear extra heavy life burdens, in addition to any other previously existing hardships or disabilities. It is extremely sad to then feel misjudged by some of those who should have the most knowledge of the pain and hardship of the roles of their special and beloved women. He made the weakest, most fragile, women into the Daughters of God/Goddess, as His/Her Handmaidens, Priestesses, and Prophetesses while they were also Mothers and Grandmothers of their families, as true Matriarchs, while bearing their loads as deserted and cast-off Wives, Mothers, and even as Step-Mothers, the most dreadful name of all, besides Mother-In-Law.

None of these roles had pre-planned and written training manuals. These generations of women ("The Amazonian Ishas"), as well as the many single fathers of children, were required to write their own Job Description Manuals, written in their own blood, sweat, and tears. In order to survive it all, one needed to know how to hear and to follow Directives From Heaven. *Thus, the Called-Out, sometimes virtually cloistered, lives of the older holy women and men, (the Veterans, the heroes and heroines, of an undeclared, invisible, terrorist War upon our Families) who still desire and choose to be still and Alone With Him in the Edenic Garden of At-one-ment with their Significant Other.* We are speaking of those husbands and wives who were forced to choose between values not of this world and the luxuries of America family life. Prayer Closets were chosen over luxurious household amenities such as sunken bathtubs and theater tickets by many of these mystically contemplative Seekers of God. The Calling is a very real one to those who have been chosen and asked to walk in the footsteps of the Holy One. *When they saw their roles with God threatened by the ways of the evil ones, they chose to walk alone with Him as their spousal support systsem when their own husbands or wives chose the things of this world over their responsibilities to their spouses, marriages, and children.*

It is possible to see all of these societal changes as being positive adjustments to make us a more spiritually-aware nation and world. We Americans have always been disgustingly and notoriously obsessed with the acquisition of money and power. This recent transition to the seeking of wisdom and divinity for their own sakes is wonderfully refreshing and fulfilling.

By our long, sad, and arduous struggles, we may yet come into the understanding of who we are in relationship to God, and to each other, and to find peace within our own heart-centered souls. *Eventually, we will all be required to come into oneness with Him, as His People, His Disciples, and His Brethren of every nation, kindred, tongue, and religion--a multi-cultural, multi-faceted, spiritual Body of the Cosmic Christ.* This is the ultimate goal and pivotal apex of our relationship with Him. We are in an at-one-ment role with our Savior. These changes are not meant for evil, but to bring us into our roles as part of the Heavenly Family, and into Friendship with Jesus. It is His love and His peace which will conquer all the inequities of this world. We must come in oneness and unity of the Love of God which has prepared us well for our Life Destinies. *Those who have suffered unusual hardships as single parents, or as secular or monastic nuns and monks, priests and priestesses of God, are still apart with Him, as examples of those who have gone through the special Refining Fires of His Testings and Trials in order to be His Disciples. They have taken up their heavy crosses to follow Him forever.*

References: *Ordinary People As Monks and Mystics* (Lifestyles for Self-Discovery); Dr. Marsha Sinetar; Paulist Press, 1986.

WE ARE ALL ISHA

When we become older women we find we are expected and required to understand ourselves and others in order to guide them through life to return to their first estate, Heaven's Gate. If we have sought divine guidance, gifts, and fruits in our lives, we must share with others who seek "How to also be filled and blessed with these attributes of the divine nature." I have always believed we are to love the Lord our God with our whole body, mind, and soul, and our neighbor as ourselves. This is the Great Commission of the Master to His children. It is our duty as His to share our lives with others. If we are not required to literally lay down our lives for others, it is my impression that those to whom much is given, much is expected. If we have been shown many things, suffered and also been blessed hugely, we must share these things with others. Thus do we share the joyful bliss of Heaven with others. We need to let others know our heritages are not of this finite world.

Many of us have been intuited and taught with all manner of techniques, by all types of dreams, visionary experiences, and beings of the Earth and of Heaven. We desire privacy and many of us are still seeking to be brave enough to face the holy ones if they desire to visit us. We attempt to keep our sacred time and space in order for them to enjoy being with us. In other words, we want to have a home with an atmosphere pleasing to the Divine Ones.

These teachings come to us without any conscious effort. It is our intention to be so attuned to the Holy Spirit of the Father that we move and flow effortlessly in communion with the Divine Spirit at all times. We come from many spiritual pathways. We know we are attuned to the voice of the Father/Mother/All That Is. We drum, dance and sing joyously in the Beloved Spirit and our Mother Earth Gaia.

It is never my belief or intention to infer I am capable of more than anyone who seeks to know the Father. Many of us are simply ordinary (yet exceptional) woman. However, in His Spirit, I believe any and all of us can become His messengers, scribes, handmaidens and stewards, priests, priestesses, and members of His Family. As someone one said, all He needs is a "Willing Heart & Soul". These are my only attributes as one who desires to do His will and to serve Him as would a loving friend or child. It is my belief we will be learning far more about the roles of our souls in their gender roles in Heaven and and on Earth. It is my feeling we are all types of the original woman Eve/Isha.

WOMEN AS WEAVERS

The following dreams came to me which explains more about the roles of the teaching women. It is also true that many women fear spiders even though it is symbol of the wise woman as the Great Weaver, and of Writers. It is obvious from the following dream that the Holy White Spider hoped and expected me to be able to show it love and to be able to touch it. Women are said to have fear as well as the loving attributes of motherhood. It seems obvious to me I failed the test of my fears of spiders.

48. HOLY WHITE SPIDER

Dream: 1996-1999

In this dream, the Divine White Spider appeared to me. I was honored and blessed to have it appear to me. However, it was a spider! I have a very bad time with spiders. My husband, who practices the laws of ahimsa (non-violence to all sentient beings), always carries each spider found inside our home to the outdoors. I have dire problems with arachnophobia.

The Spider in my dream wanted to have close communion with me. It seemed to want me to love and hold it closely to me. I loved it, but I could not hold it. I was forced, even in my dream state, to tell it, "Dear, Holy, White Spider, though I do love you, I cannot hold you as I have arachniphobia."

The dream ended. I felt I had missed a divine blessing by being unable to conquer my fears of spiders--which also included The Divine Spider. I have been very sad about this because I found myself longing to be able to hold the Wonderful Spider. Indeed, I wondered if God, Himself, had appeared to me, in the guise of a Divine Spider, as if to test His daughter's love and the ability to control, and not be ruled by, her fears. I felt I had failed my test and had earned a low score on this initiatory exam.

Later, in the Fall of 2002, I dreamed of all types of spiders, including Jade Spiders. I also learned the Spider is the symbolic creature who works with writers to spin their writing webs to capture the hearts, minds and souls of their readers. Finally, I realized the Divine White Spider came to me first, prior to my beginning attempts in May, 2001, to write books. Now, rather than fear of spiders, I am in awe of the wisdom and ways of the Divine Weaver. However, even with all my new insights, I do not know if I would be able to hold and caress a large hairy spider in spite of my efforts to conquer any fears I may be harboring in my life.

Later, I realized the Spider is a wonderful symbol of Life. She spins the Web of Life in a Circular Spiral of Life. The Spirals and Webs of Life are woven into a huge Divine Tapestry of our individual and communal lives.

****

Inspired Writing- October 25, 2002

49. DREAM WEAVER-THE JADE SPIDER WEAVING THE STRANDS OF THE WEB OF LIFE

The strands must be woven together. We have spun a long strand on our spinning wheels. We are the spinners of life. We have tried to be like wise and benevolent Mother Spiders who become Grandmother Spiders- who have become such expert weavers- that we can attempt to spin our wonderfully intricate Webs upon which our children can live and grow in harmony upon their own multi-faceted strands of their own life tapestries. However, in order to live and to grow, each new soul incarnated into each new humanbeing must weave his/her own strands to make their own Webs of Life--their own divinely-directed Tapestries of Life. We call this manifestation The Web of Life, which is an individual and communal Spiral of Life into Infinity and the Web of the Infinite. The Web and the Spiral become interwoven into a hopefully and prayerfully wonderfully-detailed, and colorfully bejeweled, design in a huge Tapestry called Life.

I, as matriarch, can spin my own silk, but I cannot spin silk beyond my capabilities. I bridge my incapabilities, and those of others I love and for whom I pray, with the Bridge of the Prayers of Faith. I pray for the Divine Weaver to weave the strands of all of our lives into the Cosmic Web of the Living upon which all of our children will find their places of birth, life, death and resurrection. The Web becomes even larger and encompasses the many-tiered levels of the Other Side, our Heavenly Home. It grows to encompass the galaxies, and worlds within worlds. It encompasses the hearts, souls, minds, and emotions of our ever-expanding universes as we are able to understand them.

Our Web grows as our minds are able to encompass more and more of the Divine Mysteries of the Divine White Spider, who weaves the grandest of all webbed tapestries upon which all of our lives hang in the Divine Balance. Like the earthly spider, we see only a tiny part of the vast expanses of planet upon which we spin our tiny, finite, webs. However, we are all one. We are connected in a massive matrix of web sites on a huge tapestry of existence and never ending creation, birth, life, death and resurrection. The strands of the web are all connected.

The writer's Jade Dream Spider must direct this Grandmother, who lives in The Heart of a Secret Garden with her Beloved, to know how to see how to spin a web big enough upon which to hang the woven strands of her life dreams in order to show the perfect order of her God-directed life. Until she connects these strands, she only sees a hodge-podge of many events and people: births and deaths, disabilities and addictions, dreams of glory, educations, hardships, pain and agonies, humble beginnings and lives intermixed with great blessings, rewards, and joys, fears, turmoils, wars and rumors of wars, divine mysteries and divine directives for life. Our worlds are ones full of the great events of life and death interwoven throughout of all the souls who intertwine their Life Webs into one great interwoven Tapestry of Eternal Life. There is a divine design and plan. We all must prayerfully Bridge the Gaps of our multi-stranded Tapestries, as we live our lives in an ongoing Spiral of Life--the lives of the Living Souls, who are parts of the Living Over Soul.

We must not forget to believe in the Power of our Dreams. The futures of our lives are built upon our strong faiths in the powers of our dreams. Without faith to believe in our dreams and our prayers, we cannot spin strong strands for our Webs of Life and Great Weaver's Tapestries of our interwoven lives. We must play our roles to independently attempt to spin our own Divinely-directed strands of web to build our own lives into a Web of Living which has the strength and continuity to Bridge the Great Abysses over which we must spin our Webs. We are the Spinners, the Weavers, and the Seamstresses of our own sections of the Giant Web of the Living Tapestry or pieces of a hand tied quilt. They are built with great intricacy, beauty, strength and power in the Divine Spirit of the Living Over Soul of the Great Weaver. Each dream must be attached in it's proper position upon this Web, for each dream and prayer is a building block to strengthen the Power of the Web. We want to build strong bridges for our children. We must use all of our dreams and prayers of faith to build a mighty Bridge of Faith to the Heavens. We must bridge the gaps left by those who do not believe in life in this world or in the one(s) to come. They have no sensory organs, minds, bodies, souls, beliefs, faiths, dreams, or prayers to sense or desire the need for a Web, and a Bridge of Faith, to complete the Tapestries woven by the Great Weaver. We must be the human Spinners and Weavers of the Strands of Life here and in the world(s) to come. We are the co-artisans of this world. We are the co-creators of dreams which we live. We are also those who pray without ceasing for powerful connecting bonds to hold our lives together. We pray for the Divine to lead and to guide us as we bless others. By so doing, we bless all, and are blessed by all. We work individually, and together, to build a peaceful and whole New World, even as we pray daily for peace and love to bond our individual webs of life into our inter-connected webs' spirals of the living in a wonderful world of a long-awaited Kingdom of Heaven upon Earth. We believe, dream, and pray for the wisdom to daily build our Bridges of Faith to span the Earth and the Universe in the wholeness of our lives.

We weave the strands which are the Keys to Life. The Keys to Life help us to better understand ourselves and others. We can then see a Divine Plan to all that is our reality in this sometimes dark world of illusion and delusion. Our lives have meaning only when we take time to weave the threads of our lives into a Bridge of Faith. Faith is a Divine Gift. Faith can believe for all things to become true, even as can the faith of a small child. We must become filled with faith to dream, and to live, the "impossible dream(s)". Our lives become miracles for others to see. They can then learn how to build their own beautiful intricate Webs of Life, as they Spiral through the heavens living beautiful meteoric lives--part and parcel of all that is, the Tapestry woven by the Divine Weaver. We must forever weave our strands of life as if we are in accord, and of One Spirit, of the Great Spirit who is over all--The Holy White Spider creating the Web upon which we are created called Life.

****

50. THE ANCIENT SPIDER

Dream: September 16, 2004

I hoped this was the last of my spider dreams. I was attempting to sweep down ancient dusty webs from walls of my empty house. The webs were from an old and very dusty giant spider with very long thin legs. I was eager to finally rid myself of this last aged spider. I was given to understand this is the last of the "Spiders" of my perhaps overburdened soul. I have led a very full and long life. Much of it has been wonderful. As with so many of us, I am carrying a heavy load of many things within my soul. Our hearts, minds and souls are carrying far more than we were ever made to carry. This was definitely a soul and psyche cleaning dream. It spoke deeply to me of the ending of a long and hard cycle of life, preparatory to a better life here and/or in our Heavenly Home. It was very therapeutic in spite of the unpleasantness of seeing a huge dusty spider of long lineage.

PART II
THE MASCULINE MONSTER VS. THE DIVINE FEMININE

51. THE MODERN MINOTAUR

Dream: March 1, 1990

Prior to this amazing dream, I had been studying Kabbalistic symbols and meanings for several days. I was deeply engrossed in the whole topic.

It was amazing to have my cozy sacred studies interrupted by this amazingly insightful dream image of The Modern Minotaur, as I label this dream creature. Not only is this a personally insightful topic but one which is interesting and instructive for other women–and men.

The dream opened with me being at a hotel in an unknown city. At the hotel was one of the most powerful man, a former acquaintance and "friend" who was an entrepreneurial businessman. He was the type of mentor many younger men desire to emulate. He also seemed to be one of those dangerous men. So were the other men in the room with him.

Into that hotel dining room I saw him bring a huge, mythical Minotaur Bull with the face of a handsome man. Unlike the Minotaur of the movies, the face of the Bull was extremely handsome. I was amazed at his daring venture. Why?

I sensed these men were going to goad that Titanic Bull, a creature of mythological fantasy, out into the world to attack, rape, frighten and even destroy women I knew. At this time, the men seemed completely unaware of my presence, as well as awareness of themselves and of their evil intentions.

In the building adjacent to the hotel were other women I loved, such as my mother, daughter and a small, older, red-haired feisty woman I did not know. I frantically ran to gather all of us into some type of safe area. I remember thinking in the dream state that we typified ALL WOMEN, of ALL ages, in ALL the eras of the world–past, present and future.

Somehow we all managed to squeeze ourselves tightly into a large van owned by one of us. We drove around briefly, ending up parking directly in front of the windows of the hotel restaurant where the men were seated.

I was able to glimpse several men I felt I almost recognized. Two men by the window recognized us.

All during the dream, we experienced a great feeling of abject fear of the Bull, so like the mythological Greek Minotaur. It was gigantically huge, powerful and looked to be completely out of control in a state of blind rage.

The men saw us. At that time, they released the awful Bull upon us simply because we were women. All of the men seemed to feel threatened by women and hated all women.

The Minotaur charged madly out of the hotel entrance in a stance of violent attack. However, he seemed to not see the van and ran past it in his blind rage, even as if the van was a matador.

The older, red-haired woman leaped from the van and ran after him on her high stiletto heeled sandals. She gave him a hard jabbing kick into one of his huge haunches.

Much to our utter shock and surprise, as we watched this whole scene from the safety of the van, this caused that mighty monster to drop to his huge buttocks, looking like a huge seated man, who then burst into tears and began to weep copious tears. It seemed as if he would never be able to stop. We seemed to sense he wept, like a human man who was suddenly startled and fearfully made aware of his own grossly repulsive and hateful behavior.

The message I got from this interesting dream seems to be the fact that many of our beloved men, steeped for centuries in patriarchy and machismo, have been rendered incapable of being whole men and whole human beings. They are not able to understand or become androgynous and balanced souls as they might wish to be–if they knew how. Instead, by their misuses of their masculine power roles they have dominated and ruled the world until all vestiges of the beautiful, the merciful, the feminine–and even God–have been removed from this beautiful planet.

Could it be possible they truly need, and secretly desire, women to stop being fearful and dominated into infantile futility as adult women? If we take upon ourselves our truly adult feminine roles, respecting ourselves and other women, aware of and requiring our own rights as human beings, will we be able to bring these poor, blindly enraged and unaware male monsters into their own roles as sons of the Divine? Would they respect and love us if they are shown our powers as royal priestesses and daughters of the Father/Mother/All That Is?

The Poor Bull, no longer viewed as a Minotaur, continued to weep endlessly. I sadly realized there are far too many Modern Minotaur Men who do not know how to overcome their own deeply ingrained evil natures. They see themselves very often as the horrible gargoyle rather than the wonderful soul and man they could be. Many of them are terribly frightened and forlorn men who are dangers to themselves and others, especially women.

We must be strong women to help them to find and love themselves once again in their God given roles as Sons of God. Perhaps then we, as women, be able to aid in the loving rehabilitation of our lost mates, our beloved men.

It must be noted at this time that the dreamer does not believe all men act like a Minotaur. It is also my belief there are many wonderfully loving, aware, balanced and whole men who are filled with the Spirit of God who need no instructions or rehabilitation as human beings or as men. However, there are far too many misogynous men out there who send fear into women's hearts. They need our loving assistance as women. Many of us are mothers, sisters and wives who need to concentrate on being loving women to our guys. I see many people as being bruised souls who need loving counseling in order to be able to fill roles as balanced people and souls, as well as to be able to see themselves as happily whole men and women fit for bonded adult relationships with one another..

The whole myth of Ariadne, her father King Minos and her mother Queen Parsifae who mated with the Divine Bull and conceived the Minotaur is a very interesting story. Greek tragedies often held answers to the questions of the human condition.

We will find there are also many wonderful fantastic heroes in our worlds to balance out the image of the Minotaur–the ultimate symbol of Evil Male.

PART III
WOMEN AND GODDESSES

GODDESSES RIDE BICYCLES

It is my belief women have been forced to be very creative in order to survive. They have used all types transportation in order to function in whatever type of world in which they have lived. We know that human women ride horses and bicycles. They also drive automobiles, pilot airplanes and space shuttles.

Ishtar was a a goddess who flew a space vehicle before copious written records were kept upon this planet. I also know a woman with the name of a goddess who rode a bicycle. Since that time I have desired to write a book entitled "Goddesses Ride Bicycles." I have had many dreams of women riding unicorns and miraculous horses as have happened to me in my empowerment dreams. The feeling of actually being astride a huge Roan Horse which is capable of being your complete protection against all unwelcome advances from nasty human males is wonderful. I know other women have also dreamed of this same Huge Horse with the same coloring as their Miraculous or Divine Protector.

I also saw myself and two other beloved women being given three beribboned white unicorns to replace our fancy bicycles with ribbons. In this visionary dream in 1991, or thereabouts, we were all wearing long flowing Grecian gowns with flowers in our hair as we sat astride our beautiful miraculous steeds. We had been given these marvelous and holy steeds as rewards for our merits.

In a couple of dreams I was in flight training such as was at Pensacola, Florida for Naval Aviators and then flying co-pilot with my "dear friend" Hillary Rodham Clinton who was piloting the small plane as we flew straight up the steep side of a very high mountain. I knew we would be fine as "Hillary was in the pilot's seat". It was an unusual dream to say the least. I do not personally know Hillary or Bill Clinton. However, at the time of their election I had two or three dreams of them and of events to come. Hillary can truly qualify as a very wise and wonderful woman, politician and perhaps even as a goddess. She has behaved like a wonderful woman and a daughter of the Divine–a goddess. He simply treats us as His daughters, to the point we almost feel as if we are called small goddesses of the Great and Holy Almighty God–the Manifold All-Encompassing All That Is–The Ineffable Other, and a myriad of other appellations, titles, symbolic meanings and powers. Who can define such as This One, the Beloved Weeping Father we wish to nurture and to love wholeheartedly. To know Him is to love Him, even as we love His Son, who came to bear witness to the Father, as the Firstborn Son of many children. Jesus is our Sibling.

This is not to say humans are equal in power to the One God, or that we espouse the beliefs we are God Almighty. No way. We are His children, created to love and to be His royal dynasty and priesthood. We love and adore Him/Her/All That Is, even as He shares Himself with us in at-onement and communion. We are full of humility as His daughters who simply aspire to learn to be conformed to the image of His Son, the Beloved Lamb of God, slain for the sins of this dark and unbalanced world. We desire to serve Him in the beauty of holiness (wholeness and loving balance) as His daughters who are the mothers and wives of His sons. Indeed, I have found I have been able to do anything in His powers, as His daughter, which He wishes me to do and to be. His strength is truly made obvious in the weakness of this very fallible and weak handmaiden.

PROFESSIONAL ROLES & OFFICES:

Women are also Teachers, Counselors, Doctors and Nurses, Oracles, Psychologists and Psychiatrists, Writers, Photographers, Painters and Artists of all types, Attorneys and Accountants, Historians, and Political Leaders, Soldiers and Aviators, Ministers, famous Religious Leaders and Professors, and all types of family roles such as Wife, Mother, Grandmother and Great Grandmother. We have not yet elected a woman in the office of the President of the United States. We have woman in roles as Governors, Mayors, Senators and Congress Women. It was not until the 20th Century that American women were given the right to vote in National Elections.

Goddesses are in a league all of their own. Mary is called the Queen of Heaven, Mother of God, Queen of Angels, and other marvelous names. It is obvious some women become known as goddesses by their roles as women, such as in the case of Jesus Christ's mother, Mary. In addition to the roles of Jesus mother, there are those who also remind us of the roles of Mary Magdalene and the other women who were the backbone of His early church.

He assists us to be whatever, and whoever, He desires us to be. Do not lose courage. Simply turn to Him in prayer. If you have problems with a male god, ask to know how He wishes you to address Him. He wishes to personally hear from you. He loves and misses you very much. He is not like the worst examples of human beings you could ever find. He is wonderful, counselor, prince of peace and becomes a multitude of beings in order to attract your attention and to win you back into His family group. I know many who cannot pray in the name of our Heavenly Father. They must seek the feminine avenue to Him through Mary. Many souls have been damaged by their relationships with their fathers and other male archetypal figures. Imagine the damage done to the psyche of a young child by an abusive father or brother.

It is my personal belief there is soon to be a wonderfully joyful huge family reunion of all of those who love Him throughout this whole world and the worlds of the Cosmos. I smile, and almost giggle aloud with anticipation , thinking of that time many of us are eagerly awaiting. I could sit here with tears running off my chin with the pure ecstasy of delight of it all. We are blessed, loved and saved from all evil.

It will not matter so much who we are professionally. It will matter if we love one another with His love. Do we miss and desire Him with all of our beings? Do we miss Him and Heaven with all our hearts. I know I do. This world is not my world. I am simply one of those simple hardworking and overtired souls who has suffered and bled too much. I feel like I'm a little too battle scarred to bear much more. However, I know He can give us new life out of His strength and healing powers. I desire and will myself to live to be and to do whatever is His divine plan for my life. This is the whole goal and desire of my life. I long for His Presence as some long for the company of a group of partygoers. I think there are many who feel even as I do. We want to be the healers and beacon lights as long as we can do so. Above all else, I wish to fulfill whatever role in life He desires for me. I am so happy to hear of the ways He has been empowering my sisters. We truly need Him . Therefore, great thanks are ours for our many blessings in all facets of our lives. His strength is truly made perfect in our weaknesses. All types of hindrances can be overcome–whether age, finances, education or low self esteem.

We are proud to be wives and mothers. We are overjoyed to be considered those who love and serve Him. We are proud to be His women. We also believe He wishes to see His beautiful little daughters treated with equality and justice. He does not want any of His children to be buried alive at birth, aborted without cause, or hindered from filling His divine roles in their occupations or elected offices.

"Without Him I can do nothing; yet, with Him, I can do all and everything He desires."

SECTION V THE DIVINE FEMININE

PART III WOMEN & GODDESSES

52. ATHENA

It is absolutely mandatory that we know there are earthly goddesses who have unusual modes of transportation. We usually think of goddesses riding horses and other regal types of transportation. This is one goddess who rode a bicycle. She inspired me to write this section which I lovingly entitle "Goddesses Ride Bicycles". My book on my life as an older earth woman/goddess and crone will not be complete without Athena who is all of this and more. She is a loving archetype of the strong goddess of wisdom .

I have changed the name and altered some details of this altogether exceptional living Goddess of Wisdom and Crafts. This Athena was no 'exception' to the traditional roles attributed to the ancient goddess. She excelled in her gardening, sharing her harvests with the poor and needy with whom she worked. She was always deeply concerned for the well being of her neighbors. She used her legal skills as well as her green thumb and healing hands of the Reiki Master. She was ageless with her white hair and wise visage. She rode her bicycle all over the area in all types of inclement weather. She seemed to have the powers of the Goddess Athena whose name she had been gifted by her Eastern Master.

She and I found magical times sipping our hot cups of tea in a local holistic coffee house and spa. We loved to pretend we could see the salamander in the embers of the open fireplace. We blended into the woodwork as the two older crones lost among the heaps of international newspapers, books and customer avidly playing chess. I truly believe we will have such wonderful gathering places in our Heavenly Home. Athena was one of those people whom we like to emulate for the many great attributes of her multi-faceted being. We were inter-faith sisters working for many of the same social issues. We cannot buy our salvations with our work. Athena knew one puts one's faith and life into action for the good of all. We show forth divine love by so doing as our hands are given to do. Our hearts are full of love for our neighbors and His souls everywhere. They are wonderfully many.

We are His beloved daughters, strong of minds, bodies and souls. We practice the stoicism of the powerful Goddess Athena, she who was born as the daughter of Zeus with wisdom, stoicism and powers beyond human understanding.

It is my belief this wonderful human woman personified the Goddess Athena in a very archetypal fashion. She made me realize the powers we have in Him, even if our "wheels" are those of a bicycle. Many wise people of the world know the values of the lowly bicycle over the expenses and accesses of the motor vehicles which pollute the atmosphere and keep us from exercising our bodies.

It is possible to realize why human beings revered the altogether idyllic feminine whether in the body of a living woman or in that of the Goddess' image. Athena is seen as a powerful and wise goddess. Many women would do well to attempt to emulate her ways.

To me, she shall always be remembered in the image of her living daughter with her name. When William Quan Judge came in my dream and spoke so warmly of Helena Petrovna Blavatsky, I was thrilled by his words about her, "Beloved lady, no one like her." I feel this way about this wonderfully individualistic friend with whom I shared such happy times. Many years later, I miss my times with Athena, a human archetype of the wise goddess whose name she bears. There is none other like her.

53. ISIS

DREAM: Early in the 21st Century

Many of us are of Christian or patriarchal monotheistic religious heritages. However, there are those who have never stopped believing there is also a feminine entity or nature connected with the godhead. Many of us have no desire for, or comprehension of, thinking of deity in the form of the Goddess as well as God.

Sometime in the first three years of this Third Millennium, the 21st Century, since the birth of our Lord and Savior Jesus Christ, I had an isolated question about the existence and role of a goddess figure. It was several months later when I awakened with the most bizarre of dreams.

I was given the dream vision of an awesome female entity as described below:

> "This impressive entity was wearing a huge Egyptian head piece, even as one sees in museum pictures of Isis. Her headdress was not that of Hathor. I knew this was the All-Encompassing Goddess. The name Isis came to me.
>
> She was wearing a loin cloth under which I was shocked to see a small penis. I wondered why. It was later when I discovered information about Isis that I realized this image was shown to me so I would connect her with her miraculous reconstruction of the penis for the resurrection of her husband Osiris.
>
> Isis is known in many different parts of the world under various names as the universal Goddess figure."

Isis was one of the most amazing dream figures I have ever been shown. I am still pondering the many facets of the study of goddess lore, as well as Isis and all the meanings of herself as the Goddess. We are told to seek and to expect answers to our questions.

Shortly thereafter, I found myself overpowered with a great desire to find "My Mother". This is a startling thing for a woman with my religious training. However, as an eternal soul with my heart attuned to the Manifold God and the Cosmic Christ, I know there are many things on Heaven and Earth more than we each can understand. I am His "Little Child". I still wonder about the ways of the world and of the destruction of the feminine. In the beginning was the Goddess before she and her followers were destroyed by the powerfully warlike male supremacist dominated societies. Perhaps when all the horrible polarizations which occurred at the time of the "Fall" are healed, we will again know the feminine touch of the Shekinah who was said to have fled the Earth at the last cyclic time of the "violence of man" when the world was destroyed by the Deluge at the time of Noah. We are once again living in a time of extremely violent "natural brute beasts". She wants to help us but cannot bear to be near such types of souls.

There are many of us who value our sisterhoods and matriarchies. We know we are mystics, psychics, healers and much more. We are the Daughters and Priestesses, the Handmaidens of the Ineffable Other, the I Am, That One of the multi-faceted personality. Perhaps He is the He/She of All That Is. Perhaps the Triune is the One, in all ways. We know there is much more for us to learn. Many are the names of the One. There are many women who wonder why they do not have representation in divine circles. The Catholic Church realized those new converts to Christianity were worshipers of the Goddess. Thus, the Church allowed Mary, the Mother of Jesus to be seen in the role of the divine feminine image. Those of us in the other faiths do not have the reverence of the Virgin Mary as part of our doctrines. We have no divine feminine. We see a Holy Family without the feminine. This seems very unnatural to those of us who are believe women play a very large role in families. Some of us can seriously weep as we ask "Where is my Mommy?" Personally, I am part of a large family full of strong, enterprising and attractive matriarchs. All of my beloved women are full of the Spirit and are attractive women. If we are not Catholic women in the Western World, we do not have a Divine Mother, a Divine Female Figure. Why?

It is not our Lord who has told us we are lesser if we are women. We are His divine creations. We are worthy companions to His Son and those others who are His sons. We are the daughters of the Family of the Divine.

Perhaps we must broaden our view of All That Is.

54. PRIESTESSES WEAR VIOLET ROBES

Dream: December 5, 1990

I saw a goddess, or perhaps just a wonderful woman, with long curly auburn hair in an apartment. Her pets all began to return to her through a torn screen door in her home. There were kittens, cats and a dog, for a total of 10 pets. I thought of meaning of the #10=Perfection. A Perfect Number of Pets? To some people this would be a menagerie. Not so to this vibrant woman. She was a true woman of the Earth. I loved her.

In the next scene I was then praying for her and her daughter (or another woman) that they would have a safe journey as they traveled.

In the next part of the dream I saw myself using some type of holy image or vessel, such as from a Jewish temple, for other people. Again, as in another dream I had of a Holy Censer (used to burn incense for prayers), I feel as if I am holding a priestly office.

I knew many of the people for whom I was praying were women connected with a group with a goddess cult, using violet as their special symbol. (Note: I was shown a real violet flower to make sure I did not confuse the color violet with purple or lavender.)

I saw large piles of violet dresses or robes, long or short, simple or ornate. Each woman came and picked a dress from the heaped up piles of dresses. These woman seemed to be secular teachers, if not holding high orders as priestesses and teachers. Each dress had its own meaning denoting social and spiritual statuses. Violet, I learned in my research, is the sacerdotal (priestess) color.

While I was with the auburn haired woman at her apartment, I saw flames appear on a chair like a throne. There were two rows of flames, on two levels, about 2-4 feet high. They were spiritual flames and were not visible to everyone. There are many messages yet to be researched regarding this section of this dream. I believe all or part of it is regarding the high offices of goddess and priestess, as played by women. Indeed, this scene may have to do with the Goddess Isis, the supreme Goddess typology. This dream is one with a variety of meanings. The throne may mean the lap of the Great Mother, the Queen of Heaven, The Seat of Authority. What does it mean for each of us? I'm quite sure each of us will have our own messages. I am still working through stacks of reference notes.

At the time when I had this dream in 1990, I knew very little about any of these topics. I proceeded on with my personal studies of many spiritual pathways. I knew little to nothing of the studies of Wiccan, pagan, Celtic, women's and goddess paths. In fact, it was in 2001 when I finally, late again, read the wonderful Avalon Series by Marion Zimmer-Bradley.

I was left with the one profound message for myself and all women that we are all to regain our original and proper roles as priestesses (goddesses and daughters of the Father, Mother, All That Is?). If we desire to do so. I continue to love the color violet and wear it to show my special dream-inspired belief in our special roles as women. The question for all of us is do we have the bravery to dare to be fully actualized women and priestesses who are willing to attempt to take on our divine roles and offices? This is a wonderful dream. The question I have is "Do we all know this?" Do we use all of our gifts to bless and to heal others? We have our duties as priestesses returned to us. These duties are those of serving and performing good acts for the good of all human beings.

It is my belief that this dream in no way jeopardizes our relationship to the All Omnipotent Father God. It simply is a restoration of the inalienable rights of women to their rightful roles as women in their hierarchal roles of wife, mother, grandmother and priestess in our spiritual and cultural roles. If we treat each other as gods and goddesses, princes and princesses, we will again see the beauty of holiness in our marital relationships and in our communities. I believe we are to again start training for our return to our Heavenly Home. The Beloved Father is not threatened. Why should any man fear the beauty and wholeness of the Holy Father and Holy Mother in his women?

As I began to type this manuscript I remembered the dream of my auburn-haired grandmother who is in Heaven, in her high priestess robes, laying her hands upon my head and blessing me. She was never more than a humble and loving matriarch. However, I had the divine dream of her in Heaven in the mid-1990's. Perhaps she was even the woman in this dream with all the pets. How intricate are the finely woven webs of the Great Spider.

Flower: Violet - Modesty, Fidelity and Purity and is a powerful charm against evil.

Ancient Greeks and Persians used it to heal both the heart and the head. It cures the floating light-headedness that goes with being in love.

If our dresses be the color of violets, which mean only the most modest, faithful and pure, why then would any question the offices of the Holy Women of God?

The key to Him is Love. The key to Life is Love. If we be Love one to another, we will not commit the sin of idolatry of ourselves or of others.

We will not break the Beloved Father's heart. We will love and serve Him in holiness as His daughters and priestesses.

55. DIVINING OR SCRYING ARTS

Dream: 1990-1991

As an innocent child of God, I was very shocked to see people using a household wall mirror to invade the privacy of others. First of all, I had no idea such a thing is possible. If it is indeed possible, and I am told this is so, why would anyone wish to intrude upon the lives of others without their permission? If Love is our Key to Life, we would not do so.

After experiencing this dream I began to research such arts and found that the art of scrying was quite a common tool of various types of magical practices. Viewing was done with water, mirrors, crystal balls and other agents. It was a commonly used tool of those such as the priestesses of Avalon–and of anyone with the ability to "See" in such a way.

It is my belief as a modern woman accustomed to the usage of telephones, fax and other communications and transportation, all means available to us in this modern age, that we do not think of using some of the older means of investigatory communications and transportation simply because we no longer need them.

If one lived in the middle of the American or Russian deserts and plains or the Australian Outback before one had telephones, automobiles and airplanes, one would practice all manner of telepathy, remote sensing, teleportation and levitation devices and arts available to humankind at that time. The heart and souls of loved ones are always missed and desired to the point of loved ones being willing to dare to die to locate a lost loved one. It is no wonder so many pioneer ancestors looked as though they were medicine men and woman. They found ways in which to heal and assist themselves which are now forgotten by many.

Young soul, fear not to seek the wisdom of the ancients. By such learning, one may save one's posterity forever. Those who will not learn from the Old Wise Ones and from history must repeat their mistakes over and over again. Humility is the best teacher. Humility seeks wisdom like a thirsty wild animal. The thirst for wisdom is not proud–but is full of humility and the desire for knowledge and discernment–both lost arts.

My first judgment of this dream was based upon fear. I can now see this message as a valuable warning of the need to hold fast to our ancient spiritual gifts. It is my teaching to seek gifts not for power displays but for the need-to-know realities of everyday life. If we forget how to build our own fires we will freeze to death. If we cannot speak to the wind or the mind of God, or the mind of a loved one, how can we locate them when all is chaos around us? Learn from the ways of the people of the Earth. They have not completely forgotten the old ways, the ancient watchers, the star designs in the Heavens, or the ways of the traveling mind, soul and body. Neither have the All-Seeing Eyes belonged only to the Father of All. If we have need to see, we will see. If we have need of other sensual powers of mind, body or soul, simply ask and received divine training.

If we need to know how to find a certain design in a sandal, ask Jesus. He wore lots of sandals. He will be an expert in sandal designs. The same holds true for asking to know how to be well of a certain illness. The answer is yours. Simply ask the Manifold God/Goddess/All That Is. The answers are forthcoming and are simply understood. We simply have not, or know not, because we do not believe all things are possible to those who love the Lord and are called according to His purposes.

Misusage of spiritual gifts is sinful. We must not attempt to intrude upon the privacy of another. Neither must we command another's soul to change or to obey our demands. Even the Father leaves us our own freewill. This is why one is to seek to know the Giver of spiritual Gifts before one asks for Gifts. Gifts without paying the dues of apprenticeship to the Giver of spiritual Gifts is being needlessly careless and foolish. Each Gift has its own rules for proper usage. They are learned in the Wisdom Schools of Heaven and of Earth. One does not turn a novice student loose with a powerfully dangerous weapon. Rest humbly and prayerfully in the arms of the Divine Teacher who will make sure you are properly trained in the tools of Divine Warfare. We are to wage wars using His love, before we ever enter the fields of spiritual battle. "Vengeance is mine, and I will repay," saith the Lord.

I do believe if we have a "need to know" reason, we will have our own magic carpet or astral travel permit as is deemed necessary by the Father. If we need to know or to see something or someone, we can "know" things rightly, without intrusive scrying into their hearts, minds and lives. We need to pray always about guidance of the Holy Spirit with Gifts of the Holy Spirit. Wisdom and moral responsibility are mandatory laws with Gifts.

I am always so pleased to have His divine mysteries and insights shown to me. We need to know the world in which we live. This gives us armor and protection from such arts and practices used irresponsibly, intentionally or accidentally by the ignorant dabblers or those who wish to bring evil into the world.

Thank You, Father.

56. THE HOLY WOMEN OF EAST & WEST

Dream: 1990-1991

This was a marvelous inspirational dream. I dreamed of purified women in iridescent white garments.

The setting was that of the square plaza of my own hometown in No. California. The number four was definitely to be noted, as it means the divine quaternity, the number of totality of being. There is also much more data herein to be researched.

Along the western side of the Plaza stood a row of Eastern Islamic Women in iridescent white longer garments, with crimson red "girdles" tied below their breasts as with Japanese obi ties. The ties was made of soft crimson velveteen cloth. In the dream state, I believe I was to understand these girdles denoted these women were married or in a patriarchal society. Of course, the Islamic women live in patriarchies. Theirs are monotheistic Islamic cultures.

Along the northern side of the Plaza stood a row of Western Women, also garbed in iridescent white shorter robes and dresses, about mid-calf in length. They did not wear "girdles". Their unbound, free-flowing hair and uncovered heads and faces denoted the freedom they had as Western multi-racial and muli-religious women of the world. In spite of their differences, seemingly all of the women had won the favor of the Father God. We were in balance and harmony, equally, in totality of the Father's Spirit.

Therefore, we had all been deemed worthy to wear Heavenly garments of iridescent white, proclaiming our Holiness and Purification, even though we were all just Ordinary Women of East and West. I felt greatly thrilled and honored for all of us as women.

The dream showed me we were prepared for any Wedding Feast–Earthly or Heavenly. Even as I have been shown to have won other awards of excellence for our spiritual growth at initiatory levels, as with the Master Numbers symbolisms, I was shown we women were doing our "homework", and were all being deemed approved as Holy Women, as well as in our roles of Handmaidens and Priestesses of the Most High. We are One in His Holy Spirit.

I hoped our men were also Seekers of Truth and Wholeness. May God, the Great Spirit and Allah heal and help us all. May we all be made whole and deemed worthy to wear the iridescent white robes of the Holy Ones. Let us continue to pray without ceasing one for another. We may not pray at given times each day. As Christian women, we are taught to pray without ceasing–as in every facet of every moment of every day.

My Islamic friends may pray several times a day and keep Ramadan. Let us remember to keep the Sabbath Day as often and as much as we can. This day was made for our health and well being by our loving Father. We may even realize we will need to learn to keep other holy days. Dear Father, please continue to lead, guide and teach us your ways. Cover us with Christ's Holy Blood and Your Angelic Armies. We will seek and find you in the Beauty of Holiness. We will always pray in Your Most Holy Name. Amen

57. THE DIVINE FEMININE

Dream: December 1, 2004

This was perhaps a vision of the eternal role and plight of the Desirable and Divine Woman.

She was a beautiful, long legged blond woman wearing a flowing hot pink dress. She held a long stemmed bright pink flower in her hand. She was running ahead of evil men and was out distancing them.

This was again simply a scene of the plight of the holy and beautiful in the realms of the worldly.

This message seemed to be one of victory over evil. Perhaps we will still yet overcome the wiles of evil to be able to be attractive without being seen by some as a seductress of innocent human men. This is a ludicrous view held by many who do not know one can also be attractive and be God's holy woman. It is possible for women to be modest and pure in their appearances, words and actions. The divine woman is full of His Spirit and lacks nothing in integrity, wisdom or learning capabilities. She should be fairly remunerated for her labors. Many woman have been forced to become the wage earner due to the losses of their husbands to disability or death. Therefore, the women have been forced by necessity to provide for the needs of themselves and their families. Some have faced harassment from others. How can anyone judge so unfairly? Children come first before the approval of others lacking in wisdom.

SECTION V THE DIVINE FEMININE

PART IV
WOMEN & MEN/PARTNERSHIPS

58. RUNIC MESSAGE

Dream: Fall, 1991

The message was in a strange form which I finally discovered was that of the Runes of Odin. This was such a hard dream to decipher we found several possible messages. It was only after my marriage and moves I realized the message was about my own marriage, partnership with my husband and the journeys I was to make. This dream was most interesting and insightful.

SECTION VI
SPECIAL MESSAGES FOR OUR TIMES

SECTION VI–SPECIAL MESSAGES FOR OUR TIMES

PART I MESSAGES

59. CASSANDRA

Early one morning in January, 2000, I received a strangely worded message:

"You are Cassandra" OR "You are (like) Cassandra."

Careful research unearthed the ancient story of Cassandra, one of the 12 beautiful daughters of Hecuba of Troy. She, as the most beautiful of Hecuba's daughters and his own priestess, caught the eye of the sun god, Apollo. He promised he would grant any wish if she'd have relations with him. She demanded the gift of prophecy. Apollo granted Cassandra's wish. However, after she had received his gift, she refused his advances. He kissed Cassandra and thereby cursed her. Everything she prophesied was true but her messages were received as unbelievable by those who heard them. Her own brother Paris refused to hear her warnings not to go to Greece. When the Trojan Horse was brought into Troy she warned her brother and his armies of the dangers of the horse. Instead of believing her prophecies, they ridiculed her for saying Troy would lose the war.

When Troy did lose the war she was taken captive to Mycenae as a concubine of the Greek King Agamemnon along with their two children. Legend has it they were all killed by King Agamemnon's wife Clytemnestra and his other family. In other myths where Cassandra is said to have survived and lived a long life as a prophetess, she later was known as the goddess Alexandra ("Helper of Men")

(*The Book of Goddesses and Heroines*; Author: Patricia Monaghan, 1981, 1990)

It is also very apropos the government named the global plan to educate the public of the dangers of Y2K ("Year 2000) The Cassandra Project. There were valid concerns on an international scope that the older computers would not be able to change dates–without upgrading–to the year 2000. They were rightly concerned their dire prognostications would not be deemed credible in order to prevent "The end of the world as we know it" (TEOTWAWKI).

It is still a mystery to me why He felt he should say I am Cassandra. Yes, I did go into a state of shock and not give forth the prophetic message I requested July 10, 1967. This is the only way I broke my promise to the Father. Therefore, I felt it was imperative to publish that selfsame message and very earnestly began to prepare it for publication in as short a time as possible in order to bless as many people as I could reach as soon as possible. This I completed in April, 2004. The title of His Message from 1967 is "*Beloved: Part I–The Garden Message and Part II–In The Still Of The Evening*".

60. THE STADIA

Dream: Sometime later in 2000 or 2001

I was standing underneath the bleachers of a stone "stadia" talking to those who had come to ask me questions about themselves and their lives. They were keeping me so busy answering their questions I was having trouble getting out to the speaker's area where I was to address the audience in the stadium.

(Note: I realized the word stadium was given to me in Greek. It seemed as natural to me to know the stadium as "the stadia" as it does for me to know I am able to call the great Greek writer Pindar "Old Pindar". I have never studied him or his work in my university classes. *Perhaps I have lived as an oracle in an ancient Greek lifetime. If not, this is simply a very insightful message to let me know how Cassandra, or others like her, may have lived.)*

61. THE PLACE OF THE ORACLE

Dream: Sometime in 2001 or 2002

I was walking through a natural wilderness setting in which were several natural stone areas. I knew I was going to the area where I would be speaking to people. *(Again, this area seemed very familiar to me. I've always wanted to go to Delphi as if it held some very special meaning for me.)*

62. WOWETSIN

Dream early in Spring of 2000.

This is an inspired message given to me as if I were to perform some type of duties or roles with Indian people. I have asked Indian elders if such a name has any meaning for them. There is always a meaning known only to our Beloved Father's Spirit. It is my great desire to know what this very special message means for my life and/or the lives of others.

63. THE BLACK BULL & HIS CALF

Dream--Spring, 2001

I was standing in the yard of my mother's home in Northern California with a small boy and a small girl. We had been discussing our plans to move from California to Colorado. They had told me these things had been necessary in order for them to fulfill their destinies as a couple. While we were yet discussing this family exodus, we observed the whole sky began to fill with the massive images of a Black Bull and its Black Bull Calf. We realized they symbolized WAR. We stood in shock, numbed by the horror of it all. We were horrified in the dream. This is no dream. It is real, and my horror has only increased as War remains a huge reality in our lives.

It was some time later when I finally realized this symbol is in complete opposition to the White Buffalo and its Calf which represent an upcoming Age of Peace. Many Native Americans and others such as myself watch all of these things with intense interest and sadness. How long must human beings fight each other? White Buffalo Calf Woman came to these tribal people and brought them the usage of the Peace Pipe. Peace is gone. We eagerly await its return with the return of the White Buffalo Calf and Jesus Christ, who was called the Prince of Peace. He called those of Peace, the Peacemakers, whom He called The Sons (and Daughters) of God.

There have been great polarizations of people and values eversince the Beginning of Time.

It is the great desire of those of peaceful natures that there once again be Peace on Earth, as was in the Garden of Eden–"in the Days when Men and Animals could talk."

64. HEAVEN'S DESTINY

I. Dream: November 14, 2003, 2:53 a.m. Words: "CLAY TABLET" (I continue to wonder about the meaning of this one. I do know our lives are like empty clay tablets until we live our destinies. This is an ongoing personal study of my own.)

II. Dream: November 14, 2003, 4:51 a.m.

In this dream I found I was seemingly a beautiful Grecian goddess wearing a fuschia colored Grecian draped gown. I had a drape of cloth over my shoulder. My hair was blonde or red blonde, which glinted in the sunlight.

Lines of men watched every move I made. I was a priestess, or was a well known woman who held high office. I was desirable and beautiful. I was happy in my feminine role of wise and beautiful woman.

III. Dream: November 14, 2003, 6:22 p.m.

The Dream continues.

I was very involved in working with Life Planning Programs/Destinies. I seemed to be very happy. The dream scene was one of very happy times spent in the warmly enchanting setting of an area like unti Greece or a like setting in Heaven. The colors were bright and vivid. So was my life with my friends and associates. Perhaps this is why I still feel so drawn to enchantingly beautiful tropical climates with their sociably warm people. I'd love to find a dress the color of the lovely draped dress I was wearing in this dream.

Special Note: There will be those who will only be able to see dreams as psychologically inspired messages. These dreams truly seemed to be of prior, or even future, lives lived on another planet if not on Earth. When I interpret my dreams I take into consideration the many types of dreams which are received by those who are truly into dream research. Some dreams which are taken by many as simply "nonsense" topics which are truly deeply important encoded messages. One uses dream research books as directed in the Spirit to understand each individual dream as a special message for life.

There were acacia and eucalyptus trees towering around the palisade making a truly beautiful world in which to live. I was standing on a second floor veranda of the palisade. The setting is so lovely one wishes one could preserve this Edenic scene forever.

Meanings of Dreams:

This dream seems to be one from myself to the Father, and my waking self. Last night's dreams seem to be of me in Heaven–prior to–or after–this lifetime.

I don't want any presences except His or those of my loved ones. Love is very important to me. Adulation of other desirable men hold no joy for me. Neither does a powerful position or the homage received therefrom. However, I do love and desire to do things of worth for the Lord.

Actually, in Heaven where all are saved, are we removed from the ongoing Wheel of Life, Why would there be a need for anyone to work with planning Karmic Life Plan Destinies? What of reincarnation, parallel and other dimensional lives. We have much to learn.

This would make those types of jobs obsolete–unless–Einstein's Theories of Relativity make repeated lives never ending for everyone. (I must again study Mr. Lightman's book, "Einstein Dreams".)

Sadly, this world of Grecian palaces and balustrades ended–as did my life as a desirable goddess of that era. This seemed to be an exhilarating life memory of my own lives or the lives of some others. They were very interesting lives to observe. As with all messages of this type, we must simply ponder all of each one of them and await eventual interpretation by the Beloved Spirit.

65. MEMORIES OF EARTH'S CREATION

Dream–September 26, 2003

I was remembering being an angel involved in the original creation of the Earth. I was flying around (seemingly without wings) trying to find my friends and relatives. I had become lost in a darkened terrain on Earth. (It is also possible I was given the impressions of those who had been angels at the Creation.)

We had come in several different color coded units of angels such as these combos:

1	2	3
Purple	Pink	I cannot remember the colors of this angel unit.
Lavender	Purple	

These were called Alpha Groups or Dominant Color Groups.

As explorers of this alien terrain, we had been frightened by several types of natural geographic and biological things native to the planet. I especially felt I remembered the very real fears we experienced when we flew over the Earth at night. The roiling wild waters of rivers and waterfalls when viewed without lights, in natural colors such as blacks and dark blues, were very frightening and dangerous areas over which we had to fly.

Also, some designs and patterns of wildly flowing water looked very much like the facial features of large creatures such as dragons, or large reptiles such as tyrannosaurus rex. (At this point in the dream I was able to draw a design which explained how the features of a creature such as this might appear to be seen in water with vortexes, etc.)

In my dream, we were still, to this time, trying to find our family members. We are still trying to find each other now. I could see several of us flying around looking for each other at this time.

We even jumped up and down in front of windows of houses attempting to be able to look inside to see if our loved ones were inside buildings.

These seemed to be such real memories to me it is hard to express them. After all, I was feeling as if I, as an ordinary human woman, knew of being an angel involved in the creation of this planet. This dream is a large and very bizarre topic of which I have dreamed and remember as if they were my own lifetime experiences.

As I awakened, I remembered how much and how strongly I love a well known woman political leader. She is like a dearly well known friend whom I love and miss very much, as if she and I, as long time friends, are separated at this time by our present life destinies.

This dream was very realistic, yet to dream of being one of many angels lost and stranded upon this planet gave one a very strange feeling which remains with me even as I relate it here. Once again, I believe I have 'tapped into' some other being's life. If I have been an angel which has been in existence from the "Beginning" to this current "End Time" it is truly not a life of which I have any awareness then or now. However, it has been a most interesting experience.

****

66. DANGERS FROM WILD BEARS & PANDAS

Dream--August 17, 2003, 3:21 a.m.

There seemed to be a grave danger of bears entering the abodes of human beings whether they lived in caves dwellings or mammoth houses.

Some people feared entries by bears through upper floor broken windows.

Some cave dwellers were concerned about bears coming into their simple cave dwellings as well. (Meanings: Literally, perhaps humans who live in the habitants of wild creatures are endangered by wildlife. Symbolically & spiritually: Bears are good medicine signs. Pandas means one must stop feeding your worries, they will go away. Caves mean marital happiness. A calm atmosphere, or defeating hostile oppositions, mean circumstances will gradually improve or be ended. It is my belief this is a former life experience of someone. It can also be simply a viewing of life on this planet in another time which is being shown to me for my edification.)

****

67. CARING FOR SAFETY OF HUMAN BEINGS

March 27, 2004, about 4:42 a.m.

I was working with others to assist with the "salvation" or collection of human beings, some plants and creatures from the planet.

I was shown lines of people and plants.

(Upon awaking, I was reminded of several others dreams I have had of leaving this planet with others. Is this something I've done in another age or is this mission for now?)

****

68. REMOVAL OF HUMAN BEINGS FROM EARTH

March 27, 2004, about 6:42 a.m.

The words: "Noetic Sciences"

Couples were meeting at a large room at someplace like an airport. I seemed to see a couple from the early days when I was a young wife of a Naval Aviator. Later in this dream, I thought I also saw other couples from several decades prior when I was a military wife.

We had all been able leave all of our earthly possessions (with the thought it would be OK to do so even if we didn't leave Earth). We seemed to all be awaiting our take off to another world.

(As in other dreams of this time, there was a snowstorm in the dream. In fact, I seemed to have missing time after I awakened. There were also a variety of symbolic messages and divine synchronicity happenings.)

****

69. WE ARE THE BELOVED'S LIGHTHOUSE BEACONS

May 24, 2004

"We Are The Beloved's Lighthouse Beacons to Bless Believers."

I awakened with this Message as the Lord was speaking:

"Fear not, for I am with you, to keep and to hold you in my arms of protection. I shall not leave nor forsake you. You are my daughter. Blessed be your name for you are Mine when I make up my gemstones of My diadem. You are forever Mine, forever and for always.

Blessed be your name even as Mine is glorified as The Beloved. I am the Beloved son of God , slain for the sins of the world. Trust not to your own understanding. Trust only in Me.

My Response: (Praises be to the Most High God! Amen)

****

70. WAKING MESSAGE FROM JESUS

August 12, 2004 —early a.m.

(You are my dear daughter–):

"Remember to tell them I am coming soon."

****

71. JESUS CHRIST AS A GIANT GOLDEN CARP

Dream - mid-1990's

I saw a huge golden carp swimming steadily up a steep waterway. He never faltered. He simply kept on swimming.

I wondered about the carp and realized the Huge Carp is the Fisher King, our Lord Jesus. He will not be deterred in His Ascension. He will overcome all obstacles and reach the highest levels of enlightenment. I think of enlightenment because The Golden Carp seemed to be an Asian symbol of Him. Perhaps Jesus and Buddha are both teaching us how to have peace on Earth. Enlightenment and transcendence are accomplished by filling ourselves with love and truth. (It was a marvelous theophany for which I am most grateful.)

72. SCRIPTURES ABOUT JESUS CHRIST:

Who's son is Christ? Luke 20:41-45

Son of God: Mark 1:11 And a voice came from Heaven: "You are My Son whom I love; and with You I am well pleased."

No Home: Matthew 8:20 "Foxes have holes and birds of the air have nests, but the Son ofMan has no place to lay His head."

His Home: John 18:36-37 His kingdom is not of this world..."I came to testify of the Truth..."

Light: John 12:44 "I have come as Light..."

Our Savior: John 3:16 "For God so loved the world He gave His only begotten Son that whosoever believeth Him may be saved."

Our Rebirth as a Child of God: John 3:3

Worship: John 4:21-24 "...Worship in Spirit and in Truth.""

73. THE MESSAGE FOR THIS TIME

Waking Words & A Message

September 2, 1004, 7:14 a.m.

Words:

Faery Realms
Balaam's Ass
One More Time
Can't Get Enough
Sexton/Sextant

The Message:

"Hold tightly to your seat and I will talk to you.
Don't you know I still love you with an all-encompassing, never-ending love?
Ours was a divine love. None can take it away.

Q. When were you born? Do you know?

A. No.

Then do not tell yourself or others what they can or cannot be.
You know a tiny bit.
We know much.
We know you are as ancient as the days are long and endless.
You are from days of old.

Don't tell others of things of which you know nothing.
Hold tightly to My hand.
I will lead you in and back.

You are My child. I know your heart. I made it.
Hold tightly to My hand and see great sights as we navigate the realms of the Heavens and the Nights of great awakening.
Soon all will know as you know.
Tell them as I told you.
They perhaps will desire to hear and will listen.
They are hurt and angry at themselves, one another and the Father.

They hate Me because I, too, am His even as they try to hate you and your words.
Do not hesitate.
Shout it loud and long.
They will hear, grow and learn.
They, too, will see Heaven and we will all be One once again.
Even so will I come into their hearts and they will learn Wisdom and Truth.
Never has it been so dark.
Soon it will be as if Night has never been Hold tightly to My hand.
I will guide you all through this plane of existence back to the Father's Realm.

Elfphame you say.
What is Elfphame?
You will soon know.
Much will be revealed.

You talk. So did Balaam's Ass speak.
Many who are as dumb as the Ass will speak with the Words of God, the Father.
Soon we will again be together where you desire to return.
I and we have missed you greatly.
Lean not to your own understanding on this level of existence.
We have not forgotten. You have forgotten.

Hold not to your own tools of knowledge.
Hold closely to Me and I will continue to show you mysteries of Earth and Heaven.

Soon it will not be Night's Darkness.
It will be Lighter than a New Day Dawning.
I will be your Light, your Way and Path.
My truth will be like a Sextant to guide you to your original destination.
The veil will lift and Avalon of your Heart will be yours once again.
Faery Realms will be re-opened to the to the worlds of human beings.

Be ye whole, even as we are whole in the Oneness of the Holy Spirit.
None can live as His without Light,
Truth & Love
Love and it shall be granted.
Come therein by the Gate of Love.
Rapture shall fill your hearts.
Death will be no more.
Time will not matter.
See Me and you will find Me.
I am your King forever.
As we drink and eat of the fruits of the life-giving Tree of Life and Wisdom.
Be ye whole even as I am whole and holy.
Night is passing.
Let there be Light and Joy Everlasting.
With Glorious Days unspeakable.
Who can tell of sights divine without knowing they are Mine

Come to Me, Children.
Open your child eyes wide and see the fantastic sights of your Father's Home.
Quarrel no more.
His tears will dry.
There'll be no way to cry with tears all assuaged and dried.

Come thou into Our Father's House.
He will bathe, dress and feed you.
You will have the Father's Rest.
Hold to My hand.
I will lead you on a tour of My Father's House.
Place your foot upon our doorsill and I will lead you in, Dear One.
It is wonderful to see you at long last.
Come into Our House and dine.
Eat and watch our screens of lives divine.
Bask in the All-encompassing Father's Love.
Ours is Forever Love.
Enter–Please.

74. TEACH US YOUR WAYS

Waking Message
June 19, 2003 (Day 260 of Prayer Vigil)

"Teach me Your ways."

"Does anyone ask Me to teach them My ways? No! They are so busy attempting to teach others their ways, which they think are My way, they have no time or inclination to ask, learn, and live My Way."

"Due to the years of many centuries spent in seeing darkly through a dirty mirror, they have not been able to see Me or themselves and their roles in the Heavens.

In your dream you were shown a large group of interior groups joined to a traveling circus caravan.

Each act of the circus was an individual pathway of faith.

Each group of performers acted out their faiths to the others.

I watched, as did you. They were entertaining to themselves and others, even if no one ever understood or espoused the others' views of Me and the Path as they know it to be.

I watched, they watched, and no one asked, "Show me Your way, oh God."

I waited. I watched. I love them and guided them to Me if I could steer them from their own ways to Me and Mine own way(s).

As you know, you made a rice dish as demonstration of My path for lesbians or homosexuals. We must make sure our rice is not bitter rice.

You saw a wooly headed mammoth rather than an elephant. It shows that these things have thus been since the antiquities of your world(s). (Ancient Wisdom).

You also saw many other symbolic people, rituals and events.

These are the ways of them all, not My ways.

I seek those who seek to know Me. Thus will I find them.

Everyone is busily attempting to lead others to Me.

Seek Me first. Then will you find Me.

You are like the blind trying to lead the blind. Like the several blind men in the cave, all heard, saw and felt the outside world as they envisioned it to be–as the blind envision and define the realities of the world. Thus do you see Me now.

Love and seek Me now and you will find Me–not your own ways.

75. WAKING PRAYER

Early-12:53 a.m.. (Day 242 of Prayer Vigil)

Prayer–as Thou risest up and sitteth down,
Lieth down and walketh each day through life.

Holdeth no hand but Mine
And you will know you are My own.

Holdeth no might but Mine
And you will know My power.

Think no thoughts but of My glory,
And you will know My glory, healing and powers.

Tell no one of Me,
And be alone;

Tell them of Me
And be My own.

When I make up My pasture full of sheep
You will know honor, fame and glory

As a Son or Daughter of God (and Goddess).

Hold no other god as idol.
Idolatry of all else is not of Me.

Neither is idolatry of My name.

Amen.

****

76. WAKING PRAYER REQUEST

Day 222-Prayer Vigil

"Pray for the peace of Israel."

****

77. DREAM

June 15, 2003 - Day 256 of Prayer Vigil

Young Asian girls and other teenagers were being imprisoned as sexual slaves.

My Impression:

We must know the dark horrors of this world's people BEFORE cataclysmic destruction comes to them all and the world is resurrected and reborn as a New Earth in a New Heavenly position. Our God knows everything. As His own children, we, too, need to know the things that disturb Him. Therefore, we must first be made aware of these atrocities in order for us to know how to better pray for the world.

****

78. A CONVERSATION WITH THE BELOVED

March 10, 2004

My Question: "Who is evil and who is good?"

His Answer: "I cannot call any evil, just "My Child".

My Question: How, then, do we know who to follow?"

His Answer: "Obey the Laws and you will know."

****

79. LOVE

February 27, 2004

"There is chaos on Earth due to the lack of Love, which thereby causes over abundance of Hatred, Prejudice and Violence." (The old Sixties song is evidently true, "What the world needs now is love sweet love. It's the only thing that there's just too little of.")
****

80. INSPIRED SCRIPTURE MESSAGES

(In response to my depression and prayer for solace.)
August 1, 2003

"Perfect love casts out all fear."

"The prayer of a righteous person availeth much."

Mark 9:42-50
"Have salt in yourselves and be at peace with one another."

Mark 10:28-31
Topic: The rewards of renunciation.

Mark 10:14-16
"Let the little children come to Me. Do not stop them; it is of such of these that the Kingdom of Heaven belongs. I tell you solemnly anyone who does not welcome the Kingdom of God like a little child will never enter it."
****

81. DIVINE HEALING

August, 2003

"And then He healed my son and gave him a whole new heart valve!"

We can be as believing and trusting as a little child, and also have medical verification of His wonderful miracles which are still happening. My son was preparing for surgery to replace his heart valve. He was also receiving prayers from his church and his family. The Father heard and answered our prayers. He is still an all-knowing God who continues to perform miracles. Jesus said, "You have not, because you ask not." Let us remember we can still come before the throne of grace and discuss our concerns, needs and joys and give all of our praises with Him, who created all.

We must have the faith of a child, for we are His children. He created us and can heal us of any and all of our earthly transgressions and illnesses–our often infirmities. If we have faith the size of a grain of mustard seed we are told by our Lord we can move a mountain. He also told us we can do greater things than He did–but do I see us believing His words?

****

82. FLASH OF LIGHT

Dream--
August 31, 2003

This dream seemed to show horrible things to do with nature. I saw a flash of light .

There were meetings being held all across the nation attended by those who work with these environmental and Earth changes.

There seemed to be a doomsday awareness and worldly souls were preparing for doom and their own deaths, especially if they held high offices of questionable roles to do with these things.

As I awakened it was as if I were perhaps a Native American spiritual leader. I was encouraged to see beautiful women praying like Madonnas instead of performing evil deeds. I was encouraged that spirituality was not all destroyed.

As the dreamer I also was encouraged to see these things in spite of the extreme dangers I saw around me.

I know we can overcome all in the Blood of the Lamb, Jesus Christ.

Thank you for this special dream, Lord.

Amen.

****

83. NEWS STORY

September 2, 2003

<u>An asteroid is to hit the Earth in 2014.</u>

(Is this the flash of light I saw in my dream of August 31, 2003. Is this one an example of Divine synchronicity?)

****

84. A MESSAGE

Waking Message
December 25, 2003, 2:50 a.m.

Song: "There is joy unspeakable and full of glory, full of glory.
(Repeat this line.)
And the rest has never yet been told."

Q. What is Your message(s) this time, O Lord?

A. I am speaking to you as never before of things to come, of glory and purpose, and times within times. The knowledge of these is unknown. The glory of these is unknown. Times within times is Mine to give. <u>None can question that which they do not understand</u>. (True!)

I am God, Creator, Force and the Ruler of all–the Times, the Eras, the People, the Forces of Evil and Good. Great are My ways and powers. Do not question. Simply obey and learn My ways above all ways.

Horrors fill the Earth and the heavens. Heaven is not of these. Heaven is joy unspeakable and full of glory and the same has never yet been known.

Know ye not the ways of Heaven are not the ways of Earth?

<u>Earth is but a place to live and do that which is righteous</u>.

If not, you will go to Hell, a place of fire and damnation for those who fail their life testings.

Many are called, but few are chosen.

Seek ye first the kingdom of God or all <u>these</u> things shall be added to you.

<u>Seek ye first My heart and soul and you will find life, and it more abundantly</u>.

I am not always reached. Sometimes I am saddened and tired by your Earthly ways. I have sought you all long and hard. I am tired. I am lonely and alone. I am sad to be rejected and shunned. I have done no wrong.

I am your own.

Such, too, are all of those unjustly accused, maligned, shunned and even killed, worldwide. Truth and justice must reign supremely or there will be chaos in our lives and kingdoms.

<u>Mercy can be had for those who are deserving</u>.

Those who are evil ((d)evils) are unjust and deserve the justice of the fallen ones of Hell. Evils are their ways. They are devils.

Speak no more of things to come for all is not ready.

This is a time of horror and evil. Great is the power and depth of horrific evil.

Stay apart and pray as the Death Angel covers the land(s) with sinful chaos.

(I hope I'm wrong on this one, Lord.)

Yes, you are, but not really, Child. I will show you what I am to do very soon. See not your own finite understanding or ways.

I am your God. We are one. You think you are blasphemous. I think you are Mine, my Child, my love.

(Thank You, Lord. Amen.)

****

85. SEE-ERS

Message
December 25, 2003, 6:13 a.m.

"See-ers know so much more they are able to see an actual accident and see MORE than the normal actual event.

They are also allowed to see the additional extraneous events seen by peripheral and other visionary abilities.

They know and see ALL–not just the events seen.

When we see–we see all sorts of extraordinary things not seen by the human eye.

"See-ers see Me."

They see who, what, and where I am.

They see when there is no vision at all for others.

They see the Living God living among them.

They see the Kingdom, the Power, and the Glory of Me in their midst and as a Dream to be dreamed."

(Amen.)

****

86. A DREAM OF JESUS MEAL

December 27, 2003

Jesus was in the dream. He was asking someone to pay for a meal.

He went several places and was not well met, but He did not become angry at anyone.

The dreamer didn't have anything to give to Jesus. However, the desired meal was prepared by Jesus by the offering of His own body and blood.

In addition to being desirous of someone to pay for a meal, Jesus had been looking for people to come in. He was wondering who was going to help to pay for this banquet or feast. He figured He would break even and everything was fine.

The second time people came in late and it was more full. It was getting late and He was wondering how He was going to pay for all of it and some were coming late. He again asked the Dreamer who was going to pay for the meal. The Dreamer and Jesus commisserated. The Dreamer told Jesus he thought He was the greatest.

Jesus thought and His loving thoughts changed the world from dark to light when He did this. He made a descending motion with His arm and things got brighter. This is the descent into incarnation.

Jesus' clothing looked to be salty or dusty as though He'd been working in them–perhaps as a carpenter, or something.

The emotion He expressed was that of sadness because some of the people had missed the Banquet. Jesus's first worry seemed to be about who was going to be at His Feast.

Dream #2.

Jesus was just being with us at a picnic or something like at a family outing. We can be in His presence unlike being at a secular meal. We were to simply hear and obey His message:

"Be still and know that I am God."

****

87. HIS SIGN IN THE HEAVENS

Dream - 2000-2003

I saw His Sign in the Heavens. (I was surprised to see His Sign as the Cross. Somehow I had never really thought about the scripture that talks of His Sign appearing in the Heavens.)

He was descending to Earth slightly below His Cross. He was below the tops of the mountains west of my home. I realized this means He is almost here, if we are thinking of His actual physical Return.

I realized the Cross was not the stark Tau cross. It was the Cross of the Church. This dream is one to ponder at great length due to the nature of world events at this time in history.

88. WALKING ON WATER

"We Must Learn To Walk On The Water"/An Anti-Fear Training Visualization

A Message–1982

It is important to use the vision of Him walking on water. It will build our faith to see ourselves attempting to walk atop the mountainous waves of life's dangers and cares. In order to be able to maintain our needed fearless walk, we must keep our eyes directly upon the Master's face. We must look deeply into His wondrous eyes fearlessly and walk over all dangers in our lives fearlessly.

****

89. "I'M COMING SOON."

Waking Message From The Lord Jesus
August 12, 2004

"My daughter, remember to tell them I am coming soon."
****

90. A WARNING MESSAGE OF IMPENDING TIME OF WAR

Dream: August 22, 2004–2:41 a.m.

1. Many had been called into the military services.
2. Women were weeping and looking for work.
3. There were stores selling gun sets for individual purchase and usage.

****

91. CHAOS THEORY–

Later--

Thoughts of Chaos Theory and "The Butterfly Effect". Is it possible to extend this theory to include the terrible stark realities or events at this awful time in our history which can be changed before they escalate into rumors of war and overt nuclear annihilation? We are told the prayers of the faithful are of much worth. Let us not stop praying. We need consolation and those who will stand up to face the Giant. Perhaps instead of a strong and powerful Giant, we face a vulnerable, aging, toothless and disabled hierarchy of evil.

****

92. LOVE AND ITS MEANINGS

"Forever love yields purpose and goes to the "bones" (even after death)."

"True Love"– forever true.

****

93. A BLESSED OLD HYMN COMES TO COMFORT US

August 14, 2004–driving to work

<u>"Love Lifted Me"</u>

"Love lifted me. Love lifted me.
When nothing else could help.
Love lifted me.

I was sinking deep in sin far from the peaceful shore.
Very deeply stained within sinking to rise no more.

But the Master of the Sea heard my despairing cry.
From the waters lifted me
Now safe am I.

Love lifted me. Love lifted me.
When nothing else could help
Love lifted me."

Praise God for His much needed divine message to us this day. Amen.

****

94. MORE THOUGHTS OF LOVE & ITS MEANINGS

August 24, 2004

God is Love.
Love is Forever.
Love is True.
Love lifts us up from death and despair.
Messages from the Scriptures:
Love is Kind, Patient, and without jealousy.
It is Loyal, Unconditional.
It simply exists without logic or thought of reimbursement or return.
Love is the Key to Life.
Without it we perish.
Love ends prejudice, hatred and wars.
Ended wars = Peace on Earth
Goodwill to all humankind.
We must add a lot more Love into our Recipe for Life.
It is tasty and nourishing.
It is everlasting and never grows old with spoilage.

He is Love.

****

95. LOVE IS FOREVER,

TRUE & LOYAL, NOT JEALOUS,
UNCONDITIONAL & FORGIVING,
MERCIFUL,
FULL OF FAITH,
HOLY & WHOLE.

****

96. OUR DESTINIES

I.

1. Study to show ourselves approved.
   (A workmanship which needs no corrections.)

II.

2. Obtain self and global knowledge and awareness of ourselves as human beings.
3. Seek and we shall find (ourselves, each other and the Creator).

III.

4. Love the Lord, our God, with our whole heart, mind, body and soul–AND—
5. Love our neighbor, as we love ourselves.
   (The question is this, can we unconditionally love ourselves?)

IV.

6. Forgive so that we may be forgiven.
7. Forgive ourselves and others.
8. Forgive and love our enemies.

V.

9. Peace on Earth could be ours–if we love our neighbors and enemies as we love ourselves.
10. If we see each other as all being Seekers of Light and as Children of God– Who will be our enemy when He reigns in Love and Light?

****

97. "BLESS YOURSELF AND OTHERS"

August, 2004

Let blessings flow all around upon every part of Earth and Heavens.
Let us bless the Father, Son and Holy Spirit.
Let us bless each other in loving grace.
Let us harbor no thoughts of jealousy, fear, or hatred.
Let us seek wisdom and light.
Let us be filled with Divine Light and Love.
Let us be blessed beacons of Light.
Let our Lights glow brightly in darkness
While blessings flow unrestrained
Cleansing all from filthy lies and ugly thoughts.

Let us be Holy.
Let us bless and not curse.
Let darkness become the Light of the Dawn Star.
Let us be wrapped in Wings of Healing,
Blessed and Protected from all strife.

Let us sing a New Song of pure delight
Blessings have washed all taints from off our garments.
We are cleansed and holy, healthy and blessed.
Blessings have overcome curses.
Blessings have opened the blessed Red Road to the Pure Land of the Great Spirit.
Of such is the Kingdom of Heaven.

****

98. WHO ARE WE & WHO DO WE FOLLOW - THE DIVINE OR DEMONS?

Scripture Message: Beware the leaven of the Pharisees and the Sadducees.
Matthew 16:11
Dream - August 30, 2002

The setting was a Pacific Coast sandy beach at the mouth of a river, perhaps in Northern California. There were several types of war vehicles such as a truck or a tank on the flooded beach, even as I now remember seeing in a dream the prior week. Even as I was observing the flooded beach, I was horrified to see the breaking of a huge tidal wave shown above the top of a very high mountain peak along the Pacific coastline west of my viewing area.

When I saw this huge wave, I quickly decided to hide inside a craggy cave atop the eastern slopes of the huge mountain. Seemingly, I believed I might be safe in the cave. I now see the cave as being the hiding place given to me by Jesus, even as I see disaster coming to our actual coastlines. He told us to beware if we dwell in the coastlines, and falsely believe ourselves to be safe. We can be hidden from all dangers inside the Cleft of the Rock of Ages we call our Lord. However, do we have time to warn others before this massive tidal wave strikes our nation? Perhaps it is already too late. We are inundated in the filth of this world, rather than being baptized in the Spirit of God, in Living Water, the Living Word, and the Light of His Divine Spirit. Do we have time to save others from like fates?

I am very concerned about my family, my Christian heritage, and our American civil liberties. I re-read this dream today as I begin to write of a topic very dear to my heart, the wellbeing of the souls of my children and grandchildren. Who and what are we leaving as our posterity? As a mother and a grandmother, I am concerned.

I have always loved the Lord Jesus as my Savior. I participated in services as an active member of the churches of the Pentecostal Evangelical Fundamentalists for over 21 years from 1965 to 1986. I wanted my children to know and to love Jesus Christ. I always felt I was not wealthy, but I could give them the wealth of the Rock of Ages, the Prince of Peace, our Savior and Lord, Jesus Christ. He would give them eternal life in His Holy Spirit, and we had the hopes we would all dwell in the House of the Lord forever, as His siblings, as His joint heirs, all of us as the Children of

God. I took my role as His sister and sibling very seriously. I also realized we have duties to be His priests and priestesses, if only in secular monk or nun roles, as His disciples. We are to be responsible for teaching and keeping the younger souls safely anchored in His teachings. I wanted to offer the best gift to my beloved children and their children. I believe this Gift of my Savior, His Salvation and Reward of Eternal Life, was the best gift I could give to my children- or to anyone. As an innocently and truly believing Christian mother, I prayed and trustingly left them in the care of the leaders of these well-attended, fastest-growing American churches.

I had warnings. I could not believe they were warnings of such horrors to come to our nation. I had always told my children of my Gift to them. It was the only gift I could give to them, but the best gift I treasured the most. This is my gift of His loving salvation and forgiveness of my sins. He offers us the wonderful chance to be freed from the karmic Wheel of Life. He redeemed my soul, therefore, I must help others to also be set free. I feel this is the greatest gift I can give to my children, and to all others who do not know of His great Gift of Salvation.

Little did I know that these "Houses of God", many of whom prided themselves on saying they were the only churches who preached the "Full Gospel", had become filled with some confused leaders who had seemingly exchanged their divine birthrights for positions of recognition, "filthy lucre", and political power in our American capitalistic society. These modern pharisees call themselves "The Moral Majority", "The Righteous Right Wing", and a number of equally disgustingly inappropriate titles completely lacking in humility. Who gave them these names?

Our Lord has many groups of believers who all strive to follow His Way of Truth and Light to the best of their abilities. He is the Shepherd of many pastures. There are many denominations of His church. The Bride is preparing herself everywhere on Earth to prepare for His Return. Each group has special needs and concerns for our society. There are even more lists of evils which could be made if we are all allowed to share our views on life and the needs of our people and our society. There are also many holy people who are not Christian in America. God has smiled upon them also. If He accepts and loves them, why should we judge anyone? This is not our place to do so. He has repeatedly told us He is the judge of all–as would be the role of any good father.

They have caused great divisions in our families, churches, communities, nation, and in the world community. Why did they do this? The people they attack are their own family members who have never stopped loving Jesus or His teachings. We have not changed into evildoers and monsters. We are those who still love Him and His followers. We are all attempting to love and to serve Him. Some may see one group of sins. The other groups may see those and other sins. Let us concentrate on the "mote in our own eye". He will judge all of us. We are to love and forgive one another and share holy kisses. He never liked pharisees and hypocrites. They are no more appreciated now than in His time. Many of us feel very strongly these things will cause the fall of our nation. We must not be divided and thereby conquered. There are those groups who love to see our divisions–especially at such crucial times in world history.

Then, and now, I wonder "Where has Jesus gone?" He is still alive and well. It is very wonderful to feel His presence and to know He is with us. Who are these very ordinary men and women who do not see their own faults? We must ask ourselves to remain humbly His children, loving one another with His love. ("Beware the leaven of the Pharisees and the Sadducees." - Jesus Christ, Matthew 16:11, N.T.)

Who are we? Here are some of the guidelines given to us by our Lord by which we may ascertain our pathways.

Do we know and practice the universal teachings of the *Ten Commandments*? (Exodus 20, O.T. See Glossary.)

We are also saved and forgiven by *His Grace*.

Jesus said you will know my people by their *Love- His Divine Love*.. (I Corinthians 13:4. 7;)

Are these people filled with God's divine Spirit? (I Cor. 14:)

Are we showing the *Fruits of His Spirit* in our daily lives? (Galatians 5:22,23, N.T.)

Are they practicing the *Gifts of the Spirit*, (I Corinthians 14), even as they love Him and live the *Fruits of His Spirit*? (Gal.5:22,23, N.T.) They go together. Without the unction of the Holy Spirit, we are not His miracle workers.

Do they know who Jesus said were the *Children of God*? Check out His

Beatitudes. (Matthew 5, N.T.)

We are also those who give, share, bless and help others, even as we would ourselves, our loved ones, and our neighbors. He tells us if we do these things we are also doing them to/for Him.

We are not to judge others. "Judge not, lest ye also be judged."

We are not saved by these actions, but by His grace. However, there are those who do not know Him, but who live as He wishes them to live. He will decide and judge which of us are His when He gathers together His own flock. Who will be called to the *Marriage Supper of the Lamb*, and to enter into the *Gates of Heaven*? These are the decisions to be made by the Father, not by humankind. We are not to live as pharisees, judging and slandering others in the name of Christ. He has nothing to do with such behavior. He wrote on the ground quietly, even when the woman who had commited adultery was brought before Him He said, "Let you who is without sin cast the first stone." Let us leave the decisions of the Father to Him who is all merciful, fair and just, who knows the hearts of all. If He dwells in the *Temples of our Hearts*, He does indeed know us very well.)

We are NOT to *slander, libel, backbite or abuse others.*

Our Lord hates these things.

We are to seek *Wisdom.* (James 1:5; James 3:17, N.T.; Wisdom, The Apocrypha, O.T.)

We must protect ourselves with the *Armor of God* (Ephesians 6:10-19):

Loin Cloth - *Truth*
Breastplate - *Righteousness (or right ways to live)*
Shoes - *Preparation of the Gospel of Peace.*
Helmet - *Salvation*
Shield - *Faith*
Sword of the Spirit - *the Word of God*

Who are we? Who are we worshiping and following--Belial or our Lord? We must carefully seek to know to whom we give the allegiance of our hearts, minds, bodies, and our eternal souls. This is our important task to know as believers in the Divine, and in Eternal Life. To whom are we betrothed? Who is our Savior? Who do we love, adore, reverence, worship, and emulate? Is it our Lord Jesus, as The Word, incarnated in human form as the Christ? (We are taught He came in our forms to be able to better understand His creation.) If we are showing forth spirit forces other than His, we are not His people. Are we, instead, behaving as the natural, brutish, human--the evil one?

Who are we? We must strive to prayerfully discern the Spirit of Truth. He is our Way, our Truth, and our Light in our Lives. We must not be deceived. We must not lead others astray as we blithely seek our own ways. The pitfalls of the Enemy are many. We are to pray for discernment to know who we are, and to whom we give our lives. To give away our Temples, in which His Holy Spirit dwells, is to dishonor ourselves and our Creator. The moneychangers, the pharisees, the unclean, and the unbelieving soul must not rule in our Holy Temple. Our Temples are not made with hands of humankind. Our hearts are the inner Holy Dwellings in our Holy Temples which are created for the indwelling and praises of the infinite Creator. Our hearts are the peacefully contemplative places of worship to which He requested entrance so that we may dine and commune together as One Spirit.

Thus are we to be infilled and led by the Holy Spirit of our Divine Shepherd, if we are the Sheep of His Pasture. We hear and recognize the Voice of our Shepherd, our Master Jesus Christ. His love covers all. We are His by His love. We are to be recognized by our peace and our love, our mercy, fairness, goodness, faith, joy, faith and temperance. We will show forth His Spirit upon our visages, and in the actions and words of our lives, if we spend precious time in solitary communion with Him. We want to walk in His steps, led by His Spirit, protected by His angels. We want to be known as His people, the sheep of His pasture.

Will they recognize us as His, or the followers of devils? Do we show forth the family heritage of our Lord's Family? We must each ask ourselves this important question. Who do we follow? Who are we?

When children tell us God doesn't see everything we do, either because he is not able to do so, or because He has no real interest, I must quickly tell them this is not so.

There is a truly All-Seeing God that does indeed see and know all about us. We are being very completely and carefully monitored, much as our own scientiests are now able to monitor wildlife, fish, and the like. Why is this so hard to believe when even finite human beings can place tags and tiny chips into their own bodies or those of their children and pets? Now, we can know the scriptures are accurate when they say not one hair of our heads or a small bird's feathers fall to the ground without the knowledge of the Father.

If one wishes to know if there is a real Satan or Devil, one needs only to start truly seeking to follow the Master's purest teachings. He will make his infernal self very real to you, for you do not concern him until you make a strong stand for the Divine and His Divine Will in your own life. If you are seen to be a threat to the throne of Satan, or to his demon forces, you will know there is a real Satanic Devil and his hordes. Devils watch us and attempt to alter our life destinies. If we are seen to be staunchly strong foes, we will be noticed, and fought by demons of the evil one.

Also, you will be truly drawn closely to the bosom of the Divine by the hand of the Lord Jesus and His angels, if you call upon Him, His Name and His Blood to cover you from all evil. He is our staunch advocate, protector, and older Brother who truly cares about our safety and well being. He will be right there to guide us out of temptation and danger. However, we must call upon Him in order for Him to come to our rescue.

He will give His armies of angels charge over you lest you fall or are be killed by one of the darts of the enemy of our souls.

We must study to show ourselves able to discern between God and Devil. This is why these words must be written - just to refresh those souls who have memories which are failing them for fears over what things may be coming upon the Earth at this time. There are those who would fulfill the worst of all prophecies, as well as wage wars in the name of Jesus or Allah.

Seek to know Him, and the Holy Ones. Do not seek to follow the pathways of darkness, lest you become ensnared in the webs of the demon spiders who will entrap and kill your very soul.with their devious machinations of minds, souls and bodies.

It is our profound prayer that all will come to know the wondrous power of the Living God, not the horrible wiles and ways of evil, the devils of this once Edenic world, who now rule and reign until His Return. They have little time in which to work. Therefore, they are very fearful and angry at God and His Children.

Let us always feel blessed to be able to call ourselves the Children of God, and our Heavenly Family which is of a royal and priestly lineage, and to never seek to be the sons (and daughters) of Belial and his infernal demons.

We must study to show ourselves able to discern today who we will follow and who we are as spiritually-endowed souls.

We offer our lives, prayers, and this book as a testament of our love and concerns for all humankind. We are sincerely your Friends and Family from our Heavenly Home, who both love you all so much. It is our desire to assist to be messengers of light in the darkness of spiritual ignorance.

99. THE ASIAN MANSION

June 12, 2004–6:22 a.m.

Many mansions are wonderful places filled with everything but His Spirit. I just entered one via the most bizarre dream setting I have ever seen.

We had seemingly rented a new dwelling. My first awareness was of being in a new dwelling and someone knocked at the door. I went to the door and asked who was there. The male voice said, "Chuck". I said, "I don't know anyone named Chuck" and refused him entry. He then tried his key in my door. I was very glad I had not opened the door to this unknown person.

It was at this time I decided I wanted to explore this new home into which we had moved. It was like no other dwelling I had ever seen. The walls were covered with colored inlaid metals, stones, china tiles, and many other types of the most expensive, heavily ornate, shiny substances. It glowed with pictures and colors of all types. The area I believed to be our apartment area was relatively simple. It included a kitchen, a bedroom, a couple of writing areas with desks and lamps, a living room with a huge fireplace covered with a metal screen. When I went to look for the bathroom, the whole scene changed. I went down a stairway to a very ornate, small bathroom. At this point, the whole dwelling expanded to include a myriad of very beautiful rooms such as the ones in the area I thought to be our own apartment.

First of all, I realized there were several other people sharing this mansion with me. I found there were a variety of people working around within each ornate room with its own very securely interior design with no windows to the outside world. They seemed to be household staff member performing a myriad of duties for the owner of this beautiful home.

The house seemed to be arranged with many levels, rooms, and designs. The exclusive design of the mansion was that of ancient Chinese affluence. I wondered why I was here. As I became acquainted with each person I began to learn of their religious beliefs and much more. There were several areas set apart for worship of the many deities of Asia. It appeared to me that each deity had a personal altar area set aside for its own exclusive worship.

In addition to the altars of the deities, there was an area with animated female dolls, which were truly living beings. They each had the abilities to harm anyone if they did not like the person. I realized one of them did not like me at all. She was preparing to bite me with a mouth full of bloody teeth. She was horrifying. I made a safe exit from this area.

During this whole dream state message, I was also aware there was a Chinese Empress dwelling within the confines of the magnificent dwelling. The whole building and its inhabitants were insulated within the confining walls of this windowless building. The affluence was obvious. The light was not.

The affluence and piety was within the walls of this home. The Lord Jesus had no place for His altar. I was sad. There would have been light, joy, and a feeling of His love rather than fear of ancient Chinese deities. Many of these were representative of death and the dark fear worlds. I judge not, because there is much I do not know of His creation. I only know I was living in a house in which He had no place to lay His dear head.

I know my Lord, the Beloved, who loves us all so very much comes to dwell within our hearts. Are we willing to give Him even a little space in which to dwell? He doesn't ask or require very much space. However, personally speaking, I try to offer Him a cozy, peaceful, holy home, even if it is humble. I try to imagine my home as a place where tired angels and a busy and exhausted Lord could feel comfortable and welcome to come in and rest anytime.

I am still pondering this dream. It truly expanded my consciousness, as well as giving me a waking headache. I am asking for His Message so that we each may have expansions of our consciousness to be able to learn and to grow in His wisdom and truth.

This was a world like none one finds in America. The building seemed to be in a sparsely built, multi-racial, neighborhood in a foreign land. It was not the world known to many in our world. However, He knows all about this home and its occupants. I believe He also loves them. We must expand our knowledge to include other brothers and sisters of the Third and Fourth Worlds. We are all His Children. We will be hugely blessed as we open our hearts, minds and souls to encompass our global community. Heaven's Gate is open for us all to enter therein. There will be joy unspeakable and full of joy. We will dwell in His Presence forever. He is great. His House is big. It is large enough to encompass worlds within worlds. He has many sheep which are not of this pasture.

My Thoughts & Meditations Regarding This Dream:

1. The first, and perhaps foremost, teaching was that we must always be diligent in our efforts to maintain our personally safe and sacred space and time. No strangers should be allowed entry into our personal homes and hearts. Neither should we share our lives with those who will enter

our homes and hearts without our personal invitations. Our hearts and our homes are the temple of the Living God.

2. This may not apply to this dream in any way. However, it is a good safety precaution which goes well with #1. Additionally, if a woman lives alone, her safety may be more completely assured if she will hang pictures of males relatives, even deceased ancestors. This gives a message to others that she is not an isolated, lonesome, and thereby unprotected, woman. This simple, old-fashioned habit of hanging up one's family pictures ("rogues gallery") may be less expensive than a security guard or system, if one does not have husband or adult children. 3. The whole house was more than I can describe at this time. I cannot believe what I have seen and experienced in this mansion.

4. This dream message is one that will require prayer and meditation.

5. In my dream research, I do know this dream of Chinese and their home does include very good and auspicious symbolic messages. At this time, this means this is a very important message from our Lord.

It is of great importance to know who is the Master of each home. We must keep a holy safe space in our hearts and in our homes in which the Spirit of God dwells. If we do not allow Him room in our homes and in our lives, it is a grave concern He will not find a room for us in His Heavenly Home. Let us remember the purpose of our lives is to realize we are His Children who are to be infused with His loving Spirit and light. We are of His own family. Let us remember to always take time each day of our lives to thank Him for breath, life, faith, and all that is. To pray without ceasing is holy and wholesome. This is the way we were made. We desire to honor and to serve good. He is good. He is God. He must have access to the inner parts of our homes and our hearts, minds, bodies and souls.

One of my latest messages was one of being allowed to share the extreme grief of our Beloved Father. I will insert this message at this time. What do you think we should take from this message? I am heartbroken by His broken heart.

****

PART II
TEARS OF OUR BELOVED FATHER

PART I--SPECIAL MESSAGES FROM OUR BELOVED FATHER

100. A SHOCKING MESSAGE OF OUR FATHER'S SORROW

Dream Message: July 16, 2004

Our Father is weeping in great gushing tears too great to be understood by any of us. I observed and then was allowed to physically share in His grief. I thought I would choke and die. His grief is too great for a human to experience. Our nasal, throat and sinus passages are too small for us to experience such a massive sorrow. The message is that Our Beloved Father is deeply concerned and is sorrowing over His created children. My heart broke as I observed My Father's sorrow. My next thought was that I wished to make Him happy, not sad. What can we do to change His sorrow to happiness? I am honored He allowed me to see and to experience His sorrow. I am not the only one who has been allowed to share in His grief. He is showing Himself to those who love Him, in all parts of the world. When a Father weeps, children must be concerned. We are His Children. Why is He weeping? We must take heed and ask Him to direct us how He wishes us to serve Him. We need to know about His sadness. This is a message for all of us. What can we do to make Him happy with us and our world? The topic for this book is to help us to learn how to change our attitudes and values for our life destinies so that we will be able to change our Father's unspeakable sorrow into "Joy unspeakable and full of glory". We will sorrow when He sorrows. We will be joyous when He is glorified and praised for His great goodness to us as His children. Many of us are bruised and wounded from terrible losses of spouses and children. We, of all His Children, have empathy for our Heavenly Father's great grief. His grief is ours and we, too, are in uncontrollable tears of mourning.

Sections of this book were written in a spirit of great weeping. This is because several of us have been given visions of the Father in the depth of agony and tears. We are His children. He is our eternal Father. Our joys and sorrows are of interest and concern to Him. His joy is ours. His sorrow is also ours. We are His family. Large families share joys and sorrows. We must know why He is grieving. It may be our faults. We may also be incurring His displeasure. We need to know so we may have a chance of changing our ways and thereby saving ourselves from destruction.

Let us help our Father clean up the Gardens of our souls. He is concerned with every part of His Garden. Our gardens are full of rotten decking, overgrown areas, weeds that flourish among dying flowering plants, and all manner of encroaching insects and wasps. The spiders are simply huge. They do not spin intricate webs like the Great Weaver of life. They are simply frightening and give us terrified delusions and insanity. We are horrified and full of panic over the cares of life and of the dreadful things which are happening to the innocents of our world. Everyday, we are told there are many terrors assailing us. Some of these terrors are real. Many of them are simply figments of the minds of other frightened souls.

The beautiful world He gave us is sometimes making us feel lost and forlorn. Her oceans roar and overflow the land masses. The human beings murder, make war and fight endlessly. Her wonderful gardens of paradisial beauty have been denuded of their glorious life giving foliage. Creatures wander in wilderness and even our cities seeking food for their young. Humans are killed by them because humans have moved into their natural habitats.

In spite of all of this, our Father is in control of all that is and ever shall be. We are His children. We trust in Him. He is our Father and we are His Children. We are eternally grateful to our caring and Beloved Father who is overcome with sorrow and tears for His Children and His beautiful creation. Our Father is deeply concerned for us. We must mourn with Him for ourselves. Our hearts are sad for His heartbroken tears.

My concern may not be your concern. After all, to many I am an ordinary women, like anyone of your neighbors. In our modern world, scribes and stenographers are not in elite professions. We may also wear other hats. Some know us as those who know things from the Father, Son and Holy Spirit. Our Lord was not understood or accepted as Messiah by some of His own family and friends. Many of our loved ones may not know we who we are and what our divine destinies are in their worlds. We are also simply family and friends.

He knows some of us have been allowed to share in His suffering and tears because we asked to know and to love Him. We must again remember the words of Jesus when He preached in His own hometown of Nazareth. He read from the texts quoted in Isaiah. They asked Him to heal their ill. He responded that a prophet is not accepted in his/her own community. This is why the prophets performed their miracles in other areas. This is the reason so many who wish to share do not. It is obvious even our Lord was not accepted in Nazareth, but was known as Joseph's son, rather than the Son of God who had come as Prophet and Messiah to save His family, friends and neighbors. His is also our pathway.

This is why a personal decision must be made by each person to know if they really want to know or care that our Heavenly Father is indeed tearfully sorrowing for His creation.

I will include several scriptural messages regarding the reasons He may be grieving. Have the ways of humankind changed since they were written?

"Unless you become as a little child you shall not enter in to the Kingdom of Heaven."
"OF SUCH IS THE KINGDOM OF HEAVEN"
(Jesus Christ, N.T.)

The Message of the Father's Weeping is one of the most shocking messages I have ever received. There was one other I will not even give a number in this book. However, I believe it is pertinent for this dark time in history in which we are dwelling, therefore I will give the shortened message below:

THE MOST HORRIFYING DREAM MESSAGE–
Date: Probably early in the 1980's.

I was an Asian man attempting to climb up the sheer rock face of a Pacific Coast mountain to escape those who were attempting to capture all Asians and Gays. Individuals were being indiscriminately kidnaped and loaded into trucks in the cities. The trucks carried them to their deaths in wilderness. It was like atrocities of the Holocaust re-enacted within our own time and space. These atrocities were being done in an American city such as Los Angeles and other large cities.

The additional messages are not needed as they were too horrible to describe herein.

101. YES, HE IS CONCERNED ABOUT ME AND ALL OF US

Dream and Message: July 16, 2004
'More Tears Of The Creation & The Creator"

It was a no win working situation in the midst of a mass of co-workers. One thought they had been given a simple job task. After attempting to complete this simply sales label or ad, one found even this simple task could not be completed because all the instructions had not been given to the typist. I was horribly disgusted and stymied that even a person like myself who had been a secretary for 35-40 years wouldn't be able to type this simple notice. The reason was "Lack of information about how to complete the simplest task, such as this one." I awakened very disgusted, stymied, and frustrated, feeling horribly cheated and mistreated.

My husband awakened and asked me to record his dream.

He was mumbling, speaking too lowly and was dictating at a speed too fast to record. I kept telling him this but he was too asleep to hear or understand me. He went blissfully back to sleep. This is like those who are too untaught and lacking in information to understand what we are trying to tell them of politics or religion. There is no way to get their attention because they are too asleep or too busy with the cares of life to be able to stop and comprehend the mysteries of God untaught in this lifetime by our teachers and instructors. We are placed here with a huge job to do without instructions. Many of our co-workers, friends and loved ones are too unaware, non-thinking, uninterested and poorly endowed with ambition or ability to seek further insights. Then, when they do think they should seek to know, they are misled, confused and left with no way to find the answers to their dilemmas. We are horribly confused as newly arriving souls. There is no one to teach us the Way to God. The Master and the Master Plan, the Guide Book, is hidden or lost in chaos and the misery thereby incurred by such separation from Wisdom, Light, and Awareness.

My husband was satisfied with having found me in his dream. He was overjoyed (and so was I). He knew we would find each other again. This is like those who get a small satisfying piece of spiritual insight. They are very satisfied and go back to their non-seeking effortless bliss of satisfaction with any morsel of food that they get, like a satisfied pet dog who receives a bite of food from their master. Some of us are like this with our Divine Master. We even become egocentric and have over inflated egos over any tiny bit of spiritual insights we discover laying around for us on the floor like a bit of discarded meat on a dirty floor. We grab onto that piece of meat like a dog keeping and preventing another dog from stealing his personal morsel of meat. We seek bites from the Master's table. Sometimes meat is accidentally dropped on the floor. As the woman said to Jesus, she wanted to be at least be able to be like the stray dog eating meat from His table. Some people even become so puffed up with pride over having their own store of meat they feel they must defend it from others. Some also feel they must have obtained all the meat there is to obtain. Therefore, they must guard it and not share it. Some feel they must share and foist even their partially eaten and half spoiled meat with others. At least these are loving enough to care about their brothers and sisters.

This is what I am facing as the "Weeping Mother", who fell in love with the Weeping Yogi statue. She recognized herself. He even wears the Phrygian hat of the servant was shown to her in a dream many years ago. In her case and that of Jesus, they are the "Suffering Servants". The Phrygian hat was given to her in the 1990's as a special symbol of servitude. They come to humankind as servants, counselors, healers, helpers, humanitarians who love and serve even as they offer their lives for the good of all, and for the salvations of many.

This morning, after I recovered from playing the role of "Suffering Creation", I became "Suffering Creator". This was a massive, macrocosmic view of All. As I slowly came out of dream state, I began to be shown these two days of messages are a massive view from each perspective. Because all of this is a new perspective, it may take longer to explain to us clearly from our finite, partially aware state of beingness.

First of all, I was enraged to find Life is Chaos, with no answers and no escapes from the idiotic whims of a demented Creator. I was disgusted and desired to be nothing. I would rather be dead or completely annihilated than to live with such a Chaos Theory of the Creator and of Life.

Second, I became the Weeping Creator. As my son had seen in a vision, the Father was weeping with unrestrained, gasping and rending sorrow for His creation. Very rarely could He show us this manifestation of His all-encompassing grief. Human nasal passages, throats and sinuses are simply not adequate to give us a bonafide manifestation of His sorrow. He is the All-Encompassing, Manifold and Undefinable One. He wants to share with us but cannot. He is alone in His massive, rending, suffering and grief. He wants to be with us even as I was shown in my Message from Him in 1967. I try to express His desires to others. They seem not to comprehend His feelings unless they are completely lost in His Spirit. He misses us. He weeps for our lost and frustrated sorrows as His creation. He knows many of us cannot find Him due to the lack of information available to them. He understands their abject horror and frustration with their incarnations in human form. They feel like lost pawns in a chess game. They feel like an abandoned and lost pin ball machine ball. They feel like a lost computer image of a man involved in an endless game of chance or a never ending war game. Therefore, life is awful and they wish escape–even in death, which is hopefully an end to life forever. In the case of those who drive with road and life rages, they want to die so much they feel they are helping themselves and others to thankfully be dead and free of this world of chaos and horror. However, they seem to forget their fellow drivers have not desired death. Perhaps they even see the bigger Plan of Creation and of their own Life Destiny. They know they must live to tell others of Him and His Way and Plan for their lives on Earth and in the world to come. Also, those who drive madly down the roads and byways of life need to remember that automobile accidents do not always end in welcome and desired death. Many of these enraged drivers, and their fellow drivers, are left maimed and crippled, perhaps living like living statues in a world teeming with activity.

Oftentimes when I awaken in horror, I am immediately shown why I had to suffer such torment. Such was the Message of this day which also included yesterday's message entitled "Tears". Tears is the message of this Veil of Tears, Earth Life in 2004. I wish to give hope and life to those who walk in tears, who empathize as Weeping Yogis. They love the statue because he is an image of themselves. We learn best from our experiences. If He can give us simulated experiences in visionary or dream states, perhaps we do not need to live an experience in order to learn from it.

The Message of this day is another confirmation of the Divine Love of the Father rather than leaving us in a Veil of Tears thinking we are a pawn in a game called Life. We are not pawns or human toys created for the perverse pleasures of a cruel and demented Creator Deity. This is what our religions have taught us. Those with large brains, who are functional and healthy souls cannot agree with many religions as they are currently being taught by their messengers and teachers. This is because the blind man is attempting to describe something he has never seen and, therefore, cannot describe. Until He infuses us with His wisdom, we are like blind souls trying to save other souls from someone or something we know nothing about. We cannot talk of Heaven when we know nothing about it. This dream message came to me in early in the 1980's. Those who try to describe and tell others of something, or someone, they know nothing about are not those who should be attempting to tell others of things unknown and unseen by themselves. This is what is being done by well meaning teachers and ministers, evangelists and children of God. They are His. Now they want to go out and tell everybody about their Daddy. Daddy is so BIG. Daddy is so BIG they have no way of describing Him. This is the same with His Plan of Creation, His Creation, the Fall, the Loss of Paradise, and of His Plan to Regain Paradise which was Lost. We have some pieces of a gigantic Puzzle Plan.

Let us humbly and lovingly seek to know Him. He will teach us His Will and Way for our lives and destinies. LOVE IS THE KEY. Without Love, we argue and fight with each other. Let us seek Him, for HE IS LOVE. IF WE SEEK HIM, WE WILL FIND HIM. HE WILL COME AND DINE WITH US. WE WILL FIND THE LOVING AND SANE CREATOR RATHER THAN THE GOD OF CHAOS. HE IS THE IMAGE OF WISDOM WHO SEEKS TO TEACH US AS HIS OWN CHILDREN. AS THE GOOD FATHER, HE WISHES TO TEACH HIS CHILDREN HIS WISDOM. AS THE GOOD FATHER, HE WISHES TO TAKE AWAY ALL HURTS AND SORROWS.

My visionary dreams of this day are no longer sorrow and chaos. They are believable dreams of hope for a BRAVE NEW WORLD. We can see this is His Plan. He has promised us the fulfillment of this dream. He has shown us chaos and hell this day. He has also given us the answers we desired last night before bedtime. I see Him as my Father. I am once again one in His Spirit. I am once again able to sing His praise in a better place. He has brought me back Home again, once again His Child. We must become as a Little Child in order to enter into Heaven. He is love. We are bruised and broken children who sometimes feel like the broken toys of a full grown errant Father God. He is not insane. Our minds simply need to become expanded enough to be able to encompass the Living God, the Creator of All. Our souls grow bigger and so does our Love. He is Love. We become Love. He has again saved us from the demented demon of fear and ignorance. He is our Savior. We are His Redeemed Children. He paid the price for our education and release from this Prison of Servitude to Darkness, whether entities or thought forms. We are His sane and beloved Children of the Good God. He is not insanity, death, destruction, chaos, darkness, unwholeness, unrighteousness. He is merciful, righteous, faithful and kind. He is just and fair. He is altogether wonderful.

"WEEP & PRAY FOR WE WILL DIE AND YOU WILL BE NEXT"

Our Father is speaking the saddest of messages to us as His Beloved Children. Thus has He spoken over and over again to His wayward

Children. We never seem to hear and obey Him before it is too late to stop the chaos caused by our own disobedient actions and words. We have again broken His heart. This wound is more than even He can bear. We are a danger to ourselves and others. This is not new. It is simply more than He can allow as the wise and loving parent.

We have become so evil we would kill even Him rather than admit we are lost and destructive souls. We are so evil we do not even know what evil is. We do not know who He is. We do not know each other. Therefore, we cannot love one another. Neither can we love Him. He is not our Beloved Father because we do not care to know Him. Indeed, in the latter part of the 20th Century there were those who adjudged God the Father to be dead. Instead, we sang a song to the Living God, and called Him holy. Where are those ancient prophetic songs now? Instead of beauty and holiness we have exchanged our birthrights for "a mess of pottage". This simply means we were so hungry for food we gave away our divine heritages for material world life. What is life without Divine Life in the Home of our Father? What is Heaven without Him. What is the creation without the Creator?

We are now alone. We have finally continued in our evil hating and quarreling ways until even our Father is ready to chastise and abandon us. I know, for I, too, am heartbroken. As parents, we withhold the rod of correction when our children are young. We reap chaos. We do not wish to hurt their flesh or bruise their feelings. We go through all manner of horrible things to spare our children the discomforts and sorrows of life. Our Heavenly Father has also done the same with us. There has come a time when even our Father can no longer allow us to play alone. We cannot play together without fighting among ourselves. He will take each one of us apart one from another as one does our own fighting children. We will be removed from our play areas and taken apart for our "quiet times".

Many of us have been alone with Him for many years seeking to learn and to grow into the types of children with whom He can share Himself. If we are too busy with our senseless lives He will not take time to teach us of Himself. We must grow into Seekers. Those who wish to know the Father will be allowed to come in close to His wonderful loving heart and arms. He will embrace us with His never ending, all-encompassing love which is more than can be comprehended by unloving human hearts. Our minds cannot comprehend Him for He is as a father is to a tiny child. Who can comprehend this large entity known as Daddy? Who wants to know anything more about Mommy except her loving nourishment? We are like tiny children. We are not progressing in our growth. We are like so many under developed children. We are retarded in our growth. We are autistic, tongue tied, alone and anti-social. We are injured almost to the point of being lost. Yet He has not forgotten us. We are so young and so sick we do not know how very ill we have become. He has been attempting to let us know of our own need for healing. We will not listen. It is almost too late to heal and save us from ourselves. If others do not injure, maim and kill us, we will destroy ourselves.

He has spoken loud and long by His Messengers the Prophets. He has let many of them learn about the messages they are to give by becoming living Messages of Doom. Each of the great prophets were allowed to feel the pangs of the pains they saw coming upon their people. Judgment always begins at the House of the Lord. Many of us saw His judgment begin to come upon this land many years ago. We saw the pouring out of the angel's censer in the early 1980's. We prayed to be covered as Judgment went out of it across our beloved land. Our sins had finally reached to the very heavens. Many of us, like so many journalists and teachers, ministers and professors of wisdom, were also caught in the backwash of the huge tidal wave which flowed across our land full of the evils of the depth of the Sea of Life. The sea teems with life. Not all of it is full of life giving energies. The messages of Tidal Waves became part of our Message of that time. Many of us literally moved inland to escape the terrible forces of this powerful inundating Wave. Those who attempt to save their lives by running are lost. Those who stay to face death are the wiser ones. To die is to live. What is life without Him? Nothing.

This how He feels about us. He would rather destroy us to save the Earth and a few healthy Children. He cannot save all of us if we refuse to listen and obey Him and His wise instructions. One time I dreamed I was frantically trying to save my whole carload of children from the dangers of an advancing tidal wave. I knew it was coming. All the signs were there. My teen aged daughter refused to hurry. I was so concerned for the good of all my children I felt I would be forced to leave her. I actually wondered if I would be forced to leave her to the Wave in order to save the rest of my children who had already obediently climbed into my large sedan. I was frantic with my loving fear and concern for her safety. I didn't want her to be lost. She is my beloved daughter. However, at the very last few moments available to us before the Wave arrived to destroy my whole family, she finally finished combing her hair and primping. I managed to save them all. I tearfully beseech everyone to listen to this story. Please come into safety of our Father's arms and let Him rescue you before it is too late. I continue to remember my frantic concerns with fearful heart. It had reached the time when we would all be lost if she did not heed my call. This is the time in which we now live. If we do not heed the warnings of our Heavenly Father, we will all perish in the raging seas of filthy waters which have overflowed our lands. We did not escape the Wave after all our efforts to save our own lives. I can still see that House by the Sea, built too near and upon the washing, swirling, pounding surf sand. We must attempt to escape the raging ocean waters which have overflowed our land. Is there still a little time allotted to us in which to outrun and escape this massive Wave?

This is no longer a future prophecy. This is like our lives. We must build our sacred homes upon the Rock of Ages. A house built upon rock do not become caught in the raging seas of life. We must seek with all our might and efforts to escape the cares and dangers of this life. We must come apart into our safe areas. We must enter our safe prayer closets while the horrors cross over our land. Perhaps we have reached the time "when no man can work". If we will not listen to the warnings from our earthly parents, we will be turned over to our own devices. We will be caught in all manner of evil perversion even as has already happened to so many of our beloved children. Will we never stop and learn from the mistakes of others? No. We must each experiment until we are endangered by our own foolhardy ways. As a young mother I loved my tiny darling children so much I offered to suffer anything if I could only learn and thereby save them the sorrows of suffering. I'm sure my prayers were heard and answered.

I have tried to take their troubles from them. It is many years later and I see clearly I did not help them. I have foolishly and needlessly dared to endanger myself by attempting to learn so they could learn from watching me make mistakes. I was very loving and protective. I was very altruistic and serving. Perhaps I was very wrong. I was a young mother with small children. I had no real knowledge of His created children. He gave us all free will and I took it. I learned of Him. They learned of Him also. This is why our wise Heavenly Father lets us have free will, experiences from which we learn about living, and then offers us His forgiveness when we sometimes make mistakes while we learn. Many of us know how valuable is the experiential learning we do as students of life and university studies.

We have a grave and festering wound in our American society. It is part of our national creed to believe that everyone is to be allowed freedom of religion, politics, speech. In fact some of us adamantly believe EVERYONE OF US requires, deserves, and expects equal human rights to freedom of speech and choice. This is especially important to those who desire to help the world to find and to know Him. It is important to be wise, loving and tolerant. Our nation was formed because the new settlers were seeking freedom of religion and worship, as well as political freedom from the oppressive systems of the Old World they were leaving. At this time we are suffering from a very frightening turn of events. Our Constitution and its carefully prepared contents are being ignored by our current governmental leadership. After years of strange teachings in our churches, some of our people now follow the teachings of radical fundamentalist leaders. At this time, it seems to many of us that no one except those who believe as they do are acceptable. Unfortunately, it is a well known fact that those who become obsessed with their own perfection are called "True Believers". Those who isolate themselves into their own "virtuous and perfect" roles and pathways are unfortunately often eager and ready to accept the words of radical religious and political leaders. Many genocidal purges have occurred when such a leader rose to power. None of us learn from observing others experiences if we are not eager to learn ourselves. Our own experiences are much more freshly and painfully remembered However, whenever we sincerely pray with concerned and breaking hearts, He does hear and answer our prayers. I know He has always heard and answered my heartfelt prayers. He even hears our quiet, shy, non-seeking prayers, whether we wish Him to do so or not. We are not alone. We are being very carefully monitored. We are His own Children. We are members the Family of God. He does not leave us alone to our own dangerous play. He sees and warns us of dangers. If we do not listen, He attempts to save us from making dangerous mistakes before they are made.

The Father is weeping because we have broken His huge Father's heart. He is weeping because we continue to misunderstand and curse Him, His Creation and each other.

We have dared to seek and to find Him. So have you. However, some of us are not allowed to also be His Children. Your hearts are too hard. Your minds and souls are full of self love. There is no room for love for children, aging parents, or each other. Tiny babies are not safe even after they are born. The innocent adult children of others are falsely charged, imprisoned and even unjustly executed for crimes they never committed simply because they have not yet been tested for matching DNA. Then there are the terrible atrocities perpetrated against the weakest ones. Where are our loving, natural, affections? This is frightening. Has He already turned us over to our own devices with the evil one? Everyone has their personal "laundry list" of unacceptable immoralities.

I do know we are walking on thin ice with our Father. I am very concerned He is now ready to let us "sink or swim". He may be willing for all to die in order to attempt to save a few, selected and whole children.

As I said, I awakened at 4:57 a.m. with the words, "We will be the first destroyed, but you will be next". To me this meant, "You can kill those of us who are different from you in our pathways to Him. However, we are all His Christian children. They will come for you after you have unjustly killed your brothers and sisters."

If He does not speed up the cosmic clock, the Angel of Death will come for us all before we take time to see "The Signs of the End Times". Let us turn our eyes and prayers to Heaven and all be filled to overflowing with His loving grace. Listen, children, while your Father yet speaks. If we wait for His hand of power, you will be very sorry to see Him coming to chastise and punish us all. He may be forced to turn us over to our bullies and our enemies to abuse and kill us.

We are too stupid to know who our real enemies are in this world if we are so unloving and uncaring as to not even know we are abusing, insulting, and killing our own Christian brothers and sisters in our own nation. If one cannot discern between those who are His in America and do not know geography, how can we know if we are at war in Iraq or Iran, Afghanistan or Pakistan? If we do not recognize the Master's voice we cannot tell if He is living among the people who call themselves Hindus, Muslims, Jews, or Buddhists and other groups? If we do not know Him, how do we know who He calls His people? All of these are also His own created and chosen children. If we are fearful and ignorant we will never desire to meet, interact with, and to truly know them as kindred souls. We are missing wonderful relationships and deep, long lasting friendships with our neighbors. Our natural natures prevent us from daring to share this planet with those who look and live in different fashions from ourselves. Fear and ignorance endanger our kinships as well as our friendships, thereby causing us to be an ancient endangered species of Planet Earth. We must stop being so backward and fearful. Fear breeds prejudice because we do not know anyone who has different skin color, eyes, hair, religious, political and cultural differences. Our psyches are absorbed in self examination which sometimes causes us to believe our ways are the best and only fashion in which others can think, live and be acceptable to others and even to the Absolute, All-Encompassing Overall Spirit we call by a variety of different names. Not only do we have individual names for That One, but some groups of believers see Him as being made exactly in the image of themselves in all ways including religion and politics.

He says He is Love. Perfect Love casts out all fear. Fear is not of God. Those who know this know Him in Spirit and in Truth. Jesus tells us "The Truth shall set you free." This is true. *We are known by our love if we know Him. We will recognize Him in souls all across the Earth–even those of diverse religions and cultures.* He is love. We are love. We are all one in Him. We have wonderful union of souls in spite of our differences. This will allow us to fearlessly seek to know one another. *Friendship will mean we can be peaceful seekers of wisdom, and new friends. New friends are not enemies. Without enemies, we will realize we are safe and well.*

Before we can have peace, we must make peace with ourselves and others. We must love and forgive one another. At this time, we are all very angry with each other because we have been arguing and warring for centuries. How long will it take us to make a loving and peaceful world of light, wisdom and (w)holiness? We have no time left in which to make war. Let us bury our hoarded rage, anger, jealousy, hatred, prejudices, and wars instead of the beautiful children who are the "cannon fodder" of our wars. Let old men who sign their signatures to documents for wars be required to fight those wars themselves, naked with their swords, in the deserts to which they send our sons and daughters. Wars will end. If love and mercy are in our homes there will be no abuses which cause some to commit murders and mayhem.

Let all of the attributes of His Holy Spirit be ours. Let us become the Children of Light, no longer the Children of Darkness. Let His Divine Light expose all Darkness to Heaven's Light. Paradise beckons. Let us leave the deserts and ride the high places of the cosmos with the Children of Light. We have no time for angry divisions and wars. Those who seek to divide and conquer our souls will not overcome us. "We will overcome" all evil with the Blood and Sword of the Lamb. We will win by being and living as His Peacemakers, Wisdom Seekers, and His Children of Love and Light. Hold high the banners of Truth and Righteousness. Do not be part of evil. Come out from among them and be separated unto Him. We have been released from the Pharaohs of the Egypts of this world. Moses is not forgotten. Neither is our Lord. The sufferings of all the holy ones of all the centuries cry out to Him from beneath His throne saying, "How long O Lord, how long must our blood be shed?" Bloodshed must end. Those who invent and wage needless war and use us as pawns in a massive cosmic and global chess game are like horrible bullies waiting to be bested. We are told He has fought and conquered even this battle. It is time to gather together for His Feast. Let us join hands and be on our way. Our Father and older Brother have shed too many tears over us. We must stop crucifying our Lord. We must wipe away our Father's tears, along with those of our older Brother, and those of our entire world family.

Since we each have our own individual families, let us begin at home, with our family members. Let us forget ourselves and our hurts. Let us concentrate upon the greater good of all. This will bring Heaven to Earth, so that His kingdom, which is us, can come into existence. It is my most profound prayer that we each become full of His peace. *Let us have peace and let it begin with me.* This is my heartfelt prayer this day. We truly need Peace on Earth and Good Will in each of our Families as well as on Earth. These are some of the ways we may be able to accomplish this giant task:

I. GRIEF.

It is deeply held belief that most of us have been going through lifetimes of extreme losses and sadness. We have all been suffering so long and so continuously, many of us have not had time or funds to seek professional help. I feel we have gravely injured souls. Many are suffering from ancient unhealed traumas of all types. Included in this group of souls should be those who have been cruelly mistreated due to the holocausts and genocides of racial and ethnic groups. We have abused those of the Third and Fourth Worlds. We have abused the children, the aged, the disabled, the poor, the stranger and the homeless (often made homeless by the insatiable greed of real estate entrepreneurs and others).

We cannot have peace on Earth until we let these martyrs know we care. The Earth must be healed. We must apologize to the Earth and the creatures for our gross injustices. We have enslaved, abused and murdered many in the names of the Holy Ones. We have had Machiavellian Codes and Rules for our lives and our governments. The western term "The ends justify the means" must be replaced by "Evil means can never bring good and holy ends or results." Our Super Powers are sliding into Collapsing Empires. We are regressing in obsolescence and atavistic levels of advancement. Soon we will be like so much aged dust blown away in the winds. We forget history even as we forget each other. If we forget history and each other, we also deserve to be forgotten. The truly beautiful souls of this world are those who came to serve and to perhaps suffer for the sake of righteousness. Some of these beautiful souls are Mahatma Gandhi, Martin Luther King, Jr., Rosa Parks, Mother Theresa, and many others beyond comprehension. There are many 'ordinary' heroes and heroines, who are unnamed and unrecorded in the annals of world history. There are beautiful, even hurting, souls who need solace. Let us be solace to others. Learn and live empathy! By so doing, you will be one of those known as the Peacemakers and Healers of this sad world. This sad world was created as a Divine Paradise. I want to see it as Paradise.

There are some things we must do before we can feel better and be healed. There has been nearly enough emphasis on showing each one who mourns truly loving consolation. We need loved ones to give us loving empathy and words of understanding. We may have had counseling. Perhaps we need to shed tears together. Many of us have untreated, thus unhealed, hearts. Heart attacks might end if we would hug another and speak words of heartfelt empathy to another.

1. LOVING EMPATHY. Empathy is not sympathy. It is living the other's sorrows and hurts, even illnesses of the body. If one is not able to empathize with another, one is not able to understand another–including his/her grief. We must learn to empathize with ourselves and others in order to be healed. Yes, I am sad. Yes, I am hurt and angry beyond words. Yes, I rightly feel so upset I can see myself with blood oozing from every orifice, including the pores of my skin. This is because I see myself beaten and abused, almost to death, by others. I know why now why some have sought to take their own lives. Yes. I can understand why even one who does not desire or approve of suicide can want to walk into the ocean and not return. Inquisitors and demons are still with us. Spiritual war still rages. We are like lambs led to the slaughter in this Hell world called Aviche in the East. Yes, many have suffered so many awful sorrows they feel like Job. Not all have sinned. Some were the abused and discarded angels and saints of this world. If you cannot feel for yourself or others, please find someone to help you do so.

Go to a loved one and with your whole heart be able to sincerely say "I am so sorry for all that has happened to you in this lifetime. I wish we could have a healing time of sharing and prayer." Many souls have gone through hideous things in their destinies which have left huge, unhealed and festering, sores. These sores need to be cleansed before they can heal. First is love. Love has not been given to many when they went through awful traumas in their lives. If one goes to war or to outer space, debriefings are required to help the returning adventurers recover and make their transitions back into daily life. Some people have had therapists, friends, and ministers. Most have needed and desired loving nurturing and consolations. How can one console when one has never been consoled? This requires empathetic hearts, minds, and souls. Empathy is love. Consolation is needed and is very helpful. Empathy says with all truth, " I hurt and suffer with you. I know you must feel so brokenhearted over the loss of_________________. Let us pray and weep together over these terrible losses in your life." If we cannot feel for another's sorrows, we need to pray for empathy, which is living love one to another. Many of our people have been unjustly robbed of fathers, mothers, siblings, and, above all, spouses. In our orthodoxies, we have instead judged, ridiculed, and had little or no understanding for the broken hearts of those who lost beloved spouses to divorce. Also, this doesn't matter whether the partner was same or different gender. One is still dealing with a broken heart. Many of us are so hurt and damaged we have had little time to seek and find healing for ourselves. We must pray for the loving ability to attempt to love and to help others.

2. SORROW FOR OUR ERRORS. This is the beginning of wise things to do. If we have hurt anyone, let us become truly sorry for them and their hurt, even if we cannot condone or accept horrible deeds or words We must ask for forgiveness for our sins.

3. FORGIVENESS. We must forgive ourselves and others in order to be forgiven.

4. FORGETTING. This is the hard one. Forget to keep score. Love the one who made the mistake. Sometimes one needs to not completely forget evil, lest it again happen to others - even by the same one who perpetrated the first atrocity upon another.

5. MOURNING. It is necessary to mourn one for another. Let us take all our cares to our Lord in

6. PRAYER. Pray without ceasing for ourselves, others, and the world(s) as a whole. We need divine help and communion. From our concerted, ceaseless, ongoing prayers come

7. HEALING of all evils. This means we can be healed in minds, bodies and souls. We can be made whole and thereby are holy. We can then face life and live it more

8. ABUNDANTLY asking and receiving fullness and fruition of our life destinies. It is not our destiny to be so abused and punished. Many of us are worthy of punishment. It is a rule that the innocent are forced to suffer with the guilty. Too long has this been a planetary norm. It must change and end. It is time for separation from evil. We must choose whether we wish to suffer or to live abundantly. I choose abundant and blessed life of the Father/Mother/All That Is. I desire the Glory of God to be mine. Jesus came to bring us redemption, healing, forgiveness, forgetfulness of our sins, abundance and glory. I think it's time for us to live as if we were Children, Priests and Priestesses of God. Perhaps it's time for us to grow up and come of age so we are able to be ready for communion with Him.

8. GOD IS BLESSED AND LOVING. He is not as many have been taught. He came to give this world life and it more abundantly. The Father I know is not the evil, punishing, horrible God personified in many negative scriptures. He is love. He is goodness, sanity, truth. He is merciful and just. He is understanding as the Counselor of our souls. He is our Advocate. He is Wonderful. He is the Mighty King who is

indwelling in our hearts. He wishes to know and be with you as an Eternal Friend. He is Beloved.

All separations and polarizations, our war stances, must end. Lord Jesus help us all! Our Father is in abject horrible mourning over His children. My mother mourns the losses in her family. So do I. Happiness can be His and ours. Dear Holy One, please hear our prayers today, we pray. We seek you now even as we desire to know You better and to be with You in a better place. Let us begin to seek to know our other family members. And all of the Children said, "Amen", and joyfully accept Him into their hearts and lives as Savior, Lord and King. His teachers and messengers are first in this long Bridal Procession to the Marriage Supper of the Lamb, our joyous Reunion with the Father, the Three in One.

Dear Ones, let us love one another, even as He loves us. By so doing, we are His worthy and desirable Bride. There are many of us who long with great gushing tears for the time when the Creator and the Creation are again re-united. Too long have the Bride and the Bridegroom been preparing for their Marriage Feast. Too long have tears of longing for an end to the Separation coursed down our cheeks. Let us be Yours forever, Dear Father. Wipe the tears from the faces of Your children and take us Home. There is no place like Home!

Scripture Messages:
Malachi 2:17
Malachi 3:1-5; 3:13-18
Malachi 4:2 & 3
Malachi 4:16

102. THE CARES & TROUBLES OF EVERYDAY LIFE

We are His children and we want to love Him with all of our hearts, minds, bodies and souls. We are very concerned that all would know Him and be His. We desire His will in all facets of our lives. We try to be filled with all the attributes of His divine nature and the gifts of His Spirit.

Instead of ongoing, continual days and nights of victories in Jesus, we find ourselves overcome with very real obstacles and fears. Our testings and trials rob us of the joy of our salvation. We feel the glory of God all around and upon us and then we go into the blackness of the oppressive cares of this life. Our concerns are so grave they make us wonder if we'll be able to survive the economic fears as well as the global weather and war conditions. The oppressive fears are real. They are so real it is very hard to hear the still small voice of reason that reminds us "Perfect love casts out all fears." Fear is bypassed by mind numbing terror. Horrors of loss of vehicles, homes, possessions arise. We feel we are alone and trapped in a black universe of depression. Panic has overcome us. We are practically catatonic and immobilized with fears. We are frightened we will not be able to function to accomplish even the basic chores of our lives, much less be entrepreneurs with insufficient income. Our fears become mountainous. We begin to think of all the things which could happen to us in our whole lives. At that point, futility sets in especially if we have no income from employment or inheritances. We feel like we are forgotten. We know others who were frightened were willing to do anything to make sure they and their loved ones are able to survive. Nothing else is more important.

We awaken in tears, write in tears, mourn and pray in tears. Life goes on. Blessings are ours. We must count them. We must seek the scriptures of the ancient teachers of wisdom. We must remember to awaken and to give thanks for all that is ours. We must "Count our blessings, one by one" in order to "see what God has done." We cannot walk atop the huge "waves" of the cares people of that era. *First of all, he sent the retarded and mentally ill to the death camps*. Some of the next to go were any of those spiritual and religious people he felt might be able to thwart his powers. Others he hated were the Jews, the Gypsys, and all non-blue-eyed races he deemed to be racially inferior threats to his dreams of an Aryan Utopia. Millions of people lost their lives during his insane reign of terror during those Holocaust years.

We must ever be ready to guard and protect our innocents from the dangers of others and dangers of life if we look at the waves. We must "keep our eyes upon Jesus–look full in His glorified face". If we do so, we can truly walk through all the horrific and terrifying things of life knowing "the things of this life will soon be passed, in the light of His glory and grace." We must learn where our sources of power and praise exist. We must "put on a garment of praise for a spirit of heaviness; and life up our hearts in and prayer" to the Father. We must sing Hallelujah to the King.

Perhaps we were full of the Lord and the Father. Perhaps we were wishing to help to ease His mourning for the lost and dying. We wondered how we could do this. Instead, even as we thought such concerned thoughts for our Father, the fears for the cares of this life assailed us. Do we see patterns of attack here? Are we pawns to the fear lords of this world or do we reject all fear and walk across the seas of life victoriously keeping our trustful gaze upon Him? We must decide we will conquer our fears by our faith in Him. Faith is His gift to us. Take it and use it like a Shield. See Ephesians 6:10-19. Use the Word of God as your Sword of the Spirit. Your Breastplate is Righteousness. Your Helmet is your Salvation.

Concentrate upon reading and studying what the Lord Jesus said and did. Read a red letter edition of the New Testament. Be careful of dogmatic views and orthodoxies which are questionable. Many hands have had worldly interests in the preparation of this Holy Bible (aka: Holy Book). Do not argue over words if you do not know what they mean. Study and seek wisdom. Be concerned about your own soul first. Then you may worry about the sins and souls of others. You must personally know Him and His teachings. Pray without ceasing to know Him. He is our Treasure. Ask Him to lead and guide us into wisdom regarding our economic concerns.

Some of these may be beyond our control. Perhaps we are living under the control of others who may not be interested in the well being of us or our loved ones. We must be studious to learn about laws and politicians. We must attempt to cast our ballots for ethical and wise leaders. We can always attempt to obtain and retain our own powers over our own lives. We can pray without ceasing. We can attempt to conquer our ignorance and fears with His help. We can humbly realize we are His, but we are also His children in need of instruction. This knowledge should deter us from acting as if we are wiser, better, more holy or loved than others. Hypocrites and hypocrisy are not blessing Him. They are blessing themselves prematurely. They are an annoyance and a sadness to others who can only look to Heaven and say "Father, have mercy upon me. I'm simply Your fallible and humble servant." Some of us may never be his business managers or entrepreneurs. We are simply His loving children. We are those who teach of His wonderful wisdom, justice, mercy and love. We want everyone to know Him. We need Him to direct us as our money manager.

There are many things which separate our souls from His. Pride goes before a fall. Humility is a proper garment for a child of God. He tells us we are His family and friends. This is a great honor. However, let us not forget we are flesh. Let us not forget our proclivities to fall into error in our daily lives. Love is the Key to knowing the Father. Let us empathize with Him and His sorrows. If He weeps over us, perhaps we need to ask Him how we can become more obedient children. Let us take time this day, and each day, to give Him our repentant heart and soul. Let our hearts be full of loving adoration of the One who loves us, but who also sheds great tears of sorrow for us.

As we take time to adore Him perhaps the Shekinah Glory of God may fall upon us. We are told we have His protection even while we sleep. Perhaps, one morning we will awaken and find all of our cares and troubles of this life are gone. We will clearly see our fears as delusions given to us by evil spirits and people to alter our reality and relationship to Him. We must show Him we are loyal children who trust in Him to take care of all of our needs and concerns. Thus, as Jesus told us, we will become like His little Child. It is hard for some to love. Others have troubles being a child. A little child has no cares and concerns. Our Father cares for us.

103. "THE TERRORS THAT COMETH BY NIGHT"

There will be those who never have to awaken in the middle of the night beset by gut-rending concerns for the fact they cannot meet the financial needs of their families. In addition, there are no healthcare benefit programs for many of us. We are relegated to the heap of those who are unworthy and unable to survive in our advanced society.

Many years ago, when I was a new adult university student in the late 1970's, my beloved Psychology Professor, James D., told us a nation is judged by the ways it does, or doesn't, provide for it's women, children, aged and disabled. At that time, I was the wife of a San Francisco Bay Area Certified Public Accountant. I was not a completely endangered woman at that time. Now I am.

I am now labeled and stereotyped as"Senior Citizen", aged 65, going on Medicare yet paying exorbitant fees for medical coverage. I was forced to draw my Social Security benefits at age 62 due to an almost fatal bout with a type of pneumonia not halted by my pneumonia shot. This was in January, 2001. In August, 2001, my beloved husband had a relapse into the throes of his disability. A few days later, our nation was attacked on September 11, 2001, by Islamic terrorists flying airliners into the World Trade Center in New York City. Eversince that traumatic national event, all our national budgetary funds have been channeled from the other needs of our citizens to wartime budgets for our War on Terror, including our Attack on Iraq, in the Spring of 2003.

At the time my dear husband again became ill, we applied once again for his former disability benefits since he is now too ill to work. The usual procedure is denial of the first request for benefits. Naturally, we were required to make an Appeal for Disability Benefits. However, my husband had been deemed to be disabled ever since he was a young man in his late teens or early twenties--over 25 years ago.

As a wife, mother, grandmother, and the daughter of a disabled mother in her late 80's, I am tired of being given the run around when I ask for basic benefits for clearly disabled people. I am brokenhearted over the plights of the poor in this nation. No other advanced nation in the global community makes its citizens become so frustrated, frightened, debilitated, and disabled before help is given--if at all.

As a sometime human rights activist, advocate for the homeless, student of Psychology and the Social Sciences, and an employee and Medi-Cal Eligibility Worker with Social Service and Mental Health

Departments for over 20 years of my 40+ years of full-time employment , I am very concerned for my beloved people, as well as for the unmet needs of ALL who unjustly slighted by these questionable services and benefits. This nation will be judged for it's heartless, unfeeling, lack of care for those who need help the most. There aren't enough statistitians to record the untimely suicides and deaths of whole families due to the mistreatment of the poor and needy. What of the lost, trapped, abused infants and children?

Some people must read and watch horrible living situations in order to attempt to know about the plights of the poor. I don't have to do so. I have worked with these situations. I now live as a lower class citizen in America, the land of the free and the home of the brave, along with decorated veterans of all the armed services, the aged, the children, the physically and mentally disabled, and the homeless - due to the shameless greed of many of our citizens.

There are many people who do not yet see life as it is for us, and will also, God forbid, be similarly for themselves. Their medical, dental, eye care, and prescription drug needs will also be unmet in their older ages, IF someone does not take responsibility for these needs NOW. We wonder how many members of the Senate and Congress have little, if any, real awareness or concern for the plights of the everyday disadvantaged American citizen. Their own incomes and benefits are insured for their lifetimes even as many of ours are not. If they have time to do so, perhaps some of them will notice the plights of their own parents and siblings.

Personally, I am very tired of waking up in the middle of the night, trying not to be overcome with blind panic because we have low income and no benefits. We are truly fit to become Soylent Green. We, who are deemed and labeled as 'Worthless Eaters' by those elitist thinkers, may prove to be the best of America's assets and benefits just by 'being there' for everyone to use for their own experiential learning and growth. However, I, for one, was never a good masochist. Ever have I told my children this fact. I believe it is time for all of us to do something by standing up as a group and shouting, "I'm mad as Hell, and I'm not going to take it anymore!" The movie was correct. We need to get gutsy and DO something to help ourselves and others. We need to become actively supportive of our advocacy groups. WE MUST DO SOMETHING. There's this old time saying "God helps those who help themselves". Sometimes the weak and ill, the aged and the little ones, cannot help themselves. We must help them, thereby helping ourselves and our grandchildren. In the Old Testament of the Bible we find Moses required others to help him hold up his arms to Heaven. Let us help each other to raise our arms to Heaven and our Great Counselor, Therapist, and Protector.

104. PREJUDICE

The Psychology of Prejudice is in force at this time in America. We're living the "don'ts" of such a textbook. It is an incredible time for one of us who have studied the dangers of prejudice.

Those who have studied about prejudice, genocide, ethnic studies, history and political science are not seeking to be labeled by some as "Humanists". We were seeking to learn what makes the world's people behave as they do to one another. These are very important topics in the social psychology of humankind. We must learn to overcome our ignorance and fears of those we do not understand. This is the behavior of the animal nature.

The Keys to Death are listed in the progressive order of their growth: Jealousy; Fear; Dehumanization of the "Other & Them"; Harassment & Abuse; and, finally, the generalized consensus of the right to Imprison, Institutionalize, and Destroy "Them" in the name of some national or religious cause. The end result is Death by Execution, War and/or Genocide. The final annihilation of the "Other" is Genocide of whole cultures and nations. Example: the white man's attempts to destroy the Native People in America starting with their families, tribes, languages, cultural and religious traditional values. Our U.S. Constitution was based upon the Native American laws on this continent. Theocracies and Racism are the Keys to Death of the Human Rights of All.

Seeking Truth and Living Love are the Keys to Life in the Spirit of the Father of All. Only by our obedience to His heartfelt desires can we stop His Tears. Let us seek Him. He will lovingly teach us His Ways for our world. We are told by Him "Perfect love casts out all fears." This is true. If we wish to shine as beacons to a dark world we must keep the Oil of the Spirit, freed of the cares and the trials of this world, in our Spiritual Lamps. Let us all put aside the darkness of ignorance and fears and live as the Lights of Christ in a darkened and fear filled world.

105. BAPTISM IN HIS TEARS

Loving is not all romance and joy. Loving is to become one with one's beloved even in sorrow. When we received our spiritual baptism in His great and unbelievable capacity to love us, we were in awe and adoration. When we become close enough to Him to share His sorrow, we are still in awe adoration of our incomprehensible all-encompassing compassionate and empathetic Father in the Son, through the Comforter, the Holy Spirit, the Shekinah. If we are a child of the Holy Ones, we are part of their suffering, as well as their love. This is how we become One in the Spirit. Not only are we enraptured by Divine Love, but we are also enraptured and in awe of Divine Suffering.

It is only by love's strong powers that we are able to bear the sufferings of one another. This is how He was able to come to Earth to become One with humankind, to become at-onement and our atonement so that we can be set free from our bondage to suffering and pain. He transmuted our sin to wholeness. He took our pain upon Himself because He loves us so very much. We are His family. We are His Beloved, and He has become completely Our Beloved Lord by His great sacrifice in order to again bring us Home to Himself. Instead of a Garden of Delights, He entered into this world where we learn first hand of pain, sadness, suffering, loss and grief. We are hungry, cold, angry, hurt, jealous, abused and harassed and cursed with all manner of awful plagues and torments of mind, body and soul. He loved us enough to enter this world with us in order to let us know He wants to show us how to be free to be His own in all oneness of Spirit, mind, body and soul. He is our Beloved and we are His at long last when we release ourselves unto His loving healing ministrations. He is the Great Counselor, Great Physician, and Beloved Bridegroom.

A human husband suffers the birth pangs of his wife. So, too, does our Beloved suffer as we suffer. Empathy comes from love. Love can enter the doorway to all types of suffering because it is strong enough "to boldly go where none have dared to go". It takes love and boldness to venture forth from the womb to become a dweller on this strange planet. He comes in human form over and over again in order to finally conquer death and the grave. In the old hymn, we sing the words "Love lifted me. When nothing else could help, love lifted me." This is so true. His love lifted us from the darkness of ignorance, lies, jealousy, crimes of all types, loneliness and shame, horror, panic and death. "Death where is your sting?" Christ tells His Beloved that death, hell, the grave, and darkness will all disappear. He will become our Light. We will bask in the Light of the Son.

If we, as fallible and frail human beings are able to love enough to draw the suffering, pain and illnesses of loved ones, and even strangers, to ourselves, how much more can our Beloved Lord take our sorrows, sins, and sufferings upon Himself, as the Anointed One? Have we not an unbelievably wonderful Savior who heals us from our infirmities? True. He is truly our Beloved. We are bound together with Him by His great love. He then becomes completely at-one, in deep communion, as our own flesh. He bears the wounds of our incarnations upon His own flesh. It is possible for us to bear the wounds of others upon our flesh if we become full of Him and His Love. Love draws all unto us, to itself, to Him. We become truly His. We become infused with His Love and the Power of Love. There is Power in the Blood of the Lamb. Suffering is the last bond of this Earth plane to be destroyed. When we have conquered all fear, lying, death and suffering, we will be free from all of our tears. When He is freed from the bondage to this planet, the Father will no more weep for the suffering of His Children. We are told we are no longer strangers. We are His own Children. A parent mourns with a child. So, too, does our Heavenly Parent(s) mourn for our hurts and sorrows.

It is important that we mourn with our children, and they with us. This is our family bond of love in action. If we have no love, we have no empathetic bonds with one another. We are strangers. We must draw close to one another in love, thereby sharing with each other's needs and sorrows, as well as knowing the joys and blessings, which we share with those not of our close family units. Families share everything if they have love enough to dare to be empathetic and close as a family unit.

Many of us have been divided by different factions and cares of life. Let us overcome all divisions and separations by His love. He will help us to share, to care, to commune as we did before the enemies of peace and love came between us. We will not be conquered by fears...many of which are contrived by those who wish to keep us divided and apart from His Love.

We are His Beloved. Let us once again become Beloved to each other–even as our Beloved Father enjoins us to so do at this time. Even more must we seek Him, as we see the darkness, the fires, the floods, and evil spreading tentacles around the world. Let us spread bonds of love, peace, joy and faith around our beautiful Earth. Loving is sharing even sufferings, as well as joys, with one another. We must be part of the Holy Family.

Suffering will end. We will again walk together "In the Still of the Evening", communing as only loved ones do. Daring to love is not easy. Sometimes we enter into grave dangers when we dare to love. If we do not take a chance on love, we will never taste its sufferings. We will also never taste the delicious fruits of love. We will never drink ambrosia with our Beloved in His Garden of Heavenly Delights.

This Message is one written in the blood, sweat and tears of Earthly sufferings. It is also written because we also know of His Divine Love. Love conquers all suffering and strife. Wars will end. The Earth and human life may be changed. The Way, the Truth, the Light and Love never change. We are the immortal lost souls He has never stopped loving. Paradise was thought to have also disappeared and could not be regained. His is our eternal Father. He is all in all. He is our Beloved and we are His forever.

106. THE LORD'S FAST-- ISAIAH 58

The Fast Of The Natural Human

Shout it aloud. Do not hold back. Raise your voice like a trumpet. Declare to My people their rebellion and to the House of Jacob their sins. For day after day they seek Me out; they seem eager to know My ways as if they were a nation that does what is right and has not forsaken the commands of its God. They ask Me for just decisions and seem eager for God to come near them. " Why have we fasted, they say, and you have not seen it?" "Why have we humbled ourselves and You have not noticed?"

Yet on the day of your fasting, you do as you please and exploit all your workers. Your fasting ends in quarreling and strife and in striking each other with wicked fists. You cannot fast as you do today and expect your voice to be heard on high. Is this the kind of fast I have chosen, only a day for a man to humble himself? Is it only for bowing one's head like a reed and for lying on sackcloth and ashes? Is that what you call a fast, a day acceptable to the Lord?

The Fast Of The Lord

Is not this the kind of fasting I have chosen, to loose the fetters of injustice and untie the cord of the yoke, to set the oppressed free and break every yoke? Is it not to share your food with the hungry and to provide the poor wanderer with shelter–when you see the naked, to clothe him, and not turn away from your own flesh and blood? Then your light will break forth like the dawn, and your healing will quickly appear; then your righteousness will go before you, and the glory of the Lord will be your rear guard. Then you will call, and the Lord will answer; you will cry for help, and he will say: Here am I.

If you do away with the yoke of oppression, with the pointing finger and malicious talk, and if you spend yourselves in behalf of the hungry and satisfy the needs of the oppressed, then your light will rise in the darkness, and your night will become like the noonday. The Lord will guide you always, he will satisfy your needs in a sun-scorched land and will strengthen your frame. You will be like a well-watered garden, like a spring whose waters never fail. Your people will rebuild the ancient ruins and will raise up the age-old foundations; you will be called Repairer of Broken Walls, Restorer of Streets with Dwellings.

If you keep your feet from breaking the Sabbath and from doing as you please on my holy day, if you call the Sabbath a delight and the Lord's holy day honorable, and if you honor it by not going your own way and not doing as you please or speaking idle words, then you will find your joy in the Lord, and I will cause you to ride on the heights of the land and to feast on the inheritance of your father Jacob. The mouth of the Lord has spoken.

107. THE SHEEP & THE GOATS-- MATTHEW 25:31-46

"When the Son of Man comes in His glory and all the angels with Him, He will sit on His throne in heavenly glory. All the nations will be gathered before Him, and He will separate the people one from another as a shepherd separates the sheep from the goats. He will put the sheep on His right and the goats on His left.

Then the King will say to those on His right. Come, you who are blessed by My Father; take your inheritance, the kingdom prepared for you since the creation of the world. For I was hungry and you gave me something to eat, I was thirsty and you gave me something to drink. I was a stranger and you invited me in. I needed clothes and you clothed me. I was sick and you looked after me, I was in prison and you came to visit me.

Then the righteous will answer Him, Lord, when did we see You hungry and feed You, or thirsty and give You something to drink? When did we see You a stranger and invited You in, or needing clothes and clothing You? When did we see You sick or in prison and go to visit You?

The King will then reply, I tell you the truth, whatever you did for one of the least of these brothers of mine, you did for Me.

Then He will say to those on His left, Depart for Me, you who are cursed into the eternal fire prepared for the devil and his angels. For I was hungry and you gave me nothing to eat, I was thirsty and you gave me nothing to drink, I was a stranger and you did not invite Me in, I needed clothes and you did not clothe me, I was sick and in prison and you did not look after Me.

They also will answer, Lord, when did we see you hungry or thirsty or a stranger or needing clothes or sick or in prison, and did not help You?

He will reply, I tell you the truth , whatsoever you did not do for one of the least of these, you did not do for Me.

Then they will go away to eternal punishment, but the righteous to eternal life."

"Whatever you did for one of the least of these brothers of mine, you did for Me."

AUTHOR'S RESEARCH NOTES–THE TEARS OF OUR BELOVED FATHER

108. "IT'S A JUNGLE OUT THERE."

How far has humankind progressed since the dawn of creative evolution? Fear, aggression, hatred, violence, territorial behaviors are still deeply part of the human psyche.

No matter how well one is educated, one must guard against acting exactly as our primitive ancestors.

Fear is the key to all ignorance. Ignorance is fear. Avidya. Ignorance. This makes one a danger to one's self and to others. Until we conquer it, we shall never be able to escape this plane of existence. We are to be Seekers of Wisdom. Wisdom frees us from sin and ignorance.

No matter how esoteric and enlightened, one must conquer fear. Fear is not of the divine–however one defines That Ineffable Other(s)/All That Is. Fear of the "Other" is not enlightenment. The truth shall set us all free to love, understand, and to eventually BE part of All That Is. Love of Him and His ways gives us love for our neighbor. Love is caring enough to be open to learn all that we must in order to be set free of all prejudice and hatred.

One sees the fear in all of humankind's spiritually enlightened religious and political groups as well as within the radical cults and sects. There is something infantile, animalistic, territorial, frightened, and atavistic within even the most modern psyche. Human beings tend to seek and require acceptance by "A Group". Therefore, I see we will never progress beyond fear of one another. Everyone else–the Other–is different from us and our "Group". Different is not bad. Our God is Manifold. He created a diversely symbiotic world. We are all one in His Spirit no matter the color of our skin, or our pathways to Him. We are all His Children. Wisdom and education teaches us that we can truly find holy unity out of great diversities of cultural, racial, and even religious differences. The Key is Love. He is Love. He is our Key to Peace on Earth.

I thought of myself as theosophical until I realized to some this is simply another group of those who must form their own small group in which to again establish their own belief system base. We are theosophical, inferring, at first knowledge, "we are accepting of all others", since theo=Divine or God and sophia=wisdom, both of which combined mean godly wisdom. It is a beautiful, eclectic, symbiotic, manifold word which encompasses more than many members are capable of understanding. It is a name to die for, and they have. However, if we must die, let it not be for the cause of an organization, but for the Way, the Truth, the Light, and far MORE...MORE THAN WE CAN NOW ENCOMPASS. We must be set free of ignorance and lies in order to see the light of truth and enlightenment, which is not based upon ONE in-group's biases. The name is beautiful and the word is wonderful! Let us love one another.

The Holy One tells us "To seek truth is to seek God". To seek truth is to find wisdom. What more can one desire? He is our Treasure. He is Wisdom, Love, Go(o)dness, (W)hol(i)ness, Beauty, Sanity, Mercy, Joy, Peace, Temperance/Self Control, and Faith. He is the reason those of us who know Him as our Beloved, are deeply dedicated to Him and His teachings. He is our Beloved. He is the reason we follow Him as His disciples, His younger brothers and sisters, all of us making up the family of the "Manifold" Father. Wisdom is sometimes called the Shekinah, Sophia, the feminine appellations of the Divine Nature and Spirit of the Divine Father/Mother/All That Is. How can we define a Living Spirit? We are eternal spirits who are part of His Spirit. In order to know Him, we must become like His Spirit. There is no question of this. It is an Absolute. Absolute surrender to Him and His Will and Ways is the choice of each of His Children who have free will to make our own choices. This can be good if we are good and obedient children. Material world children must learn obedience to wise, holy and noble earthly parents as training for obedience to the Divine Father. Children love to obey those who personify Him. When I was left alone with two small children I began to prayerfully wonder what I would do with them as they became teenagers. The still small voice of Lord said "If you are fair and loving all will be fine." What a comfort those words were to me over the years when the three of us walked as a family "one day at a time" with Him. He was holding and carrying us through the many adventures, testings, trials, and blessed times in those formative years of our walk with Him. He truly was closely walking hand in hand with us, supporting, loving, nurturing, and molding our souls to love and adore Him, as well as to desire above all else to be His obedient and willing Children.

Not all have such a Family. It is a great Gift to know the Treasured Parent who also is the author and finisher of our Faith in His Divinity, as our Lord, Savior, as well as being Father God. He is all that He personifies in His Beloved Son Jesus. Jesus came to Earth, choosing to incarnate in human form, in order to know His Beloved, those of His siblings who are also of His Divine Family. He suffered and died for our sins (errors) we make in our lifetimes. He also came simply because He couldn't bear to have us suffer without Him and His understanding and comforting Presence being eternally with us to lovingly protect us from sin and danger. To know Him is to love Him. How can one not love all that is Good? He is able to save and keep even the "least of these".

Some of us have been called out to truly walk, talk and live among the "least of His", the beloved ones He came to bring Home to Himself. He came not to the hypocrites, pharisees and those who are lost in their own worlds of material values–even in their own religious congregations. They shall have their rewards in this world.

The Sheep who have gone astray are not only in the "highways and byways". He will find His invited guests for His Wedding Feast. There are also those of His Beloved Ones who, out of fear and their desire to be a member of a church, are lost in them. Some of these pseudo religious institutions have grown fat off the blood of the innocents. Souls have been stifled, stymied, trapped and lost while seated within the confines of dwellings made by men and ruled by thieving ministers of the Gospel of Our Good Shepherd. Oftentimes, sheep are very gullible, slow, fearful, and easily led to their deaths by predators. There are those who are predators who seek to infiltrate even the houses of God's people. They seek the Children of God, who are left like innocent and unaware lambs to be caught and devoured.

We must seek Wisdom. Wisdom is God. He never told us to forget to seek Wisdom. Indeed, we need to seek Him and His wisdom even more as we see there is little time left before the Day of the Lord. He promised He would never leave nor forsake us, "even until the End of Time". He has kept His promise. However, many "Signs are in the Heavens", and the "Day is far spent". The signs are upon the Earth and are seen in the Heavens. "All is now ready." He is seeking His Beloved.

His Beloved Sheep are lost. Many of them have gone astray even while seated in the pews of their own churches. They have gone to sleep, even as His disciples fell asleep while guarding Him as He prayed in the Garden of Gethsemane. Not all are asleep. Many are wakeful. There are also those who have not been able to fit themselves completely into the molds of this world and society. One of the ways mental illness is defined is by the ability of the person to fit into the mold of the social norms of society. In this society, there may be many who cannot follow Christ and bend their knees to the evildoers, many of whom lead flocks astray. Flocks like to be good sheep. They do not wish to be sheep who stray and require the sheep dog to run after them barking at their heels. It is easier, as well as safer, more cozy and comfy, to be a good sheep...even if one must have an unworthy and unprotective shepherd. However, the Sheep of His Fold recognize His Voice. This is the Key to finding the Good Shepherd. If we know His Voice, we will follow His Commandments. They do not always lead us to membership in a religious organization. We are His Temple if He indwells our spirits–lest any man/woman should boast of holiness by attendance upon Him in a building made with human hands. He has made and indwelt us. We must therefore be holy, even as He is holy. Wholeness and holiness go together. He is Holy. He desires, expects and requires us to also seek to know Him and His Holiness. If need be, we are "Called Out" to walk alone with Him. When we are shown where His People dwell, only then can we affiliate with that Sheepfold. His Sheep know His Voice. "Be ye wise. In fact, be ye wise as a serpent, yet harmless as a dove." Wisdom and peace go together. There are many who are living as "Called Out Ones". I know they are out there living in the highways and byways. I have worked, lived, and dwelt among them as well as living in the household of the rich who begrudge us the least of their possessions, even if we serve them. Those of us who sometimes have chosen to take less, rather than to take too much, are also the Sheep of His Fold. There are many of the "least of these" who are the Lost Sheep who have been left stranded without good shepherds to care for their needs. Our Good Shepherd has never left nor forsaken us. We have been ignored, even slandered and libeled, because we will not follow other than The Good Shepherd. There are also ones of us who are too ill and disabled to be able to find a sheepfold. We are lost because those evildoers decided to rob them of their rightful inheritances due to selfish decisions of those who care not for the widows, orphans, disabled, aged, women and children, mentally ill, the veterans of many wars. Indeed, they have been robbed of proper medical, spiritual, emotional and educational care. Without education and medical care many beloved souls have been left without jobs and homes. Many in this land do not realize how very close these same fates are to themselves. Be not deceived. Anyone can become ill, poverty stricken and very needy, without funds to replace teeth and eyeglasses, without dental and medical care of all types. Wealthy real estate entrepreneurs have become rich because they practiced the perversely obscene business rules of a society which adjudges their behavior to be sound and sane. They fit the social norm of this planet which is sometimes called Hell. They are too obsessed with their selfish goals in life to know or care if they are His or not. Yet, all alone, cold, hungry, ill, unclad and unhoused, exist those who love Him and His ways, His wisdom, His truths, and are the "least" of His Beloved Sheepfold. He said He came to save the Lost, the Poor who are also poor in their spirits (if not in their hearts), who are needy, thirsty, hungry, ill, poorly dressed and perhaps have no real home of their own. They live among us. Some walk among us as the Invisible Men and Women, of all races, religious pathways, cultures, languages, and the world, even as Thieves (who shared crosses with Him), some carried beggar bowls as the sanyasim (the Holy Beggars). Some had lost teeth, eyeglasses, their minds and their souls. Some of the "least of these" consciously know they are His examples to a sin-sick society steeped in treasures not of Heaven but of this material world.

One day I saw it as it was. By this time, I had realized about seeking His Treasures. However, I was literally led to stop at a very expensive department store in a wealthy suburb of one of America's most affluent cities. In His Spirit, I saw this store, like so many others in America and the wealthy cities of the world, as looking like a Pirate's Giant Treasure Chest full to the brim with precious stones, clothing, and all manner of wonderful treasures. Those who sought such treasures arrived at the doors of this Temple of Treasures in inordinately expensive automobiles, thus showing all who they were as worldly minded people, able to shop and to buy from this manmade Temple of Doom. I couldn't afford even one item that day. However, my gift for that day was to see it as the deadly trap set to ensnare the unwary within its devouring claws. So, too, will some try to claw their ways out of the morass of filthy greed, lust, and unspeakable sins. "Seek now whom you will serve. Will you serve God or Mammon?"

109. "THE LEAST OF THESE"

How would He begin? This is the question I have this pre-dawn morning. How can I tell it like it is in the ways He would like us to discuss this very special topic I know is so dear to the heart of my Beloved.

He loves "Them", even as He loves all of His beloved children. We are all His siblings and are part of His family at Home. Therefore, He came to bring them the same loving blessings He has for everyone.

Why are they different? They are different because they are His and He is the "Manifold God". They are living lessons. He came as "The Suffering Servant/King" in order to show us an example of His loving humility in action. Some of us have been very remiss in not noticing that He also was born in someone else's manger, among the beasts of the field. He had no place to lay His head. He tells us even the foxes have holes. He had no home of His own. Again, He has recreated the same situation. Indeed, it has never ended, for the poor have always been with us from the beginning of time. How can so many beloved Christians not see the example He gave us? It was not accidental He is portrayed as coming to Earth as the "Holy Beggar", like a Hindu sanyasim. He is the Prince of Peace, the Fisher King, the Beloved Savior, and many other beautiful names. He also knew very well the ways of the poor and needy, the disabled, the poor, the hungry, unwashed, unclothed and unhealthy poor and homeless.

In this modern age we must think once again of the end results of sin and greed. If we treat another in any way but a holy, caring and loving, sharing, fashion, we will have caused many to lose all they have and become homeless, sometimes very holy, beggars among us. This is what has happened in America the Beautiful, the land of the free, and the home of the brave. We have forgotten the all-seeing, all-knowing, God of Heaven. These are His Children, His kings and priests. Many of these have been unjustly treated. Many have died. They have agreed to suffer in order that we all may learn that we have helped to create their suffering. Therefore, let us not take too long to learn our lessons. They have been with us far too long. Many of them have died attempting to teach us the paths of righteousness. I believe many of us have been raising our hands to Heaven saying, "Please record this!" and "How long, Lord?" Judgment is already the heritage of America and we still seem to be unaware, unrepentant and, above all, blissfully ignorant and unashamed of the errors of our uncaring of our now acceptable daily attitudes and treatments of "Them", the silent, downtrodden, homeless among us. They have been among us since some slightly greedy entrepreneurs decided they wanted to make sure they had fine homes...sometimes more than one elegant home. Many lower income people were first squeezed out of their low rent homes onto the streets. This began in the 1970's. Wherever there were those who needed much, and cared not for their neighbor as themselves, someone else lost their lodging and became homeless. The Father saw and wondered how long this would continue. He wanted all His Children to love each other and live together in health and happiness. He had never taught them that greed is best. They listened to their own dark inner voice and said, "I need to have whatever I want, even if someone else suffers in order for me to have more than everyone else." It is obvious this selfish playmate is not a team player. There are no special treats given for bad behavior. Why, then, have we patted these nasty children as if they are good children. They do not deserve a sweet treat. There is also no way to sugar coat this inequitable and unholy situation in the self-proclaimed "Greatest Nation in the World".

110. OUR FATHER KNOWS

This is written for those who often feel alone and lost in a dark world and universe. It is my wish to let every person, young or old, know we are created and kept by a lovingly protective God who truly knows all about us, including our every thought, word, and deed. He is known by many names and by many who know His Voice and His Presence. He speaks to our hearts. He knows who we are and everything about us. He is our Heavenly Father. His are the all-seeing eyes, the all-hearing ears that are always aware of the needs, joys and fears of all of His created Children. As one of His earthly mothers, like an 'Older Earthly Guardian' of my children and grandchildren, I dedicate this book to all of those who lie awake in the darkness fearfully wondering if they are alone. I know we are not alone.

Why do I write these things for others to read? I guess I'm one of those who cannot bear to hear of a problem without attempting to fix it. Also, I am accustomed to writing my thoughts in order to organize my own thoughts and to make any needed change in my bad living habits.

Recently, a young man shocked me tremendously when he said,

"God doesn't know or care about what I do."

This statement immediately made me begin to think of all the memories from my own lifetime of walking as a Child of God, my Heavenly Father.

#1 - We only think, and sometimes even hope, God does not know anything about us.

Our scriptures tell us He knows if one hair falls from our head to the ground. He knows when a sparrow dies. Nothing is unknown to God.

The All-Seeing Eye (the Widget Eye) is a universal symbol of the all-seeing Eye of God, the all-sensing, feeling, aware Living God. He tells us we are His and that He cares about everything about us.

He tells us He loves us as His Children. We are part of His household as Sons and Daughters, who are also His Royal Priesthood. He tells us He misses our times together in The Garden of Eden. He wants to commune with us as His Friends.

Yet, too, He is as protective as the Mother Eagle who will carry her eaglets upon her own back as she flies high into the heavens. He has the all-seeing eye of the Eagle. He sees and knows all we do, say, or think.

He knows our hearts' secrets. If our hearts are indwelt by His Holy Spirit, He also knows that.

However, we are also safe from our very polite Savior and Our Heavenly Father.

"The Earth is the WALRUS of God's Eye." The word walrus is a combination of the words Whale and Horse, thereby signifying it is so huge and powerful as to mean it is like the two power symbols. It is the Power Station or Planet upon which He places His Eye, His caring, and help. Never fear for Big Daddy is here.

He knows and sees all, even as we have for uncounted centuries the others who watch us from the skies. He also knows all about those ancient astronauts, even as He care about the well being of those of His brave children who make flights to the stars and the Moon. He knows we see Mars, even as He sees all about us.

We tag wildlife, fish, family pets, and even our children with tiny microchips placed into their bodies in this century. This helps us to better chart their life patterns and to preserve and thereby save them from the unknown dangers they cannot know or sense.

We are not alone! I cannot stress this too strongly. We must be aware there are others who also watch us with intentions of harming us and our civilizations.

The Divine Records and sensing devices are of ancient origins. Our technological advances have all occurred in the 20th Century of this Fourth Sun/World of Earth's creations. We have had computerized records for little more than 50 years. There are those indigenous tribal people who have no idea of our continents, nations, cultures and religions. The United States is considered to be one of the modern world's socalled Super Powers among the nations of the world. These people have no idea of our God, who is known to the Western World by our own distinctly definitive names.

The Eagle is well known to the world's tribal people. It is known to most of the world's peoples as the Heavenly Bird which is said to find fish even if it is high in the heavens, where it is said it can fly to the very throne of the God. The All-Seeing Eye of the Eagle is thought to be able to see even the Deity in Heaven. If the Eagle can see Him, surely He can see us as well as the Eagle.

Another high flying, all-seeing bird is the Hawk. One night I was praying for world leaders. The Red-Tailed Hawk appeared to me that night in my dream. Its shrill scream awakened me to attempt to interpret my dream. Much to my surprise, I found that Hawk is the totemic bird of all world leaders. It intercedes for them with the Highest Leader in the Heavens, God. It's obvious to me that God heard and answered my heartfelt prayer for healing upon the Earth, beginning with divine guidance and protection for our world leaders.

These two huge raptor birds are the largest of the birds of the Kingdom of Flying Creatures. Seemingly, we do not see the fantastic flying creatures such as dragons, rocs, and garudas unless they appear in dreams.

The Whale is the largest of the denizens of the Sea Creatures. It is said to be like Sheol, deep in the Earth. The Horse is the human symbol of power of the Animal Kingdom, even as the Whale is the power of the Sea. Humans define the power of their vehicle engines by horsepower.

Thus, when I dreamed the Earth is the "Walrus" of God's Eye, He revealed to me one of His mysteries of our own planet being His recognized Power Center. Our beloved Planet Earth (aka Gaia) is evidently known as His own powerful living biosphere.

I believe all of the Creation is part of That Holy One we call God. We are all parts of Him. He tells us this in our own scriptures. The Immensity of the Manifold, All-Encompassing One is incomprehensible to us with our presently finite awarenesses and abilities.

Personally, I have no doubt that all my thoughts, deeds, and words are known by my Heavenly Father, as well as by my older brother, Jesus Christ. In fact, this awareness has been made so real to me I would not dare to even pretend to myself that we do not serve The Living God.

WAYS TO KNOW HE KNOWS

1. If we venture forth into dark realms and endanger our souls.
2. Worship Satan and devils. (Our God saved us from them.)
3. Give a place in our hearts to dark entities and become infilled with their spirits, not the Spirit of God.
4. Practice rituals intended to elicit the notice and connection to other spirits other than the Holy Spirit. Our God does not condone our divided attentions to other spirits besides His own.
5. Worship the world and all it offers. The God called Mammon rules those who sell their souls for all that is offered by the material world. They forget the teachings of Jesus and live as 'normal' human beings who are no longer infused by the Holy Spirit of God.

MY PERSONAL EXPERIENCE

My first meeting with Satan, or some other powerful demonic force such as himself, was when I was a young wife and mother in my early twenties. I had joined and been baptized into a strongly cultic religious group.

Two of my family members had come to visit me to attempt to dissuade me from making further commitment to this church. We talked at length.

It was later when I went to the darkened back rooms of my home that I felt the "Presence of Supreme Evil".

I was understandably terror stricken and ran back to join the others. Evidently, I had attracted the notice of the evil ones because they had hoped to have my soul caught in the webs of the pathway I had mistakenly chosen as my own. Being lost forever in a spiritual labyrinth is not my desire for my life lest I become lost in it and lose my soul. I can attest to the fact that there are forces and powers as evil and as real as those of our Lord. After that beginning experience with evil personified, I can never again harbor a doubt there are evil entities dwelling in the midst of us - if not indwelling the fleshly tabernacles of our own bodies in which dwell our souls and minds. This is why I know exorcisms are as real, and as needed, as they were when our Master, Jesus, performed them upon those bound and entrapped by devils. In the case of the demoniac, the devils asked to be sent into the swine rather than be sent to Hell.

He came to set the captives free. This means ALL of us. Therefore, "be ye free in the powerful Name and Blood of Jesus!" If you need to be set free from demonic forces, call upon the assistance of those who know and seek healing for all from evil forces. We need not remain in bondage to those of darkness. Read Isaiah 58.

In July 10, 1967, I was a newly divorced young Christian mother with children five and seven years old. I was still living on a U.S. Naval Base in the middle of the Mojave Desert of California where my husband had been stationed as a Naval Aviator.

I had felt very sad and shy the day before at the Sunday church service. I felt I'd had the interpretation of a message given in tongues. There was no one else who came forth with the message.

It was the next morning while preparing breakfast for my little ones when I silently prayed to Jesus to be given the the Message I had not given the day before.

Suddenly, I had a mountain of words piling up as if behind a dam ready to be released down a spillway. I grabbed an empty stenographer pad and I began to write at top speed for that day and several others. I still receive inspired messages from the Lord. Perhaps it is because of my many years of communications with Him that He has become my Beloved Best Friend. I have also written Messages from Him in a book which I have entitled *"Beloved"*.

The point I wish to make is that "He heard my silent prayer in my mind!" It doesn't need to be a verbalization to get His attention, and His answers, to our prayers. When I received the book-sized "Garden Message" from God in 1967 I was so shocked I simply closed the three steno pads and carefully stored them for the next 35+ years. My life became a very busy worldly life. It was not until 1985 when I again began "a closer walk" with the Lord once again.

I must again state that He heard my prayer in 1967. He remembered my prayer request, the huge body of writings, and me. He remembered I had made a Promise. We are told to never make a promise unless we intend to keep it. This is truly the message I got from the Lord, because by May, 2001, I finally realized He had truly meant I was to give that requested "Message" to those who need to hear it. He had not forgotten any part of our communications in 1967. He had patiently waited for me to become an older wife who had grown children. Thus, I was able to have the time to listen to His Voice and to perform the work it requires to publish His Message abroad. I cannot stress strongly enough of how He values our heartfelt communications, our love, and our loyalty to Him and His Message of Salvation. This is part of The Great Commission He gave us when He ascended to the Father.

He asked us to "Feed My Sheep". We are also to become like Fishers of Men. Read the Fisher King Grail stories, as well as the Holy Scriptures. In other words, if we are willing to do His work, He truly wishes to hold us to our promises given. We serve and commune with a Living Heavenly Father/God. He will remind you, one way or another, of your relationship. Time is nothing to Him. Much to my shocked surprise, I found and now strongly believe He has a memory longer than an elephant's memory.

ANOTHER BIG PRAYER HEARD & ANSWERED

It was early in the 1970's when I again thought I needed to pray to Him but I forgot to ask as a Daughter of a Kingly Father. I was weeping for formy children and myself never foreseeing that a choice without asking the Will of my Father was not an acceptable plea.

I learned a gravely hard lesson. One must be bravely willing to ask for the Divine Will for any part of our lives. We have forgotten that we are His Children, His Priests and Friends. We do not realize we are not to make careless choices in our lives. We are also the Temples in which His Spirit dwells, if we come from spiritually active families, and have made promises to love and to serve the Living God.

The message I got from this real life experience is that He hears and answers our prayers, even if we do not pray carefully, or with Him in mind at all. God does know us and our ways. He knows all about us because He created us.

No one will ever love us as much as does our Heavenly Father. He is the most nurturing of parents. As Earthly parents, like older Earthly guardians of our children, we have our ears and eyes continuously attuned to the cries and needs of our own babes. No human being is more just, fair, merciful, caring and loving than is our Father in Heaven.

Our Heavenly Father is also the unquestionably best when it comes to being a Counselor, Therapist, Advocate and Attorney, Judge, Jury, the Master of all paths to Him, Who knows those of All Truths and Faiths. He is the Giver of the Gift of Faith. If we are Seekers of His Truth, He will give us Truth and thereby set us free to know Him as Friend, Parent, Savior, and Creator. I have no doubt He is my All-In-All God/Goddess/ All That Is.

He owns "Cattle on 10,000 hills...", as well as being Creator of this planet and those of the Cosmos. He is the ultimate Landowner of real estate! Who is more wealthy than our God?

He also created and understands all the many holy laws of integrity and ethical ownership of real properties of all the business worlds of all that is. He also knows the terrible dangers faced by His Children from the sins of greed, lust, fear of poverty and loss, and of rulership of others. The combination can cause even His nicest and most holy Child to go astray into the evils of the god Mammon. Mammon can take over rulership of business tycoons causing them to cheat and exploit their workers, their communities, this world's peoples in all types of vile ways. Many people have not read, or may have forgotten what they read, of the messages of healing and rescue for the poor and needy in the Holy Scriptures. That is why it is so very important to read and to study "What Jesus said and did." If we do not study to show ourselves approved, He will be forced to tell us, "Depart from Me, for I never knew you. You are workers of iniquity." (If we are not fair, just and truthful, we are none of His.) *He told us He wished us to prove our love for Him by following His teachings.*

We surely do not wish to become insane due to the mindless and careless misuse of our powerful God-given powers and gifts. *Read about King Nebuchednezzar in the Book of Daniel.*

Lust for vast political or economic powers can cause even the most beautiful of souls to become ensnared in a selfish world where self-empowerment reigns before their love of God's Ways and His Will. These selfsame Spirit filled Souls can become filled by evil spirits. They can become the worst of tyrannical rulers and even warlords. The innocent virtuous can be stymied and stifled into utter frustration by the evils of this world. However, Father God does listen to the prayers of the virtuous, whom He came to guide, guard and to save as His own.

The world of the altruistic (selfless) and peace-loving souls would not be run as this world is functioning at this time. These are those who want nothing more intensely than to have the Kingdom of the Holy One ruling and reigning upon Earth. These are the Seekers of Truth and those who desire peaceful rapport within themselves and their own households, as well as Peace On Earth Good Will to All, and Love from and for God, ourselves and our neighbors, even as we love ourselves. If we have no love for ourselves, we cannot have extra love to share with others. We start by going to the God of Love for Love. If we serve Mammon, we will not be filled with God's Divine Agape Love. We may be filled with the love of Narcissistic Self Love, or even Eros the Romantic Love God. We may even have huge amounts of Filial Love for our families.

Agape is the Highest Unconditional Love for all that is Holy. God is Love. Therefore, be infilled with His Spirit and dwell forever in His boundless, freely offered, Love for all humankind. You are His Child. He loves you, and all of us, with love too great to be understood, much less described herein. Love is wonderful. Let us be baptized in His Love.

God hates Lies and the making of any type of untruths. We must be honest in scrutinizing our own intentions of heart, mind, and soul. Honesty with ourselves is very important. We do not wish to become a child of Belial, the Prince of Liars.

For these was the Lake of Fire prepared.

Insanity, Lies, False Accusations and Accusers, Slander, Libel, Gossip, Gluttony, Thievery, Murder and Mayhem, Arguments and Quarrels, and Wars, are not the True Nature of the Divine. *Read Galatians 5, in the New Testament, to discern between the behaviors of the 'Natural' and the 'Godly' person. Read also the Beatitudes of Jesus' Sermon On The Mount to know "Peacemakers will be called the Children of God".*

Much as with the martial arts of the Zen Patriarch and Master Bodhidharma, self-defense is taught in order to avoid and to survive brutal attacks. However, as with even Peaceful Warrior Prayer People, sometimes even these defense masters can be stronger than the attacker realizes. Our defenses are strong in His Spirit, which is never to be underestimated for prowess.

Jesus Christ also answered many of His accusers with a gently inscrutable Zen Koan-type question. Human beings were not ready to understand Him, as the Cosmic Theanthropic God incarnated in the flesh of a human being.

There are still many who would again attack Him and denounce His Perfected Teachings as blasphemy. They didn't know Him then and there will be those now He will not know as His own. They are still as lacking in wisdom, truth, and love as they were then. The prince of this world is still wreaking havoc with the souls of human beings. He still tells us, "Listen before it is too late."

I know without any doubt that He knows, hears, sees and smells all the evils of humankind. The All-Seeing Eye never slumbers nor sleeps. Neither is He deaf or dumb.

He still *Speaks* to our hearts, minds, and souls, even as He *Hears* and *Sees* us and all our intentions and thoughts even before we know the desires of our own hearts and souls. He also wants our souls to be a "sweet savor" or smell to His nostrils. He tells us He will spew us out of His mouth or nostrils if we say we are "holier than thou". Jesus showed us how He hated pharisees and hypocrites.

As one can see, even the scriptures speak to us of the Five Senses of the Divine who tells us He is that I am. He also comes to us in the God/Man form of His Son Jesus Christ, our Lord and Savior.

He is still the Living God who loves and ministers to His own created Living Family of this world. He also says He has Sheep which are not of our pastures. What might that mean? Let us ponder and reason together. This is one of those bigger, more mysterious and intriguing questions to be pursued prayerfully as an honest Seeker of Truth and the Master. "Seek and ye shall find, knock and it shall be opened unto you."

There is also no way to escape the love, the beauty and the holiness (wholeness) of our Creator God.

"Holy and worthy of praise is He. Praises to His Holy Blessed Name!"

When I was a newly-born Christian attending a Pentecostal Christian church in the Mojave Desert of California, I heard lots of people say "The Lord said this"..."The Lord told me that"...and other statements like these. They made me very interested in being one to whom God speaks. At that time, I felt very unaware and stupid about such a topic. I became convinced I needed to learn to know the "Voice of the Lord". I prayed endlessly to know His Voice.

Later, I learned all of these impressions were from Him - His special telepathic message to my mind and soul, sometimes felt as a thought, or even as a still, small, voice. He wants us to desire to seek Him in order to find Him, and to know His Voice. In regard to our relationship to Jesus Christ, the only begotten, firstborn, Son, our older Brother, and Savior, we are told we hear His Voice as our Great Shepherd. We are called the Sheep of His Pasture.

We may receive messages clearly in the middle of the night, while we sleep, or to awaken us to learn of things He wants to share with us. We could also be awakened to keep us safe from all types of dangers. Sometimes we'll be given messages by our Guardian Angel/s. We are guided and protected by The Holy Spirit, God the Father, Jesus Christ and His Angels.

When we receive one of these personalized messages they are unforgetable and one would never again doubt that God is really the Living God. He has never changed. Human beings have efficiently, carelessly, and unthinkingly written Him out of their highly technologically modern hearts and their lives. He has never left us. Jesus told us He would be with us even until the End of Time and the End of the World, as we now know it. After all, He is the Creator of this Matrix we call Earth Life. He created all that is and ever shall be. He knows of all dimensions, worlds, people, and all the beings and creatures of the universe. He is the all-time Head Scientist, Physicist, Mathematician, Geologist, Counselor, Business Expert, and Advocate, as well as the Chief of Divine Police of the Earth and the Cosmos.

He also told us He would send the Comforter, the Holy Spirit, to bear witness to Him, to counsel and to comfort us, after He had to leave us here on Earth when He returned to the Father in Heaven. He told us to tarry and we still tarry to be completely infilled with His Holy Spirit in order to be able to obtain the Gifts of His Holy Spirit as are recorded for us in II Corinthians 14. As the Children of God, these are our rightful Gifts as His disciples and priests. We are born again into the Holy Family of God, by our rebirths in the Holy Name of Jesus Christ, the Savior of the souls of this world. He is said to be the "Firstborn of many brethren (and sisters)". We are His brothers and sisters in the Family of God.

We were created to bless God, the Earth and Heaven, and each other.

Where have we gone awry in our pathways? We must constantly look at ourselves to make sure we have not become tainted with the gifts of Mammon, rather than the Holy Spirit of God.

Jesus tells us we can discern which souls are those of the Children of God by their Love, and the attributes of His own Spirit (spiritual values and nature) in their lives.

We must not be duped into lethargy or the acceptance of lies from spirits and spiritual forces not of Father God's Holy Spirit. We are to attempt to learn and to live like Jesus. He is our perfect example of how to live as a Child of God. We are told we must "Study to show ourselves approved (by God), a workmanship which needeth no correction" (from our Heavenly Father).

We are told we must be Seekers of His Truth and Wisdom in order to be able to stand against the lies of the 'Enemy of our souls' - Satan and his hordes of demonic forces.

Thus, with these injunctions from the Lord, I was impressed to read what Jesus said and did. He is truly our perfect example as God's Son who came to live on Earth as the one we call God/Man: Meaning: God who came in human form in order to know how we live and die. Our God love us enough to send His Son Jesus to personally learn of His creation. What great love must this be to come to such a primitive planet from the beauties and comforts of Heaven?!

As I read the things Jesus said and did, I began to see Him as my Master and Savior. His teachings are mine. Since I had not been allowed to become entangled and mired in the doctrines and tenets of religions and denominations, and the ministers and leaders thereof, He alone is my Rabbi, Teacher, Lord and King - my All in All. I am His disciple, His sheep, His sister and His handmaiden. We are friends. I attempt to never hurt Him.

Therefore, after many years of being His, I see I am one of those Christians who sees God in, of, and about everything. I see the Creator as pantheistic, as being wholly indwelling and part of all of His creation. We are all part of All That Is, which is another way to define God. He indwells our bodies, our Earthly Temples not made with hands...lest any man should boast of building our temples with finite hands. We are the Temples made with the hands of the Infinite.

If we seek Him, we will find Him. He knocks at the door of our Temple to gain entry into our Temple, into the Holy of Holies - our Hearts. He is very polite. If we choose to not answer to His rapping at our Hearts' doors He will not forcibly break down the doors to aggressively gain entry into our private worlds. However, He wants to be asked to visit and to commune with us as He did in the Garden of Eden with our ancestors Adam and Eve, strolling each evening with them "in the still coolness of the evenings". He tells us He longs to once again walk in at-oneness with us.

To have such a One as our Friend is a Treasure of Great Value. My heart and soul are overflowing with the bounteous goodness My Friend shares generously with me and all of us who wish to be His friend.

As with any protected Children, we are carefully watched, listened to, and heard. We are learning how to be Children of Heaven by attempting to emulate and copy the ways of our God and our Father and of our older Brother Jesus. As the younger siblings we have a very wonderfully archetypal Big Brother - Jesus.

111. HOMELESSNESS & OTHER SAD REALITIES OF THE HUMAN CONDITION

It is my great desire to assist myself and others to better understand some of the reasons for us to re-evaluate our own lives, as well as the worlds in which we live. Perhaps if we can learn from our long diverse life experiences we will be able to create a better world in which all of us may find a "good life", health and the pursuit of our individual dreams and aspirations. Perhaps we will even work together as a global community of nations which decides to "beat their weapons into pruning hooks and plowshares." We will ban and outlaw violence and wars forever. Each of us will live healthy long lives in peace and happiness, without concerns for others seeking to use and abuse others in the patriotic and religious fervor of grandiose delusions of power hungry egomaniacs and tyrants.

Insights for this era of American history. Read only if you are interested in learning some things not known by everyone about those called the "Invisible People" of our modern, high tech civilization at the beginning of the 21st Century after Christ's birth. Many of you are educated than myself in this matters. As always, mine is the everyday experiential view of a woman of this era. Perhaps I will be able to help someone else to know they are not alone. It is my grave concern many are becoming progressively depressed, catatonic and hopelessly lost in lies and rhetoric which does not truly let them know theyare not alone in their troubles. Neither are they the only causation of their massive problems with finances, health care, housing and survival needs. Truth will set everyone free to see who and where they truly stand as victims in a selfish society. Abused people lose hope. They even acquire "The Stockholm Syndrome". This simply means they become so lost in their own terror and pain as to reach the point of defense and support of their captors. What on Earth is happening?

"SUGAR COATING FOR A BITTER PILL"

This is the personal title of this section I will call this fictionalized story "Love Forever True". It is my humble attempt to make an unpalatable pill so that one may ingest it in the easiest fashion possible.

1. This is the U.S.A. –but not ALL families have beautiful family homes.

2. Sorry Folks, the Poor, Needy, Disabled, and Aged are part of society.

3. Time, death and Income Taxes still exist.

4. Medical Insurance is only for those who are given full-time hours. Most employers attempt to keep from having to pay for the high costs of medical and retirement coverage for employees. Therefore, few employees are given full-time employment. If they are on jobs which pay very well by the hour, those employees are expected to pay for their own insurance benefits. Many governmental leaders do not have personal family concerns about Social Security or Medical, Dental and Vison Coverage. Their Plans are the best. Their Federal retirements are also safe.

5. Evildoers are very much alive on Planet Earth. There are Believers as well as Bureaucrats who think nothing of robbing the poor, children, the aged, or even their own families. The selfish cannot obtain enough for themselves, even if they are wealthy. The needy are many. They are not evil. Many of them are poor due to the selfishness of others who are truly poor in all aspects of their lives. God knows all.

6. Liars still abound. Those who face liars all their lives can recognize liars.

7. Many of those who are disenfranchised now are really the holy ones in disguise–observing and suffering for all so that there are those who will learn and grow by their sacrifices and sufferings. The Life Reviews of many will be altered by their attitudes towards "The Least of These".

This section is to be a fictionalized story of real homeless people and their lives. This section of messages are fictionalized and "sugar coated" for easier consumption by those who have tender feelings for their own healths as well as for those who are called "the Invisible People" of America. All of the typical happenings of human beings, and homeless people as a whole, are true events many experience daily. The names and locations have been changed to protect the innocent poor souls who just happen to be too poor to afford a dwelling place in which to store one's possessions and self within the safety of protective walls. Everyone in America has grown up being told we are guaranteed inalienable rights of speech, religion, homes and jobs. This is the American Dream. Not all Americans are able to afford even a simple living area of their own. They have a very hard time having even their "basic survival needs". What happened to their dreams? Nothing. Many of these people do not have any hope of quality of life or life at all. Some are mentally and physically ill. Some are dying alone, cold and abused. There are many disabled, veterans, and addicted souls. There are also many people just like us who are "falling through the cracks" in our failed wars on poverty.

There are many who think the financial grant programs should be handled by private industry and churches, rather than by community programs through city, state and county programs. This is not a good idea becuase many churches have t eachings which would make many people think poor people are also evil. This is false teaching, but it is very much believed by various groups of Christians at this time.

In addition, due to these types of biased thinking, some of these churches do not make contributions to homeless shelters and food banks. Perhaps these needy souls are now defined as "untouchables".

Most of the evangelical shelters require those who receive shelter and food also attend their church services–thereby insuring they have given the residents of the shelter every chance of becoming acquainted with Jesus Christ. The bad part of this is there are homeless who are believers in other pathways who are also homeless due to various valid reasons. They may also read other holy books. Many of these shelters do not allow any holy book but the Bible.

There are those neighborhoods which strongly refuse to accept homeless shelters, care homes for retarded, sex offenders, and the mentally ill in their neighbors. We see the validity of these concerns. We also see the plight of those disenfranchised souls who are the invisible and forgotten needy ones among us. It is very hard to hear others denounce you stating they do not want you in their backyard (NIMBY). What neighborhood will accept these people? They are still our brothers and sisters.

Who will take the time to get acquainted with these people in order to see them as one of our Father's children? He wants us to open our hearts and lives to others in order to become acquanted with these of His children. Prayer is the key to knowledge, wisdom and the ability to know how to work with and to bless "the least of these". He must be closely working with us and them if we are to bridge to gaps in our national and local governmental social programs and our privately funded sharing programs. Love is the key. If we treat others with respect and love, we may be able to assist some people to become actualized into their highest self realization.

If one needs health insurance, it may not be available. If one is well paid and employed, they may qualify for medical, dental and eye care insurance. If one becomes ill and is bankrupt, there may be nothing.

Basic automobile insurance coverage may not cover the repair or replacement of one's own automobile, which is the only vehicle available to supply the needed transportation for a low paid family. However, automobile insurance premiums may far exceed the ability of many low paid workers to afford them.

These topics are not happy ones. Neither are the lives of those forced to live in under these mediocre conditions.
****

LOVE FOREVER TRUE (#111-continued.)

CHARACTERS:

GABE W.- University Sociology Professor, who also teaches music courses. He is a widower, fairly well endowed with income, a nice home by the Pacific Ocean in Santa Cruz area. He is an educated man who knows the ideal values of this world, as well as other worlds--past lives, or the Other Side. He has a young daughter who needs a tutor.

CELIA S.- She is a Student at the U.C. Santa Cruz who tutors fellow students. - She is a pretty blonde and blue-eyed U.C. student, shapely, very sweet, nice, ethical, spiritual, intelligent and altruistic, as well as being a great tutor. She is also a spiritually aware and attuned soul. She is the daughter of a typical middle-class, working man's family who live by the typical American work ethics of those who do not understand the realities the world in which they live. They still believe anyone can do anything they wish to do in America. They must believe in the infallibility of our values or they cannot live in sanity. Our heroine has been forced to get out there and live by the realities of our affluent and greedy society. She is trying to fend for herself against overpowering odds. Housing costs have caused many single people, students and employed people, single-parent families, as well as disabled, and unemployed indigent people, to have no way of affording housing. Sometimes a couple of people can house mate, thereby making it possible for each to live in a real as the "Homeless". No one wants them, or their shelters, in their back yards.--NIMBY means "Not in my backyard."

THE OPENING SCENE: She lives in a well-used seaside grove where college students and even local professional people who are unable to afford homes camp out very discreetly at nite. People camp out at night because they cannot afford to pay rent.

In the first scene, Celia is shown sweeping the ground with a tree bough to hide all traces of her presence from any walking by, police authorities, etc. Each small grove is used as an apartment or house. At any rate, our heroine is one of those people who is temporarily down on her housing luck. She and a group of university friends are discreetly sleeping out in their sleeping bags and small tents in a little noticed thicket near the local community college in Aptos.

However, in order to survive without housing, one must be very careful to avoid notice by local residents, their pets, or their children, as well as the local police and sheriff's departments who patrol these types of areas where people may be sleeping out hown as being deftly returned to it's natural appearance. The ground is sandy with pressed down grassy areas. Each occupant does his or her own sweeping. Each leaves quietly and drives off in their individual vehicle. They are comrades in their poverty. They are our own people, in our own land, just down on their luck in a greedy world too busy and overworked to notice them/us.

Since it is summertime, they are not forced to sleep in their vehicles as what is known as "Vehicle Homeless"--the level of status above the indigent street person without the shelter and protection of an auto. Many of them had been sleeping in their vehicles during the winter months, using as little fuel energy as possible - usually simply to use the heater to warm their chilled bones. Sometimes they are able to cook at homes of friends and relatives. Sometimes they buy fast food, and carry food with them.

Whenever they gave a homeless friend a ride on a cold night, they turn their heater on as high as possible, usually at the request of their chilled passenger. They feel badly when forced to let that other less fortunate person out to live basically in the elements. Some have told horrible stories of being awakened at nite to find themselves being nibbled upon by rats. Some who had deeply injured areas of their bodies with supporaton, and bloody bandages, found to their horror they had attracted predators larger than rats. One person who had recently had heart surgery slept in a "smelly" cave in the mountains of Colorado. She seemingly didn't realize she was fortunate to have slept alone in the cougar's den. Many tears flowed over that story.

Celia had worked in a local homeless shelter where she met a young man who seemed drawn to her. He came and sat at the counselors' tables and discussed his neo-Nazi views openly with her. He eagerly told her of his belief there would soon be race wars beginning in America. She was stunned when she realized she hadn't noticed his German military boots and uniform earlier. She was so startled by his appearance her response to his statements of his desire for the race wars to start was to say to him, "How would you feel if many of your friends here in the shelter were killed?" He immediately became enraged at her words, arose angrily, sat down across the room and glared at her all evening. The next afternoon when she came to work, he and a friend angrily screamed ugly and hateful names at her. She realized he had seen her as a blonde, Aryan, possibly Nazi sympathizing person. Indeed, she had Germanic, English, French, and other European ancestors, as well as having a name her father had told her was possibly "dangerous".

She was heartbroken to see the women and children, the girl with a wheelchair crawling onto a bed, among the rows of other beds, and the other very ill, aged, and mentally ill souls who were forced to resort to such lodging rather than be on the street. One mulatto woman, an opera singer, with her 10-year-old son of a Middle Eastern father, her husband, from whom they had been forced to hurriedly flee from the Bay Area with their pet rabbit, were staying in the shelter.

One night Celia met a wonderful group of down and out Native Americans. She was wearing her well worn silver turquoise ring which had been given to her by a dear friend, Hawaiian wife of a local Indian tribal member. They seemed to feel it was a powerful stone ring. They asked her to join their circle as they sat in an area of the shelter. The leader of the group was a pock-marked Sioux man who called himself Sundancer, as he showed everyone in the group his chest wounds from the ritual sundance ceremonies in which he said he regularly participated. The Lakota Sioux Sundancers dance for the healing of their people, in much the same roles as one who intercedes like a healer, Bodhisattva, or savior figure.

They talked of many things as a group. One Tlingit Viet Nam vet, sadly and with tears, told of his sadness and horror to find that he was the soldier in his unit who was able to make the sadly accurate decision in his unit as to which of the local Vietnamese women and children were being sent as living timebombs and who must be killed to save their unit. The Tlingit man said he missed the "breathing of the whales" in his native lands in the Northwest.

Later, Sundancer told her of his wife and children who were called by tribal titles such as Prince and Princess, of his love for sage teas, and that he was a grandson of Chief Crazy Horse. Later, he briefly sat in her simple car beating his hands on the dashboard as he regaled her with his proficient native drumming. She would not soon forget meeting such a man. The next day, she prepared food at her mother's home and took it to him and his friends who were in need of hot food to eat. She found them where he had told her they would be on the side streets near the Bay. They seemed very happy to have simple homemade bacon sandwiches made by the hands of a homeless counselor, who they did not know was also homeless. Sundancer told her he would like her services as a helper they needed in S. Dakota with his Sioux people. She wondered then where her destiny would lead her sometime in the future.

While Celia worked at the large city shelter, she also collected beautiful poems and recorded thoughts from those who stayed in the Shelter for a Homeless Newspaper. Many are the holy ones who live, and die, at the mercy of an uncaring, unaware, selfish society. There are holy beggars and prophets on the streets of every town in America, even as there are holy beggars and prophets in India, the land of the holy ones. One beautiful black man told her someone had told him "This is the planet where they kill saints." Many do not see the Holy Beggars, the Invisible Homeless, in America.

She received several treasured certificates for her work with the homeless shelters. However, few, if any of her co-workers knew she herself was houseless. She had relatives and friends with whom she often stayed. All of her worldly possessions were stored in a local storage center. These storage rooms cost as much as rental costs for whole homes cost in the past. However, she kept many of her personal items and books with her at all times. She had her automobile, but no way of affording even a cheap apartment. However, though she was hard worker, they never received enough funds with the Homeless Task Force to give her a needed income. Her small stipend from a beloved deceased aunt made it possible for her to provide transportation for other homeless who lived at the family shelter where she worked as a volunteer assistant to the Shelter Manager. After all, since she was herself fallen into hard times, how apropos that she should work with such as herself. We've always been taught that experiential training is always the best.

Indeed, about six months before she met and began work with the homeless, she had been given a dream in which she was shown herself and her Mgr. at the Shelter, working as social workers together. The unusual part of the dream was that those who showed her this prophetic message were from a huge, brightly lit Mother Ship seemingly from another world. Later, after she began to do this work, she remembered the prophetic dream of her destiny for the following two years. She and her Mgr., now her good friend, loved to watch the movie *Thelma & Louise* together. Only those of the sisterhood of poverty, who are intelligent and daring women can enjoy and understand such a movie. They both knew why the heroines in the movie chose death.

Some of the sexually exploitive actions done to the poor were incomprehensible to people who never have had to live on a low income, or without funds, at the mercies of society and/or their families attempting to have their basic survival needs of housing and food met.

One day on the streets of America could quickly drive a tenderly reared person insane with the sudden need to locate some type of protection from the elements, and their on how to meet their needs for food and drink, water, bathroom and bathing facilities. These are things most people take for granted. These are the immediate needs of someone who is forced to survive on the streets and highways of anyplace in the world. These are people who do not have drug, alcohol, physical, emotional or mental handicaps. There are many of them out there trying to survive each hour of every day in all types of terrains and weather conditions.

There are those who are caught in the bondage of incestuous family situations. In additon to that, the mother may be suffering from poor self esteem and cannot meet the survival needs of herself and her family. She has been so abused through verbal, sexual and emotional abuse that she cannot take care of herself, much less others.

The retarded people of all ages are especially vulnerable to all forms of exploitation by unscrupulous souls who have no regard for themselves or others. This is a major problem. There are some single parents who have found a partner simply because someone is lusting after their attractive retarded child, and the family home, vehicle, and other property. The unscrupulous step parent may not love or desire the new spouse at all. They are simply being very openly, if not deviously, taking advantage of the disadvantaged in wisdom, if not material resources provided by a deceased spouse for the innocent family members–now at the mercies of a human predator.

There are those who are so very loving, innocent religious souls who live alone, with or without a vehicle. A vehicle is a very important protection against predators who try to exploit anyone who is vulnerable. It gives its owner a quick means of escape, as well as protection from the elements if one is stranded without proper lodging. However, at this time we will explore the lives of those who live alone. Perhaps they have friends or family who have not been careful to keep them safe from those of questionable reputations. In fact, some of the nicest people have no concepts of who or what is normal and right. They have lived and worked with such a variety of dysfunctional and imbalanced circumstances and people that they may even allow such unfit people into their own personal circles of friends and acquaintances. This can lead to infiltration of their safe family unit with dangerous elements of society who may even have intentions of sexual and marital involvement with those innocents in a family. Such is the case with those who do not practice methods of securing their lives so that they always maintain a inviolable safe space, or zone, into which no outsiders are allowed. These wise people always keep safe time and space for the protection of themselves and their families. Decisions must be made carefully to never allow those of questionable repute into the family's tribal circle. This is practicing good self preservation and survival skills on a larger scale than the personal. These are the duties and responsibilities of the wise parent or leader who is the protector of a given group. Many parents are not fulfilling their duties . Perhaps they don't know how or what to do.

Those who are separated out, alone, and looking vulnerable are fair game for human predation. An example of this is that there can be several nice, sweet, loving types of even holy women living in an area. One human male predator can prey upon all at the same time, causing them to live in fear for many years, or lifetimes. These nice women are the type who would be too embarrassed to "make a scene" by letting someone know they were choking in a public restaurant. Some few would die rather than speak out due to shyness. This is the case with the every innocent prey of sexual predators.

Human predators are very devious and covert. They will make use of all manner of underhanded and nasty tactics to work their ways into the close proximity of those they have decided are to be their prey. They arrive before dawn and very late at night. They have access to the home of their prey because an unthinking family member introduced them to their prey. Perhaps they saw someone and immediately and selfishly formed an obsessive fixation on some physical, or other, attribute of the prey. Sometimes they stalked someone to find the "object of their affections". Perhaps they practiced dark spiritual acts to "make" the person love them. They will stop at nothing to get whoever, or whatever, they want in life. They may even rationalize "the end justifies the means", for some this is an All-American adage for life . Therefore, it is fine for them to "make" someone become their sexual pawn. One man who is polygamous can become like the harem master of many unprotected females.

Prior to the times of homelessness, Celia had been an elected Secretary of the local chapter of the N.A.A.C.P., while attending the local university. One of her professors in Afro Studies was also her Advisor for her Bachelor of Arts degree in Social Sciences. He and she were both on the Board of the N.A.A.C.P. and were actively involved in local civil rights issues.

At one time, she worked with other vehicular homeless who staged a sit in on a local beach. These beautiful people held large gatherings at their meals which included the whole tribal gathering linking hands in prayers before their meals. It was a special group of interfaith and inter-religious Seekers of the Holy. Among the campers, there was one group who had a cozy, well-made "hootch"*, complete with a real stove.

This was a wonderful place for others to gather out of the piercing cold nights of the northern California beachfront dunes. These people suffered great dangers from locals who loved to come out at night to shoot their guns into the vehicles of sleeping homeless. Indeed, one night Celia, Kara (the Mgr.), and others, sat in her vehicle on guard duty trying to catch those who shot their high powered guns into others' simple homes--their vehicles. One beautful family had bullets hit very near their sleeping children's beds while they slept in their huge bus which was their home.

This large group of beach homeless told her they were very concerned for the safety and wellbeing of others who were not yet suffering as they were at that time, a decade ago. These dear souls said they had already learned how to live in vans and cars, as well as knowing how to build fires, care for normal human needs and desires, cook meals outdoors, and much more. They were genuinely concerned and prayerful over the dangers they sensed were coming upon America. Yes, the Holy Beggars are among us. Are you able to recognize them? They are here in all our own communities.

Indeed, even the Director of Social Services and the local Health Dept. said there were no homeless in his local city. He was so uninformed and so stupid. Anyone could have shown him areas where whole settlements of homeless lived--whether under overpasses on the ledges above freeways, under bridges by the Bay, under bushes and trees in local forests, or perhaps in or around his own house or stairwell? Many people in our over-indulged nation are blind, deaf, dumb and stupid as their inanimate and worthless idols. Our gods are the gold, power, lust, greed, and prejudice of this modern material world. He was elected by ones like himself who worship these goals and idols.

One of her co-volunteers, also on the local Homeless Task Force, who had access to the Grateful Dead music group, wrote a letter about these beach homeless, many of whom were Grateful Dead people. The Group sent a check for $10,000.00 to the Shelter for their people.

Some church leaders and church organizations who have falsely taught others to believe that one must have done something wrong if one is homeless, disabled, or poor, do not donate funds to assist the homeless of America. They seem to completely forget all of Jesus Christ's requests to feed and clothe the poor and needy and to give a drink of water to the thirsty, as if to Him, or His angels. After all, this is the nation which believes itself to be His own Christian nation.

****

This morning was another beautiful balmy day by the blue Pacific. She picked up her bedroll, disguised as a normal school backpack, along with her books and personal items.

She quietly and carefully walked to her parked older vehicle, a run-down, older yellow convertible in need of vacuuming and repair. The black cloth top fits poorly and does not keep out all the elements of weather. She gets into the car and drives away to her place of employment. She arrives at the home of Gabe Winters, where she counsels and tutors his daughter Rowena.

Celia could live as a group home counselor in one of those homes. However, she wants the freedom and mobility of this position not in an institution.

Gabe has become enamored with Celia. He wants to see her again. Somehow he locates where she hangs out in the daytime at a local seaside gathering place called Zelda's at Capitola Beach. He locates her seated by the sea, slowly sipping a cup of French Roast coffee, wearing her sunglasses and looking very attractive as she chats with friends.

Little does he know how life in the richest nation of the world has treated this fine woman. She is without a lodging due to the exorbitant rents charged by property owners for any piece of rental property in this day and age. Indeed, the descendants of the rich and famous, down on their luck, can be found sleeping in their vehicles or in wooded and sandy groves by the sea, such as in Southern California (and many other areas worldwide). She is one step up the ladder from being a completely down and out street person. She is known as a "Vehicle Homeless Person". She is not an alcoholic, drug user, nor is she mentally ill. She is simply too poor to rent a home in which to live. As has been stated, there are many others like her in this affluent modern capitalistic nation. Those who do not wish to know hide their heads in the sand like ostriches.

Celia hangs out at local restaurants and beach houses so she can have access to toilets, bathing and washing facilities, food, drink, warmth and good company. As with J.K. Rowling, author of the Harry Potter books, she also needs a place to study which has nice ambience and good coffee. When she leaves Zelda's she can always go to a better study area, such as the nearby coffee house or book cafe. Gabe knows something of these alternative lifestyles. Would he know what to do with her if he knew how she has been forced to cope with her hardships in life. However, in spite of all this, she always tried to be a proper single woman, not given to promiscuity. Her mind and her soul were as attractive as was her body. However, many were the lechers who pursued her simply for her sexuality as a very attractive woman who is also a mother and a grandmother.

Our emphasis in on what a wonderful person she is. She has done nothing wrong in life except to be poor. She is spiritually, physically, emotionally, and even educationally, a wonderful woman. She is a top notch student and employee. She is employed. Her income is too low to afford to live in our society with it's material world vices of greed and it's God Mammon. After all, this is the American Way of Life.

Gabe only knows he wants to know this woman. He is younger than Celia, but he remembers a different age, with different values, and cultural awareness. People have not all sold their souls for greed. He is one of those wonderfully bright men who recognizes the higher qualities of Celia. In addition to all of this, they seem to recognize each other from someplace. Both of them wonder about where they had known each other before. They are each believers in reincarnation and in other worlds. They wonder if they have been together in prior lives. Have they been friends on the Other Side prior to their present life destinies? However, the age difference matters less to each of them than the thought of not being together. They each recognize the other as their soul mate. In fact, Gabe seems to remember having a vision of Celia when he was a 15-year-old boy in Michigan. He saw her, and he was asked by the Spirit if he would help her, for he was shown visions of her hard life. However, he had not been shown her homeless plight in his precognitive visions.

She is his student in one of his Music Appreciation courses at the University.

He is not one of those professors who attempt to meet and to date any new and pretty female student who comes into his classes. He is a stabile, mature, very respected and intelligent man, full of awareness of himself, and women and their feelings about being treated as sexual objects to be lusted after and used by men rather than as individual people, with brains, souls, AND bodies.

However, there is a real thing between this couple. They have been attempting to pretend they are not aware of the feelings they have for each other. He doesn't know how to begin pursuing her. She doesn't wish to become the Professor's "Item". She is a serious student intent on obtaining her degrees in order to better be able to help others as a social worker,

One day, he pursues her when she left his home after visiting his daughter.

He locates her. What does he do now to get her attention?

Celia seems very happy and sociable as she sits in the warm sun at one of Zelda's umbrella tables on their outdoor deck by the beach. She reminds him of someone he knew when he remembers a time when he was composing music based on everything he saw, spontaneously and effortlessly as an accomplished musician and composer. He remembered his long shoulder-length hair and clothing of Mozart's era.. H knew he had loved her then. He still loves her, though he does not know who she really is.

He parked his auto at the curb, but was slow in getting up his courage to exit the vehicle. What was he to do after he seated himself at an adjacent table at Zelda's? Should he begin a very logical conversation about the music class? That was a good opener. Also, since the course involved a study of musical instruments of the world, it would allow him to show his extensive knowledge of these specialized instruments.

Sauntering was hard. He wanted to rush over, cup her face in his hands, and kiss her on the mouth. That was out of the question. How to appear nonchalent when one is feeling anything but calm. He knew how he felt about her. How did she feel about him? Did she, too, think of him as deeply, and from past memories, as he did of her? He lost his courage as he thought of how foolish all of this could be. Surely he must be suffering lovesick delusions, if not of insanity those feel who remember other times.

His plight has ended when she sees him approaching and asks if he would like to join her at her table. What luck! God must be in His Heaven today. Surely all things are done well when one walks daily in one's ordained and planned personal spiritual life destiny This is the way he lives--in the ongoing flow of the Divine Spirit as he knows it.

He sits down at her table casually, as if it were his natural place to be. He felt they were like a couple who had been as one for centuries. What were her thoughts?

As an opener, he asked her: "Do you have any questions about the course?

Celia quickly replied: "No, but I truly would like to know I could call upon you at any time if I do need to ask questions. Thank you for your concern. I really like your course. I've never seen so many wonderful musical devices in all my life! Do you have a collection of instruments?"How many do you own yourself? The ice had been broken.

Now, where do we go from here?

He tried to steer the conversation into something a lot less academic.

Gabe: Have you studied philosophy? Which author is your favorite?

(He wanted to ask her of her spiritual and religious, even metaphysical knowledge. Was she psychic, a healer, a dreamer? Who is she in this lifetime?)

Do you go to hear local speakers, or to local operattas and plays? If so, perhaps you would like to go to some of these performances and we could discuss more about your interests in music. If you are interested, I would be glad to assist you to build a superior collection of references books and tapes for your own library?"

(He felt like a fool, babbling on with any topic that came to mind, just in order to remain in her company forever.)

Much to her surprise, she realized this was a man who liked her. In fact, it seemed he was truly desirous of her company. She shamelessly began to think of how she'd love to be seated in the sand alone with him, behind a large piece of driftwood sheltered from any rising afternoon sea breezes. Perhaps they could share a bottle of wine together, or a get-acquainted kiss. Why did he seem so familiar to her? In fact, she also began to visualize several hours of enjoyable time practicing to see how their lips felt together. She didn't know what to say. What could she say? This was her professor. However, they seemed to be communing as if they had always known each other. Perhaps they had known each other - perhaps forever.

Her response: "I think I'd like that. Also, I really do want to learn much more about music. My fields of study are in human services and health care professions. However, music is one of the healing tools we need to learn to use to heal ourselves and our planet. Sound is the Music of each person's soul, or Sphere, according to Pythagoras. I am just beginning to use music to heal my emotions. I have learned it is also used to heal our bodies as well. Indeed, we are very much helped and often healed by usage of aromatherapy, music, light and touch accompanied by our prayers. Affirmations and meditation can keep us well. Indeed all of these therapies alone, or separately, can heal us from mental, emotional and physical illness. The laying on of hands is also a healing art, as with reiki, massage, and other healing arts."

Gabe: "Have you ever considered learning to play a musical instrument? If so, which one?" (He seemed to remember her playing a small Celtic harp in another time.)

Celia: " I play nothing but my CD's and cassettes for music at this time. However, I seem to have an overpowering desire to have and to learn to play a small harp. I almost feel I could easily learn to play it. When I read *The Mists of Avalon*, by Marion Zimmer- Bradley, I felt completely thrilled and excited as I read about the ballads played by the Druidic bards, the priests and the priestesses of Avalon. What is your personal preference of instruments? Do you play any instrument yourself?"

Gabe: "I strum a guitar rather poorly at this time. However, when I was a teenager I had my own music group. We did gigs. I need to get a new string for my guitar and start to play again.

Do you think you would play a harp if I attempted to obtain one for you?"

Celia: "I don't know if I'm smart enough to learn to play any instrument. However, I love the very thought of even owning a harp of my own. Maybe I have memories of times in Heaven when I could play a harp proficiently.

Do you remember such worlds? Indeed, do you believe in such places as being real? Do you remember living before? If you do, what do you remember that you would feel free to tell me? I have a blockage of my memories of other worlds and lifetimes. However, I do seem to dream of wearing very ornate and fancy dresses of extreme affluence, with large full skirts. Indeed, these dresses with full skirts are the only types of clothing I ever wear in these dreams.

Also, I seem to feel close affinities with certain parts of world such as the Middle East, the southern parts of Europe, California, the South, the Islands of Hawaii, and more. I love the ocean surfs and seascape living. I love to study bizarre, ancient and little used languages if only for the numerological meanings of their alphabets and metaphysical meanings."

Gabe: "I seem to have memories of knowing you for many lifetimes, as well as in our Heavenly Home. Do you remember me? If so, what do you remember about our times together--if indeed you are able to also know these things? I am very deeply interested in your responses. I feel like we've known each other forever."

Celia: "When I lived, I fear I may have lived in the times of the French Revolution. When I traveled to Europe I seemed to have terribly sensitive areas of my neck whenever I saw a chopping block upon which people had been beheaded, as with the one at the Tower of London where Anne Boleyn and others lost their heads for daring to cross the reigning powers of that time. I hope and pray these are not true memories.

If so, I pray we never again have such Dark Ages before we have times of enlightenment and Renaissance once again. I wish I could remember more. However, as my religious studies instructor told me, "Sometimes it is better we do not remember our prior lives. This implied to me that we truly do not know what we have said, done when we lived or of how we died when last we lived. Ignorance may be bliss."

Gabe: "I am intrigued by your insights. I somehow felt we would have much to share. Is it possible we have been born as soul mates? I've heard that our soul mates stay in Heaven while we live on Earth. Somehow I find it impossible to believe you would ever let me be here alone."

Celia: "Maybe I haven't left you. However, you did come before me. I was always so thrilled by the scenes in *The Blue Bird* with Shirley Temple. I see us together in the Other World, before we both came to this world. You hated to leave me, even as did the boy in the movie. I wept when you had to leave me. I feared we would never again find each other. I cannot believe this is all happening, yet it may be we have again found each other."

She suddenly realized she had little time to get to her sleeping area before dark. They had talked the afternoon daylight hours away. The sun had dropped until dusk had fallen. She also had become frightened by the intensity of their newfound feelings for each other. She didn't want a cheap and transitory relationship with Gabe. She realized she had found her beloved Gabe with whom she wished to share her life. Their love for each other was based upon shared interests and values--apart from the love of two human bodies for one another. They had waited for perhaps centuries for each other. Why should they feel hurried and take a chance of losing each other forever? She knows she must make some small excuse to cover her real need to leave. She cannot let him know she is homeless. She fears the alienation that will occur if he knows she is without socially acceptable lodging.

She quickly rises from the table and hurriedly makes her excuses to leave knowing full well there may be problems finding another way to be together to find out where their relationship is going after such frank sharing of their innermost feelings for each other.

Celia: "I really must go. It's been the most wonderful afternoon in my life. I feel like we've miraculously found each other and I'd like to see you again if possible."

Gabe: "Celia, I cannot believe I've found you only to lose you once again. We can't let this happen. When can I see you again?"

She quickly responded "Perhaps we could meet after class tomorrow to share more of our thoughts. What about meeting here again at 4 p.m.? I think I could make it easily. How would this work with your schedule?"

She has no intention of taking a chance on never seeing him again in this role. She is falling deeply in love.

This is not a love at first sight thing. This is the recognition that she has always loved this man. They have simply been separated by time and space for a season of time. Since their destinies have been arranged so that they can once again be together, nothing must hinder the progression of their relationship in this incarnation. She is full of hope, yet fears separation and the loss of him in her life. She is in love beyond all everyday ideas of what love means and how it can become a divine relationship written in the heavens for perhaps all time and eternity. She knows they have a date with destiny.

Gabe: "I 'll be here tomorrow without fail. I know we must see each other again." Arising from the table he gently pulls her to him. As he breathes in the fresh scent of her hair, he realizes he has once again found his true love. He makes a vow to himself to never again let her escape him. Their lips meet briefly, but with a deep bond of love.

Celia wants to melt completely into his arms, but she gently releases herself, turns and lets him know with a smile, a gentle nod and wave that she will be there the next day. Her heart is so full, she fears she will burst into tears of joy, and a small degree of fear that this has all been a dream and they will never see each other again. After all, he is a solid citizen. She is a homeless student. She knows about a world of people of whom he may know nothing. After all, she has her feet firmly placed in two worlds, the one of acceptability as an employed university student, and the world in which her family lives. Her world and her income place her out among others like herself--the "New Poor", along with the one-parent families, and others of the socalled minorities who are really the world's majority populations.

This is the socalled Fourth World unknown to many upstanding, well-intentioned, and uninformed American citizens who would be shocked and unbelieving if they did know the stark realities of their seemingly well-ordered, high income, religiously-based society. After all, this is the Land of the Free and the Home of the Brave. It is a dearly held tenet of our American creed that everyone can live in abundance no matter what their real beginnings. Such is not the case, as any of those who open their eyes, ears and hearts know.

****

Celia suddenly realizes she is blessed this day. She had earlier arranged with her dear friend Francesca to be able to visit with her this evening. It is too late to easily reach her thicket and set up her simple camp. In addition, it is time to do laundry, to get a real hot bath, and to take care of extra hygiene needs in the comfort of a real home. She is supremely grateful to God and to her longtime friends for their love and understanding of her plight. She has known Francesca since they were children in the first grade.

She remembers another dear friend had given her a bag of freshly picked, homegrown tomatoes still warm from the garden. This will make a nice hostess gift. Perhaps they can share a homecooked BLT sandwich, and catch up on news and conversation.

Francesca is very fortunate. She is able to live in a small mother-in-law apartment on her parents' property. She knows the realities of today's world and realizes how blessed she is to have a virtually rent-free lodging. Her father insists she only assist with utilities, phone and a small amount of upkeep and maintenance of the family property. She realizes her family are her protection from the cold, heartless and sometimes dangerous world Out There. She realizes the beautiful safety and protection she has in family and her extemded family of relatives and friends. She also realizes her responsibility to assist her less fortunate friend. She praises God for her bountiful blessings but has been taught the laws of sharing with those who have need but as you are safely able to do so. She knows what a wonderful person and soul her friend has always been. She also knows Celia would do the same for her should her life ever change as drastically. She knows she and others like her could easily be in Celia's circumstances in spite of the best precautions humanbeings can take. Life's surprises are there for everyone to share. Living has no insurance policies except we are told we will not be given more tests than we can bear. She loves Celia and Celia knows she will never change her feelings no matter what status, income bracket, illness, or trauma she faces. These are the characteristics of a True Friend. Francesca reads of Christ's words and actions. She believes we are to do unto others as if we do them unto Him, the Best Friends of anyone's soul and lifetime pathway. She puts her faith into her life choices, words and deeds. She, as a Christian believer, knows she to love and serve others as she is able to do so. Loving is the law of Christ, the only law that never ends no matter what life brings, what miracles ones does in the name of Christ, or the prophetic or healing gifts of His Spirit. We are saved by His Grace, not by our good deeds. However, we are told our good deeds are part of our normal expression of our love for Him and all who love the Spirit of the All-Encompassing Father. His children are the multitudes who show forth His Spirit, even if they do not yet know His Son Jesus as their Saviour. Francesca loves Him with all of her heart, mind, body and soul. She wants to be His disciple, friend, and spiritually engrafted younger sister in the Family of God. She loves Him and Celia with all her heart. Never thinking of all these things consciously , she automatically lives the laws of love everyday of her life. She is His. She knows she is a Daughter of the King of Heaven. She is a gracious and willing hostess and lives her role of handmaiden/priestess of the Living God, showing forth His love and eager role of world server for all to see. Her attributes are His Spiritual Fruits shown forth in her daily life. She shares His blessings with all as she is able to do so. With these deeply engrained rules for living she is also a very wonderful friend.

She knows the importance of offering food, drink, bathing and laundry facilities to those who have need of them. Francesca proceeded to prepare a quick and wonderful snack for both of them, including sharing her pitcher of freshly-made lemonade. She is eager to hear of Gabe, and the amazing conversations Celia and he have shared that afternoon. She sees the hand of God in all of these events. Perhaps Celia is about to be blessed and kept safe by their Heavenly Father in even greater ways than she has known for awhile.

Celia cannot yet comprehend the miraculous events of her day with Gabe.

She is deeply touched and blessed by his love and the love of her heavenly Father. She finds herself in happy tears of joy whenever she thinks or speaks of Gabe and her Lord.

She offers profound prayers of thanks to God as she drifts off to sleep in the freshly-made bed offered to her by Francesca. She may not always have a real home or even yet a real church of her own to attend. However, she knows she is Christ's. She knows He loves and cares for her no matter how frightening life sometimes may seem to her or her loved ones her are concerned for her safety. She is grateful for every blade of grass on her beautiful world. She is glad for life in spite of the hardships and concerns she faces as a poor working student.

Alternative lifestyles are not always understood, applauded, nor assisted in our affluent society. The first thought is that someone must have done something wrong, rather than that Celia and others like her may be living lives so blessed as to be gifts from a loving God who gives them unusual awarenesses, testings, and trials (in order to place them in His divine fires in order to refine them as into golden vessels in His temple) so they may learn and grow in wisdom and become priests and priestesses in His divine Home and Kingdom. Celia had been told one time by her beloved psychology the very true adage, "Only the wounded physician can heal." Christ is the supreme archetype of the healed Fisher King. He was wounded, healed, and has become our type of the Divine Healer. He is the Divine Priest-King who acts as the High Priest who bears all our illnesses and sins upon Himself. He is the Hierophant because He has holy office to do so. Celia knows we want to become like Him. His Cross is ours.

She tearfully reads her Bible and a Guidepost she had in her backpack before allowing herself to sleep.No matter what the circumstances, she tries to read and pray each night. In the morning, she thanks God for each new day, and prays for those with whom she will share her life that day, as well as for the world, world leaders, and His Divine Wisdom, Love, Justice and Protection for all. She is also His beloved sister, and a Child of the Father. Long has been her life path as His. She knows He loves her in spite of the hard times into which she has fallen. She knows there is a Divine Purpose for everything that happens in our lives if we walk obediently with Him--not seeking our own glory or will. Celia has amazingly been able to dedicate her life completely into His care, and is eager to have only His Divine Will in her life. Others have so young have not been as brave. The complete renunciation of one's own selfish desires and will to Him is the hardest of decisions for most of His children to make.

The end of a long day has miraculous and blessedly come to an end. Tonite is a blessed time of thanksgiving. Celia will sleep and dream well this night. She dutifully places her journal, pen and eyeglasses conveniently handy on the bedside table. She sets her alarm for tomorrow's busy day of classes. Her last words are for thanking Him. "Goodnight Dear Lord. I am yours and You are mine. Thank You for Gabe."

She turns over in her cozy bed and places the care of her soul into His hands. She knows we need to pray for divine protection, as well as knowing He and our angels are always with us to guide, protect and keep watch over our actions and words whether we are sleeping or awake. What a wonderful Friend is our Lord.

It is not unusual for Celia to be blessed with wonderful dreams from His Spirit. Tonight will not be the exception. He continues to speak to us in dreams and visions, even more so that ever. She knows her scriptures and believes He has never changed. It is only we who have changed due to our modern, often false, teachings. It is only our inabilities to know and to believe in Him which separate us from a closer walk with our Beloved. (Read and study about this type of Spiritual Walk with Him.) He has never left us alone. It is only us and our modern teachings which separate us from His Divine Presence. For those who love and serve Him He is the same, yesterday, today and forever. He is always closer than our own breath. He speaks to our hearts and souls whether we are awake or asleep. Sometimes a we sleep safely in His dinine care, we cross over to the Other Side in our dreams to share visits with our loved ones who have crossed over into His Divine World. We look forward to our redemptive return to our Heavenly Home. Above all, He is her Friend who sticketh closer than an earthly brother. He will never leave nor foresake us. He will give us strength and fortitude to overcome all adversaries, even Death, in the power of His Name and Blood.

In fact, Celia was given her own special message of hope and love from the Lord. He knew her life was changing. At that time, He gave her a very special message for her life. He spoke to her heart and told her, "As I was with Moses, so shall I be with you."Over the years, she had finally become more and more aware of the intensely close relationship of friendship shared by God with Moses. Having God as a friend is the best message He could have ever given her. The words of the old hymn, *What A Friend We Have In Jesus*, was very real to her. She knew that "Without Him she could do nothing. However, in Him, all things were and are possible." This was part of her repertoire of special verses she used to keep her heart strong in His Path, walking by faith in His footsteps.

With these thoughts, she drifted off into a deep sleep safe in the arms of Jesus, in the safety and protection of the family home of her beloved friend who is like her sister in His Family. Celia sleeps soundly until she is awakened precisely a moment before her alarm goes off. (She hates alarms.) She is awakened by following a very insightful dream. She begins to obediently pray that the Lord will give her the divine interpretation of her message even as she records it in her journal. This is the message the message in her own words:

Dream: *Feeding the Multitudes*

I was in an indoor setting with many rows of wooden bleachers with dirt flooring throughout. There were a variety of people seated in this seemingly safe and quiet place. They were hungry. I tried to find food to feed them. All I could find were dishes and bowls full of leftovers. Somehow, I fed them from leftovers and from new food which seemed to keep appearing from someplace. Other people either brought it to us, or it just kept appearing as needed.

I felt very handicapped to be able to feed all these hungry people without new, clean and fresh, food. Also, I seemed to have mislaid my spectacles again. I was unable to truly see how to locate, prepare, and serve food to them all.

Even the wild creatures started to come into this safe area. I saw a wild white wolf enter and dart off to a safe corner. Later, I saw a corner area where two or three wolf mothers lay safely nursing their litters of pups. Someone felt safe enough to go over and pet the wild mothers.

Those people who had found their way into this safe area seemed to be the peaceful people who some do not wish to recognize as God's children. They were those who could be called liberal, hippy, homeless, mentally ill, those who drink liquor to excess, and others. They, and I, wondered if we were safe anywhere. We wondered if we would be able to find food.

We, however, found there was food, if only leftovers, prepared for us. We knew we were loved and cared for in miraculous ways.

When I awakened, I was horrified to realize this is like our world at this time. Many of us have been forced out of our stadiums and home churches. We are out on the highways and byways, without our church homes. We are those lost sheep and wild creatures He will have to go out to find. He will preach to us and feed us with an endless array of leftovers, and "New Wine and Food" as well. We will be cared for, privately, and secretly, if need be, by our loving Saviour. We, too, are the Sheep of His Pasture, of which He tells us He has other pastures. He came to Earth using His whole life as a teaching tool from which we are to learn His values.

Who was our Master? What are His teachings that are not the doctrines of devils? To know Him, to know His Voice, His Ways, His Truths, and His Light of Life, are the necessary goals of our lives. If we do not know *Who* He is, or *What* He came to say, we do not know *Why* He came, or to *Whom* He came to show forth His Ways. He is too big for this world. He loves, protects, and is merciful to many who have no teacher or master. He is Jesus, the Christ, the Bastard Son of Mary, the Firstborn Son of God the Father, who chose to send Him to incarnate in human flesh so that He might know who we are, how we feel, think, hurt and die.

He is our Lord and Savior. He came that none would be lost. He nurtures and feeds us as He cares for His sheepfold. We are like His lambs who were lost from the sheepfold, pushed out by uncaring ewes to be devoured by predators..

We have the "Other Part" of the human soul. We offer ourselves, as did our Lord, as human sacrifices for others. We are not obsessed with fame and glory. We are very often forgotten and ignored because we do not force ourselves upon others. However, we are strongly against being forced to share our lives with those who do not follow His teachings. We read our Bibles and see a different Christ. We know He came to tell us things we are not being told by our many power-hungry, anxiously fearful, divisively active church leaders. They have no idea of how many of their fellow spirit-filled Christian brothers and sisters have become the vast, silent, stymied, stifled and oppressed underground church in hiding in AMERICA, the Land of the Free and the Home of the Brave.

Neither do they realize, nor do they care, that they are ignoring and abusing the human, cultural, political and spiritual rights of these same groups of people simply because we also still believe in our American Constitution and Bill of Rights as the inalienable rights of all Americans, not one chosen group, prepared for us by our Founding Fathers. Our beloved ancestors lived, suffered and died to make sure that we and children, their posterity, would never lose these inalianable rights.

Many of the ancestors of our families fled from the oppression of the Old World to this New World to seek religious and political freedom. Where has it disappeared? Who has taken it? How long must we eat leftovers and crumbs from the tables of our elitest neighbors who proudly tell us this is all we deserve. I was warned of this many years ago. I did not understand. We are all the Sheep of His Pasture. Our Lord has not changed. Our one-party, one-Christian church, American pharisees and hypocrites of today have legislated us right out into the highways and by-ways of this so called free world in which we all live. Do you even realize we are missing from your churches? Do you wonder why, and do you care? Do you want to know what we see?

Until you are full of His love, His wisdom, and His ways, you will not know why sometimes half of your family members will not sit in the pews beside you. You accuse them of being liberal, demon-possessed, unholy, evil, and other awful appellations. Who are they? These are your loved ones who would have been willing to die for you, even as enjoined to do so by their Lord Jesus. These are the same people who tried to show you His love, His healing touch, His miracles, His exorcisms, His prophecies and much more. You do not come to us for teaching, healing, preaching, and blessings. If we pray, you ignore our prayers, as if He does not hear our prayers. You even dare to question and perhaps blaspheme against the Holy Spirit by questioning the ongoing operations of the Spirit working in the lives of those who are not of your same political party. Why? It is impossible to locate such scriptures in any of the various translations of our Holy Bible.

Who are you to judge who He hears or chooses as one with whom He will share Heaven? Who are we to tell our Heavenly Father and Older Brother anything? We are the Clay, not the Potter. He said we are not to be vengeful, for Judgment begins and ends with God. He is the only one who can destroy the soul, however, He chooses to go out to the highways and alleys rather than have any be lost. He fed His sheep upon open hillsides as by the Sea of Galilee when He was here and lived among us--even as He lives within our hearts today. He feeds us Manna and Quail even as He did other refugees in another Wilderness, the Desert called Sinai, with Moses. Moses was a Friend of God. I am thrilled to believe and feel He is my Friend. He comforts us in our aloneness, even as He welcomes and nurtures the wild beasts of the wilderness as His four-legged friends. He welcomes even the Holy White Wolf, as well as the one with White and Blacked speckled head. We should listen to and observe the ways of the wild wolf who rests securely safe within His protective covering. We are safe. We are secure. We are fed even as we go in and out of His sheltering walls. We eat well from simple fare, but we are fed. We learn new things because we are a new creation. We are those who walk alone with Him, in the still, cool, evening hours. We are in the Garden with our Beloved. We are not alone in the Wilderness. We are fed and led as His own. He, too, knew one is not seen as a prophet in one's own family or hometown. They tried to stone him in Nazareth. When He offered His life for all of humankind, they crucified Him with thieves, to whom He offered Paradise even as He died. He was resurrected because His life was lived to teach us we also will be resurrected to life again in Him. We will walk in the Gardens of Heaven with our Beloved for all eternity. As with Lazarus, he was the simple beggar, accepting crumbs from the table of the Rich Man. However, God knew Lazarus was His friend. He gave him eternal life.

When they told others not to come near them for they were too unholy to share life and spiritual things with them, they lost those souls as friends. However, the Lord offered them higher, and closer, seats than those who shoved them apart from their own virtuous person. The Only True Friend anyone needs is Him, even if one walks alone from all unholy remnants of humankind. He may become the preferred choice of Friend (and Savior) of many who walk alone, ostracized from acceptance by those who are pharisees, the virtuous, the holier-than-thou ones. Scriptures tell us that God said He would spew such as these from His nostrils. He does not like hypocritical behavior, or spiritual pride, in His own children.

Who are we to shun anyone? We are an engrafted Branch. We are the Lost Sheep He saved many years ago. Our ancestors were poor pioneers of this great land. We are to forgive even our socalled enemies. Oh, God, how we wish they knew we love them so. Love is not logical. Money is not our God. He is. Would they also shun our poor, scruffy, holy great-grandparents? We are shunned because we believe we have the same human rights of free speech, enterprise, religion, and political party as was written into our Constitution. We are citizens of the world in America. We are of all races, colors, cultures, religions and ideas. We believe we are free to each worship in our own way as we were offered in our Constitution. We believe we are all God's Children. We are all His Creation. We sit humbly at His knee, wherever He chooses to be with us. We, like Mary, spend all our time alone with Him, eagerly listening to only Him.

We all want to eat at His Table, even if we eat the crumbs and leftovers which fall from His table. We still believe in being part of our one Nation, Under God, however we define God. However, it also seems our personal, individual, prayers and votes do not count. Someone else has decided the take our votes and prayers as their own.

We have been made to play the role of Scapegoat for all the sins of our neighbors; as we are slandered and libeled unceasingly by fearful and hating people. We are now being made to play the role of Sacrificial Lambs of God, even as our Lord also bore the sins of many upon Himself. Thank you, fellow Christians, for helping us to become His martyred disciples, who are still your neighbors, and family. You have been helping us attain His glory. Thank you, though you know not what you do. Thank you, Jesus, for blessing us with even this sad, broken-hearted, existence based on fear, prejudice and intolerance of soul-sick friends and loved ones who no longer share their lives with us. However, I do not thank those who have divided families thusly so that the words of a grandparent are not deemed wise and wonderful by children and grandchildren, now being led by and overwhelmed by the mountains of prejudicial rhetoric of sometimes insane church and governmental leaders who teach doctrines not known by some of us who have long studied and researched the ways of the world and of our Lord.

However, I do have to tell you all, our prayers, and our votes, continue to be heard and answered by our Holy, Omniscient, and Omnipresent Divine Lord and Savior Jesus Christ, who came to bear witness of our Father in Heaven. So, too, did they kill Him when He chose to be our Advocate as an Adversary against those who felt there were no human, political or religious rights for us as gentiles, or of those others who dared to cross the orthodoxy of Sanhedrin, Jewish Priesthood of the Temple, or the Roman Church, and now a Machiavellian time of atavism beyond the acceptance of all enlightened people of all races, kindreds, tongues, and religious pathways.

The teachings of Christ were given us as a fulfillment of the Law and the Prophets. He came to bring us into the Holy Family as Children of God. We are no longer servants and mongrel dogs. Now, through His Grace, we are Family. We are saved by His Love and Grace. The Old Testament Laws have accused us of guilt of breaking all the Commandments, even if we only broke one of the Laws. In the New Testament, the Good News of His Salvation, He says He remembers nothing we have done. If we ask Him, He forgives us and He has taken our errors from us forever so we may enter into the Holy of Holies, even as Priests, and as Holy Heirs to the Kingdom of the Great God. If He has not condemned or ostracized us, why do some feel we are not fit to share His Table, in His House, here upon Earth. We know we are still His Chosen Ones. No one can separate us from His Love and His Salvation of our souls. He still saves and heals us.

As He said, He would go out to find His Guests for His Marriage Supper if His invited Chosen guests did not choose to come to His own intimate gathering of His Son's Wedding Party. Are we all going to be there? Let us don our wedding garments in preparation for His Feast even though we may be outside, in the alleys, all alone from our brethren and sisters inside church homes we all shared. We, who eat sparingly now, may soon dine on rare cuisine. Some of us are wealthy and well-known believers. However, some of us who have had our pews and seats filled by others may not be recognized by our slim gym-exercised figures; our identical, well-groomed, barber shop haircuts; our purely white, bleached, teeth; our healthy, nurtured and doctored, bodies; our designer clothing, large homes and vehicles, all washed and pristine, parked in front of model church buildings. Our only desire and hope is that we are all deemed worthy to be recognized by Him. Our prayers and votes are for the poor and the needy, those of different skin colors, cultures, and even religious paths; the lost, dying, disabled, aged, women and children--the socalled Minorities of the world--who are really the Majority. His people are a diversely beautiful group of people of all stratas of life on Earth (and Cosmos?).

Open your hearts and your doors now while there may still be time. Do not turn away such as these. By so doing, you may have offended some of these little ones. These may be our Lord, His angels, or your own ancestors and grandparents, in disguise. If you do unto the least of these, He tells us we have done these things--good or bad, helpful, or not--unto Him. To whom are you closing your hearts? He tells us we must become like little children in order to accept and enter into the Kingdom of Heaven. Will we be able to enjoy Heaven, or, instead, will we attempt to tell even Jesus who He is to be in His Own World? At this time, we tell everyone exactly how Jesus, and the Father are to be known and followed. Do children tell the Father how to run His own Home?

We, as faith filled, needy, small ones without any powers, will overcome all evils with His Blood. Are your hearts and lives covered by His redeeming, protective, Blood? We were being fed and nurtured, even on leftovers. Are you being filled with His Spirit? Are you His Friend? We, as Children left to wander in the Wilderness, are walking with our hands linked within His. A child is proud and happy to walk safely with his/her parent.

We feel like well-loved little children. We know our prayers are heard by Him. We know our votes are registered and counted by Him. We are those who have been fervently asking Him to record all the evils we have seen perpetrated upon His people everywhere for decades. We know He has heard and recorded our requests in His divine Record Books of Life. He knows He is loved and desired above all else with us. This is why we can walk alone in the Wilderness of America without our own seat in man-made pews. We are of a church not made with hands. We are those who have gone through many long years of refining fires, storms, floods, earthquakes, wealth and poverty. Many of us feel as if we are no one without Him. Thanks be to God for miracles. We are healed. We are His.

These experiences were a very disturbing, enlightening, and uplifting dream. I wept copious tears for those many seeking souls and even wild creatures I was so fervently attempting to feed from the crumbs and leftovers, even as we all shared this protective simple and rough shelter in oneness of the Spirit. The dream was an epiphany of His love. I thank Him for His marvelous love and healing powers.

I was so blessed by this dream. I came at a time when I needed confirmation of His love for us who are having problems surviving in the hard economic times we are facing in this nation. I realized that I was not cast out and ostracized by Jesus. The only ones who question my education, political views, sanity and goodness, are those who also have the unbelievable audacity to question my salvation and my spiritual gifts. The thing that hurts the most is that these selfsame people are those for whom I would have given my life without a second thought. I have lived my spiritual life in front of these I love the most for a very long time. There is grave concern on my part for the souls of those I love. If they question someone who has always loved Jesus and His ways, and who has been filled with God's Holy Spirit for many years, will they not also be very unfair and judgmental with those who are strangers?.

The ways of the pharisees were not acceptable to our Lord. How can anyone believe oneself to be better than another brother or sister in Christ simply because he/she belong to a certain political agenda. Do they not remember the Constitution of our United States and the Bill of Rights contained therein?

However, I must hurry and prepare to go to my classes. Will I see Gabe again? If so, how will he act towards me today. Yesterday when we were together at Zelda's he dared to bare his soul to me. Will he be brave and strong in his resolve to have me as his, or will he be overcome with shyness and remorse for his impulsive expressions of his love for me? Will I see him today at all, or ever again? I am overcome with love, while

I also face the fact that he may disappear out of my life completely. Lord, please lead and guide me this day. Amen

Celia thanks Francesca for her friendship and hospitality before she leaves for her classes. She and Francesca have gone through many of life's adventures together. They value each other as true friends, perhaps for all eternity. It's late so she must hurry off to her classes.

As she drives past the groves which she sometimes shares with her friends and fellow students, she notices one of her friends walking out of the local 24-hour cafe. She knows he has spent all night in the cafe cramming for his exam. She also knows there were probably other homeless people in that cafe. Where else can those without their own homes be warm, have a table which they can use to visit with friends or to read and study? Some people who are in pain and who use alcoholic drinks to cover their pains if they have no medically prescribed pills available may also spend part of their evenings in a favorite bar until it closes. After that, if they so desire, due to weather conditions, illness, or whatever, they leave the bar as it closes and proceed to the nearest all nite coffee shop.

Celia knows of one friend of hers who has lived his whole adult life in his own van. He worked in wilderness recreation areas in food services when he was a younger man. He is now in his early sixties and he is still living in his van.

When he was a young man in the Sixties, he suffered a "splitting" of his mind, as he calls it. He either suffered a mental illness caused from illicit usage of drugs, an altered state of spiritual consciousness which stayed altered, or he became ill with the onset of a genetic emotional disorder. He was handsome and well built. She wondered if he had spent time in an institutional setting such as a monastery, ashram, or even a mental ward or a prison, since he maintained a very private, soft-spoken mystique. He said he had been a father. He never spoke of marriage. At his later stages of life, he looked like an older Native American medicine person, rather than a local Irishman who probably was a descendant of Druids. Due to his back injuries, he drank quite often to numb the pain he suffered sleeping in a metal vehicle for most of his life. He has been a construction worker, so this is a natural result of his lifelong bodily stresses and injuries. However, he loved to keep his van's living areas very neat and his bed made up with pretty bed linens. He is one of her good friends. They have shared many experiences together in their roles as spiritual brother and sister. She had met him at a local family bar to which her university instructor had taken group after class one night. He had taught her much about the sub-culture called homelessness into which she later was forced to enter.

His spiritual gifts are many. He is but one of America's Holy Beggar & zealous Wisdom Seekers who would all have been very accepted in India. There are many American homeless and mentally ill people who would be seen as very intelligent and holy in another, more spiritually and academically advanced society of the Earth.

Years before, in one of her psych courses, Celia had been very shocked to learn the means used to define if one is mentally ill in our Mental Health Centers. The definition of being mentally ill is "To not be able to fit the societal norm" of their own society. Does this tell one we need changes in our nation?

It is a sad reality that there are many on this planet who see normal Americans as citizens of one of the most backward, ill-informed, stupid, non-spiritual, and hardly religious, evil and decadent nations of the modern world. We have high technology, and we rule the world with our military might, backed by our presently abundant wealth. However, to others we may be seen as were those souls existing at the historical Falls of the Great Empires of the Greeks, Babylonians and Romans which dominated the others nations of the world at those times. We are considered to be stupid despotic warlords and spoiled, over-wealthy demagogues. We do not learn from history. We are like spoiled, undisciplined, children who are lacking in the naturally normal restraints and affections of less rich, more ancient and civilized nations. We are hated and feared, even as our universities are used to educate young leaders of those nations, and who go home and take back their own countries governments of others who also wish to share in our bounty. We are seen by many to be the utopian dream nation all have sought throughout the ages. As it is with any desirable person, group, or nation, they are worshipped and revered as world leaders even as they are lusted after, and desired as slaves to those less fortunate. Love and Hatred do indeed make strange bedfellows.

Many who are homeless are different, desirable, and abused by those who do not understand them,. Since some of them are different than the societal norm, their souls with their special spiritual and mental gifts, are suspect. They are hated and abused by many who do not understand them or their roles in society. Prejudice lends itself to it's own specialized study in human behavior. The one who is different is always seen to be a frightening threat to those who are ignorant. This is a normal animal fear instinct. This is why most homeless people learn to become lost in society. Their secrets are kept, as to their locations, lifestyles, and sometimes even their real names.

Celia's long-time friend is an exceptional person. He is simply without any affordable housing which is deemed acceptable by our affluent society.

Indeed, he has a partial university education, as well as being a personally well-read man. He looks and acts like any other. Some know he is homeless. There are many who will never be privy to that well-guarded secret. Those who are mentally ill also attempt to protect themselves from discrimination and abuse by not divulging their illnesses to others who do not understand anything about these things. Ignorance is bliss. To those who may suffer from the abuse of the ignorant, it is an unnecessary evil. Why not become educated as to the special realities in life--your neighbors who dwell among you, stifled and stymied by the unnecessary ignorance of lazy neighbors who never realized Wisdom is to be sought by all--not just a few to whom she is their ideal.

He is a devotee of his religious pathway which is the Bahai faith. The leader of the Bahais was Baha Ullah, who is believed by his followers to be Jesus Christ who has made His Second Coming, unknown and unaccepted by the Christian world. He lived and died. His monumental tomb is located atop a hill overlooking the seaport city of Haifa.

Celia hasn't seen him for a long time. She is concerned for his well being. However, when she thinks of him, she usually finds herself running into him someplace. She misses him. Celia is always very sad if she fears she has lost contact with a friend. To her a friend is a friend for life. But enough of her friends and homelessness as a study. The Lord said they would always be with us. However, that does not mean we are to treat them as the invisible men and women to whom we blindly turn a deaf ear and a blind eye. We are to offer to assist if we are able. It is even fun to give when we have the least ourselves. God sees and knows all. He tells us He loves that type of open-hearted giver who does not keep score on generosities shared in life with others. It is only all right to remember to thank others who assist ourselves.

The day is like any other, EXCEPT for Gabe. She cannot wait to see him. She hopes she will be able to concentrate on her work and lectures in her classes. She knows she has never felt exactly like this before in her life. She is truly in love with Gabe. She believes Her Lord has saved them for each other. A miracle is afoot. She can feel it in her heart, soul, and even within her logical mind.

Celia realizes she must make a plan carefully for her day if she is to meet Gabe at Zelda's at 4 p.m. Her classes go smoothly though the hours drag by slowly until she can be on her way off the campus. The afternoon was one of those days she called "blue-green blustery days"--the kinds of days which literally call to nature lovers everywhere.

She remembered to grab a sweater from her car as she got out at Zelda's. The winds tend to rise between 3-5 p.m. near the ocean, and she didn't want to catch a chill or spend all of her time with Gabe running indoors to the Ladies' Room.

Gabe was early as she also managed to be. Seemingly, after years of not finding each other, both of them had their intentions to make up for lost time, and to not lose each other ever again.

"Hi! How are you?" His voice sounds joyously alive and happy as he greets Celia. She tries hard to cover her bubbling elation at the sight of him. She wants to burst into one of those silly, school girl grins.

As with many of those "accusing voices" we all carry with us, hers had exceptionally depressing as to her relationship with Gabe. Celia never suffered from low self-esteem, but she truly found her current plight to be demoralizing and depressing as a houseless single woman. In addition, though she felt in no way to be unattractive, she also has the normal human insecurities suffered by those who are newly in love.

Together at long last, the hours had passed very slowly for both of them. In fact, each second of each minute seemed endless. This is the sweet delight of those who find themselves completely, enamoured and fascinated with another significant other. In the case of Gabe and Celia, this was even worse. They felt themselves to be star-crossed lovers with an ancient relationship beyond the comprehension of many people. However, whether as a star-crossed lover, or one who bumbles through life mating carelessly, loving completely and wholeheartedly, without shame, love can be excruciatingly painful, even as it is the delightful nectar and the healing balm for the soul and heart. For this type of relationship, parting would indeed be eternal sorrow.

Celia knows the Son of God knows her every thought and feeling. She knows Gabe and herself have not met miraculously to again be immediately separated. She knows this within her own heart.

She also knows they both share an impatience to be together as a couple married in His spiritual bonds of holy matrimony.

How to make a loving, long-lasting relationship become a reality is the question even as it is a problem. Wisdom, love, kindness, forgiveness, fairness, goodness and many others of the attributes of the nature of God must be the graces of a joyous, merciful, an faithfilled (and thereby faithful) soul as one prepares for establishment of a star-crossed relationship and marriage.

It is of most importance that the husband have the respect of his wife. She must also be loveable in all ways in order for him to love her. These are the ideals of an idyllic marital relationship, however, since men and women are not perfect, it is possible they may err from time to time.

Both Celia and Gabe had spent many lonely years as single people analyzing, researching and learning the do's and don't's of good romantic relationships. Knowing each other as respected and loved friends was on top of each of their Lists. Each soul must realize it is a divine creation dedicated to living as a developed, wise, and holy (whole), fully-actualized soul--even if it lives alone as a monk, nun, or single adult. In fact, it is of utmost importance for each soul, married, single, widowed or divorced, to attempt to become the most nearly perfect creation possible. By so seeking to be like our Creator, we honor our Maker, our Savior, and Friend.

Celia truly felt it was important for her to always strive to be as "properly single" as it was for her to be "correctly married". No other choices were hers, howbeit hard it was to follow her own personal prescription for her own carefully-lived life. Of course, some people never have these concerned choices to make in their lives. Those who are crude, impolite, mean and ugly do not have problems outrunning suitors or lechers.

Celia's heart is full of love for the man she assumes Gabe to be. She knows it is important to be sure who he really is as a man if she is to consider him as her prospective husband and eventually as the father of any children they may have together.

There can be no negative large questions about each other as one enters the times when lasting decisions are made regarding engagement and marriage.

It is also the loving responsibility of each partner to at least attempt to continue to be and to look at least as much the same as possible as when one meets each other. One also should not use spells and prayers against the will of another in order to draw someone else to one's self. Neither is it ethical to attempt to delude the other person as to one's true nature or appearance. Both Celia and Gabe had known others who could not control their negative behavior patterns in order to sustain courtships through acceptable lengths of time to know one another enough to be able to form stabile marital relationships. They knew it was good they both lived in the same city so they could explore each other's patterns of living, and get acquainted completely before they made any lasting decision about their relationship. Many of those who are unsuitable for marriage try to hide these facts from others. In fact, many of those with the worst habitual behavioral problems try to find unsuspecting strangers who live in other areas away from their own communities. For such as these people, it is absolutely necessary for them to do so in order to find anyone who will take a chance on them as a partner.

Rule #1 - Make attempts to never date anyone at a distance from yourself. They may not be as they want you to think they are. This is one of the age-old secrets kept from the unwary by those with unsavory lifestyles and "skeletons in their closets".

Also, Celia recognized the dangerously insecure natures of those men (or even women) who may form an obsessive stalker's attitude for one. Many are prone to call on the telephone and to hang up simply to selfishly and compulsively keep track of the person who is the object of their affections. This can cause the person so pursued to feel very insecure, frightened, and prone to become paranoid over such a situation. Obsessions of the unstable, insecure and unsocialized person may change them from simply a strange and lonely person into a dangerous predator who literally stalks another, whether they are desirous or aware of their predator or not. It is important to avoid such "fatal attractions" at all costs.

These types of relationships are not partnerships. They are ownerships and harassments by those who must control others and situations in order to feel secure as people. Indeed, these are not strong, secure, or stabile individuals--whether men or women. Yes, women can also stalk another--whether of the same or opposite sex.

Celia's code for life was to "Be careful!"! Those who are innocent and ignorant are prime targets of those who exploit others for sexual or financial favors through money or any type of property they so desire. After all, to some, something is better than nothing.. Many are the lewd, even criminally dangerous, worldly-wise people "out there" who lay in wait like a wild beast attempting to see who they can lure into their traps. The unwary, the innocent, and the unwisely ignorant person, often with a head stuck in the sand so as not to see bad things or people, is fair game for such a devious, conniving, soul. Unfortunately, this aggressive type is far more common in the civilized world than many nice people would like to know. These human predators exist among even those who masquerade as holy and virtuous, whether rich or poor. They can be those who are good salespeople, aggressive business persons, and the like. They are known to go to churches for the sole purposes of finding untouched and sexually safe young people. This is a very sad fact of life. There is much murder, mayhem, sado-masochism, perversions, incests, and white collar thefts in upper-middle class America than one would ever like to know about.

Celia and Gabe are mature souls, neither of whom are desirous of living in a sick relationship together. They want to stay away from questionable people and behaviors of such types of souls.

Both of them live their lives as souls who are totally dedicated to paths of holiness and righteousness, yet do not act as if they are pharisees or hypocrites incapable of sin. They are mature souls who know anyone can do anything given the extremes of stressful living. They are accepting of themselves and others as fallible people who are simply attempting to be like their Master. They believe in the higher karmic paths of love, light, and wholeness. Perversions are available and can be pursued by any unwary, inquisitive soul. They know this. However, no matter how careful, anyone can stumble and fall into evil without in any way seeking it. Only the wary ones, protected and guided by the Holy Spirit, will survive to fight another holy battle of the soul and flesh for him or herself and others.

Celia knew Gabe was a respected man in his community. However, she knew she would continue to meet him in public places for as long as she could do so, thereby preventing themselves from being tempted to become too intimate too soon. A person who has respect for one's self and the other person is also loving and caring enough to be contemplative and thoughtful about the ways one may use to control our hormones and libidos.

It's especially hard to be apart when all one can think of is merging as one. In this world, humanbeings use merging of their bodies regularly and often forget "Merging" in Heaven is the merging of mind and soul. If one is interested in an eternal love based on wholeness and respect, as well as attractions of two bodies for one another, one must plan for this type of relationship prayerfully and well. These two desired each other as soul mates as well as lovers. Celia and Gabe are the types of lovers who require the Divine Stamp of Approval upon their lives together, or apart.

As they sat down at their familiar umbrella table, they grasped each other's hand as if they'd never let go. Coffee was on their menus but not in their thoughts.

Each find their hearts ready to burst with emotionally charged statements full of their romantic feelings for the other. The day was magical. The bright sun sparkled on the gently breaking surf. This was a day like no other. Many a couple has become mesmerized and intoxicated by the wonderfully beautiful and romantic setting at Zelda's. After all, F. Scott Fitzgerald was so smitten by his own Zelda, the woman for whom this beachfront eating spot was so named.

Many times Celia had gone there with her beloved Aunt R. and Uncle A., who she always thought of fondly as "The Lovers" They had been married over 65 years, yet they were still "an item" to each other. To Aunt R., he was always "My Guy". He loved her all those years from her first kiss. They were one of those couples one could believe had been together for eons and throughout eternity. They were "People for any season", ageless, politically and socially aware, caring and ethically sound as individuals and as a couple. Many had been blessed by their carefully planned and shared lives. After Uncle A. crossed over, Celia had a dream of the party Uncle A. was preparing for his beloved R. He had prepared a bounteous feast for her arrival, as well as a theatrical performance. Aunt R. left to be with Uncle A.shortly after Celia had this dream. What a great party it must have been! As she sat at Zelda's with Gabe, she knew they would have wanted her to be with him at the special spot they had loved so much, where they had shared such happy and lighthearted times with Celia. Celia felt as if Gabe and she were having a celebration of their long and happy marriage, while she and he were hoping for the same type of relationship for themselves.

While they were alive, they had spent time on the beautiful beaches at Santa Cruz. Uncle would play his banjo as a crowd gathered to listen to him play, seated in his natty brimmed hat from the Forties, with tie, blazer and slacks. What a charming couple. They loved to go to hear the Dalai Lama when he came to the area. They loved the redwoods and the Indians of northern California. He was a photographer with Eastman. She was his faithful and adoring wife who was always there for "her Guy".

"Hello, Hello, I missed you!"---Two conversations overlapped. They shared their dreams, interests, eccentricities, and their pet peeves. The day ended finally at 10 p.m. There was little time left for any place for Celia to go except to an all-night study session at the 24-hour cafe. She dreaded the thought of no sleep time. However, it was too dark to check out her fellow campers at the grove.

Homeless women are statistically an endangered species. They are fair game for all types of predators, especially human males. Those women who do not have the protection of a vehicle injure their feet and legs from their continual need to stay mobile and out of the clutches of those who seek them as prey for sexual attacks. Celia was sad to hear many homeless women have injured legs and feet from their unprotected situations. If one is without funds, one cannot just hang out at a cafe without buying something in order to have the amenities of a table and chairs, warmth, light and safe surroundings and companionship if need be. There are many people with backpacks at all night cafes. Many students congregate in cafes and libraries to study. Homeless people, and maybe even angels, love to go to libraries and cafes. In fact, the angels, as shown in several popular movies, seem to prefer the hallowed, quiet, halls of wisdom and learning at universities and libraries. There are many souls who need safe havens, including churches, if they are indeed sanctified places of refuge.

Celia had been learning many things by experiencing homelessness. She could not imagine why she had to go through this period of her life.

She had worked with Social Services and Mental Health Agencies, and knew about the needs of each human being for basic survival needs of housing, food, and clothing to be met in order for life to exist on even the lowest rung of society's ladder of success. Survival, to some, is the most basic of success stories. This invisible sub-culture is all around everyday citizenry across this socalled wealthiest nation in the world. This all became part of our lives on a massive scale during the years of the Great World Depression of the early 20th Century.

Then there were a few very good years some call The Classic Era of the Good Life in America from the mid-1950's through the next two decades following World War II. Celia called it the most abysmal times she had ever faced alone.

"Gabe, where are you tonight? I so want to be with you, but I don't want to cover a lot of distance between us too fast." She & Gabe know they will be together forever, if not in this life but in the world to come. He is her Beloved even as her Lord is her Divine Beloved. Theirs is as pure as the white rose of true love. No one can ever separate them again. They will walk the paths of Heaven with Him forever. We know their divinely planned meeting will end in a lifetime of spiritual happiness. We know they are bonded as a couple. They will overcome all obstacles by their shared beliefs in the All-Encompassing Beloved Father. We will all now leave this dear couple in His care. Their lives have been ours briefly in order that we might learn something about the plights of the homeless and those who dare to seek relationships with others.

****

Do we dare to hope the love of human beings for their neighbors will be sufficiently powerful to overcome the plights of the poor and homeless among us? There are many selfish people who are willing to do anything in order to make sure they are affluent and well established in all of the world's socially acceptable business and religious communities. We hope so. Celia dares to hope there may be a miraculous ending to the ongoing plight of the homeless of America. Is there a chance she and Gabe may be able to truly build a life and family together? How can se overcome the stigma, and very real confines, of her living situation? She is horrified to realize there no futures at all for some of us. No matter how bright, beautiful, educated or not educated, working or not, there is no way to afford to have even a small dwelling of one's own. There are others who have selfishly helped to inflate the costs of renting and buying lodging far beyond the reach of the working poor of America. There are many fine mothers and fathers who would like to give their families a "real" home. Some have only a vehicle such as a car or a school bus. Some have very modest low-rent housing in tenement or ghetto areas. There are those who do not realize many apartments and mobile homes are priced far higher than the salaries of those who are working in low paid jobs. Many well qualified employees feel fortunate to have employment. Oftentimes we find more real joy and thankfulness in the humble homes of the poor. Their families and friends are their treasures. He is the Shepherd who cares for those who are living in poverty and disability. Sometimes we find more real thankfulness and sharing in the hearts and homes of those who are seen to have nothing. It is mentioned in the Holy Scriptures of how the rich man wonders at the ingenuity of the poor man and his family. Those who practice good tribal laws of sharing and caring will overcome all dangers because they have love one for another. Love, again, is the Key to making our lives a Heaven rather than a Hell.

We have also knowledge of those families living sparsely who gently rear their beautiful children as wise, peaceful, empathetic and kind human beings. They help them getting established as young families. There are also some selfish parents who become fearful about taking care of their children. Sadly, one or both of the adults may force the child onto the streets to try to survive. What do you suppose happens to that dear young and innocent soul? Imagination should give the answers.

Then, if one or both of the parents are not heartless, selfish, ignorant or insane, or are addicts, and many are, there will be the reinstatement of a National Armed Services Draft Board to snatch these youngsters from their safe homes. Many of these were kept from their less spiritual neighbors. The brightest stars, the treasured posterity of poor families, will be taken to be used as "Cannon Fodder" by those who care not as much for peace on Earth as that their warlord positions in the annals of history be insured forever. These will not be known for their Heavenly Treasures, but, instead, for their powerful positions in the historical War Records of that violent training world called Earth/Avichi or Hell World.

It is obvious we have sucked the last bit of sugar from our bitter pill. Reality is not easy to face. Therefore, we sugar coated a slice of life called "Homelessness" and a world where the poor and the rich grow up together. There are many other horror stories to be sugar coated and fictionalized in order to spare the innocent from embarressment and shame. The question is, "Who should feel ashamed?" We are penalizing the hurting poor and needy, the disabled, the aged, the veterans of our many wars, and the children of all of these. We are treating "the least of these" (and our Lord) very badly at times. It is time for us to remember the teachings of the Beloved Spirit of our Father.

How dare we call ourselves God's people? We are not His until we begin the fast He requires. (Isaiah 58) He requires us to give to the poor and needy, to serve and to heal, to treat fairly and truthfully, and to set all these captives free. We are not a just and holy nation unless we treat even the least of these as if they were our Lord. These are His own words. I am just a scribe who listens to the words of my Beloved. We are His Beloved if we hear and obey His Commandments.

We must pray for His divine love to enable us to understand the plights of the poor and needy. If we do not learn from our life experiences, we may not understand that all of these are also His children. It was the author's joy to work with various Human Services Departments for many years. There were several times when I remembered I must think of each person as if they were an angel, or even our Father, in disguise. It is our desire to never harm nor offend "the least of His". This means we are to treat all sentient beings with the love and respect we would show to the Creator or His Messenger.

One day a dear Christian lady was standing in line with a young man who appeared to be homeless. She was finding herself feeling judgmental thoughts until she heard the Father say "He's also one of My children." Thus will we know if they are His. They will be known because of His love in their hearts and the smiles upon their faces. This is not to say that all of these are safe. Many of God's homeless are also emotionally of physically ill. There are many beautiful holy ones who are "Sojourners", as if they were "A Stranger" in a strange world. Perhaps their worlds suffer not because of greed and selfishness. Instead, they came to help us who suffer from the dis-eases of this beautiful world. Perhaps some of the poor and needy are really angels and the Lord testing us.

There are many homeless saints in the streets of one of the most affluent nations in the world. Perhaps some of them are here to test those who know not the ways of the poor. If those who have been richly blessed will not learn the way of the Good Samaritan, they may reap a harvest of destruction in their nation and loss of the precious immortal souls of themselves and their loved ones.

"HOLY PSYCHE--EXPANDED REALITIES OF THE INFINITE SOUL"

OTHERS OF THOSE INVISIBLE PEOPLE

It is important to realize many of the homeless of America are simply unemployed workers who have lost their jobs for one reason or another. There are also many disabled of all types, including those who are emotionally and mentally ill. Drug and alcohol addictions exist. There are also some of these people who rely the pain numbing influence of alcohol to be able to bear ongoing pain. If they do not get proper guidance with their living and medical needs, they rely on street drugs, as well as alcohol, to cover their physical and emotional pain.

The street does not reject women, children, old men and women. It welcomes any who walk into it with, or without, shopping cart of tote bag. In fact, life is not kind at all. Some people lose their own homes to abusive housemates or spouses. They may not have anything. This is why hygiene kits and resource lists are of utmost importance to the person without a money, a tooth brush and toothpaste, hair care items, eye glasses, or any clothing or warm outer garments and boots or good walking shoes. Things others take for granted such as a hot shower or a bath room are not taken for granted by the homeless. They have learned these things the hard way--through personal loss and lack. God help us all!

There, but for the grace of God, go any one of us. The trauma of being homeless, without food and sustenance, and support group(s), is enough to drive many a tender and innocent soul into premature insanity. It is very hard for any of us to be forced to face the grim realities of our Earthly existence. To do so is to symbolically open Pandora's Box. For some sad souls, they see nothing left in Pandora's Box...not even "Hope". These souls feel doomed and destroyed. They believe, and it may be true, that nothing remains available to them except more disability and a long, hard, dying process. Truth is stranger than fiction, and just as violent and cruel. The plight of the homeless is a hellish nightmare. Many of the homeless are the holy and the innocent ones.

We must look within our hearts and locate compassion and empathy. If we have not lost these Fruits of God's Holy Spirit, we may wish to pull them out of our heart centers and prepare to use them creatively to assist these dear ones, many of whom are of our neighbors, or even those who are our own flesh and bones. Homelessness is not discriminatory. It can be the plight of any of us. We may be forced to love and serve one another, even as we would wish someone else to do unto us should we meet with such suffering in our lives. To love is to care. To care is to give a drink of water to the least of these dear neighbors. It is obvious from His Words that He also loves even the least of these as His Beloved.

112. MORE INSIGHTS– THE SAD DEGRADATION OF NATIVE PEOPLE

Depression & Futility
Dream: October 21, 2004, 5:15 a.m.

I went to bed thinking there was a special message coming this morning. I had no idea it would involve the people of my heart, the ones I love without knowing exactly all the reasons why.

The Dreamer's Thoughts:

Perhaps because my soul has been adopted by their souls as our people adopted their children out to strangers and sent them far from their homes to attend the white man's schools. They often married into other tribes and lost their own family's tribal cultural, linguistic and spiritual heritages. Some see it as a planned program of genocide of the native people of America. One hopes this is not true. However, destruction of the buffalo was considered a good way to starve these strong people of the this Good Red Earth. Some very great hunters such as Buffalo Bill helped to make the plains where the buffalo lived become drenched in the blood of these noble and respected ancient creatures. In fact, they were killed until they became all but extinct. Is it not just that there is a herd of buffalo kept at Buffalo Bill's burial areas? All of this based on the hateful statements of ignorant white men who dared to think and say, "The only good Indian is a dead Indian." Is it any wonder there are many people who wonder if the white men are devils? Not all Indians have agreed that "It's a good day to die." Many of the children of white men of those awful killing times have been adopted to know Indian ways, to weep and to work for Indian causes. Blessed be the names of the holy ones who have trained these initiates in the mysteries of the holy tribal people. The ways of the Great Spirit and the great laws of life of Buddha have sustained many of us when they took our Lord and re-crucified Him and us in His land called America–the "Land of the Free, and the Home of the Brave." What a mockery of all that is holy to any holy soul.

Justice will be done. Great is the Spirit of the People of the Holy Book, the Books of Life and of the Keepers of the Tribal Records. All is not lost. All is not sad. All are not statistics in social work reports. We are all the children of the One who knows and sees all. These people know of the Watchers and the Star Maps. They know of the Maid of Peace, the White Buffalo Calf Woman and return of the White Buffalo Calf of Peace on Earth. They know they will overcome, even as the Blacks of African American heritage sing this song of their victory over the atrocities they have also suffered at the hands of evil White Americans. They smoke and they dance to bring these things to pass. We have not given up. We will simply become stronger in the powers of the Holy Ones. His Peace will reign forever. We believe the evils of those who are sad, fearful and dangerously ignorant will perish as Earth renews herself and her creatures. Resurrection from death is for all who love and practice holy right ways of living. The Good Red Road leads to Paradise for all.

In the dream there seemed to be two roles, that of the hurting and entrapped American Native person and the sadly hurting person trying to help that person. I felt the hurt, the sadness and the feelings of futility and wounded pride of the man who was trying to show me his terrible plight. He was entangled with the laws of this nation from the time he was a small child. He felt owned, controlled and degraded by social and correctional systems which had no understanding of his personal and cultural needs either as a man, a father, or as an indigenous person who lives as part of nature–not separated from it as does the white man and his culture. His roles had been usurped by harsh laws and unaware systems and people who do not know how to live in their own cultures, much less his.

I was being shown lives–like drawers of lives–rather than as one human being to another. Each drawer, or file, was just another set of terribly sad circumstances. In one drawer I shared the sadness of a father who had a small son with bullets in his head despite the man's attempts to protect him from the terrible frustrated rages of neighbors who could kill him as they sprayed bullets over the neighborhoods into other's homes and children. This wasn't even Wounded Knee. This was just day to day life in the world of the disenfranchised poor Native American. I felt heartsick for the person whose life was placed in a file drawer and also for the person who wanted so much to help and could not help. Small band aids could not cover the massive wounds of the all of my poor people. I know this. I have worked for many years with the never ending plights of the poor and homeless.

The fathers were often not even allowed the protection of their own family members. Not only had they lost the protector role of their families, but they had also lost their roles as husbands, fathers, chiefs and priests of their families, their tribes and nations. Their souls are sad–whether in the land of the living or if they view their families from the Other Side. The ancestors will once again come forth. Rituals and religions will be once again resurrected even as their bones are resurrected. It seems Indians and whites may learn much from one another. Respect is needed for the original natives of this land. The white man must learn of the powerful gods and rulers of this continent. They are not all gone. They are patiently awaiting the time to come forth to tell their story of the way things must be. The hierarchies of heaven and earth have been disturbed. The souls of the land, the people and of the heavenly hierarchal rulers have not been heard. They will be heard. Everyone deserves their "Day in Court", not just the poor Indian who, along with all the poor, are sometimes forced to steal in order to feed himself and his family. Those white leaders who rule do not know the people. They do not even know themselves. If they were forced to put upon their own feet the moccasins of any of these poor people–even another like themselves of poorer status–they would not know how to feed themselves. They, like the rich man, of the white man's Book, would not know how the poor man survives. Neither do many of even those who love and try to assist the poor person know how life really is for those who are attempting to eke out a living so close to the earth, in a society geared to tell us only high technology will conquer all. Those people who embrace their heritages and learn to live once again off the earth will be protected by Mother Earth. Many of the "civilized" white people will die because they have forgotten the ways of the ancestors in their attempts to become rich and famous. They have not been loyal and caring of the needs of their own family members. The loss of the white man will be the gain of the red man. Many of them still are of the opinion the white man will kill himself after he has tried to kill all the other two and four-legged creatures, as well as the finned and feathered ones. When that happens, the red man will again regain his land and his god. Yes, he may see his god as red–not blonde and white, even as the African may see his god or goddess as black and incredibly beautiful, strong and wise beyond words. The Great Spirit is holy even as we must be whole to be children of this holy and just deity. His heart is many hearts and skin color is not the way to discern Him. His people are like Him in their deeds. They live His love one to another. These people inately knew His ways for He had taught them His ways even as He taught them to the white people.

I write once again in the spirit of the Indian. One time years ago as a university student I awakened telling others of the sadness of the bereaved husband and father who described the massacre of his family by the white man. His heart was broken. His frustration and sorrow was immense. He was unable to rest in the land of his fathers. He walked around that day and came by in a dream to tell me of his sadness as a ghost roaming the bloodied Earth telling the story of his ghostly unrest and of the Earth still crying over the blood poured out upon her breast.

He weeps also for the degraded destruction of his beaten and destroyed Mother, the Earth. He saw much. He is unable to rest in peace. The Earth must be cleansed by tears and other restitutions to herself and to her people. These things have not been forgotten by the souls of the abused and murdered. Neither has the soil of the Earth recovered from the bruising of her flesh by human flesh. She will perhaps finally react and call forth the denizens of the heavens and of the underworld to come forth to help her. All the voices of earth and heaven, planet and humankind, call forth their sad pleas to the ears of the Great Spirit, the Father of All. He will hear and weep before and after the purging of the Earth of her great virus of human life and her unhealed wounds of invasion and rapine of her own flesh by those who saw themselves as the white supremacists created by their gods of greed and lust to attempt to dominate and control Mother Earth and all the other souls who lived freely upon her breast. It will be a tremendous surprise to such souls to realize they were not the only ones loved and empowered by the Great Spirit of all. The spoiled angry ones will learn much–hopefully not before it is too late for anyone to live upon the beautiful mounds of Mother's breast.

There have been books written about the Native American people. Beyond all these efforts, it will take the empathetic and healing hearts, hands and words to make recompense to the hurting souls of these people. Prayers must be offered to the Great Spirit who created and can heal the hearts of the earth and of her people everywhere. The world is bathed in the blood of the innocents who simply believed in their God-given rights of free will to live and to die happy in their own lands with their own people–without the intrusion of strangers who lusted after their lands–and had no desire to truly become friends and neighbors. The ways of the socalled civilized strangers were not the ways of the truly civilized and religious socalled primitive people of these continents of the New World–more ancient than any. Her nations were uncounted and reached into the several hundreds. Her rulers were the proud and unabashed heroes of their domains. Great were the deeds and cultures of these lands. It is our great desire to once again see all of the people living in harmony upon the breast of their Mother with no remembrance of the brief interruption caused by the destroyers of all peace on Earth–the hordes of those who would invade, rather than visit, any land upon which they would place their feet. Peace can only be held by those who are full of the love and wisdom of the Great Spirit.

If our pioneer people had been able to take time to get acquainted with those who lived on this continent for many centuries before their arrivals they would have been less fearful of everything their neighbors said and did. One example of this is that the drums and dancing were taken to be war dances. Perhaps if they had visited with native people they would have been shown many of these dances were those done by the tribal members in order to attempt to make sure the earth stayed balanced. Thus the measured cadence of drummer and dancer. Many of these people knew the earth was given to alter her rotation on her axis and to become "unbalanced" and to wobble. Prehistoric tribal memories and records told of times such as the white people had forgotten. The native people made sure they never forgot those times described by the storytellers as the times when the earth fell over or moved out of her normal rotation cycles. Thus, they ritually danced to make sure they helped to keep the earth turning at a safe rotation cycle. Wisdom and tactful communication could have helped white people to be less fearful. The people of this continent all have records of several other Ages of earth life prior to the singular event the people of the Middle East and Far East remember as the time of Deluge, the Flood of Noah. The Meso-American people know of at least four Ages prior to this Fifth Sun Age. The prophetic warning for the Fifth Sun is destruction by Fire this time. ("The Fire This Time", by Afro-American author, James Baldwin.)

We must pray for peace upon this planet. We must be at peace with ourselves and with each other. We must see ourselves as all connected and family units of one massive Tribe of human life, living at peace and at-onement, in close communion with ourselves, the Holy One and with all others.

We must always remember we are all Children of the Great Father. We are not statistics. We are all human beings who are worthy of His loving concern. None must be made to feel like lesser souls of a lesser god. We are all the Children of Royal Lineage and Priesthood if we seek to know and to follow the Good Ways of the Great Spirit of All.

This book is written to share truths that will set all souls free to walk in the truth of the Eternal and Universal Spirit of all who are Seekers and Lovers of That One, The Manifested and Manifold God. Truth shall set us all free. This is my goal for daring to share with such a diverse group of souls. I worship the Divine One in the spirits of the Sufi, Gnostic, Buddhist, Theosophist, Native American and, above all, as a sibling of my Beloved Cosmic Christ. We are all created with the Blessings and Love of the Beloved Father of all. I love all His creation as one who sees Divine Beauty in all paths to the Center, which are those of Light and Love. We do not wish to live in bondage to a theocratic system of government. We are not rebels and terrorists. We are His Children, created by His Love. His Truth will set us free to live His Love for all to see and to learn of the Blessing Path. We wear arm or head bands of all who are persecuted for the sake of the inalienable rights of freedom and righteousness. The author, at this time, claim citizenship with all those who are denied equality of personal rights to life, liberty, speech, religion and governmental choices. It is my firm belief that the laws of this continent have always been those of equal fairness for all tribal people who love and seek the Great Spirit. I claim my membership as one of His adopted Native American children. I stand in support of the rights of all the North American Indian tribal people. I also claim my birthright as a citizen of the United States of America. My Anglo-American heritage is long as one who can claim genealogical ties to many of the European and Middle Eastern areas of the world. Several of these ancestors signed the Constitution and Declaration of Independence of the United States of America. I claim heritage in Colorado, California and wherever there is one who has no one to represent them. It is my desire to make a vow to do my duty to my Heavenly Father and to all His Children everywhere. I want to serve Him and His Will more than any other desire in my life. It is my desire to assist others to know and to find the One who loves and comes to everyone who seeks Him. This is a divine promise. It is a free gift. It is my intention to give anyone who desires to know of Him a wonderful chance to hear of life that is stranger than fiction which can only be lived by walking closely in the Spirit with Him. Yes, the Holy Spirit has not left us. We are not alone. We are led and guided even as Moses was led and guided through the Wilderness of the Sinai Desert.

I carry the banner of hope and truth for all who feel as if they were disenfranchised and unrepresented by our national government or religious organizations at this time. We must stand together for our highest values and rights. The tongues of evil ones speak lies and slander. Black is white and white is black. The virtuous weep with frustration and rage over the injustices done in the names of the Holy Ones. We must pray for our enemies and attempt to do good to those who persecute us unjustly in the name of our Lord Jesus. They do not realize they also persecute Him and His other lambs. He has sheep of many pastures. They hear His Voice and do not walk alone, ex-communicated and forlorn. They walk in the Shekinah Glory of His Spirit of Truth and Light which will set all free.

I speak as a daughter of the Earth. I am representing Him in the many roles I play as His daughter who desires Him and His will above all else. There is nothing else but Him. I am no one and nothing. He is everything. I love Him in everlasting adoration as my Savior. I serve Him as His daughter who now claims this land for His Great Spirit in the name of the Native Woman, Wowetsin. I am His daughter, washed in the Blood of the

Lamb of God who was slain for the sins of the world. I am baptized in water, the Holy Spirit and in the Love of the Father. I beseech That One for the sakes of all who love right ways. We are all His creations--whether two legged, four legged, feathered or with fins. The colors of our skins are all His creation. We claim equal human rights for all.

In the words of Richard Oakes, "Alcatraz Is Not An Island." We, like Alcatraz, are an Idea and a Dream. We believe for a miraculous release from all bondage and injustices. We wish to be set free to serve our Beloved Father, in Spirit and in Truth. We claim this nation for all those who seek Him in Spirit and in Truth of all nations, tongues, races, cultures, religions and nations. Our ways are the ways of the Ancients. We return to the Ways of Truth for we are told the Peacemakers are the Children Of God. We also believe "Those who worship Him must worship Him in Spirit and in Truth." His Truth will set us free to serve Him "In Spirit and in Truth, as One Nation Under God, with Liberty and Justice for All."

We are free people made so by the hand of the Great Spirit of all that is. We are looking forward with great expectation for the birth of the White Buffalo Calf. It is said this Calf will usher in a time of great peace upon the Earth.

113. MORE DIVINE INSIGHTS PARALLEL WORLDS & OTHER DIMENSIONS

I awakened with a most unusual dream of parallel worlds and other dimensions. These were not normal thoughts for me. However, others who have experienced these realities of worlds within worlds have been shown by others in their dreams, books, and movies. However, my perceptions and perspectives of life had been firmly rooted into the soils of terra firma, in a third-dimensional world, with 24 hour days and years made up of 365 days. In my dream, I saw myself living three complete lives as well as the one in which I am fulfilling this life destiny. These insights seemed very real to me in my dream state awareness. However, when I awakened, I was in a state of shocked amazement and disbelief. "My God, I had experienced, and perhaps am still experiencing, living other, vastly diverse, lives at the very same time I am also living my own present life!" This was a mind-bending thought. The currently-held religious and cultural beliefs of the perspectives on human realities held by most people in my modern high-tech world had indeed become convaluted, and blown asunder. I will try to share some of the unbelievably amazing roles I was concurrently playing in other lives shown in my dreamstate:

1. *Wife/Heterosexual Marriage*--In the dreamstate scenes I saw myself living a full life as the husband of a family, in Montreal, Canada. We were seated as a couple in our kitchen with our blonde son and daughter.

2. *Husband/Lesbian Marriage* --I was also in a lesbian marriage, as well as the relationship with my wife and family in Montreal. In this life role, I was playing a fatherly role to our two blonde sons. I was dividing my time between this role and my life in Montreal as the father.

3. *Buddhist Monks* - I was a young Tibetan male monk running and leaping happily over beautiful stone steps upon a Tibetan mountain hillside with a young woman, also a dedicated Tibetan Buddhist nun. We were advanced souls and we could fly and levitate at will. We were ecstatically happy though I am also living:

4. *My Present-Time & Space Life* - A wonderfully full spiritual marriage of great love as wife to my wonderful friend and husband. Seemingly, we have come to in this destiny for the many lessons to be learned and lived through at this time on planet Earth. We are both social psychologists, interested in human rights as social workers, deeply engrossed in our spiritual lives with goals of fulfillment of the highest

actualizations possible. We are priestly seekers and those who protect the metaphysical truths of the world. We desire the Divine Will of rightness, wholeness, truth, justice, purity, peace and love for all. We have personally chosen our marital name because it means peace, bliss, and love. We desire only that all sentient beings attain the highest roles of divine perfection such as are taught by Christ and the Buddha.

My thoughts were confused. How could I be divided as a soul into the parallel life roles? This is not part of my teachings. However, my dream showed concurrent lives. I was each one of these people. I wondered if I was hallucinating. Perhaps I am. I wondered if I had lost my sanity, or, indeed, my soul. Are these separated lives prior or ones I am to live later? Are these lives lived within circles upon one spiraling Web of Life?

Many times "I have felt as if I have lived six lifetimes in this one lifetime". I have mentioned this--generally jokingly--to several of my close friends. As one who has come to this planet to live in the 19th Century American world, I have lived in relationships named by the anthropologists, "Serial Monogamy". This means people want monogamous marriages in American Christianity. However, many are polygamous souls. Therefore, many souls have been forced into several marital roles in one lifetime. These consecutive marital roles have made many of us feel as if we are humans who must change our appearances, statuses, and positions as if we were human chameleon lizards. The selfish, cold-hearted, premeditated, changing of marital partners has become so common as to be no more than a change of clothing for some unloving souls.

Personally, I was one of those 20th Century socalled 'Renaissance' people who has experienced far more events and roles than I ever desired or sought. If I can list such anomalies in this lifetime, how do we know what other truths and awarenesses await us if we are open to new thoughts. After all, we have always been told we cannot comprehend the mysteries of the Divine.

In this one feminine lifetime I have changed my life several times--at the desire or whim of my husband:

1. Age 18-29. I was the the young patriotic wife of a United States Naval Officer/Aviator. I pinned his Naval Aviator wings upon his uniform at Pensacola, Florida, in 1959. He flew jet aircraft off Naval aircraft carriers while I sat for many lonely months of two Pacific cruises with our young son and daughter. This was a wonderful and also an awful time in the author's life.

2. *"Single Mother with Two Small Children"* - Age 29-34. This traumatic time seemingly always remains in my memories.

3. - Age 34-45.

This role brought me everything most people think they need and want in the material world, except emotional, psychological and spiritual health and happiness. I had no spiritual, political, or cultural rapport with this dear person. Since it seems I had forgotten, or had never been taught and learned, my spiritual teachings and values, I was taught by my Heavenly Parents, and I learned a very hard lesson. I did not ask the will of the Father for my life. He gave me the type of life that would teach me of Himself and His Ways.

3. *"Beloved Soul Mate's Wife*"--Ageless. When we met in 1988, we met as adult university students. We became close friends from 1988 until 1991, when we also became a couple. We were married in 1996 after our psychic and spiritual meeting 27 years prior in a prophetic vision he was shown of me and my life. My husband has followed a predominately Eastern path, while I have a Judao-Christian heritage. We are above all else citizens of Heaven, a cosmic universe and world, inhabited by a diversity of eclectic beings with whom we share rapport. We are strangers and sojourners in this world. Our material world treasures are in each other and our beloved family. Our spiritual treasures are here and in our heavenly Home. Those who walk not by the flesh alone, do not really share the same awarenesses and value systems of this out-of-balance, violent, selfish, unjust world. Greed and lust do not fit into heavenly lives. Altruistic love, mercy, forgiveness, health, joy and peace are the rules of heaven. We strive to have these values lived in our own personal lives in this world in order to assist in the cleansing of this planet. We are those who believe we must attempt to be lights in a very dark, dense, unwholesome, atmosphere filled with fear, disability, death, and horrors of all types--real or imagined. These are the teachings of my Beloved Lord Jesus. He believes in Jesus and the teachings of Buddha who says his followers should attempt to come back as Bodhisattvas in order to help to save all sentient beings who desire the higher paths of enlightenment.

114. EMPATHETIC HEALING

These altered states of reality in my dreams help me to attempt in some small ways the immensities of the worlds and natures of the Manifold Spirit of All That Is.

By the standards and norms of others, those of us who can enter these altered states in any way may be adjudged as mentally unstabile. It is important to keep ourselves with open minds and souls. Thus, if we are blessed, we may acquire some small inklings of the degrees of awarenesses which are ours, both now, and in the future. It is easy to label others experiences as insane, mis-directed, untrue, or unbelievable if one has closed psyche. We strive to walk peacefully, in holy fashion, filled by the Spirit of Love, Light and Truth, which is accessible to all of us.

I must admit, even with my personal instructions to myself always strive to be open minded and able to accept new thoughts and realities, and to not be prejudiced, I still have had a hard time experiencing, much less understanding, and accepting, the lives I saw in this mind-altering dream of altered realities very often foreign to our generalized Judao-Christian social and psychological modeling.

As a student of psychology and the social sciences, I have taken many units of classes, as well as working in the fields of mental health and social services. I have been an advocate for the homeless and minorities.

It has been my great desire to understand the hearts, minds, souls, and even the bodily differences of those who have uniquely diverse lives from my own. This is why all of my life studies and experiences have been into those of understanding of the human being--a "wonderfully made" creation.

115. DISABLING INSANITY

Seemingly, I must be subconsciously questing for the understanding I seek of the altered states of mental illness. There is much more to be learned from experiential living of another's realities than one can ever hope to obtain from a sterile text book. some do not wish to dirty themselves with the realities of mental illness. I must, for a live as the wife of one of God dearest souls who is adjudged to be emotionally ill. Evidently, my Lord has answered my prayers for wisdom and guidance to be better able to help him and others.

Just one day prior, I dreamed of my own soul's existence in other life destinies seemingly being lived in "Parallel Worlds and Destinies". The following divinely inspired dream message was a very hard message for me to receive, much less believe and accept as even my dream reality. It was shocking and horrible. It also helped me to feel the emotions of one who is truly mentally ill.

THE NEXT DAY'S DREAM:

"I had been dropped into a world of insanity. It is horrible. It seems to close in like a vise on one's mind. It is filled with fear."

In my dream, I prayed as follows: "Please release and set me free to sanity, to serve and to love you, Lord Jesus. I feel as if this world is inescapable. I must be healed and escape!"

The dream reality made me feel as if I were sick, "Oh, God, I'm too sick to eat, drink, sleep, or find a place to go the bathroom where I should go. I cannot get my clothing up or down. I cannot go to the bathroom if I don't know where it is."

In the next scene, I was driving a vehicle. "I cannot keep my thoughts (balanced) to safely drive a vehicle." (I drove the automobile through a building and out again.. I was driving with passengers from San Francisco to northern California.)

I realized "This world is one we must exit. We cannot stay in here very long. We have lost contact with reality." (I am concerned I cannot return to the real world and escape this insane world.)

I again found myself praying as if I were The Hierophant. "Please heal me, Lord, even as I had them pray in the dream, "Please heal me, Lord." (I felt I had perhaps gone too far in my efforts to work with empathetic healing principles in my desires to help and to try to heal others. Now I must be healed. I dwell among disabled and dying souls."

"Yesterday I entered the worlds perhaps seen and heard by schizophrenics. If they do not have an, as yet undiscovered, spiritual gift, *they are insane.* If I do not detach from these worlds I, myself, trained as a counselor, will also become like those I seek to help. They say "curiosity killed the cat". Perhaps I am outliving my sane lives. I feel like I have learned more than I can bear to know at this one time--or ever again want to experience. God save me eternally from this Hell I pray! Amen"

According to the questionable mental health social norms of our American society, some of these psychological and spiritual insights are considered abnormal in our country. However, in the Far Eastern spiritual and cultural psyche, these may be much more normal awarenesses to those people than many of our other culturally-acceptable norms in America.

As a long time student researcher of life and human beings and their existence on this planet Earth, I have entered other realities as well as the world of the emotionally insane. When I took over 25 units each of Afro and Native American studies, I also became so involved in my studies I was able to write course papers which made my ethnic studies professors think I was indeed thinking with the heart and soul of a black person. I also feel very much intertwined spiritually with Native American souls. I dream of totems and ancestors, even as a Buddhist or a Native American. This, I have come to believe, is part of the role of an empathetic soul involved in spiritual healing and understanding of souls. I feel very closely connected to those who have been adjudged to be insane in our modern society. It is my heartfelt belief that many who are considered to be insane in our society, will, instead, be sought and sometimes exploited, by those desiring to know more about altered realities and other dimensions as yet unobservable to human eyes. These Holy Psyches may not be insane. They may be the forerunners of those higher souls, with more evolved and used, spiritual gifts to see into the past and future, as well as into parallel worlds, due to their abilities to alter their states of reality at will. I believe some "insane" souls more sane than some"normal" people. Many are much more directed toward curing of their emotional ills whether through medications or therapies.

PART III MESSAGES ABOUT THE FATHER & SON

116. GIVE THANKS & BLESSINGS/ THE MESSAGES FOR THIS DAY & EVERY DAY

August 26, 2004

"In all things give thanks" I said.
"How do I thank Thee
Let me count the ways."

And the Still, Small Voice spoke to my heart,
"Arise and talk to Me
In the Still of the Morning."

This day, like no other, is mine in which to thank and praise God.
Some face the East or West, then North and South.
Some blow the conch and bless the Earth and her harvests.
We share the fruits of the vine.
The cornucopia of delights of field and vineyard.

Let us, therefore, bless the Creator(s) of these delights of hearth and home.
Let us arise early in the cool stillness of waking Earth
And say,
"Thank You, dear Father, for all that is. I am Your child. I love You this day."

Let us bless the Earth and Sky.
Let us bless lest all will die.

"End Thy weeping, Dear Father, and Thy sorrows.
Let us gather in Your arms as Your blessed Harvest of Pure Delights.
We will always remember to thank Thee early and late in darkness or at dawn.
You, alone, are worthy of praise.
We love You.
We are Your Beloved Children.
Weep no more Our Father.
We are finally Yours at long last.
We love You and want to come Home as Your Beloved Prodigals.
Please forgive and love us.
We will thank and love You forever, Dear Father.
In these ways will we seek to know You once again.
We are Yours.
We are Home.
We will no longer weep alone.
We are joyously reunited
At The Tree of Everlasting Life in The Garden."
****

THE TRIUNE GODHEAD

117. "I HAVE NOT FORGOTTEN MY CHOSEN PEOPLE."–EARLY 1980'S

"I am the God of Abraham, Isaac and Jacob.
I have not forgotten My Chosen People."
****

118. "I AM THE WAY, THE TRUTH AND THE LIGHT OF LIFE"

He said, "Let there be light" and there was light...The creation is obedient.

He said, "Be still." and the stormy sea was calm...The sea and winds obey Him.

He said, "I am the Way, walk ye in it."...Do we seek and find His Path for our lives?

He said, "I am the Truth."...Do we seek Him, His Truth and the freedom He gives us?

****

119. JESUS HATED--

The ways of the Pharisees, Hypocrites, Liars, Backbiters, Gossips and those who slander and bear false witness against their neighbors. He wrote upon the ground when the woman was accused of adultery. He asked "Who among you is without sin, and will cast the first stone?" No one could answer that question. I know none who can say he/she is without sin. We are told we have all sinned and fallen short of the glory of God.
****

120. THE FATHER HATES--

A proud look, a holier-than-thou attitude, an unrepentant heart, those who seek to abuse and kill His children. He hates lying, cruelty, and blasphemy against the Holy Spirit.
****

121. THE GIANT GOLDEN CARP

The Giant Golden Carp was swimming steadily and strongly up an ascending waterway up a hill. He seemed to be making progress in spite of all types of opposition.

The message seemed to be that this wonderful dream creature was shown as Jesus Christ overcoming all obstacles to Him and His own people everywhere. There were no dangers or stresses which would keep Him from transcending all types of darkness upon this planet to reach a time of complete wholeness and enlightenment for all that are His. This dream was a great and beautiful gift to show us another symbolic aspect of our Lord and Savior Jesus Christ.

****

122. GOD IS (LIKE) A MOTHER CAT.

The dreamer awakened feeling completely like a kitten nursing at the great furry side of The Mother Cat. This Mother Cat was not a simply a feline mother. This Mother was God/Goddess in the most nurturing of natural roles imaginable. There is no other mother more caring and nurturing than the feline mother. She provides all needed nourishment and cleansing for her kittens. She is loyally protective of them against all dangers, even from their fathers. She will courageously move her whole litter of kittens, one by one, to safety.

It is hard to imagine for some of you, but this simple dream scenario was one which gave the dreamer one of ultimate bliss in the sharing of this aspect of our Father's nature.

****

PART III
ANGELS

123. HER GUARDIAN ANGEL

She is now an expectant young mother. The day she saw her angel was when she was a little girl seated beside her mother on the front seat returning from the grocery store only a few blocks from her home. She evidently leaned against the door and began to tumble out of the station wagon. Her mother quickly grabbed one of the sleeves of her dress.

The angelic hand that left a large hand print on her upper thigh for all to see was also holding her from being dragged beneath the family car. She remembers seeing parts of her guardian even as she glimpsed the paved surface of the street she never touched with her body. It has been many years ago but she told of seeing a feathered wing, a sandal and part of flowing garments. This one gives this grandmother goose bumps.

****

124. THE VENETIAN ANGEL

The dreamer was in a city like Venice which had canals full of all manner of filth. There were filthy human hands reaching out of those waters, much like hands of horrible people reaching out of a Hell world. They were attempting to grasp herself and her young son to use, abuse or destroy them by pulling them into the canals with themselves in all their filthy ways. The dreamer realized her daughter was safely kept from these types of people, but her son and she were still endangered.

At that moment, when she wondered if they would escape the desperate hands, an angelic figure came to their rescue. He had come bounding up the stairs near them. He was garbed in an amazing form fitting pure white suit with a hood. His face showed through the round circle much like the face of a scuba diver in a wet suit. He had come to the protection of herself and her son. She knew they would be kept safely from the grave dangers of those in this world who so desperately need and seek help for themselves. In so doing, there is grave dangers to those who are socially and spiritually attuned and aware who wish to give them loving assistance. This is the first time the dreamer has seen this guardian. He left her with a feeling of great safety from all dangers of this world.

****

125. ANGELIC PROTECTORS OF MY CRYSTAL MOUNTAIN

She saw herself asleep inside a huge crystal mountain. She also saw this mountain surrounded by giant angels with their hands linked in a protective circle completely around the whole perimeter of the mountain. She knew she was freed from all fear and was completely safe inside this mountain. This mountain may be a type of Jesus Christ as the Rock of Ages. He is our Savior.

****

126. WARRIOR ANGEL

He saw a huge angel appear in the sky carrying a bow and arrows with heads of unusual designs. The man and woman were in a hole in the ground each absorbed in their own pursuits. The Angel raised his bow, took aim and shot the man, who died screaming.

In comparison of the Angel of Venice and this Warrior Angel, we discovered both wore the same types of white form fitting suits which looked like the wet suits used by scuba divers. The Warrior Angel was a Negro with black skin.

****

127. ANGEL OF THE RAPTURE

The sight was one of glorious ascension to the heavens by all her neighbors. She knew this was a scene of symbolic "Rapture of the Saints". The dreamer was tremendously excited and thrilled. She wanted to join another of her family members so they could hold hands and arise together. As this thought crossed her mind, a beautiful angel appeared to fly ahead of her car to the other person's home. The angel glowed with pure white iridescence in all aspects of itself. She had never seen a being so wonderful.

When the dreamer told her loved one of the much awaited (and sometimes feared) Rapture, she was shocked to find her kinswoman was not happy. In fact, she had no desire to know anything about this event.

The dreamer was horrified at the plight of her loved one. She was also thrilled to have seen the "Ascension" and "The Angel of the Rapture". No words can truly describe this wonderful messenger. It's also obvious that one person's "Rapture" is another's "Fear".

****

PART IV
MESSAGES ABOUT HEAVEN

128. CALLED HOME

She received three dreams telling her of the upcoming return of this beloved lady to Heaven. She didn't want to believe it was time for the world and her beloved family to lose the presence of this dear woman so loved by all.

1. Injury to her head & death. (The Dreamer sought to check on the safety of the lady and to pray for her and her family. This first shocking dream came within the last six months of the holy lady's life.)

2. Gathering of the family to what must have been the funeral and the special role of the Dreamer at that funeral. (More prayer time. The time for leave taking seemed to be nearing. The lady was hospitalized with a dread illness.)

3. The arrival of a son from far away. (When this dream warning came just a few days before the death of the beloved lady, the Dreamer knew there was not much time left to her beloved lady if her son was arriving. More prayers.)

All of these warning dreams came before this lady left to go Home. She had been a very well loved active church woman. Her funeral was huge. She was given a going away party like no others. Her children revered and loved her. She had left small notes around the home to let them know SHE knew she was also preparing to leave very soon. This, to me, was one of the most wonderful of "Calls" from Heaven. She was evidently prepared and ready to return to her other offices in Heaven. Great was the honor felt by those of us who were blessed to know her and to share in her life, and her death. Everyone knew she would receive resurrection after to new life. We were all greatly blessed to be part of her circle of loved ones. We all love and miss her and look forward to again sharing our cups of tea with her in her cozy Heavenly Home.

129. PART I--INVITATION TO A FESTIVE FAMILY REUNION

Dream: Early 1999

Theirs was a special marriage. They were lifelong sweethearts. Many years before, as a young couple they had opted to not have a family due to the dangers of tuberculosis in his family. They shared all types of life's joys (and sorrows). Theirs were interests in Native Americans and their lore, as well as in Tibet and the Dalai Lama whenever he spoke in their area. They believed in liberal humanitarian thinking and living. They believed in equal human rights for everyone. Their marriage always seemed to be one of mutual respect and love, lived in orderly and peaceful fashion. The Dreamer always thought of them in the role of the idealized "Lovers".

Theirs seemed to be a special marriage. They thought of and planned for all facets of their long lives as well as for their deaths.

He had crossed over first. This is the way she wanted it to be. She was always concerned for his well being. He was always her "Guy", her dearly beloved husband. It was a couple of years after her beloved husband's death when she fell and fatally broke her neck. She lived only a short time.

However, her death was no surprise. The Dreamer had received a dream message from her husband in Heaven several months before her death. He came in a dream to ask the Dreamer to assist him in preparation of a grand theatrical performance and feast for the arrival of his beloved wife. The bounteous table was shown laden with all manner of wonderful foods. He was young and his balding head was now covered with dark hair. He no longer wore eyeglasses. He was very much looking forward to being with her once again.

The Dreamer was surprised by the dream and again began to pray for them both. She knew this was another warning dream of the leave taking of her beloved relative.

Everything was done in an orderly and peaceful fashion, even as they had lived their lives in balance and wholeness. All details had been arranged by his beloved wife, including the disbursement of their combined ashes with rose petals at sea in the northern California coastal waters of their beloved Pacific Ocean. Their funeral in their beloved ocean near her birthplace was a true celebration of their long and loving relationship here and in the world to which they both returned as a couple. They truly lived their marital roles in such a fashion. They were a quietly unassuming wise, fun, socially aware and romantic couple. We look forward to our reunion with them and all the rest of our huge extended family in our Father's Home.

129. PART II--THE RUBY CAR

1992

This was a most bizarre dream. I found myself leaving a new car dealership driving a free automobile. I had not paid for it, yet it was mine. In the dream it was called:

"The Ruby Car"

I was in need of a new vehicle at the time of my unusual dream message. I discussed it with others and even entered contests to see if I could win a free automobile as a prize. In fact, I received some very real dreams of winning prizes during that time. This dream message remained in my memory and haunted me for years until the Spring of 2000. In the interim, my beloved 1979 Honda Prelude became completely too damaged to drive it safely. My sister gifted me with a wonderful used Cougar car. I was blessed and gave great thanks to her and to my Heavenly Father for His protection and care of my dire automobile needs.

The family began something like the Dragonfly's Dance and all decided to migrate to Colorado from the shaky lands of our births in Northern California. In June, 1996, my beloved husband and myself began our long pioneer move to Colorado driving our Cougar car. We began our long Exodus across the desert lands of Nevada and Utah. Our faithful mountain cat car made it through some large adventures before we bought our 1996 Ford Taurus GL in 1997.

We were very busy as newlyweds and with the many adventures shared with my large tribal group. We were all in Colorado but divided into nuclear family units. My husband, my mother and I became one of those units, as each family separated into their own unit. We've had new marriages and the birth of my grand daughter's son. The Father is wonderful. We were suffering but we were also being blessed in spite of national economic upheavals , the " 9/11 Attack On America", unemployment, bankruptcies and much more.

My dear Aunt Ruby left Earth to go to be with her "Guy" at her Reunion in Heaven in October, 1999. They left several of the younger women in her family special bequests–thanks to their childless and carefully lived lifetime of being a wonderful couple. About six months after I purchased our bright yellow 2000 Vol kswagon Beetle on my grand daughter's October 23rd , 1999 birthday, we suddenly realized we had received "The Ruby Car" about which I had dreamed in 1992. The car did not have ruby colored paint. It was Aunt Ruby's trust that had paid for this precious little yellow "Love Bug" automobile. We truly felt blessed and in awe of a Great God who gives us special prophetic dreams to keep us informed of the special gifts He has for us in His treasure chest of wonderful surprises.

We had it for several pristine years of driving. In 2004, after many years of attempting to survive the great family debts with one income, I was forced to sell Khepra, the Egyptian "Sun Beetle". It was a wonderful gift from two people I tend to think of with great love and respect. They had adopted some of us as their own children.

The other especially interesting prophetic dream about our marriage, partnerships and our "Journey" was given to me about the same time in Runes, about which I also knew nothing when the dream came to me. It talked of partnerships and journeys.

130. "ANGEL SPAM"

Theirs had been a special relationship on the Earth plane. Perhaps he had been designated as her "teacher of Republican right wing extremism". In spite of the differences of their ideologies, their long term friendship seemed to outlive the grave.

Shortly before his birthday, someone dreamed the words "Angel Spam". She checked her new computer to see if this meant something about the computer, though she didn't even know what spam was at the time. Sure enough. There was at least forty awful and funny spam messages. This was very unusual and she was still trying to clear her new e-mail account when the next message came on his birthday.

She was seated introspectively at her kitchen table reading and praying. Suddenly, her hanging kitchen light began to gently blink on and off several times. This was weird. The lamp had never done this before–or since. She suddenly realized this was his birthday and burst into tears finally connecting the "angel spam" and the lamp as being a special message from Heaven from this beloved soul. He was simply attempting to use electricity to let them know he was well and happy on the Other Side. He and she had always had a bond, which seems to remain unbroken. He knew she would recognize him and his obsession with computer technology, as well as the synchronicity of his birth date with the "Angel Spam". Always a jokester even in death! He also knew she wanted to know her prayers for his salvation had been heard. He knew she would be worried about his soul's well being. It was a very wonderful message he gave her in those two special greetings from Heaven.

It might be noted right at this time that the Dreamer/Writer has never sought to have access to Heaven, Hell or any other prophetic or secret lore. It is my belief we are reaching the time when we will have access again to other planes of existence and will no longer fear death, even as was prophesied by our Lord Jesus. He also said time would no longer exist. I think even that is being altered.

****

131. A PHONE CALL FROM HEAVEN

Message From Heaven - Early 1990's

She had been a favorite auntie. One of her nieces asked to know if she was all right immediately after her long life. Immediately, upon the end of her prayer, the phone rang.

The youthful female voice on the line was hardly audible as if from a long distance. She and others in the family had said they wished to communicate from the Other Side. She did. Hers was an unusual name. This is the name for whom the youthful woman was asking. We know this was our now youthful and communicative auntie calling to let us know she was doing fine on the Other Side.

This same niece has had communications from many on the Other Side.

****

132. BLESSINGS FROM HEAVEN

The Dreamer was shown her paternal grandmother in a Heavenly Realm atop a Holy Mountain perhaps. The face of high cliffs held carved out picture frames (like huge icons) showing images of great leaders and priests wearing high head dresses. She was wearing a flowing robe and ornate head dress.

Grandma laid her hands atop my head and gave me her divine blessing. I have never felt more honored. I also loved and missed her more than ever. She had lived humbly in her mother and grandmother roles on Earth. It is obvious to me, that all are not as others assume them to be.

This was a blessed time for which thanks are not sufficient to show our joyful happiness.

****

133. A ROOM IN HEAVEN?

Dream: about 1985

The Dreamer awakened from seeing the most wonderful black and white marble floors in a room with the most beautiful of diaphanous draperies blowing in the breezes as walls. The scene was altogether wonderful. The question is: Is this a room somewhere upon this planet, or, instead, is it a bedroom in Heaven?

****

134. BELOVED DAD (EARTHLY FATHER)

December 26, 1903–April 2, 1956

The day my father was killed was my first meeting with death. His was the first funeral I ever attended. He looked like a painted man. He was. The logging truck had run over him after he seemingly was forced to jump after the brakes failed. However, if I had not seen his body, I would not have believed he had really been killed, in view of the repeating dream I had for many years. Many years later, I learned my sister also had been dreaming exactly the same dream.

OUR IDENTICAL DREAMS ABOUT OUR FATHER::

We each dreamed Dad was not really dead. We both had the impression he had just gone away due to hurts in his life. The dream was very real and left both of us feeling as if he were still alive and it was a possibility that he would return.

My sister hadn't gone to his funeral. We were both having a real problem with this repeating dream. I knew he was gone. The painted man was not my real father in the coffin. As I said, I was truly glad I had gone to his service because I knew this was only the shell of my Dad. We discussed our identical dreams at length. Whether it was our psychological comfort, a prophetic dream of his reincarnation either in this lifetime or in another, we both shared this ongoing, identical dream for several decades. I believe this is probably a very common denial dream which comes to those who have suffered the sudden great traumatic loss of a close loved one.

MY OTHER DREAMS ABOUT MY FATHER:

I have had several other dreams of him in the past 50 years.

1. In one dream, he brought me a sweet roll in a paper bag, as if he were bringing me a loving peace offering for leaving us both so suddenly. It was an unspoken, telepathic message of his love for me.

2. I had another dream of standing on the hilly drive in front of our old family home. We knew we were together surveying our family's properties.

THOUGHTS OF REINCARNATION:

At times I wondered if he had been reborn into another person now here on Earth. Sometimes I see similarities of his personality, desires and attitudes in a young man in our family now. However, this could be due simply to genetics–not an incarnation. I do know I wish very much I could have known him better. I was only 17 years old when he left us. It was too soon for me to get to know him as an adult. I was the one to greet the messenger from the mortician's office. I consider that statement I had to make that day to my Mom, "Mom, Dad has been killed" was the saddest, most shocking, statement of my whole life. I still feel the sadness of being forced to give my mother such a shocking and terrible unexpected message. We had absolutely no warning of his death, except Mom had mentioned feeling she should buy insurance on the automobile loan and to keep all bills paid up. Thank God for His warnings to her. He truly goes before us to lead and guide us through the hard times in our lives. We must listen to His quiet voice.

Many years later at a large military party at the home of friends, I found myself in their bathroom weeping my heart out for the loss of my father.

I look forward to seeing him again, and perhaps getting to know him much better together in our Heavenly Home than in this lifetime. I know we both shared interests in literature, writing, unusual studies and sci fi. I do believe he is well and happy in Heaven with all the other relations. I wish he could have been here to visit with my children and me. It is my belief my only sibling, my sister, and I have perhaps been severely damaged by the sudden loss of our Dad at such a crucial time in our young lives.

POSTSCRIPT:

A couple of days after I finished the initial draft of this writing about my father, I had a most unusual dream. I wondered afterward, with my new knowledge of the Other Side, if he had not seen me writing and was letting me know how happy he was to have me thinking of him and writing of our lives together. I think he knew and he evidently decided to share something more with me in this dream I had of us together again–in another lifetime.

THE DREAM–Late in 2001:

I dreamed we were together at Christmastime in the Elizabethan Era at the time of his beloved Shakespeare. We were at a local pub garbed in the clothing of affluent people of that time. Dad was definitely wearing a fancy outfit of an aristocratic gentleman, who was loved for his ribald wit and sociability. He as very outgoing, happy and seemed to be enjoying himself tremendously as a popular person of the times. In that lifetime, I played some type of role that was close to him, as I did in this 20th Century lifetime. My Dear Friend, from this life, was also there in that lifetime with me. I saw her seated over in the corner of the room looking like her usual beautiful self wearing a pure white, satin dress. We were discussing things together as we do as close friends in this life. In the dream, I left the pub with Dad.

This dream may have been triggered by my thoughts of my father as I worked with the writing of his life and death. This may be partially true.

I have not included all aspects of this dream. Divine ethics seem to let me know this is something I must not do. However, it is indeed tempting to do so, as some of the things I have been forced to leave out, would prove to others that knew him and know me that he is indeed communicating to me from the Other Side. I do know I suddenly have this inner feeling he knows about my life and my writing. I know he is very happy I am finally allowing myself to think of him and to give him recognition as my father, as well as being a wonderful human being loved by many who knew him. It is pleasant to him as well as to me. The dream message was a beautiful remembrance of a former time together, for which I thank our Heavenly Father.

I came to this world as if I were as a tabla rasa, someone who remembers nothing of Heaven, or of possible former (or upcoming and parallel) lifetimes. Therefore, as a private, old world gentleman he is, he now wished to share some private insights of himself as a man as of our former lifetime together.

135. A GALA PARTY IN A "LITTLE CHILD'S HEAVEN"

Dream: Early in the 21st Century

The Dreamer was an expected guest at a large social function held in a building in another world–whether Heaven, another planet or dimension. The darkened room was full of guests. She was not sure if she had newly arrived in Heaven, or, instead, if this was a social gathering. She found herself attempting to locate an old friend from almost 50 years prior. She had experienced an earlier awareness of his passing a few Earth years prior to this dream scene.

While she was doing the usual party socialization thing, as one would do on Earth, she began to notice some striking differences. This was not a world where there were absolute "No's" and "Impossibilities". She knew she was indeed in another world when she observed living stuffed animals upon the couches, as if she were in the land of the movie entitled "Toy Story". It was as if Heaven really is a place such as only one who is able to become as a "Little Child" would appreciate and love for the pure joy of unspeakably wondrous life everlasting. This world seemed to be one in which you would be able to see and to do whatever one was able to imagine. As a childlike human woman she was thrilled to see these charming creatures. It was truly a Land of a Child's Imagination.

Recently, the author became aware of the fact that a child who is a new arrival in Heaven would perhaps not be looking for a dear old human friend. Perhaps, instead, a small child would be looking for his or her beloved doll or teddy bear upon their sudden return to their Heavenly Home. How wise and wonderful is our Heavenly Parent who has placed these dear toys where they will easily be seen upon the couches in the areas into which the child will be entering upon their arrival.

It is obvious we have covered topics from stuffed toys to Elphame and faery realms such as are in the fictionalized teaching series such as *The Lords of the Rings Trilogy* in our many years of divinely instructive messages from Heaven. Seemingly, there are divine truths which are perhaps ancient realities hidden within necessarily fictionalized stories This is even as the author of this book has attempted to hide the real life suffering of the homeless in fiction. Those who are accustomed to reading fiction wish to read about terrifying things and of horrible human suffering as if they only happen to someone else. Some of us love to see wonderfully marvelous fictionalized beings and events as realities. Perhaps, if we indeed must become as if we are little children to enter into the Kingdom of Heaven, we will have the joys of being with our toy animals as well as with our beloved pets from our lives on the Earthly dimensions. It is the author's impressions that He and His multi-dimensional worlds are wonderful. Sometimes we must bend our minds in order to be able to encompass all that is and might be; but we can do so only if we are able to open our hearts and our minds to think and to act as if we are a "Little Child" we have always been in Him. Wonderful!

136. THE AUTHOR'S THOUGHTS REGARDING DEATH AND OUR HEAVENLY HOME

It is my belief that many Americans attempt to delude themselves into believing disability, aging and death come to all others except themselves. It is a complete denial of all scriptural teachings of every great religion on the planet to treat both topics as if they do not exist.

This again , is an attempt to remain as little children not yet ready to be fed with whole and holy adult food. How long must we feed ourselves the food of babes? It will be a wonderful time when adult human beings again are in tune with the creation and their own bodily rhythms. We accept marriages and births. We do not wish to mar our perfect world with visions of disability, aging, and death. We are a culture which wishes to see and experience only health, wealth, beauty and perfection. There is a grave concern for those who refuse to see realities of all types. There are things we cannot change unless the New Millenium teaches us new ways to obtain desired healing, longevity and interaction with other worlds. Transcendence of the bonds of this world must be achieved before we are allowed to enter those other worlds of the pure Whole Ones where ignorance, violence and self have no place.

The author has seen and experienced dream vistas of multi-dimensional creations consisting of both parallel and simultaneous worlds as well as worlds within worlds, and ongoing worlds–all of which seem to be part and parcel of His creations. These topics are mind boggling and incomprehensible to many of us. Much more study is needed. Now we discuss Albert Einstein's relativity theories in depth. Quantum Physics and General Relativity Theories seem to validate the realities of these worlds many of us have been shown.

We have forgotten more of this world than should ever have been allowed to occur. One reason may be that leaders with simplistic ideation do not know what is missing of the knowledge of life and of death. Death is closer than most people desire to know. It has never been my intention to delve into the spirit world. However, I have been given messages of the upcoming deaths of loved ones, as well as of their ongoing lives on the Other Side. A couple of souls have evidently required further prayers. Thus, even though the author has not been taught to pray for souls after death, she does so because there are those who seemingly request and need prayers. One cannot refuse such a request.

Some people study of the death and the planes some souls enter upon death. May our hearts be stayed upon Him and filled with His presence. When we leave this world, let us keep our heart and minds upon Him. We must practice control of our fears in order to consciously desire to be with Him, if we are not in a swoon. If in a swoon (coma), we trust Him to be there to walk through the Valley of the Shadow of Death, or that His angel(s) will be there to escort the helpless vessel during this time of transition. There are wonderful stories of these types of visitations. Above everything else, remember to seek to "Go to the Light of Christ."

The night I began to enter the realm within The Black Dot, I thought I had entered the beginnings of a death state. Mindfulness was very helpful. I realized one must relax and trust one's soul to the One. Immediately, I was back in this dimension. It was a most startling event. I have had discussions with those who have accidentally astrally projected as little children. The child was met by a little dwarf or elfen man who sharply told him "Get back in there!" There are some adults who have used psychedelics who have met with frightening creatures in those astral planes. It is my belief we need to learn to overcome mindless fears at this time. There are things beyond our comprehension on the Other Side. If we are enraptured with our Beloved Lord, He Himself, or His angelic messengers will introduce us to these new wonders. Death's sting will be gone. We will joyously be with those we left behind and who have returned ahead of us. These are my visions of the Other Side. Other souls may learn other things. If a sad soul is restless and seems to show itself to you, pray for it and ask it to seek Him and to go to His Light. There are some disembodied souls who do seem to inhabit certain dwellings and areas of our planet. We pray to understand and help them if you become aware of them. It is our belief we don't attempt to reach out to interfere, nor we attempt to dabble into the other worlds unless they present themselves to us. At this time, we seek the wisdom of our Father. My belief is "In Him I can do anything I must do. Without Him I feel unable to do things of great danger." This is simply my personal view of my role in the order of things big and frightening to my soul. There truly seem to be creatures we have not yet become acquainted. Prayer may be needed. We will be guided and directed.

Many modern humans have desired to tune out all that offends their pristine sensibilities. We can only pray one for another. Some realities do not change. We must be brave enough to take internal and universal journeys of the soul and mind. Let us prepare to meet our Divine Rulers of the Divine Realms–possibly within our own hearts and souls.

PART V
MORE PROPHECIES & SCRIPTURE MESSAGES ABOUT THE SORROW OF OUR FATHER

****

137. OTHER THINGS WHICH CAUSE HIM TO WEEP

Holier-than-thou behavior and words	See Isaiah 52:10-12 & Isaiah 57:1-2
	Isaiah 65:5-7
Fasting in the natural vs. His Fast.	See Isaiah 58

Sabbath Day - non-observance of His Day of Rest. Many scriptures.

****

138. PANDEMIC INSANITY

August 31, 2004–all night

It was a restless night interspersed with what seemed like one case of insanity after another. The Father knows and sees all. Perhaps I was allowed to witness these things because this is what He sees all the time.

It is indeed a time like no other when "Their hearts will fail them for fear of the things which are coming upon the Earth."

It must be noted also that "Their minds and souls are also failing them for these selfsame fears."

****

139. ENDLESS QUARRELING

September 2, 2004

Parents have great troubles with the quarreling of their children. This causes family arguments. There are times when it becomes so uncontrollable as to be dangerous to the well being of the entire family structure and the members of the family unit. His is a large family unit. Is it not possible to empathize greatly with our Heavenly Father?

He made laws by which we are to live peacefully.

Before He did that, as a trusting parent, the first son of His creation killed his brother. Now, while He is hoping we will not destroy each other completely, it is our concern He is weeping in pure frustration of seeing and hearing so much chaotic quarreling among His own children.

The children seem intent upon not attending instructions in Wisdom, even as some of our own children occasionally may not treasure wisdom of elders, teachers and parents.

Love conquers all evils. All of His laws are the Laws of Love.

Quarrels cause great waves of venom to encircle the globe. Perhaps He knows we will not stop even with this planet but will spread our venom throughout the vast reaches of the cosmos.

We all know parents, as leaders (like "Older Earthly Guardians") of the young, are often faced with very hard decisions. Sometimes it is even a hard choice between the survival of one or of the whole family. Our Father may be weeping because this is now His hard parental decision. If He cannot control the unruly hoards of sparring and fighting children, He may be forced to send some to correctional schools, prisons, or outer realms for the protection of the good and whole children who are being abused and threatened by their actions. This is a serious thought. Who is the good and acceptable child? Who is not? These are thought provoking questions. What would you or I do if we were the Father of All?

140. THE GRAIN OFFERINGS

Dream: October 2, 2004 (The 2nd Day of Prayer Vigil.)

In the dream I was in my own home. There was a Native American Medicine Man seated on the floor with several grain or seed offerings to be blessed and prayed over to the One God, the Great Spirit.

People were all trying to cleanse themselves and to find long ceremonial dresses for robes. I was aware this was my friend and his people. They each began to receive spiritual calls to come for the ceremony. By this time the yard, as well as the house, was full of small groups of people gathered to make seed and grain offerings to the Great Spirit.

This suddenly reminded me that the Grain Offering is to be made for Sin. I, myself, felt like offering up myself as the grain offering–even as Jesus Christ –became our Grain Offering for the sins of all. I realized why He offered Himself for the sins of all human beings. I understood why the Sundancer offers himself on the Tree for His people. I knew why the Buddhist Bodhisattva offers their life for the well being of all sentient beings.

This dream was given at the time of the Jewish Feast of Tabernacles. Are we not all His children? Many tribes make many sheep folds. All are washed in the lifesaving Blood of the Lamb, if they so desire to accept it as their covering from sin. He knows His own sheep and no one can take any of them from His flock.

Scripture Messages: John 4:21 Those that worship Him shall worship Him in Spirit and in truth.
Psalm 19:14

141. NATIVE AMERICAN VISITORS

Two Dreams: November 30, 2004

7 a.m.

Several Indian leaders had come to our home to ask us to assist them with documents involving ownership of their lands. They requested both my husband and me to assist them in various ways. His involved usage of his wonderful writing skills.

8:51 a.m.

The Native American leaders came back to show my husband the beauty of his work.

I was shown the possible dead face of a white man with his face painted as if for war. He had large dark green design painted upon his chin.

I thought of our Native American neighbors and of all the suffering they incurred by their attempts to welcome the European immigrants to the soil of both North and South America. These newcomers had no understanding or respect for the rights of these native people they saw as simply primitive uneducated pagan souls. Due to their fears and the barriers of language and culture they took the lands of these people, their hosts and hostesses, with no regard for their well beings. Again the psychology of prejudice had overcome love and logic.

Many of the white pioneers were not at peace with the "redskins". They robbed, maimed, killed and ravaged the native people and their lands. It has not ended.

There is a Great Spirit that knows and sees all. Some people think He only cares about one special group of people. This is untrue. In spite of all disregard for the rights and values of others, the white people may yet think themselves to be the saviors of this planet, as well as also as the only group with a "Moral Majority" of virtuous souls. "You will know them by their love." (Jesus Christ)

When the Indians danced to balance the Earth, all the white people heard was savages beating unfamiliar musical instruments in strange ways. They had never heard of those people of the Americas who were considered by themselves and others as the 'keepers' of the creation. Native people of North America believed themselves to be those who were to pray for the Earth and all living creatures whether two or four legged, finned or feathered. They asked the plant or creature if they could use it for food. They knew the Earth was unstable at times. Thus, they danced and drummed in time with the heartbeat of the Earth in order to make sure she stayed on her axis. They remembered times when she had left her given position in the heavens and there had been different positions of sun and moon, and much more. Many ancient cultures know the Earth has altered her rotation and shifted her axis at intervals of approximately every 10,000 years. The last of these massive changes occurred at the time of the Deluge. Thus the title of James Baldwin's book *"The Fire Next Time"*. This is the Fifth Sun of the Meso-American calendar which ends at 2012A.D. Modern people would do well to consult the ancients for answers to the the ancient mysteries of creation and apocalyptic times. We may be concerning ourselves with things which are not at important as the things we refuse to learn.

When the white man came to this continent they found pyramids and massive monuments as well as tepees and dugouts. They found rulers of great wealth and power as well as the noble wilderness chieftains wearing feathered head dresses leading smaller tribal units. The laws of the red man were based upon laws they had learned from the Great Spirit and His special holy messengers such as White Buffalo Calf Woman. She left and her ambassadors Deganaweda and Hiawatha spread her messages of the peace pipe ritual, peaceful prayers and living to many of the people of the 500 Indian nations of this continent.

This is only a discussion of North America. South America had been visited by Europeans, Asians and Africans. There are many questions about which continent had birthed the first of these people of these continents of the New World. European monarchs began to vie for access to, and possession of, the luxurious wilderness lands of a Utopian New World. All of them forgot these simple people who inhabited these lands had their own ancient cultures and languages, governmental laws and leaders, as well as their very deeply spiritual religious traditions. The greed and ignorance of Europeans killed the spiritual leaders of this hemisphere. The treasures of the Earth are of more value to those who worship Mammon than the holiness of hearts dedicated to the Pathways of the Holy Ones.

The innocent blood of holy souls stained the soils of Mother Earth. Their food supplies were also purposely destroyed in order to accomplish the genocidal purging of this continent of the people who loved her. The massive buffalo herds were wantonly slaughtered in order to starve His native people. Holiness was not in the hearts of those marauders who invaded her soils. However, they felt they had the laws of God Almighty upon their side due to their obsessive belief in their own white supremacy, with a special clause written in saying God had given them a destiny of subjection of the Earth's inhabitants to their rule. Do we speak with His words or those with the greedy rulers of the European community? This is not a case of shocking behavior in past centuries. There still remain terribly unethical, Machiavellian deeds which are being perpetrated upon His native children to this present day. All Indians are not good Indians. Neither are all white people followers of the gentle Master Jesus Christ. Perhaps someday there will once again come a time when a pristine new world exists and men and animals will once again 'talk'. Adam and Eve were quite familiar with communication with creatures. Our own Holy Book tells us of this fact.

America's native residents of these continents did not claim ownership of land. They believed no one can own their Mother, the beautiful planet upon which we all live. They had no concept of the avarice of the white man for ownership of personal property.

Many of these brave souls manage to survive in the most barren of wastelands, in spite of the white man, kept by the All-Seeing, Wise and Just Great Spirit of All.

One can only wonder at the meaning of these dream messages. Yes, these people do believe in Dreamers and their messages, even as do the Australian aborigines. They have existed for tens of thousands of years upon this planet. The primitive tribal people of all continents may be here long after the aggressive white man has destroyed all he has created in his own selfish greed for more. It should be noted herein there are many white people who have loved and worked with the Native people, knowing and seeing the beauty of holiness in their faces, as those of His many sheep folds. Great will be the amazement of those who see the great diversity of their neighbors in the Happy Heaven world(s). One hopes they do not also realize these are the innocent saints they killed in one of the various names of the Holy One.

What on Earth is happening at this time?

142. HIS LAMBS

October 16, 2004 (The16th Day of Prayer Vigil)

In my dream I was leafing through a newspaper in some part of the Christian world perhaps. One page showed a wonderful picture at the top of the page of a very high craggy mountain darkly in shadow. There were several cut-away views of open cave areas into which I could easily see. In the middle open hole I was shown the wonderful sight of an unseen personage bottle feeding the small Lamb of God in a large basket. I could not see whether this one who fed Him was deity, angel or human being.

I awakened joyously thinking of my pleasure that some holy souls here on Earth were still giving nurturing sustenance to the Beloved , the Lamb of God.

On the personal human side I realized there are also those who give support and nourishment to His Lambs, the little ones who need to be bottle fed the Word of God and treated as His beloved children. Some are already bearing many heavy crosses in their lives.

He asks us to feed His sheep even as He, as the Lamb of God, will be fed by our nurturing of His Lambs. We show forth His presence upon the Earth if we are love one to another.

I am so thrilled this day. This was a beautiful dream in which I was shown a wonderful scene of love in action, reciprocating, uplifting and enriching to God and humankind. Oh, Father, is it possible there will be those who will remember to care for your Beloved Son and His Sheep? We know they must be treated as a Loving Mother or Father would treat them. We must become the images of Christ to others.

In the dream I then leafed through another newspaper of an area of the world which did not love Him. It had no uplifting pictures of nourishment and care of Him or His Sheep. His Message is still ours to fulfill. We must feed His Sheep, here and everywhere, even as we continue to give nurturing care to our Beloved Lamb of God who was slain for the sins of the world. Perhaps if we fulfill the wishes of our Beloved Father His tears will end.

All suffering and shame will end if we treasure, follow and teach the Ways of the Lamb. He will no longer be ashamed of at least one group of His created children. Let us love one another, even as we are loved by Him. His Truth, Love and Light will set us free to love ALL of His children with the Love of the Father. It is my great desire to never make Him weep.

143. THE GOOD SHEPHERD

Dream: November 2, 2004, about 4 a.m. (Presidential Election 2004, U.S.A.)

His Sheep have been following leaders other than Himself. They have become entrapped in their own church pews as the good sheep who have not "forsaken the assembling of themselves together". This is the admonition of this age. "Do not forsake the assembling of yourselves together as you have seen some doing." I taught them this scripture myself.

Then I was "Called Out", like Jeremiah to be a strange watch person for the Lord. I must now "put a trumpet to my lips", even as David Wilkerson was once admonished to do so.

I believe the most darling of people have forgotten to read and to pray. They have become obsessed and exhausted by the cares of this life and by evil predator shepherds in their own sanctuaries. I believe they were too tired to realize what was happening before they were all caught responding to the demands of the loud leaders who led they astray so they could no longer hear His still, small voice. If they heard Him, they were overcome with exhaustion or had no ears to hear Him because their idols had become those of the Loud Leaders who had become tyrants, aping the ways of the Divine and speaking the lying words of the evil one.

Many sheep were heartbroken and stayed in those pews trying to assist the others. Even these strong and loving leaders also became entangled in doctrines of humans leaders following their own ideas of "How to become wise and wonderful, powerful and rich", the "wholeness" of the new gospel. Two decades before I had gone to find a book about the Savior in His bookstores and could find none. Instead, I found self-help books of people who liked pink and blue sweet and sugary country things. They didn't seem to miss pictures of Him walking atop the waves of life and such wonderful faith building visual tools for our lives. They didn't seem to wonder about why there were no books about our Master Jesus Christ. Why?

This is what was allowed to happen to those dear ones. They were made to be so worn down and tired so they would not be able to remember all the teachings of their Master, the Good Shepherd, "the Lamb of God slain for the sins of the world". Mr. Gibson tried to show them. They loudly went to see Him horribly scourged and crucified one more time. Many of the "Called Out" sheep were alone with Him, being bottle fed atop a craggy mountain, apart with Him. He had quietly come to many in the middle of the dark nights in the early 1980's, BEFORE so many wonderful ministers lost their pulpits to those who were willing to do anything to get their positions of leadership and power.

Many souls came into the flocks who were not His sheep. The sheep began to learn the ways of the world, not of His role of Suffering Servant, the Wounded Physician and the Fisher King. These are the ways of our Lord. We must take time to become reacquainted with Him and His teachings. If we love Him, we will follow His commandments and teachings. It is by these teachings that we will be known, not by our loudness, strength or oppressive ways. His burdens are light. His ways are loving, just and beautiful. He is beautiful. He is the Good Shepherd. He is also the Beloved. His Beloved hear and know His Voice and teachings. They want to know all they can about Him. They read red letter editions of the New Testament. They seek to be filled with His Spirit–none other. They know He has never stopped speaking to our hearts, in the still of the evening. He still communes with us in our heart centers, the Garden of Delights. He tells us we are His. He loves us with an eternal, never ending love.

We are all heartbroken and saddened by our great schism. Love is the key to all these divisions between us. We were both obedient. Some stayed in their churches with false teachers. Some of those same people were forced to find new churches and pastors, OR they were asked to be brave enough to come out into a prophetic ministry ALONE WITH HIM. Sometimes our hearts are being broken over and over again. Our loved ones have been told their loved ones who belong to other political parties and religions do not know Him. These teachings are not scriptural. They are not the words of our Lord and Savior Jesus Christ. Many no longer know who He is. The Father and earthly loved ones are so very sad and brokenhearted. He is our best Gift we ever had to give you. He offered Himself to you and gave you salvation. He is still here. So are those who loved Him who follow different political party lines and leadership. Their voices also have merit in our Father's House. We are also His Sheep. Conversations are good. If we hold up a talking feather perhaps we will be allowed to share our political and spiritual views once again? Thank you.

We know there is an Invisible Civil War in America. Over one half of the population of America is apart and alone being bottle fed by holy hands. When I had the first dream of the Lamb, I wondered what it was all about. I thought the Lamb was Him. Now, today, I can see those who are apart are the lambs He is hand feeding while they are out there all alone without earthly shepherds. This only makes me love Him more. He has truly not left us alone. Many of us are being enraptured and re-infilled with His Spirit. Thank you.

There will come a time when all yokes of oppression will be lifted from us. We will once again "be together again, just praising the Lord"–in Spirit and in Truth. No longer will we be led by those who love power, wealth and leadership more than they love His teachings. Mammon is a dangerous foe. He rules all those who forget Him. The ancient forgotten books were forgotten because the orthodox leaders did not wish to have Him interfering with their personal roles of church hierarchies. He wishes to interfere. He desires to set His sheep free to follow Him with no interference from other shepherds not of His Flock. He has come to set all of the captives free–free indeed–to love and serve Him in Spirit and in Truth. His love covers all. Thank You, Dear Father.

Many years ago, I picked up my orders from my Supreme Commander Jesus Christ. I was at a wonderful Seder Supper under the ministry of my beloved friend and pastor Jim Hayford in a suburb of the San Francisco Bay Area. When the Battle Hymn of the Republic was sung, these words stood out to me as my battle cry: "As He died to make men holy, let us live to set men free–His Truth goes marching on." Truth will overcome all darkness. His Light, His Truth and His Way are the Way of our Holy Shepherd. We must open wide our eyes, minds and hearts to become re-acquainted with our Shepherd. We must study to show ourselves approved, workmanships which need no correction.

He has not changed. We have been caught in heavy old dirty webs and cares of life. The demonic spider has entrapped us in her webs. We will fight no more against one another. We will again become "One in the Spirit" because "We are one in the Lord". He alone is holy. He alone can overcome the enemy spirit and bring us once again into loving union in our divided churches. What is church without one's parent or child? He asked us to know Him.

We have each been trying our best to know Him. The big question is "Who knows Him?"

He has not left us alone. He is with us to find us and to bind up our wounds. Soon we will be together as families and loved ones. We will again be His wonderfully eclectic, symbiotic and muli-faceted, multi-cultural and racial, sheep of many pastures. We are those who have washed our garments in the soul cleansing Blood of the Lamb.

We did not watch the Passion of Christ. We are the Passion of Christ. We are those who have been called out to testify that we are washed and re-crucified in His Blood. Whatsoever you have done to us, you have done to Him. We didn't need to watch the Passion of Christ. We are

His Passion. He is our Passion. We have drunk from His Cup. We have eaten His offering as His priests and priestesses. Our share is the Grain Offering. We present ourselves for the sins of all of us. We are part and parcel of Him. We are Him to this sin-sick world. We have been bruised with words. We have been beaten and killed. It has not ended. If we stand up to say, "This is His Way, follow thou in it" we will be scourged. If new prophets tell you He is here or there, do not listen. He still dwells quietly and sweetly in your hearts. He loves you. Love is the one attribute of the Father who is weeping for His beloved children. He hates to see us driven apart into separate sheep pastures. Soon He will come with healing in His wings and will draw us once again back together again. We do hope it will be sooner, than later. Many of us are very forlorn, tired and abused. He is feeding us and we are with Him, safe in the Cleft of the Rock of Ages. Do not pity us. Look to your own heart and let us see if we can once again find each other.

He does not take pleasure in the warring of one family member against another. He sees and knows all. He desires us to beat our weapons into plowshares and to again learn sound teachings.

Civil War is a harmful wound. It has been over 100 years and we are still recovering from our national schism between North and South, Yanks and Rebs, over the issue of enslavement of our black people. Do we have another 100 years to give to such issues and divisions? It is time for His Return! Are we ready and looking forward to His Return? Wars can be ended by the teaching of studies in cultural, racial and religious issues of division. The Truth that sets us free is the one of education. If we are too fearful to teach these courses we will never find each other. Boldness is the Key. Love is Bold. Love is courageous and cares enough to dare to work with the unknowable, the frightening, the different. We are not dangerous one to another. The Enemy only wishes to cause us to think this Great Lie. Our Father is Manifold. He is Great. Let us take upon ourselves His persona. Let us become His Children. If we become His Children, we will truly know Him and His Teachings. His ways are bigger than our ways. He knows His Wisdom and His Ways will set us free to know and to love one another. His is a theology full of His blessings. He is the Father of the Shepherd of the Cosmos. We are His siblings. He is the first born of many brothers and sisters. We are all His family. Let us join hands and sing, "Blessed is the Lamb that was slain...." He is our Blessed Lamb. We are all His lost and saddened lambs–divided out by tough sheep dogs into separate herds. In fact, some of us are no longer His Sheep. This is a hard reality. Are we still His sheep? Let us all once again ask Him this question. Let us attempt to hear His still, small Voice once again. Amen.

Let us think about these issues. It is time to be dressing for the Wedding Supper of the Bridegroom, the Lamb of God.

This is a glimpse of the things I have seen early this morning:

" There are those who have been taught all types of things by rote in loudly emotional and loud sessions in the wonderful convivial comradely church gatherings. No longer did their hands lift to heaven as if lifted by a heavenly hand. His people were told when and how long to lift their hands to heaven, how long and loud to shout and to praise His name. Something had changed from being led by the Spirit to being led by human leaders intending to direct His Sheep to learn to respond to other voices besides that of their Good Shepherd.

Human beings, like wonderful obedient sheep, can be trained to be an obedient flock led by new shepherds with loudly barking sheep dogs. Exhaustion and subliminal teaching is often used to brainwash dear souls. When fear of the unknown is added, we have the makings of a very dangerous time. There are many like myself who have been impressed to dare to become a "fool for Christ". His Voice is the one we hear. We have been "Called Out" to walk with Him during these times of dangerous leadership. We were the prayer group people, the Sunday School teachers and mothers of the families. We have been led so wonderfully by the Beloved Savior. He has not forgotten His Sheep. The Father weeps for the loss of His Sheep. He has awaited these times to speak directly, as in days of the ancient ones, to His own Children, the Redeemed by the Blood of the Lamb.

144. MIRACULOUS ENTITIES

Dream: December 7, 2004

There was a created area of Heaven or of the Earth where 'Miraculous Entities' had been placed to live. They were sought to assist with hard needs involving miraculous means with which to accomplish them. Their services could also be sought for financial woes. (Piles of currency were shown.) People brought their children for blessings and assistance.

This seems to show us another personal insight of the many worlds of the Father. The feeling was of goodness and joy. It was a very pleasant land.

One felt this was not a place where these folk would be arguing over their powers and having wars of evil beings over the usage of great powers. It seemed to be a place on Earth where one would be able to go to seek divine assistance of heavenly humans or heavenly beings. This may also have been the Realm of the Immortals and of the Family of God in Heaven. He was simply sharing it with us once again.

PART VI THE BELOVED FATHER & HIS CHILDREN

145. THE ACCUSER OF THE BRETHREN

Message: December 23, 2004

Let none accuse one who is saved by our Lord. He paid the price for any and all of our errors and sins in life. We can tell that nagging "Accuser" to go take a leap off a cliff. We have no part of him. We are a forgiven Child of the Father. Jesus Christ is our older Brother. He is the firstborn of many brethren (and sisters). We are of His spiritual House and Priesthood. We are His Family.

We may be an "engrafted branch", yet we are His. We have been forgiven and cleansed by His soul cleansing Blood. We are His forever. He has known us forever and to Him we return.

Many of His most humble children are the hardest beset by the "Accuser". In fact, if he cannot reach us in our own minds and hearts, he will attempt to use others less in control of their own minds and souls.

They love to hit us when we are at our lowest level of energy, courage and faith. Sometimes we feel far too battle scarred and traumatized by the cares of life to be able to stand even one more "attack". We know we live in times when "They" will spend lots of time trying to hit us where we are weakest. They know they have little time left in which to work. We are told they will rage and roar like lions.

Those of us who have walked long, sometimes lonely, contemplative and meditative lives in Him are full of His Spirit. We are also vulnerable to the attacks of those who are threatened and fearful of our unusual strengths. This is because we have been walking with the Father as if He were our earthly father. He is. Mine was killed when I was 17 years old. He has become my Father and Husband, as well as my Beloved Savior, Mentor-Teacher-Master and adored God. It is my desire and belief that I have no idols I adore more. I love Him and His Pathway. Upon that Pathway, He and I have walked for many years as Friends. Friends do not kill or abuse Friends. This is why I know humans have written certain scriptures such as "And God took Moses out to slay him." This is not my

Beloved Father God. This is an angry and hate filled human person who wrote this scripture.

"What a friend we have in Jesus; all our sins and cares to bear..." This is why I feel I can freely call upon Him to comfort us when we are under attack from "The Enemy". If we have an enemy, we must tell Jesus about them. We can toss our woes upon Him as if we were tossing Him a hot potato too hot to any longer hold. Sometimes, at the worst of times, I do this a lot. If I have a nervous breakdown over every little thing in life, I will not be here to help myself or the loved ones who are in my care.

Many years ago, I found myself becoming greatly saddened by sins I was carrying in my life. I was comforted by the Spirit and guided to write them down in a list upon a piece of paper. I was impressed to pray for forgiveness from the Father, roll up the paper and ritually flushed it away from my life. I remind myself these sins are gone forever whenever a nagging thought comes in my mind.

To do otherwise would be to seem as if I did not trust my Heavenly Lord's Sacrifice for my sins.

We are told there is nothing too large, or too small, for which He is not concerned. He tells us "You have not because you ask not." I always think my problems are less than others, therefore telling myself others deserve His time far more than mine. We are not to think this way. We miss great blessings by believing "the Liar". He is forever telling and making lies. Let us seek Him. He is the Way, the Truth and the Way. Since we have found Him, let us walk there in His footsteps. Amen

146. DESTRUCTION OF ALL OUR IDOLS–THE END OF ALL TEARS

Let us all strive to stop our unhealthy habits of living. It is time to learn and to grow in wisdom. Seek us first the Kingdom of God and we will be part of it. He has spoken. We are nothing without His Words. We are all at different stages of our humble and penitent walks upon the straight and narrow path. Some of us remember and know things others do not. More and more of His children are now beginning to remember their first estate is as the Father's children.

If we attempt even slightly to have empathy for Him and each other, we will break hate barriers around the globe. It is possible to have our planet shining with light beacons pointed toward Him. The feelings engendered by the horrid energies of those who are jealous and hate each other is hard for anyone to bear. He feels all of us all the time. This would be unbearable. Not only do we hate and fear each other, but we also turn our venomous behavior and words upon Him. He is innocent of everything except gifting us with all manner of blessings and His all-encompassing love.

It is possible to imagine a world without ignorance, jealousy, lust, greed and avarice, violence, murder and mayhem. That world is like the one I believe many of us remember from our former lives on the Other Side. Many of us desire with all of our hearts to experience the same ambience of wholeness, thanksgiving, love and peace here on Earth.

This is the world the Father planned for us. He made a wonderful world and blessed it. In fact, He called the creation and said, "It is good." He then rested on the seventh day and called it a Sabbath day forever. He created this Sabbath time for our own much needed rest times from the work and cares of this world.

The causes of many of our problems are our addictions to our idols. The Father gives us wonderful descriptions of the uses and dangers of human idolatries. Some of the best descriptions of our present idolatries are written in the wonderful Apocryphal Books of Wisdom, Chapters 13, 14 & 15. Listed below are some of these scriptures in the Books of Wisdom (NJB):

Wisdom 13:1-9 - Astral & nature cults.

Wisdom 13:10-19 - Worthless idols without any life.

Wisdom 14:1-9 - Other idols.

Wisdom 15:10-19 (This section is taken from the New Jerusalem Bible):

Ashes, his heart,
meaner than dirt his hope
his life more ignoble than clay,
since he misconceives the One who shaped him,
What is more, he looks on this life of ours as a kind of game,
and our time here like a fair, full of bargains.
"However foul the means," he says, "a man must make a living."
He, more than any other, knows he is sinning,
he whom from the same earthly material makes both breakable vessel and idol.
(The folly of the Egyptians: their indiscriminate idolatry)
–as in our modern materialistic natural Babel worlds–
But most foolish, more pitiable even than the souls of a little child,
are the enemies who once played the tyrant with your people,
and have taken all the idols of the heathens for gods,
which can use neither their eyes for seeing
nor their nostrils for breathing air
nor their ears for hearing
nor the fingers on their hands for handling;
while their feet are no use for walking,
since a human being made them,
a creature of borrowed breath gave them shape.
Now no man can shape a god as good as himself;
subject to death, his impious hands can only produce something dead.
He himself is worthier than the things he worships;
he will at least have lived, but never they.

(Our people have become as stupid, unaware and unfeeling as the lifeless idols they worship. We must again return to our worship of the Living God who is weeping in futility about our worship of our dumb idols. Idols are for those who do not know the Beloved. We have worlds of realities far beyond our comprehension with which to hold our attentions raptly for an eternity.)

147. DESTINY MARKINGS ALONG THE WAY

This is a summation of my very long personal Journey in the Spirit of the Beloved beginning in the Spring of 1967. It was at that time my marriage ended. This entire lifetime of great adventures has been marked with signs and guides, scriptures, songs and meetings with wonderful and sometimes awful people.

It is suddenly my awareness today that I have been led into all types of lifestyles beyond the one into which I was initially born into a working class family in a beautiful wilderness area of Northern California in the midst of the Great Depression.

I remember black out blinds on the windows of the family home from World War II sea to land shelling from Japanese submarines off the western U.S. coastal areas along the Pacific Ocean. Most homes included arsenals of rifles hanging upon their walls lest there was war action upon our own coastal areas. Years later I heard people in Alaska kept poisonous drugs in order to escape experiences worse than death. The children of my age group saw the first pictures from the awful Holocaust death camps in Europe. I remember feeling the "fear vibes" of that era from Pearl Harbor, death of President Franklin Delano Roosevelt, the bombs with the mushroom clouds that ended WWII and the lives of so many innocent Japanese people, and the fears of never living in a world without the pall of death hanging over all of our lives. When I traveled in the areas where Adolph Hitler had spoken so many years before, I could see his agitated face and gesticulating body language from the balconies where he gave some of his most rousing war time speeches to the Nazi youth, etc.

In 1953, I was healed from my birth defect by the new procedures used to perform heart surgeries. I was married in 1957 to my sweetheart who was a math student at University of California, Berkeley, California. He then became a Naval Aviator. I became a mother in 1959 and again in 1961. Life was still sort of the All-American Dream being played out for those of us a little older than the so called Baby Boomers from the rash of post war pregnancies which occurred when the veterans returned home from WWII. During this time I learned of life as a Naval Officer's Wife and as the wife of one who was in the Aerospace Research Pilot School with N.A.S.A. When my marriage ended in 1967, I received this message from the Lord.

"As I was with Moses, so shall I be with you."

I was alone with two small children before I remarried in 1972. I married a certified public accountant in the San Francisco, California Bay Area. I lived the life of the upper middle class businessman's wife with both of our families. I learned of all that is now happening in our nation in 2004 at that time. Due to vast differences in our lifetime and eternal goals, we were forced to part due to our vast ideological differences.

During the time I was alone and attempting to know what to do as an older single woman, I met another one who was a sign post along my pathway. He steered me into multi-cultural studies and living. I became one who was set free of many of the white Anglo-Saxon Protestant (W.A.S.P.) restrictions upon my life. I was made aware of the fact that most of the planet is not occupied or controlled by northern European people. I became acquainted with the people who many white Americans like to think of as invisible. This doorway opened to me in 1985 after I asked to be shown what had been happening in the twenty or so years prior. As I mentioned, I was told "We will show you these things but they may frighten you." This was truly the case even before things started to happen. I had also met many of the International students at my college in Santa Cruz. This opened the doorway to understanding of the many Islamic people in the world at this time.

I met them and the African and Native American people. My next meeting was with the invisible homeless people of America. Before this happened, I had begun to meet local people who had been partially or completely homeless all their lives. This was a world I had not known existed.

A couple of dreams were given me to prepare me for my work with the homeless community of my own home town and environs. The first dream reminded me that my relatives who had been forced to leave the Oklahoma Dust Bowl "would understand". I stumbled upon the movie "The Grapes Of Wrath" by John Steinbeck. I watched the pioneer Joads arrive in the California vineyards and farm lands. I realized that group of relatives most certainly would understand the hardships of pioneering and of homelessness. I also had a very fantastic dream while house sitting at a friend's small mobile near the local Indian reservation. In the dream I was shown a huge, brightly lit and beautiful UFO Mother Ship over the nearby river. It had been sent to tell me of my work with another woman I had not met. This work seemed to be as a social worker. The dream ended with a true prophecy of a snowstorm, which I had not known was coming. Within a few short months I was working with this selfsame dream state woman as her administrative assistant at a local homeless model shelter. I worked with this dear friend for a couple of years after I had worked with the local Black organization. By this time, it was becoming obvious to me that our Father had many children everywhere. I have been honored to have met some of the most wonderful people of the whole world in my life. I have also learned of some of the most horrific people, events and ageless evil hierarchies in my years of "walking in the Spirit of the Beloved". It is truly a reality that we must bear the marks of the society to which we bring our prophetic messages. We must learn we are to speak no careless prayers.

If one prays for patience, one must learn patience–sometimes the hard way.

If we offer ourselves as human sacrifices for the lives and souls of others, we will be facing many things beyond the scope of understanding of most people.

If we ask to suffer so others may learn from our sufferings, we have indeed prayed under the unction of the Spirit, or in blindly naive fashion.

If we seek to learn Wisdom and Truth, we will be filled–perhaps to overflowing.

If we want Him with our whole hearts, minds, bodies and souls, we will be at-oneness with Him. He will share His mysteries and secrets with us. As a friend, we will learn what hurts and what delights Him.

If we are the Children of Our Father, we will see Him weep, even as we are weeping. We weep together. How else can a family be.

Sometimes when we begin weeping, it is very hard to stop–even if we are finally made happy. Weeping and mourning has become habitual to us and perhaps even to our Beloved Father.

As His friends and disciples we will learn why He spoke as He spoke. We will learn His teachings even as did Mary–at His knee. We will sit listening raptly to every word He brings to us, even as I do to this day. I do not wish to miss anything He has to share with us.

It is my strong belief and desire to share with others so everyone may know how much they are loved by the Beloved. This is why I dare to make myself foolishly vulnerable to the whimsical attitudes and words of others. I believe we will only become one family when we dare to share ourselves with other–even as He made Himself vulnerable to us when He came to bear witness to the Way, the Truth and the Light of the Gospel. He didn't come to destroy. He came to set us free from bondage to age old manmade laws and idealogies not of this world. If we want to know Him, we must seek Him. The Father and the Son say come. We will then meet the rest of the Divine Family. Such are the ways of Heaven as I know it at this time. I am still learning. It is time to apply for entry into the portals of Divine Learning. It can set the captives of this planet free. This is what He came to do.

They killed Him and His prophets. We are Sojourners. We seek Truth. Thus did the African heroine Sojourner Truth see herself as a living sacrifice for Truth and Justice. She sojourned here upon this wonderful planet where Dark Ages occur upon occasion. We must be the Beacons of Light with oil kept in our Lamps, as the Wise Virgins. We must let them know He is coming soon. We must tell them to follow His teachings. They will set everyone free in His love and grace.

I can see very clearly as I assemble the many years of Messages from Heaven He has shared with me, for everyone, that He has indeed made a Divine Path in the Dark Wilderness places of life. He has never left or forsaken me. He has held my hand and led me on a long an circuitous journey through many worlds. He has introduced me to my other neighbors upon this beautiful world. He has shown me He dwells in the hearts of everyone if they will allow Him and His teachings entry. He has made me into an international, multi-cultural, inter-faith, spiritually aware and free Child of God. I am no longer in bondage to the archaic laws of ignorant, greedy and hate filled people. These are not those who will govern in the kingdom of Heaven.

If we allow ourselves to be led and guided into the mysteries and secrets of the heart of the Beloved, we may desire to enter into Heaven. We must be open to enjoy the childlike joys and beauties of Home. Those of us who love simplicity and seek to know Him will be taught of Him.

We must not judge, for thereby are we judged. I have not written this unusual collection of a lifetime of messages for the pleasures of those who wish to question, slander and judge another's spiritual experiences. I do not seek an editor, a counselor, a researcher or yet a theologian. We are simply offering a heartfelt lifetime of spiritual experiences in order to entice others to also seek to know Him.

These are personal moments to be shared with those who can comprehend the ways of the Beloved. Others will not desire to share in these conversations for their hearts will only be seared or they will be overcome with fears of wonderful things which are simply not familiar to themselves. This is why we must study to know Him. Otherwise, we must daringly leap off the precipice into His outstretched arms. By so doing, one will simply expect "To see what happens." After all, the just and faithful know this is the way they must live. I only make these personal offerings in my attempts as a counselor and teacher to whet your interests for more of Him. He is so wonderful I wish to share with everyone the beauty of the Beloved. It is time for more exercise of our minds, souls and bodies.

Let us all begin our walk in the Spirit of the Beloved this very day.

148. IN THE SPIRIT OF THE BELOVED FATHER

Dream & Message - September 25, 2004

Whether agencies, institutions or divine offices, all are dedicated to the concerns of those who are poor in spirit, minds, bodies and souls. No matter how huge or how futile the human condition, it remains the all-encompassing concern and sorrow of the all-seeing and all-loving Almighty Father. He weeps, even as we weep, because it is so agonizingly frustrating to never be able to see and end to such suffering.

We, as workers with those who suffer, are exhausted, frustrated and sometimes lacking in hope. We wonder whether we will ever see an end to such chaos and unhappiness. We hurt for bodies, minds, hearts and souls. We start out attempting with all our human abilities to cure these great social and spiritual ills. We look at them from every angle and viewpoint. What can we do? We study them from every academic perspective whether sociological, psychological, spiritual, political, geographical, historical or simply from the diversities of human perspectives as cultures, religions, racial or linguistic confusions. We analyze at every moment of our lives if we are interested in the care and cure of human beings. If we are with social and medical facilities we attend many endless meetings and write books full of analytical notes. We attempt to discuss a variety of plans in order to solve these never ending woes. We battle the constant changes of political leaders, all of whom have their own selfish or altruistic agendas. All of the administrators, psychiatrists and psychologists, myriads of counselors of all types–business as well as medically or legally affiliated–, all levels of social workers and technologists, nurses and doctors cannot put Humpty Dumpty together again. The old mythological stories tell us Humpty was a humanoid Egg. Some know Humpty was a cannon. Others see ourselves as types of Humpty Dumpty, a poor cracked and destroyed Human Being who is unable to be healed ever again. Let us not give up. After thinking of all the endless frustrations of studying, working with and facing all manner of frustrations and failures, we still must never stop working for the complete blessed healing of all of us. Our Father and those of us who work to cure all the ills of human beings know we cannot give up. No matter how battle scarred we become. We may be on abject burn-out and desire a time out as I did when I had the dream in about 1988 of The Crowd of Witnesses. We may actually seem to leave the Earth to enter Heaven through the Swinging Door early in the 1980's. We may see and experience other lives ourselves or others may have lived or be yet living. We may be able to empathetically enter any world we need to enter in order to help heal another. We may need to live as many lives as are necessary for our own salvation and those of others. No price is too high to pay for the safe return of even one beloved soul to our Father's Home. We know we are not going to be allowed to rest until all the lost souls find their ways Home again. It is easy to forget we are simply lost in a strange world of suffering and jealousy. This is not forever. It is simply one world of many. Do not give up. Help is on the way. We will work our way through all the rubble of our lives. We will not stop believing in the seemingly "Impossible Dream" of a world in which all human beings live fairly with equal human rights, housing, and other survival needs met. We will not suffer from the dangers and heartbreak of racism, sexism, agism, disabilities, death and an endless array of social aberrations (for there is no more aging, disability and death).

I have personally spent most of my adult life attempting to learn how to work with and help the plights of the poor and needy, mentally and physically ill, the lost and saddened souls of all. Today's dream scenario seemed to again show me we cannot stop caring about and working with these people, their social and spiritual issues. This is still the highest of professional concerns. It is the highest goal of the Father to see an end to all these problems.

The world has been run by those who are like the mindless, enraged and out of control Minotaur forever. It is time to give this Beast a fast and hard kick out of existence. Let him mourn forever–not Our Father and us. It is time to say "It is ended!!" He must go. Those who destroy the Minotaur will be freed from his dominion over the whole of Our Father's creation. The Minotaur is an aberration of human and divine conception, a type of the original fall of the angelic into human destinies. The ancient stories hold the keys to life as we know it from Enoch to this time. We will make sure we do not produce any more immortal copies of the Minotaur or Cyclops. Until we return to our insatiable urge to know Sophia, the goddess of Wisdom, we will see no releases from our bondage as human beings lost in the darkness of the cosmos. Wisdom will teach us of the reasons for our conditions at this time. She will teach us of what is to come if we do not alter our pathways to destruction and doom. She will also teach us we must not give up believing in, and fighting to attain, an end to ignorance, greed and selfish lusts of all types. We must not tire in well doing. We will overcome ignorance, poverty, disabilities, age, and death. We will see an end to the world as we know it. We will all be changed, in a moment and a twinkling of an eye. Our hearts will be full of the rapture of the saints because we finally realize we are saints and children of the Father. He has never changed. We forget our first estates and royal dynasties. There were those who told us these false stories for centuries. We began to forget the original stories from Our Father. When we run through the "Swinging Door" again we will once again immediately KNOW to whom our souls have ever been in communion. We have never been alone. We have always been closely watched and monitored. We have never been anything but His Beloved Children, in whom He is well pleased. He released us to go on a rite of passage called by several different terms. We cannot learn without personally entering into our experiential lesson plans. It is my belief we made those before we personally decided to come to this world to learn and grow in the graces of our Lord and Savior Jesus Christ. He also personally made His decision to come as divinity in human form in order to learn how we suffer and die. He also learned how we live, feel, triumph over disease and death, and experience love. He became human in order to empathetically know how to heal us. We will be made whole, for He has paid the price for our healing. Those of us who aspired to become social workers and psychologists also came to assist others. The doctors and nurses, as well as all the therapeutic healers of all types are all here to do their parts to save our bodies, minds and souls from suffering.

We are many. We are not giving up. Neither are our individual tears stopped until ALL is ended and destroyed which can cause suffering. Perhaps we have very little time in which to continue our work.

Personally, I staunchly intend to continue my quest for right and wholeness forever. We will continue this eternal Quest because it it a Righteous One. We stand for the equal Human Rights of All. We will mourn together until all of the captives are set free from their bondage to corrupt systems from archaic times. When all is done, we will all wipe our eyes and shout Hosanna to the Bridegroom who has conquered all of the Evil Ring Lords forever.

At this time:

Let us all sing together "WE WILL OVER COME, WE WILL OVERCOME–SOME DAY!"

Let us all attempt to see that world coming in the Clouds of Heaven.

Let us imagine we are all donning our wedding garments to attend the Marriage Supper of the Lamb.

Let us imagine a world in which ignorance, time, darkness, death and illness are no more.

Let us imagine we have found our ways Home. We are no longer like lost prodigals.

Let us again see the images of our Beloved, our loved ones and those wonderful Heavenly Homes and other edifices we have so long remembered from someplace.

Let us close the doors on the Bully Minotaur. He is but a mythic creature again.

Let us wipe all the tears from our eyes and those of our Father. It is time to be joyous!

We will eternally sing praises to the Holy Ones. We are Home once again.

We will sing that old hymn (and others) "We've got joy deep in our hearts today!"

We have all done our appointed work to aid and to save the Lost Children of God here on this planet. We have all fought the good fight. We are all victors in Christ Jesus, who is our Lord and Savior forever. We have overcome the Beast and all evil as we walk covered in the life saving blood of the Lamb, who submitted Himself to be slain for the sins of this world's souls. We are "ALL TOGETHER AGAIN–IN THE SPIRIT OF THE BELOVED–JUST PRAISING THE LORD!"

149. THE SMILE OF OUR BELOVED FATHER

November 27, 2004

One day in July, 2004, my Beloved Father let me see and share in His brokenhearted weeping. It is now November, 2004, and I realize this day how happy we will all be when our Beloved Father can once again smile upon us and tell us we have done well as His good and faithful children.

My sorrow lifts because I know no child can be happy when its parent is sad or angry. What can be done to bring a smile of joy and approval from our Heavenly Father's face?

This must be our ony concern if we realize the extreme gravity of a situation in which we are involved which causes extreme sorrow to the heart of Him whom we adore and serve, no longer servants, but as His own children.

"The Father smiled and the world was no longer in the throes of war. God smiled and the world was once again happy. He said, "It is good" and it was once again as He had made it to be.

He again strolled with us in meadows and forest lands. All war had ended. Souls flew happily to His bosom, He healed the wounded of all tribes of the world. He healed the broken hearts, damaged minds and souls of all. All are His children.

Victory was His and all were blessed and healed.

The Spirit said, "Be happy and multiply, be fruitful and holy.

See your neighbors as your friends and loved ones.

Speak no more of war.

Seek to unify–not divide families, couples, communities and nations. Be ye one Family–My Family.

All are perfect. All weep in great sadness, calling upon My Name in great sorrow.

Therefore, even as you weep, I will weep.

A loving parent does not laugh derisively while children are hurting, injured and dying.

Come now, let us reason together. Let us all be seated in prayerful accord. It is time to be breaking weaponry into plowshares.

How can there be joy while weapons of mass destruction are being created and used by any nation?

How can there be Joy and Peace while some hoard monstrous stockpiles of gold, oil and real estate while others children have no food, housing, clothing and toys?

How? How do some dare to sleep at night knowing their own evils reach to the Heavens.

I do know and see all.

I desire obedience to holy principles.

The Laws of the Cosmos will become Laws of Earth, or Earth will be no more as it is now known.

When one limb is gangrenous it must be amputated in order to save the whole body.

The tiny starving faces of African and Indian children concern Me.

Why do they not concern human parents with overweight selfish children?

Many of those dear souls are wealthy with treasures not of earthly hands.

There is nothing hidden from the Father.

He hears all the prayers of all those who love Him–whether the Bushman's child or the children of a Saudi aristocrat. He hears the tearful pleas of those who submit themselves to prayers many times each day, whether in homes, churches, mosques or synagogues.

All are of the Family of God and many are also of the House of Abraham.

Those who come to Him through Eastern paths or those of the Earth's religions are ALL His children.

He alone looks at each heart and knows each souls as its Creator and Father God.

> "Red and yellow, black and white, all are precious in His sight. Jesus loves the little children of the world."

This is one of first songs one learned in Christian Sunday Schools. It is still true. He has not changed.

We are to let our "Little Light"shine forth to light the darkness. We are to let our lights shine, " let it shine, let it shine." Perhaps if all of us let our hearts speak to one another, we'll all remember the ways of the Father before it is too late.

We have let ourselves become lost from Him due to our fear and hatred. We have forgotten to seek the Wisdom of the Father. He tells us He approved of King Solomon's selfless request for Wisdom. Solomon did not ask for great wealth. The Father blessed him because His heart and values sought the Will and Wisdom of the Father above all else.

What else is of such value? Nothing. To be closely walking and sharing with Him is treasure of unbelievable worth. To be in His Presence is the desire of those who are His children. We want to be able to make Him smile. His loving and approving smile is our delight. The happiness of the good child is to please the Father.

Our world will never be happy as long as we cause our Beloved Father great sorrow. Let us attempt with all our hearts, minds, bodies and souls to love and to bless our Heavenly Father.

It is time for us to once again be able to stroll with Him "in the still of the evening". We need and desire His Presence above all others. His is the Presence we seek when we "run through the door" into our Heavenly Home once again. Heaven would not be Heaven for many of us if we could no longer be allowed into His Presence. His Presence is the Heaven we seek. He is our Treasure. Our greatest desire must be to fulfill His Will and Way. Our destinies are His. He has created us to love and to serve Him forever. We desire to be His beloved ones. His smile will be ours and His tears will be no more.

He will help and heal us. He will become our Father once again. We will walk and talk with Him as did our First Parents. All time, disability and death is ended. Our Father's tears are gone. All have been wiped away. Thank You, Father.

150. THE GIFT OF FAITH

December 14, 2004

"The Gift of Faith is an elusive Gift.
Hold strongly to it or it will be gone."

* * *

Dreams: December 14, 2004

This morning my husband and I both dreamed of spiritual groups. His dream was of telling a group of people they are all to live as the Buddha. Christians are told they are to live as Christ's disciples. We are all to attempt to personify our Beloved to others.

I dreamed of my personal discovery of the formation of two new Christian groups. The one I was shown was full of nice people who were attempting to construct a new meeting place in my local home town theater. (I can see these sanctuaries are truly needed for those who feel they are no longer welcome in their own denominations due to the lack of religious freedoms.)

The one person in a leadership role appeared to be wearing a long robe with head dress shaped like a fish, the Sign of the Great Fisherman, Jesus Christ. A view of this person was given from the back to show the hooded robe figure of the priest or priestess. The robe appeared to be a pale purple with pink toward the edges of the hood (or mitre–the head dress of a priest or priestess of high office). It is my belief these groups would also be using other ritual items such as the crozier. There was a very loving and convivial spirit among these believers. I thought I would like this group very much. I hoped this was a group which would bring great blessings to all of His children.

Next, I was also shown a large fish out of water–seemingly beached in a shallow stream or river. It seemed to be alive. Perhaps this is the plight of our American Christian churches at this time. They have alienated themselves into becoming dry creek beds, are still living, but are lacking the water of the Holy Spirit. Many of us know we are a religion divided at this time. Some have been abused and alienated from their own families due to the hypocritical and legalistic theocratic views of some divisive leaders. Families have nothing to gain from divisions. Leaders with secret agendas have reasons for separating believers into divided camps. Thus can the enemy of our souls entrap us into warfare among brothers and sisters. This is not of the Lord.

I was given the following as a second message that seemed to me to be a grave warning for all of us:

"The Gift of Faith is an elusive one.
Hold strongly to it or it will be gone."

It is truly a time to face the Enemy of our Souls with strong demonstrations against his wiles. It is not a time to be divided and conquered by those who wish nothing more than to destroy the Faith. Let us not argue over self-righteousness and our own ideas of faith, leadership, offices of our own individual paths and denominations. Peaceful interchanges can heal the breaches made by our own fears and ignorance. All types of divisions may come between believers. Our faith is in Him. He is our Prince of Peace. Let us be non-violent as was Mahatma Gandhi in his work for Truth, Freedom and Peace on Earth. The Beloved Spirit of Love covers all and insures we have peace among us forever. Amen.

151. HE IS THE LIGHT OF TRUTH ALONG THE WAY

December 18, 2004

I am the Way, the Truth and the Light. Walk ye in it. These are the words of my Beloved Savior Jesus Christ.

If we believe He is our Way, our Truth and our Light. Let us walk ahead prayerfully upon His Path. My walk has been a joyous one. I may have come a circuitous bifurcated path. We went off at the crossroads way back there about twenty years ago and I learned much about the fact there are truly many "Paths to the Center". This is the major reason for studying religions and the vast diversity of their varieties of religious experiences. There are many books written. There are many purified and serious souls each seeking to know right pathways.

This morning, after all my studies, I am truly aware of how wonderful is His Plan of Salvation for us, His "Lost Souls". It is possible to become lost in a morass of confusion and darkness. We can be led out of this situation if we will walk in the footsteps of our Lord. He has sent us His Beloved Holy Spirit. The Holy Spirit is our Comforter, our Teacher and Counselor. We are guided and protected by our Beloved Father's Spirit. What more do we need? Why do we need to fear? We do not. It has been said our only fear should be Ignorance (avidya). This is an Eastern teaching. It is also true in the West.

There are those ancient paths which have come from the paths of the Mystery Schools. There is now our generally accepted and followed path of His Passion. We have been washed in the Blood of the Lamb, our Savior Jesus Christ. I symbolically place His blood over the doors of my home to cover and protect us. Our ancient ancestors cleansed themselves in the blood of bulls and rams. They believed in their resurrections from spiritual deaths by baptism in water, fire and spirit. Charismatic Christians of this age also stress spiritual baptism (often with tongues of fire) and in water baptism to show ourselves to be believers in Him.

If we have His Love we are able to ponder all of these things. We are taught we must study to show ourselves approved as His childlike disciple. We may come to a realization and knowledge there may indeed be many paths. These many paths may all end up with us in our Father's Heart. We have all converged into the Center–our Beloved Father. The Center is part of us. He dwells in our Hearts. He is Love. His Love is eternal and so are we His eternal souls who are attempting to find our ways back to Him whom we desire so very much.

We have been given many holy righteous teachings of how to become a Child of the Manifold God. The next stage is realization of what this means for our individual souls and the collective group soul of this planet. How are we connected to the other dimensions and worlds of His infinite universe? We have been told there are many Paths to the Center. Some of us may come from paths of His Passion or His Mysteries. We may overlap and interact. We may understand and experience a diversity of truths. The Key to All is His Love. Love is a very big word. It covers and cleanses all from sin (errors). Love is ours. Love is kind and wise. It is merciful and just. Love is our Beloved Father. He knows, sees and judges. We are not to judge on another. He sees our hearts. He knows each of us as His own.

He is our Beloved Savior. He is The Path, which is His Way of Truth and Light. It becomes narrow and hard for those who cannot walk happily in His Love, Wisdom and Truth. If we would rather argue and war over ideas our pathway is wide and ungoverned. Fear and ignorance prevents us from finding Truth and Wisdom. His Light is our Beacon. He is most literally The Way, The Truth and The Light. Light exposes and overcomes Darkness. Some few do not like to have their deeds and thoughts exposed. The Truth will eventually overcome Ignorance and Darkness. The questions are of "How" and "When"?

This is one of the topics of our ongoing walks "In the still of the evening". If we love Him, we will want to walk forever as His beloved Children in His Presence in His Garden. We have had a wonderful time learning of marvelous and magical worlds and creatures. We also are being taught by the best of all teachers. He will teach us of those things which we must know in order to enjoy His World completely. He has said "It is good." We must learn how to make it remain "His World". He is its Creator. We are His Creations along with all else He has created. We do not subjugate our Friends. Friends walk and talk together. "Friends Eat Together". We are all awaiting "The Marriage Supper of the Lamb". This is an exciting time. We will all be breaking bread and sharing His cup. I am excited. His church is "His Bride". We are His forever. We are honored and thrilled to be His.

Our Father will be smiling at long last. Our family will once again be as One Family with no barriers between us. He is our Center. We are His Children. A Child always wants to be with its Parent.

His Truth sets us free to find The Light. He makes Himself a Light unto our footsteps as we walk carefully upon His (Path)Way, prayerfully seeking Him. We are taught His Truths while we walk with Him on the Way to our Emmaus.

Only if we become as a Little Child will we be able to walk on this less traveled road. The road well traveled is paved with the lies of the fearful and powerful selfish rulers of religious and political institutions of all types. This is not to say all institutions and rulers are evil.

Our Path is straight and narrow. It is a peacefully prayerful Path. We are alone with Him much of the Way. This is the Way upon which He teaches us Truth. He is our Light whenever the Way grows dark. He never leaves nor forsakes us. He is our Beloved Friend. Whenever He seems not near, His Beloved Spirit is with us ot lead and to guide us. We are His penitent childlike students. We want to learn of Heaven. He is our Beloved Father.

Come, let's continue along on our blessed walk. We are eager to learn more of Him. He is Good. We seek the Good and the Holy. Let us therefore try to be like His Heavenly Beloved Spirit.

In conclusion, no matter which words are used, or which names define the Beloved Spirit of our Heavenly One, we believe for a miraculous conclusion of His Great Plan for the Salvation of Planet Eart. His tears will disappear and He will also wipe the tears from the eyes of all of His children of all the Earth. We are all His Family. He is All That Is. We are His Children forever.

152. "INCREASE YOUR BOUNDARIES TO INCLUDE ALL OF MY CHILDREN"

Dream: January 1, 2005
This was night full of messages.
Dream #1: 4:22 a.m.

The first message was of my long deceased paternal grandmother attempting to give me an encoded message. I , in turn, was attempting to give this message to my daughter.

Dream #2: 7 a.m.

I was to communicate with each of the adult women who were heads of households. It seemed as if we were to attempt to build bonds forever of these various households of women. While I was pondering this dream, I was reminded of the matriarchal bonds from the beginning of this world. Women have always had a natural sisterhood. They also have a divine sisterhood as the mothers of all of His divine children. This children are of great importance to the Beloved Spirit, the Father.

I made lists of all the women with whom I needed to build, or even re-build, contacts who would perhaps share my eternal existence in our Heavenly Home, as well as in this world. It seemed to me we are to become much more aware and helpful of each other.

Dream #3: 10:11 a.m.

The words seemed to continue to repeat themselves over and over again.

"INCREASE YOUR BOUNDARIES TO INCLUDE ALL MY CHILDREN"

This does not mean all of these are babies or children. All people are His children if they attempt to love and to serve Him. He also has recalcitrant and disobedient children of all biological ages. He has many children around the whole world who are His beloved children.

#1–My grandmother, who I was shown is a holy priestess of the Father on the Other Side, has come to remind me of teachings. I am to remind my daughter.

#2–We, in turn, are to communicate our loving concern to every other mother we know. They should do the same. In this fashion, we will rebuild family love in our own and every other family. We will stand united as His Family. He is telling us we are family, a village of tribal connections.

#3–He is requiring us to become as Little Children who are able to obey their Heavenly Father. He wishes us to remember we are all His Children. He has many children not of this world or universe.

He is commanding us to do away with all barriers and boundaries of religion, racism, ethnocentrism and each of our self-acclaimed supremacist values which are deeply ingrained within our individual souls. He is requiring our love to overcome these barriers between people of His world.

Are we capable to doing these things? Do we really wish to see Him in all of the people of this world?

Many of us have watched the horrors of the earthquake induced tidal waves which have destroyed the lives of so many who live adjacent to the Indian Ocean. We have seen the beauty of holiness in the faces of all of His children. These people look different than us. They also worship Him as Buddhists Muslims, Hindus and many more religions of the entire world. We have seen the Fruits of the Holy Spirit in their faces. We know they love the goodness of the Beloved Spirit.

At times like this, we know we are all His Children. His children lovingly help another, without any regard to status or race. We are all His Children if we obey His Voice.

If we have become as the divinely spiritual "Little Child" who, we are told, will be our archetypal leader, we will simply believe and obey our Heavenly Father's wishes. Good children do not question. Children do not judge their parents. They simply know they are His Children. If we love and obey Him as our God and Savior, we are His Children who know we must obey Him because He is our Father.

We are told we will not enter Heaven "unless we become as a Little Child. " We must think of what it truly means to become as a Little Child. We will be judged how we treat "The least of these" (little children, the homeless, the aged, the disabled, our family livestock and pets, and many more who are seeming "least"). He tells us as we "treat the least of these we have also done the same to Me". This is a very important thing to remember. How are we treating others? If we are mistreating anyone, He sees and knows all of these things. We are doing these things also to

Him, our Heavenly Father, the Beloved Spirit. His Holy Spirit comes to comfort, counsel, lead, guide and to teach us.

We have asked to be led and taught of the Holy Spirit, The Beloved Spirit of the Father. He is now teaching us. He wishes us to learn and to obey these lessons. If any can watch the horrors of the powers of Mother Earth these dear brothers and sisters are experiencing and feel heartless towards them, one has to wonder why we have no heartfelt concerns for the plights of so many. The world is mourning today. Black banners fly in every land. Other flags are flying at half staff for the horror of it all.

White flags are on every home in those areas hit by the tsunamis. Few families have escaped loss of at least one loved one. The world's New Years Eve celebrations have turned to a time of holy quietude, contemplation and the burning of incense, candles and funeral pryes. All those who pray are deeply prayerful. The whole world is in mourning. All people wonder if this is but one of many earthly disasters to come upon the Earth.

As a survivor of many sad disasters in my land of California, my eyes have been bathed in tears for a long time. I realize we are all very exhausted and tired–in fact abjectly suffering from post-traumatic shock syndromes. May God be with us all through these troublous times in which we are living. I would rather write of happiness an bliss. Oh, yes, in addition to horrors, we do have His blessed events also in our lives. We must shake off our traumas which make us depressed and even catatonic at times. We must rise up to pray and to live for each other as His Spiritual Children. We are His Children if we say He is our Father with His Beloved Spirit dwelling within our hearts and souls. We must help one another.

We must enlarge the boundaries of our hearts to encompass one another, beginning with those of our own homes, families and friends. We must open wide the doors of our traumatized and frozen hearts to let ourselves become compassionate towards one another–even as I have mentioned in other parts of this book.

Let us be filled to overflowing with Thy Love today. May we truly become as Your Little Child in order to better be able to learn Thy Ways for our lives. We must remember to treat others as we would wish ourselves to be so treated. (The Golden Rule)

We must remember to treat others equally. We must not decide to mistreat the poor and weak among us. Many of these are Himself. If we are walking in His Holy Spirit we are part of His Beloved Spirit, even as a small human child wishes to become part of his/her parent. Let us be filled with the Beloved Spirit and show His Light forth to a suffering traumatized world full of His Children. Let us pretend we are again all little children. This is the only way we will be allowed to enter the Kingdom of our Father. A good little child will share and help another with no boundaries made by frightened adults. Let us all listen to our Father's Beloved Spirit today.

All of my life I have been walking in faith in His Holy Spirit. I have been comforted, counseled and warned of many things coming upon the world and into my own life and the lives of my loved ones. Today My Father says He commands me to obey Him. I pray I may be able to fulfill His requests for my own life and to do as He wishes for the greater good of all of His children everywhere.

He loves and desires all of His Children to come to Him without fear or restraints. He wants us to remember His ways and His teachings. Of such is the Kingdom which is coming soon which shall be led by His "Little Child".

If we have the "Perfect Love" of the "Little Child" (the "Born Again Child of God"), fearlessly holding tightly to His Beloved Hand, led by the Father's Beloved Spirit, we will "fear no evil", for He is with us, to lead and to guide us even through the "Valley of the Shadow of Death".

We will trust Him to "Teach Us His Ways". We will no longer be a hate-filled soul, full of ignorance and rage. We will have become truly His "Little Born-Again Child". We will eagerly be awaiting the Return of Christ to rule and reign in His Earthly Kingdom which is part of the Father's Heavenly Kingdom.

We will learn of many things. We will no longer feel like "lost Sheep, who have lost their Way". We wonder and some argue over holy days and the Sabbath day. We will be taught about all of these things if we are open to counsel. There may be teachings about which we have no conceptions at this time. Let us remain teachable until His loving tutelage.

We hope to eventually see an end to all divisive arguments over the doctrines and tenets of the Christian Protestant denominations and the Catholic Church. We will be taught about each world religion and find we each know of the Father and His ways. We must seek to be led and guided in His loving instructions. We must examine those those teachings in which we find unity. Prejudicial fears cause fear, hatred and wars. We must learn from history.

153. A TIME OF SORROW

January 7, 2005

We must listen to the still, small Voice of the Beloved Spirit. The Signs are on the Earth and in the Heavens. The latest message was received as late as January 7, 2005 by one of His very wise older human children. There was a "Voice" from Heaven which spoke this Message in the afternoon and again in the night with great sadness:

"THIS IS THE BEGINNING OF SORROWS."

We located the scripture in Matthew 24:8. The next scriptures speak of a time of horrible persecutions upon the Earth as people continue to disagree over Jesus Christ, who He was and is to each and every one of us. Is this message the answer to why our Father is weeping? As we can see, it took the shared input of two people to obtain the meaning of the reason our Father is weeping. This must concern any and all of us who have been allowed to witness His unrestrained grief. There are scriptures in each of the four Gospels of the Apostles which verify we are entering a time known as "A Time of Sorrows and Birth Pangs" before His Return. These scriptures are listed in the end of the Section entitled Signs In The Earth And The Heavens. The author would love to be in error. Let us pray together for wisdom and truth. We do not wish to speak of horrors when it is time for blessings.

It is obvious it takes a democratic majority to obtain the opinions of the whole tribal council.

He has been lifted up on a tree twice–once at Calvary on Golgatha and again last year by Mr. Mel Gibson with His award winning movie "The Passion".

In addition to physically showing Him and His crucifixion, we should be lifting up His teachings. He told us we show are love for Him by obedience to His teachings. He said "I come to bear witness to the Father and His kingdom."

As we can see, it took our whole family's involvement–intentional or not—because He wants us to realize we are participating with Him as a Family. Is it not just the oldest member of our extended family received the scriptures which gave us the answers to why He is unrestrainedly weeping.

It seems others will feel it is necessary to stamp out all memory of our Lord and His teachings. He has gone and we are those who are His sojourning Bride, the church, who have washed their bridal garments in His life-cleansing Blood shed for the salvation of the world.

There has been far too much warfare fought in the beloved name of Jesus, the Prince of Peace. This is because demons do not want peace on Earth, and good will between all of His children.

Some fine professors will say all the prophecies have already been fulfilled. I hope and pray this is so–BUT–as one who studies human behavior, I am sure there are enough ignorant fearful souls to attempt to initiate another time such as the early Christians faced in Rome, or during the dreaded Inquisitions of the Roman Church. Fear and violence breed more fear and violence.

It is dreadful to be forced to think of the possibilities of such times of horror. Why kill anyone in the name of Allah or our Father, Mohammed or Jesus, or the large Church or all the smaller churches and denominations? There are many who are very distressed with the perversions of His teachings by those who have declared themselves to be His only children. Let us not have the descendants of those holy innocents who were unjustly killed at the horrible"burning times" now kill the innocents of Christ due largely to the rage engendered by the false teachings of some few who have perverted His teachings for power and greed.

Much to my erxtreme consternation I have led myself and anyone who reads this book into a terrible realization. If these scriptures have indeed to yet be fulfilled, it is my concern this is now beginning. I did not wish to discover such truths. I had hoped to eventually see the Spirit of our Beloved Father smiling happily. Instead, He is warning us of the times in which we are living.

This is not even considering all of the very large questions about Jesus Christ's birth, role as the Son of God sent to save the whole world from sin. It is obviously the year when it will be one of deep sorrow and a great test of the faiths of many. We must know who we love and serve. Why do I love Him? I leave all arguments over deeply theological questions to the Biblical scholars. I find my relationship in Him is one of trusted and tried friendship. I love His teachings because I was instructed to seek Him and His teachings over all others of men and institutions. I love Him as the Beloved Savior of my soul. I believe He is the Son of God. We are also the sons and daughters of God if we follow the Father's commandments.

If He had a marital relationship and children with Mary Magdalene, these things are not a concern to me. Celibacy is not the reason on which I base my trust in Him. I know there can be celibacy among those who have known sexual relationship. This is a celibacy of the soul, as well as of the body. The original sin was not the one of sexual relationship. It was disobedience to the Father's request to not eat of the Forbidden Tree. Obedience to His teachings is the key to loving Christ.

Our Father is weeping. Jesus and his engrafted siblings are also weeping. Please keep us from the evils of this world we pray.

The author is a simple handmaiden/scribe. Therefore, I can only trust and obey. I do not need to have empirical proofs of the veracity and authenticity of my Lord's life or teachings. He is my Friend, Teacher and Beloved Lord. He doeth all things well. I have no profession or name to uphold. I do not know what I think of many of the doctrinal arguments taught about Jesus. I simply know and love Him and His teachings.

It is no longer a mystery why so many of us are seeing the Father's tears and the terrible disasters coming upon the Earth. Let us love one another in His Beloved Spirit. The next day the author was presented with a wonderfully uplifting and inspired happy message. This, too, may be our spiritual lot in life. We simply know that whether these are true or false prophecies, or if they are personal and are not for the global family, they are still His Words. We know He has spoken and

He entreats us to "INCREASE YOUR BOUNDARIES TO INCLUDE ALL MY CHILDREN".

These ar the words of a loving heartbroken parent. Our weeping Father has asked us to open our hearts to everyone. We are to attempt to do so whether in giving to the needs of those dear children in southeast Asia, the homeless children of America or to love our neighbors no matter what their political or religious affiliation.

We must continue to pray for all of our world and national leaders. Please give us love, Father, so we may pray for even those souls who have made us feel as if we have no rights to think or to pray. We need to love and pray for even those who have made us think they may be our enemies simply because we see Jesus in different roles. Lord, please forgive us our sins even as we prayerfully seek to love and to forgive those who trespass against us. I want to hear once again the scream of the Red Eagle in my dreams. Please forgive and bless all of your children and their leaders everywhere, we pray. We want your Kingdom to come and Thy Will to be done forever, Father.

We are part of all that is coming upon the Earth whether we desire to be here or not. We see wars everywhere. There are those who argue about religious institutions. There are individuals who are fearful and argue over the respective spiritual paths of each person. It is obvious humans are given to disagreements over anything which is new. It matters not whether the arguments are over new ideas, new pathways, new governments or simply over new (or simply different) energies and manifestations of His supreme powers. We must not fear the diverse gifts of His Holy Spirit. He gives these gifts to many diverse types of persons.

Fear is deadly. It gives souls the unbridled power to kill others with untrue slanderous words and names; if not literally, as with the terrible genocidal purges and inquisitions of many innocents in ages past--judged by modern "Brute Beasts", those with the atavistic primitive mentalities of fear and ignorance. It is easy for such individuals to wrongfully label and stereotype others as "demonic". Such a terrible "label" may cause the deaths of their innocent neighbors. Perhaps these neighbors are simply daring to live, think and breathe in a different fashion as yet unknown to the literally ancient "Natural Brute Beasts". The Lord told us these times would be like those at the time of Noah. Many of us see we are now living in times such as those. We are concerned as we watch each new day approach. What new manner of evil will we see under the Sun?

Let us all try to imagine together that Love and Peace have overcome racist and religious wars. Heaven is already upon the Earth, and that His Kingdom of Peace has come and His will is being done Let us join hands with all His beloved souls with those of all nations, cultures and religions. Let us pray with all our hearts for Peace on Earth and good will to all, for of such is the Kingdom of Heaven. He taught us we are to ask for the desires of our hearts.

We do not wish to be wise in our own conceits. We wish to be full of His wisdom, joy and peace.

We are preparing the Way for His Return. We are in the birth pangs before He comes to "Set the captives free". We may be living in the days called "The Great and Terrible Day(s) of the Lord".

We must stay open to His instructions for our lives as His citizens. We will learn Truth. His Way is one of Light. We will walk in His perfect peace, which passes all understanding, peacefully serene in the Light of His Love. May these things come true. It is in Thy Holy Beloved Spirit we pray, Father. Amen

C.A., The Weeping Father's Weeping Child

He has heard our prayers and given us choices which are listed below:

I. A CHAOTIC ENDING OF THIS WORLD AS WE KNOW IT

Descriptive Scriptures: Matthew 23 (Pharisee & Sadducees)
Matthew 24:8 to end. ("This is the beginning of sorrows.")
Mark 13::8 (Birth Pangs)

Luke 21
John 15 & 16; also, the Revelation of John

Or

II. A NEW EARTH

THE CHOICE IS OURS

The Father God has given us all free will to choose this day who we will follow. Our choices are those of life or death. We can choose to make Him happy or sorrowful.

Do we choose wisdom and liberty as children and heirs of the Father, or the ignorance and destructive chaos of our friends of Earth, some of whom are "natural brute beasts"? We must awaken to new insights as if we are newborn babes of His wonderfully blessed new creation. We must all realize we are His own children and listen to His wisdom. Let us be newly filled with His Holy Spirit. We must seek to know His wisdom at this crucial time in the long history of our world. We are to be filled with all of the Fruits of His Holy Spirit. May our lamps be showing forth as beacon lights in a darkened paradisial world. All is God and He is All That Is. Let us choose Life more abundantly in His Holy Spirit. We can co-create Heaven or Hell. Let us choose Him who is the Creator of Life, Who tells us we are all part of Him-The Manifold Father God-Who is All That is. We desire and choose friendship with our neighbors and Life rather than destruction. We do not wish to return to the abject Chaos prior to this Creation of our Earth. We wish to make our Father happy with His many children.

DIVINE LOVE

When one is ecstatically in love with Him, there is no place of indecision
And uncertainty.
When we are enraptured and in love with the Beloved, there is no fear,
Disrespect of dislike.
We know we are His.
Nothing else matters but our Divine Romance.
We love Him as our Way, our Truth and our Light.
In Him are all things wise and wonderful, lovable and lovely.
He is in the role of Lord,
Savior, Son of God,
Prince of Peace and
Reigning King
He is one of the Divine Messengers of the Living-All-Knowing Father/Mother/All That Is.

"They will call Him Immanuel–God with us." Matthew 1:23

"Tell them I love them. Ask and you shall receive. Knock and it shall be opened unto you."
(Holy is the Lamb of God. Amen)

Trespasses As We

Our Father, who art in Heaven,
Hallowed by Thy name.
Thy kingdom come, Thy will be done,
On Earth as it is in Heaven.

Give us this day our daily bread.
Forgive us our trespass as we forgive those who trespass against us.
Lead us not into temptation but deliver us from evil.

For Thine is the kingdom,
And the Power,
And the Glory
Forever and ever.

Amen.
(Jesus Christ)

SECTION VII
SPECIAL INFORMATION FOR THE READER'S FUTURE REFERENCE

THE AUTHOR'S RESEARCH SUMMARY OF SOME OF THE POSSIBLE AND PROBABLE CAUSATIONS OF OUR FATHER'S TEARS

1. The Creative Father completed the formation of the Heavens and of the Earth. He created all manner of land, sea, and air creatures, including human beings. When He was finished with this wonderful work He said, "It is good." He blessed all with His loving Presence.

2. He left them to their own devices and they sinned many times. He took pity upon them and finally sent His only begotten Son Jesus Christ to release them from their neverending lives of error.

3. He came to save the lost and dying, the sinful and sorrowing Children of God.

4. His was a simple Message of Truth, Light, and of Life more abundantly: 5. He said, "If you love and follow Me, keep my Commandments:

> "Thou shalt love the Lord your God with your whole heart, mind, body and soul, and your neighbor as yourself. Do unto others as you would do unto yourself."
>
> &
>
> "Go out into all the world and give them My Gospel of the Good News–My teachings which are easy and simple to follow. I gave My life for the sins of the world. It is finished. All you have to do is believe in Me and "Try" to follow Me.

6. I came not to destroy the Law or the Prophets but the fulfill all of the prophecies of My Mission. It is a worthy mission because My Father does not wish for any of His beloved children to be lost. I am come to save them from their sins. If they will listen to My simple Message of Love, Truth, Light, and Whole Living, they will be nourished and fed by the angels of Heaven. We are giving a simple message that can be understood

by all who think and believe as a Little Child thinks and feels. Of such is the Kingdom of Heaven.

7. He said the Kingdom had already come before He left. He left us with the injunction to wait upon the Holy Spirit Counselor to be sent to us to lead and guide us from all dangers and errors.

8. He said He loved all of us, even if we have sinned and fallen short of the glory of God. He did not say we were created imperfect or evil. We are Beloved Children of God. Jesus is the firstborn of many brethren (and sisters). We are now part of His Family.

9. He goes to prepare a place for us to come to when we leave this plane of existence to return to our Heavenly Home and our Family.

10. The Holy Family is made up of all nations, kindreds, tongues, races and genders.

11. He came not to condemn the world, but that the world, through Him, might be saved. Thus, He is our Savior. We are saved by His Grace. We worship Him in our own holy temple not made with hands, lest any man should boast of the building of His temple.

12. His Commandments of the New Covenant are simple. He said They kept everything simple because they want none to misunderstand and become lost, frightened and forsaken.

13. Many souls cannot believe the simplicity of the Father's wishes. He simply wants us to come to Him as loving and obedient children. He wants us to be ready to accept and enjoy the pleasures of a wonderful and fantastic world so far beyond our own expectations we must become like a wonder-filled Little Child in order to be able to experience and enjoy it.

14. Human beings and their regimented restrictions, their orthodoxies and authoritarian religious structures will not allow themselves to be led by a Little Child. Jesus said, "And a Little Child shall lead them." Our hearts must be securely held by the loving Father in whom is no evil. He is all that is Good. He is Love. Love is not happy when any suffer. This is why The Father is weeping. Love cannot bear to observe so much unhappiness.

15. The Loving God knows there are many of His suffering children who are too ill to be able to find Him. Some of them are so injured and damaged by their Earthly incarnations they are mindlessly filled with fears, pain of all types and cannot help themselves. We must spoon little amounts of His delightful food into their hungry mouths. They are thirsty for the Water which takes away thirst forever. They, like the sad Prodigal, feel they are alienated from the Father. This is an infernal lie! He wants to prepare a Grand Reunion.

16. The Children need simply to "Come to Him and He will give you rest." He will bathe your wounded and soiled bodies. He will give you an iridescent garment such as is worn in Heaven. He will feed us all a marvelous feast at our Family Reunion, The Marriage Supper Of The Lamb. The Bridegroom says, "Come for all is now ready."

17. The Father does not weep because He hates us. He weeps because so many of us believe we are a hated and evil race. We are hateful to ourselves and others simply because we believe we are unlovely and horrible. He did not tell us we are evil and worthy of destruction. The danger is from ourselves. We treat ourselves and others as if we were not worthy of life here or in the Worlds to Come. How would we treat each other if we loved and respected each other as all being part of a Royal Household and Priesthood? If we followed the Master's teachings and refused to listen to the false doctrines of human logic, we would be set free...We are free indeed!" We would be freed to treat our spouses as Royalty.

18. If we treated Him and the Lord as Beloved Family, we would have no wars. Without hatred there would be no wars. If there were no wars and we were peacefully inclined to follow His wonderfully simple Commandments, we would indeed see "His Kingdom come and His will be done on Earth as it is in Heaven." If we refuse to accept anything less, it will be so. We no longer condone violence of any sort. Those who are of Heaven learn Peace.

19. If we would re-read the teachings of our Beloved Master and adhered to them, we would be His Sheep. Many of us have been asked to adhere to His Commandments of His New Covenant. He is the fulfillment of everything. The Creation, the Father, the Son, and we are all One. We are not adopted. If we become as Little Children, we will find peace, love

and plenty in the well-watered Garden of Our Inner Temples in which They will dwell forever.

20. The doctrines and teachings of the blind adult souls cannot lead us on a holy and wonderful path. Only a beautiful trusting, loving, and obedient Little Child will enter into His House. Thus, our current rules of adult living become obsolete if we leave out the attributes of the Holy Ones. Selflessness is of Christ and Bodhisattvas. Peace is The Prince of Peace and His Sheep. They will be called the Children of God. The Meek will inherit the Earth–not the conquerers who rape and pillage their Mother Earth. We must bless all. We must surround ourselves with Beauty, as teach the Cherokee people. Sweetly holy Children would never quarrel and squabble with anyone. Only adults with poor security and sick hearts do such things. Why would the God of Love need to punish His own Children unjustly? Why would He destroy those who love Him? He loves this Planet, even as the Walrus of His eye. Why would He feel He needs to destroy it completely? It has been remade a few times. This does not mean it is inhabitable. It simply means we must become one big happy and well adjusted Family. However, we know most families have troubles with being dysfunctional at times. As with our studies of the patriarchs, our Father's Family is not an exception to this family norm.

21. Perhaps this is one of those times when the Father is frustrated with the length of time it takes to teach us His ways. I hope and pray we learn to help Him better soon. I cannot bear to watch Him weep. Can we make a pact between all of us to make efforts to study to show ourselves ready to enter Heaven's Gate. He is eager to welcome us Home. It has been a very long separation. I, for one, very much desire to again regain and return to our Heavenly Home. Let us rid our hearts, minds and souls of all false thoughts and attempt to see Them in the pristine and simply fashion in which They desire to be known and followed. They are Simple. So is the Father and His Way. He is fond of Little Children.

He says to forbid them not. This is a Simple Mystery. Evidently, the Father and His Family will have much fun Forever as Children in a Glorious Land of Unspeakable Joy. Does this have any connection to the things many have been taught? Let us study to show ourselves as Little Children to our Weeping Father. I think He will stop crying and draw each of us to His ample lap in a great Fatherly bear hug. I think someone told many Children bedtime stories which were not of OurFather. They talked of unspeakable monsters instead of our Loving Father and of joys unspeakable.

22. He will stop crying when He is no longer accused of things He did not do. This makes most of us extremely hurt at such injustices.. Slander and Lies are not of the Father I know and love. Who do we follow? Let us scrutinize our own lives and re-evaluate our attitudes and ethics as Children of God, rather than as those who dominate everything in the fashion of violent warlords. These things are not the Perfect Will and Way of the Divine Father. They are aberrations of diseased minds and souls.

23. Let us not re-crucify our Lord. He came to Earth to bear witness to the Father and of His Truths. Let us read what He said and did. Try to love and follow Him. This is all He expects from any of us. He is wonderful. Seek Him and be found of Him. Fill yourself with His Holy Presence. Holy is the Lamb of God. He is worthy of all praise. He Father said, "This is My Son in whom I am well pleased". The Lord tells us to "Let the Children come unto Me and forbid them not, for of such is the Kingdom of Heaven."

24. Remember He also blessed the Earth and all that is. He blessed us and called us His own. He tells us He misses us. He wishes to walk and talk with us as He did in the Garden. Let us begin our walks again with Him in the Still of the Evening. It has been far too long since we have been with Him. We will enjoy being with Him once again. Come, let us return to our place upon His lap. We are the Children He adores as His own.

Jesus says, "Whatever you have done for the least of these you have done unto Me."

25. He tells us He will never leave us alone, unprepared and unwarned. He will be with us even until the End Times, those Great and Terrible Days of the Coming of the Son of God.

26. We can choose to become His own children, filled completely, counseled and led by His Holy Spirit, into a new life of peaceful joy, at-onement and communion with Him Who Is Everything, or we can once again destroy ourselves in the chaos He sees is coming. Apocalypse can be ours once again. Is it necessary for us to destroy each other and the whole Earth again; and forget our heritage as those who know we are part of the God that is All, who needs and wants nothing-- except for us to finally realize we are part of Him. He dwells within our human temples. He offered us blessings, health, beauty, wholeness, truth, wisdom and more abundant life in Him. Do we choose Chaos or Heaven? We are

<u>concerned with the sorrow of our Father. Let us this day choose to be create a wonderful New World, rather than the Chaos of our prior creation. The choice is ours to make at this hour on the Cosmic Clock.</u>

THE TEN COMMANDMENTS

(Deuteronomy 5:7-21, Holy Bible, NIV)

I. THOU SHALL HAVE NO OTHER GODS BEFORE ME.

II. YOU SHALL NOT MAKE YOURSELF AN IDOL IN THE FORM OF ANYTHING IN HEAVEN ABOVE OR IN THE EARTH BENEATH OR IN THE WATERS BELOW.

III. YOU SHALL NOT MISUSE THE NAME OF THE LORD YOUR GOD.

IV. OBSERVE THE SABBATH DAY BY KEEPING IT HOLY.

V. HONOR YOUR MOTHER AND YOUR FATHER.

VI. YOU SHALL NOT MURDER.

VII. YOU SHALL NOT COMMIT ADULTERY.

VIII. YOU SHALL NOT STEAL.

IX. YOU SHALL NOT GIVE FALSE TESTIMONY AGAINST YOUR NEIGHBOR.

X. YOU SHALL NOT COVET YOUR NEIGHBOR'S WIFE, HOUSE, OR LAND, MAN SERVANT OR MAIDSERVANT, OX OR DONKEY, OR ANYTHING THAT BELONGS TO YOUR NEIGHBOR.

****

THE NATURAL PERSON VS. THE FOLLOWERS OF JESUS CHRIST –GALATIANS 5.

A CHILD OF A DEMON DESIRES TO BE LIKE HIS FATHER

The ways of the natural human are those of sexual immorality, impurity and debauchery; idolatry and witchcraft; hatred, discord, jealousy, fits of rage, selfish ambitions, dissensions, factions and envy; drunkenness, orgies and the like. Those who live like this will not inherit the Kingdom of God.

A CHILD OF GOD DESIRES TO BE LIKE HIM

The Fruit of His Spirit should be in our lives: love, joy, peace, patience, kindness, goodness, faithfulness, gentleness and self control. Against such things is no law. Those who belong to Christ Jesus have crucified the sinful nature with its passions and desires.

****

THE TWO GREAT COMMANDMENTS OF JESUS CHRIST

HIS GREAT COMMANDMENT TO US IS:

"You are to love the Lord your God with your whole heart, mind, body and soul and your neighbor as yourself."

&

"Do unto others as you would have them do unto you."

HIS GREAT COMMISSION TO US IS:

"You are to go out into the highways and countryside to tell others of the Good

News of My Message."

(We are His disciples who are to take up His Cross and His Mission to go out into the world to become His Christed Ones to "Feed My Sheep" as "Fishers of Men".)

****

THE BEATITUDES

Matthew 5:3-11 (Holy Bible, NIV)

I BLESS ARE THE POOR IN SPIRIT
FOR THEIRS IS THE KINGDOM OF HEAVEN.

II. BLESSED ARE THOSE WHO MOURN
FOR THEY WILL BE COMFORTED.

III. BLESSED ARE THE MEEK
FOR THEY WILL INHERIT THE EARTH.

IV. BLESSED ARE THOSE WHO HUNGER AND THIRST FOR RIGHTEOUSNESS
FOR THEY SHALL BE FILLED.

V. BLESSED ARE THE MERCIFUL
FOR THEY WILL BE SHOWN MERCY.

VI. BLESSED ARE THE PURE IN HEART
FOR THEY SHALL SEE GOD.

VII. BLESSED ARE THE PEACEMAKERS
FOR THEY SHALL BE CALLED THE SONS OF GOD.

VIII. BLESSED ARE THOSE WHO ARE PERSECUTED BECAUSE OF RIGHTEOUSNESS
FOR THEIRS IS THE KINGDOM OF HEAVEN.

IX. BLESSED ARE YOU WHEN PEOPLE INSULT YOU, PERSECUTE YOU, AND SAY ALL KINDS OF EVIL AGAINST YOU BECAUSE OF ME.
REJOICE AND BE GLAD, BECAUSE GREAT IS YOUR REWARD IN HEAVEN, FOR IN THE SAME WAY THEY PERSECUTED THE PROPHETS WHO WERE BEFORE YOU.

****

GLOSSARY

AHIMSA- Hinduism/Jainism --peaceful, non-violence toward all sentient beings/creatures, including insects.

ANANDA -Hinduism-- peace, bliss, love, happiness

APOCALYPSE/APOCALYPTIC--A revelation of things to come in the socalled "End Times", or the "Great and Terrible Day of the Lord".

ASTROLOGY/ASTROLOGICAL--The study of the supposed effects of the stars and the planets upon human beings and their Earthly lives.

AT-ONEMENT - A sense of spiritual communion and holy at-oneness with God.

ATONEMENT - Payment of debts owed. Example: Jesus Christ paying the death penalty for our spiritual crimes against universal laws.

CHARISMA/CHARISMATIC--Charismatic believers; usage of "unknown languages or tongues of humans and of angels"- Pentecostal experiences and Gifts of the Spirit, such as at the Day of Pentecost, Acts of the Apostles, Holy Bible.

CHRISTIAN -Those who believe in and follow the teachings of the Master Jesus Christ.

CHURCH - (His Divine Bride) - 1. The body of believers as the Bride of Christ. 2) The Holy Catholic Church. 3) Christian believers. 4) An active member of a church.

COMMUNION - A sharing; fellowship. 2) The sacrament of the sharing of the Lord's Supper of the Bread (His Body) and the Wine (His Blood).

CONTEMPLATION/CONTEMPLATIVE--monastic - private prayer and meditation; to review or think about attentively.

CROSSING OVER --Death; Crossing Over to Heaven.

DARK NIGHT OF THE SOUL - A feeling of separation and isolation from God experienced at rare times during the lifetime pilgrims of many believers. See St. John of the Cross

DISCERNMENT (of spirits)--The Gift of Discernment of spirits, entities, human spirits and psyches.

DIVINE HEALING--Laying on of hands; empathetic healing; prayer for the sick for miraculous recoveries...which still occur even in this modern world ruled by the empiricism of science and high technology.

DIVINE ROMANCE - This is a spiritual realm where one experiences feelings of divine love for God.

ENLIGHTENMENT - The English word is used within the Buddhist context to convey the state of complete awakening of an individual. The Tibetan equivalent literally means "one who has become purified and is perfectly realized. - A fully enlightened person is called a Buddha (awakened one) who is capable of benefitting others. In the Christian context, one can also become a fully purified and enlightened soul who will be able to benefit others. Enlightenment can come to any who are serious seekers of the purity, truth, wholeness, wisdom and love of the Divine.

ESSENE - A colony of believers who lived at the time of Jesus Christ. Many of their writings were found at the caves near Masada and the Dead Sea...thereby causing these vials of parchments to be called The Dead Sea Scrolls.

EXPERIENTIAL--actual experiences, rather than scholastic studies alone.

ESOTERIC--understood by, or intended for, a few, select; secret; mysterious. When one seeks to know God, one enters into the mysterious world of the Divine.

EXORCISM--The usages of divine powers and religious rituals in order to expel evil spirits.

EXOTERIC--readily understood; commonplace knowledge.

GLOSSALALIA- utterances of unknown languages; speaking in tongues in so called Spirit-filled Pentecostal churches.

GNOSTIC/GNOSTICISM -Gnosis means Knowledge. These believers in Christ preached that each person needed to make their spiritual decisions based upon personal spiritual knowledge gained from their own experiences. There is much to be studied about these believers.

GREAT MOTHER -The all-encompassing nature of the over soul of the Divine Mother.

GREAT SPIRIT - The over soul of the Soul of the all-encompassing Divine...All That Is. Native American name for the One Spirit.

HOLY/HOLINESS--wholeness; sacred, devout, saintly.

HUMANIST/HUMANISTIC--1. A system of thought centered predominately on human interests;2. One who studies human interests or the humanities; 3. Literary Culture.

HUMANITARIAN--Concerned with the interests of all man/humankind; philanthropic. Jesus Christ, Gandhi, Martin Luther King, Jr., and others were humanitarian.

KNOWLEDGE–Gnosticism or gnosis; awareness of facts, truths or principles; cognizance; erudition; a body of accumulated facts; what is known.

LOCUTION–n. A speaking. 1. A word, phrase or expression. 2. A partcular style os speech.

MAGI–Astrologers or metaphysically Wise Men, as in the Story of the Star at the Birth of Jesus Christ .

MAGIC--1. The art of controlling the supernatural; sorcery; charm or spell.

MAGICAL--Delightful.

MAGICIAN--A conjurer.

METAPHYSICS/METAPHYSICAL–Philosophy in general; particularly the science of philosophical essential principles; abstruse or abstract principles of philosophy.

MONK - A man withdrawn from the world under religious vows or as a secular mystic or monk.

MYSTIC/MYSTICAL--Spiritual matters known only to those who have special comprehension, or who are initiated into special truths. One who believes in, or practices, mysticism. (Note: Jesus, and other holy ones are known as mystics.)

MYSTICISM--A mode of thought founded on spiritual illumination or intuition.

MYSTICAL- Example: Jesus and His people are in mystical union with God

NEAR-DEATH EXPERIENCE (NDE)--This is an event which can occur prior to the complete release of the human soul from this life incarnation. The soul leaves the body for a space of time and ascends to the heavens.

NUN - A woman living apart from the world under religious vows or as a secular mystic or contemplative woman.

OCCULT--1. Beyond ordinary understanding. 2. Secret; known only to the initiated.

OUT-OF-BODY (OBE)--Astral projection; time or space travel out of the body, whether on Earth, or to other worlds. This can occur with intent, or at near-death experiences of dea

PHILOSOPHY--The science dealing with the general causes and principles of things; a personal attitude or belief system.

PRECOGNITIVE–Precognitive awareness of events before they occur; prophetic dreams, etc.

PROPHECY/PROPHETIC--A prediction of the future.

PROPHESY -- Foretell and forth tell events in the future as prophetic predictions.

PROPHET-- One who foretells or predicts the future; a spokesperson, especially one inspired by God.

PSYCHE--The human soul. See the Greek mythology of Psyche.

PSYCHIC--1. Pertaining to the mental or spiritual life. 2. Pertaining to mysterious mental forces. 3. Sensitive to such forces.

PSYCHOLOGY--The science of mind and mental activities.

SALVATION/SAVIOR - 1. That who saves. Example: Jesus Christ as our Redeemer and Savior. 2. Redemption.

SECULAR - Adj. temporal; worldly; not of the church. Secularism, n.

SEEKER (of Truth, Wisdom, etc.) - A Spiritual Seeker is one who devotes one's life to the pursuit of wisdom, knowledge, the Divine, or the many attributes of merit personified thereby or therein.

SEER - Prophet/prophetess. One who sees spiritual entities, or experiences metaphysical awareness unseen by others without the gifts of knowledge, discernment or prophesy.

SIN/SINNER-Greek Word: harmartia=Missing the mark, or error. Also, the Babylonian masculine Moon god was called "Sin". Lying as a crescent upon his back he saw all of the "sins of humankind" .

TEACHER - n. One who teaches, a teacher, whether in or outside a school or educational facility.

TRANSCENDENCE - v. t. Go or be beyond (a limit, etc.); surpass; excel. Transcendental - adj. Beyond ordinary experience. Transcendentalism - n. A philosophy based on reasoning or intuition, not empiricism.

WISDOM--1. The power or faculty of forming a sound judgment in any matter/Having the power of discerning and judging rightly; 2. Having knowledge; learned; cunning; sagacity; experience; erudition; judicious, aware. 4. n. Wise persons collectively. A person with a wise manner, way or mode.

AUTHOR'S SUGGESTED READING REFERENCES

Allport, Gordon W., *The Nature of Prejudice*, Addison-Wesley Publishing Company, Inc., 1986.

Angus, Samuel, *The Mystery-Religions And Christianity*, A Citadel Press Book, Published by Carol Publishing Group, Editorial Offices, 600 Madison Avenue, New York, N.Y.1966

Ballou, Robert O., *The Portable World Bible*, Penguin Books, 1977.

Beevers, John (Translation by), *The Autobiography of St. Therese of Lisieux*, A Doubleday Image Book, 1957.

Bacovcin, Helen, *The Way Of The Pilgrim & The Pilgrim Continues His Way*, An Image Book, Doubleday Publishing, 1978.

Cannon, Dolores, *The Convoluted Universe*, Ozark Mountain Publishers, P. O. Box 754, Huntsville, AR 72740, 2001.

Cannon, Dolores, *Keepers Of The Garden*, Ozark Mountain Publishers, P. O> Box 754, Huntsville, AR 72740

Carroll, Lee & Tober, Jan, *The Indigo Children*, Hay House, Inc., Carlsbad, Caliifornia, 1999.

Chopra, Deepak, *How To Know God*, Harmony Books, Random House, New York, NY, 2000.

Cory, Isaac Preston, *Ancient Fragments*, The Secret Doctrine Reference Library, Wizard's Bookshelf, Box 66, Savage, MN. Original publication, 1832.

Eck, Diana L., *A New Religious America,* Harper, San Francisco, California, 2001.

Franciscan Friars of the Immaculate, *Padre Pio, Wonder Worker*, Our Lady's Chapel, New Bedsford, MA 1999.

Estes, Ph. D., Clarissa Pinkola, *Women Who Run With The Wolves*, Ballantine Books, New York, New York, 1992.

Fadiman, James & Frager, Robert, *Essential Sufism*, Castle Books, A Division of Book Sales, Inc., 114 Northfield Avenue, Edison, New Jersey, 08837, 1997.

Fleming, Ursula (Editor*), Meister Eckhart, The Man From Whom God Nothing Hid*, Templegate Publishers, Springfield, Illinois, 1990.

Fox, Matthew, *Original Blessing*, (A Primer in Creation Spirituality Presented in Four Paths, Twenty-Six Themes, and Two Questions), Jeremy P. Tarcher/Putnam, New York, N.Y., 2000.

Fox, Matthew, *The Coming Of The Cosmic Christ* (The Healing of Mother Earth and the Birth of Global Renaissance), Harper Collins, San Francisco, California, 1988.

Fadiman, James & Frager, Robert, *Essential Sufism*, Castle Books, A Division of Book Sales, Inc., 114 East 53rd Avenue, Edison, New Jersey 08837, 1997

Hancock, Graham, *Fingerprints Of The Gods*, Three Rivers Press, New York, N.Y., 1995.

Happold, F. C., *Mysticism, A Study and an Anthology*, Penguin Books, Baltimore-Maryland, 1963, 1964, 1970.

James, William, *The Varieties of Religious Experiences*, Mentor Books, The New American Library, New York, 1958.

Kelsey, Morton T., *Tongue Speaking*, Doubleday & Company, Inc., Garden City, NYC, 1964

Machiavelli, Niccolo, *The Prince.*

Merton, Thomas, *The Monastic Journey,* Image Books, A Division of Doubleday, Inc., Garden City, New York, 1978. (Other suggested books by or about Thomas Merton are: *The Seven Storey Mountain, A Seven Day Journey With Thomas Merton, Contemplative Prayer, The Wisdom Of The Desert.*)

Needleman, Jacob, *Lost Christianity*, Bantam Books, Doubleday & Company, Inc., 245 Park Avenue, New York, N.Y., 10167, 1980

Norbu, Namkhai, *Dream Yoga And The Practice Of Natural Light*, Snow Lion Publications, Ithaca, New York, U.S.A., 1992.

Noss, John B., *Man's Religions–6th Edition*, Macmillan Publishing Company, New York, N. Y., 1980

Pagels, Elaine, *The Gnostic Gospels*, Vintage House, A Division of Random House, New York, New York,1981.

Pagels, Elaine, *The Origin Of Satan,* Random House, Inc., New York, New York, 1995.

Pagels, Elaine, *Beyond Belief, The Secret Gospel of Thomas*, Vintage House, A Division of Random House, New York, N. Y., 2004.

Peers. E. Allison, *The Autobiography of St. Teresa of Avila*, Doubleday/ Image Books, Garden City, New York, 1960.

Peck, M.D., M. Scott, *People Of The Lie*, Touchstone, Simon & Shuster, New York, New York, 1983.

Rinpoche, Tenzin Wangyal, *The Tibetan Yogas of Dream and Sleep*, Snow Lion Publications, P. O. Box 6483, Ithaca, New York, 14851, 1998.

Roberts, Frances J., *Dialogues With God*, The King's Press, Palos Verdes Estates, California, 1972.

Roberts, Frances J., *Progress Of Another Pilgrim*, The King's Press, Palos Verdes Estates, California, 1970.
Roberts, Frances J., *On The High Road Of Surrender*, The King's Press, P. O. Box 763, Palos Verdes Estates, California, 1973.
Roberts, Frances J., *Come Away My Beloved*, The King's Press, Palos Verdes Estates, California, 1970.
Schaup, Susanne, *Sophia*, Nicholas-Hays, Inc., York Beach, Maine, 1997.
Shah, Idries, *The Sufis*, Anchor Books, A division of Random House, Inc., New York, N.Y. 1971.
Shahnaaz, *Dialogues With The Prophet Mohammed*, Author House, 1663 Liberty Drive, Suite 200, Bloomington, IN 47403, 2004.
Shinoda Bolen, M.D., Jean, *Goddesses In Every Woman*, Harper & Row, Publishers, San Francisco, California, 1984.
Shinoda Bolen, M.D., Jean, *Goddesses In Older Women*, Harper Collins, Publishers, 10 53rd St, New York, New York, 2001.
Spangler, David, *The Call*, Riverhead Books, New York, 1996.
Spengler, Oswald, *The Decline Of The West*.
St. John of the Cross, *Dark Night Of The Soul*, Image Books, Doubleday, 1990.
Sinetar, Dr. Marsha, *Ordinary People As Monks And Mystics*, Paulist Press, 1986.
Teasdale, Wayne, *The Mystic Heart: Discovering a Universal Spirituality In The World's Religions,* New World Library, 14 Pamaron Way, Novato, California, 94949, 1999, 2001.
Teasdale, Wayne, *A Monk In The World - Cultivating A Spiritual Life*, New World Library, 14 Pamaron Way, Novato, California, 94949, 2002.
Underhill, Evelyn, *Mysticism*, E.P.Dutton & Co., Inc., 1961.
Van Praagh, James, *Heaven And Earth*, Simon & Schuster Source, New York, N.Y., 2001.
Virtue, Doreen, Ph.D, *The Crystal Children*, Hay House, Inc., Carlsbad, California, 2003.
Walker, Barbara, *The Crone*, Perennial Library, Harper & Row, Publishers, San Francisco, California, 1985.
Walker, III, Ethan, *The Mystic Christ*, Devi Press, P. O. Box 5081, Norman, Oklahoma, 2003.
Walsch, Neale Donald, *Conversations With God, Books l, 2 & 3, Book I,* G.P. Putnam's Son, 200 Madison Avenue, New York, New York, 10016, 1996.
Walsch, Neale Donald, *Friendship With God -An Uncommon Dialogue*, A Berkley Book, Published by The Berkley Publishing Group, A

Division of Penguin Putnam, Inc., 375 Hudson Street, New York, New York, 10014, 1999. (New Books: *Tomorrow's God & What God Wants.*)

Yogananda, Paramhamsa, *The Divine Romance*, Self-Realization Fellowship, 3880 San Rafael Avenue, Los Angeles, California, 1986.

Additional Reference Materials:

Christian Bibles:

King James Version (KJV)
New International Version (NIV)
The Jerusalem Bible–a paraphrased Catholic edition
The Servant King New Testament, International Bible Society
The Apocrypha–Edgar J. Goodsend, An American Translation

Other Holy Scriptural References of the World

The Holy Quran
The Hidden Words–The Writings of Baha'u'llah
Lost Books of the Bible and the Forgotten Books of Eden–World Bible Publishers
The Book of Enoch the Prophet–Richard Laurence
The Complete Gospels–John J. Miller, Editor
The Dead Sea Scrolls and the Christian Faith–William Sanford LaSor
The Dead Sea Scrolls–Essene Texts
The Gospel of Thomas–Coptic Text
The Nag Hammadi Library–James M. Robinson, General Editor
The Other Bible–Willis Barnstone

ABOUT THE AUTHOR

The author sees herself as a child of God in a universe too big to describe. She is a seeker of Truth and Wisdom. She has been traveling a long, sometimes hard, pathway through a very busy spirit-filled life with Him. It is her desire to help others to know their positions and powers as children of God.

Celeste sees herself as a very "ordinary" person who has lived through all types of social, spiritual and political changes in America and our global community. Her personal quest to know Him has led her into realization of the unbelievably manifold nature of the Creator. It is her belief we are just beginning to tap into the highest awarenesses of the One many call Father, Mother, All That Is, the Ineffable Other. If we allow ourselves to fearlessly seek to know His Wisdom we will learn more than anyone can imagine. She believes in the salvation and divine nature of Jesus Christ, the Great Shepherd with many pastures, who has asked us to "Seek and you shall find, knock and it shall be opened."

Her very full life has included marriage, children, grand and great grandchildren. She has also been employed for most of her life with Community Social Service Agencies working with the needs and rights of the homeless, mentally and physically disabled and other minorities. She has virtually completed two Bachelor of Arts degrees in Social Sciences and Comparative Religious Studies; additionally with minors in Psychology and Ethnic Studies.

The author is a former military wife, and a civilian tourist, who has traveled in Europe, the Middle East, Mexico, the United States, and the Hawaiian Islands.

In 1967, the author was given a message of divine love for the world. This is the divinely inspired message she published as her first book entitled *"Beloved"* in 2004. The topic of *"Beloved Spirit"* is her ongoing lifetime walk *in the still of the evening lost in the Beloved Spirit.*

Printed in the United States
32683LVS00003B/43-48

9 781420 838206